*Money, Murder, and*
**Dominick Dunne**

# Other Books by Robert Hofler

*The Man Who Invented Rock Hudson*

*Variety's "The Movie That Changed My Life"*

*Party Animals*

*Sexplosion: How a Generation of Pop Rebels Broke All the Taboos*

# MONEY, MURDER, AND
# DOMINICK DUNNE

## A Life in Several Acts

## Robert Hofler

The University of Wisconsin Press

The University of Wisconsin Press
1930 Monroe Street, 3rd Floor
Madison, Wisconsin 53711-2059
uwpress.wisc.edu

3 Henrietta Street, Covent Garden
London WC2E 8LU, United Kingdom
eurospanbookstore.com

Printed in the United States of America

This book may be available in a digital edition.

Library of Congress Cataloging-in-Publication Data

Names: Hofler, Robert, author.
Title: Money, murder, and Dominick Dunne: a life in several acts / Robert Hofler.
Description: Madison, Wisconsin: The University of Wisconsin Press, [2017]
| Includes bibliographical references and index.
Identifiers: LCCN 2016041574 | ISBN 9780299311506 (cloth: alk. paper)
Subjects: LCSH: Dunne, Dominick. | Journalists—United States—Biography.
| Trials (Murder) —United States. | Celebrities—United States.
| Authors, American—20th century—Biography.
| Motion picture producers and directors—United States—Biography.
Classification: LCC PN4874.D846 H64 2017 | DDC 070.92 [B]—dc23
LC record available at https://lccn.loc.gov/2016041574

To

anonymous sources

No one loved them, or used them, more than Dominick Dunne

Writers are always selling somebody out.

Joan Didion, *Slouching towards Bethlehem*

# Contents

# Contents

viii

*Money, Murder, and*
**Dominick Dunne**

# 1

## Father and Sondheim

In 1993 Dominick Dunne was already famous for saying "he did it" whenever it came to a high-profile murder case involving celebrity, money, and privilege. He almost always sided with the prosecution against the defendant, and he did so with the same passion and unbridled partiality he honed a decade earlier when, making his debut in *Vanity Fair* magazine, he covered the trial of John Sweeney, the Ma Maison sous chef who strangled to death Dominick's twenty-two-year-old daughter, actress Dominique Dunne.

Erik and Lyle Menendez were on trial for double murder in 1993. The two young men and their two middle-aged victims were not celebrities, but they were wealthy, lived in Beverly Hills, and had ties to the movie business. Even more newsworthy: the victims were Erik and Lyle's parents, Jose and Kitty Menendez. The brothers loaded and reloaded their 12-gauge Mossberg shotguns fourteen times in the TV room of the family mansion at 722 North Elm Drive. Why so many bullets? Was it rage? Or an act of self-defense? Or both?

There was no doubt that Erik and Lyle had murdered Kitty and Jose on August 20, 1989, as the couple sat watching *The Spy Who Loved Me* on a VCR. The big question of the sensational Menendez trial was whether the father had sexually abused his two sons. Dominick said he believed without a doubt that Jose Menendez never molested his sons. He said it before the trial began, and he said it twelve years later when interviewed for a documentary based on his life, titled *Dominick Dunne: After the Party*. "I never ever believed for a second that he sexually abused them," he told the camera.

Actually, Dominick did believe the two sons' accusation against Jose Menendez, and he believed it for more than a second. He believed it for the better part of a day. September 11, 1993, was Lyle Menendez's first day on the stand in his own defense, which was based on his claim that he and his younger brother committed double murders because they feared for their lives after years of incestuous sexual abuse. Experts call it the imperfect self-defense.

The Menendez trial had been going on for a month when Lyle, age twenty-five, finally took the stand that Friday. Preceding him there were thirty-two witnesses for the defense who portrayed the two victims as miserable parents. Among other offenses, friends and relatives told the court that Kitty Menendez made her sons sleep in pet-ferret feces to punish them and Jose Menendez had once called his son Lyle a "dummy" in public.

Dominick had grown restless, and he was not the only one in the courtroom tired of hearing the litany of parental offenses—some major, many minor. Finally, Judge Stanley M. Weisberg of Los Angeles Superior Court put an end to it. "We're not talking about a child custody case here," said the judge. The defense had scheduled many more such witnesses to bad-mouth Jose and Kitty, but Weisberg refused to hear them and ordered the lawyers to call one of their two defendants to testify instead.

Once Lyle took the stand, his lawyer, Jill Lansing, asked him, "Did you love your mom and dad?"

"Yes," said Lyle.

"On August 20, 1989, did you and your brother kill your mother and your father?" she asked.

"Yes," he replied.

"Did you kill them for money?"

"No," he said. Lyle's first tears began to appear.

"Did you kill them because you wanted to pay them back for the way they had treated you?"

"No," he said. Audible sobbing now joined Lyle's tears.

"Why did you kill your parents?"

"Because we were afraid," he whispered. When Lyle went on to describe why he and Erik were afraid, he sometimes spoke through his knuckles, as if his hand could prevent him from saying the words that were unspeakable. At other moments, he put his head in the sleeve of his dark blue sweater to cry.

"He raped me," said Lyle.

"Did you cry?" asked his lawyer.

"Yes."

"Did you bleed?"

"Yes."

"Were you scared?"

"Very."

"Did you ask him not to?"

"Yes."

"How did you ask him not to?"

"I just told him, I don't . . . I don't . . ."

According to Lyle, Jose Menendez thought of their sex together as a kind of male bonding ritual. Lyle was only six years old when first raped, and he said being anally penetrated made him feel he was "the most important thing" in his father's life.

The most heartbreaking moment in his testimony, however, came later when Lyle talked about his younger brother. He revealed his father also had sex with Erik, and that he, in turn, replicated that sexual abuse by taking his kid brother into the woods to molest him there in a similar manner. In the courtroom, Lyle looked away from his lawyer, and leaning forward on the stand, he faced Erik for the first time during his testimony. "I don't understand why, and I'm sorry," he apologized to his twenty-two-year-old brother.

Erik and Lyle were not the only ones crying in the courtroom. Several jurors and reporters also wept. Dominick was not one of them. His eyes dry, he nonetheless looked ashen, upset. He shook his head. "I wonder if I'm wrong. Could I be wrong?" he asked the young reporter sitting next to him. Shoreen Maghame was covering her first big murder trial, for the City News Service, and she and Dominick sat next to each other most days in the Van Nuys, California, courtroom. They generally agreed about what transpired there, but unlike her friend from *Vanity Fair*, she could never be certain that the Menendez boys lied about their father.

Out in the hallway, Dominick repeated his "I wonder if I'm wrong" statement to another reporter. This time, he added, "I can't believe I'm saying this, but I think I believe this. I think he's telling the truth."

Unlike Maghame, reporter Robert Rand agreed with Dominick about almost *nothing* that happened during the Menendez trial. In fact, Court TV had hired Dominick and Rand to disagree, and late every Friday afternoon throughout the trial the two journalists presented opposing weekly rebuttals on camera. Crime watchers had never seen anything quite like it. The Menendez trial was only the second trial for which the cable network presented gavel-to-gavel coverage, the first being the ten-day William Kennedy Smith rape trial in 1991. On Court TV during the months-long

Menendez trial, the daytime coverage titillated more than any soap opera on the tube. It was Robert Rand for the defense and Dominick Dunne for the prosecution, with Terry Moran moderating.

In the hallway, Dominick repeated himself a third time, "I may be wrong."

Rand knew his colleague's fervently antidefense position, especially with regard to the Menendez sons, and any journalist's natural instinct would be to question such a dramatic reversal. But the two men kept to their agreement never to discuss the day's events before they went head-to-head on TV. "We wanted to keep it spontaneous," said Rand.

The Menendez trial represented everything Dominick loathed about the criminal justice system in America. It was all about a couple of wealthy brats using their money, their father's hard-earned money, to buy themselves justice and, in the process, ruin the good reputations of their victims. Dominick saw the same thing happen to his own daughter, Dominique. The defense raised unsubstantiated charges of abortion and drug use against her, and then, in Dominick's opinion, the killer got his rich boss to pay for his defense.

Dominick made it clear why he supported the prosecution in almost every case. The Menendez trial, however, proved more personally complicated for him than any other of his career. Like Jose Menendez, he, too, had raised two sons in the rarefied hot-house environment of money, privilege, and celebrity that is Beverly Hills. Dominick repeated what one of his sons told him: "Dad, I knew lots of kids in Beverly Hills who've talked about killing their parents." Dominick said the comment shocked him, and he repeated it despite the fact that both his sons later denied ever having said it. And there was something else disturbing to Dominick about the case. He said he found himself identifying with one of the young killers and confessed to being "fascinated" by him.

Erik Menendez was the handsome son, the likable one. Erik overcame a severe childhood stammer, as did Dominick; and much more significant, Dominick believed Erik to be "homosexual," a word Judge Weisberg was averse to being used in court to describe the younger defendant.

The Menendez trial compelled Dominick, for the first time in his life, to write and publicly talk about the physical abuse he experienced as a child at the hands of his own father. He linked that abuse to what happened to the younger Menendez son. "I think the hate that Erik had was with his father's inability to accept the way he was. Something had to trigger it off," Dominick said of the double murders. "I always had the theory that Erik was gay. I'm sure [ Jose] called his kid all the terrible faggot, fairy names. I never ever believed for a second that he sexually abused them as the lawyers said he sexually abused them. But he was abusive in the way my father was abusive to me."

In the twentieth century, the concept of what it meant to be homosexual changed almost as much as the words to describe and degrade it. The word "sissy" in the guarded 1930s when Dominick was a boy had been replaced by "faggot" in the less circumspect 1980s of Erik Menendez's youth.

"He mimicked me," Dominick said of his own father, Richard. "He called me a sissy. 'Sissy' is a tough word. It may not sound tough, but it's words that hurt. It lingers."

The word "sissy" fastened itself to Dominick's consciousness because it labeled his greatest fear about himself. He was not a real boy. He was a girl trapped in a boy's body.

Dr. Richard Dunne Sr. was not the only one who thought it or said it. An uncle told Richard that the six-year-old Dominick "ought to have been a girl." A friendly Italian barber told his mother, Dorothy Dunne, the same thing: "He ought to have been a girl." What remained burned in Dominick's memory is that neither parent disagreed with that opinion; no one came to his "rescue" to claim the real little boy within.

"I never felt I belonged anywhere, even in my own family. I was the outsider of the six kids," said Dominick.

In time, when he was well into old age, Dominick would put a humorous spin on his outsider status. He claimed that he came late to developing his verbal skills, and when he finally did speak, his first words to his mother were those of a prissy aesthete: "Your dress is awfully cute, Mom, but your shoes are a little bit dirty."

An old man can laugh at his youth. He cannot laugh at it when he is living it.

"My opinion of myself was *nothing*!" Dominick stressed. What hardened the prison walls of his effeminacy is that Dominick was only one year younger than his older brother, Richard Dunne Jr., who loved sports and was good at playing them. The bedroom the two brothers shared at 1720 Albany Avenue in West Hartford, Connecticut, said everything Dominick and his family knew to be true. Richard was a real boy because he covered his side of the bedroom with pictures of famous athletes; Dominick was a sissy because he preferred pictures of beautiful movie stars. Even the high school yearbook at Hartford's Kingswood School told the tale of these two Dunne brothers. It gave Richard the nicknames Tarzan and Big Dick for his prowess at football, hockey, and other rough-and-tumble sports. The yearbook editors were too kind to reprint any of Dominick's nicknames.

He did not play sports. Dominick was short and smaller in build than his older brother, and while these two Dunne boys shared strong Irish features, Richard's face in photographs is more open, rarely tense. Dominick's falls into a natural wariness whenever he is not smiling.

His escape became the movies and putting on puppet shows for the neighborhood kids. One puppet play he wrote and staged told the story of two girls, Molly and Polly, who traveled west in a covered wagon. It deeply embarrassed Dr. Dunne that any son of his would be writing for the theater, much less plays about two girls.

What Dr. Dunne failed to understand is that sissies, as well as girls, can be tough and very resolute in their pursuits: putting on puppet shows and watching movies provided Dominick his only relief from being called a little girl, on the one hand, and being compared to Big Dick, on the other. What Dominick could not escape, even in the imaginary worlds of film and theater, were the frequent beatings he received. They were not the sexual abuse that Erik and Lyle Menendez claimed. But they were abuse just the same.

In her book *The White Album*, Dominick's sister-in-law Joan Didion recalls a verse that Dorothy Dunne framed and put in the foyer of her Connecticut home. It asked God to "bless the corner of this house," as well as "each door that opens wide, to stranger as to kin."

Didion wrote that Dorothy's verse gave her a "physical chill" whenever she read it. Paranoia came naturally to Didion, who never took an immediate liking to strangers. For Dominick, it was not strangers whom he had to fear. "Something about me drove him crazy," Dominick said of his father. Publicly, Dominick would never admit what that mysterious something was. Privately, he knew. As he wrote in a letter years later, it was his "incipient fairyism" that his father despised, "and it became his business to rid me of same."

Dr. Richard Dunne was a respected heart surgeon, and if a phone call from the hospital happened to interrupt his thrashing Dominick, he took the call, gave his medical advice, and then went back to the chore at hand: "beating me with a riding crop so I had welts on my ass and thighs," Dominick claimed. "I got to a point where I told myself I will never let him make me cry."

Instead of shedding tears, Dominick decided to do something about the little boy inside himself—the little boy whom his father hated and people said was actually a little girl. As he wrote years later in his private journal, the young Dominick Dunne decided to "invent another person," and he would spend the remainder of his childhood and the first half of his adult life trying to become this other person. Looking back at what he created, Dominick had to admit, "I was a fake."

When a child decides to be another person, which aspects of his personality does he keep, if any, and which does he set out to destroy?

The little boy inside Dominick did not give up without a struggle. He sentimentalized his self-induced transformation by turning it into a religious calling. "I would have made a perfect Christ child," he wrote. Dominick also developed a very severe stutter.

Being a sissy, as it turned out, was not the only thing Dominick learned to despise about himself. Named after a grandfather, Dominick Burns, he recoiled from the family's humble ancestry. Born poor in Strokestown, Ireland, Burns escaped the potato famine of the mid-nineteenth century to move to America, where he quickly parlayed his success at being a butcher-grocer into founding a bank, the Park Street Trust. Despite his newly earned wealth, Burns never saw any reason to give up working behind the meat counter, much to the embarrassment of Dominick, who preferred having a banker, not a butcher, for a grandfather. Dominick's younger brother John Gregory Dunne described Dominick Burns as having gone from "steerage to suburbia" with all due speed. It was an understatement. In his American transformation, Burns earned so much money and gave so much of it away to Catholic charities that Pope Pius XII made him a papal knight. The city of Hartford even named a grade school after him, the Burns School, which continues to function as an elementary school at 195 Putnam Street.

While Dominick hated his father, he had reason to love his maternal grandfather, whom he and his five siblings called Papa. (John Gregory Dunne spelled it "Poppa.")

"He had an enormous influence on my brother and me," Dominick recalled. "Early on, he taught John and me the excitement of reading." The Dunne children took turns spending Friday nights at their grandparents' house, and not out of pure affection. Papa paid them fifty cents apiece to listen to his readings of poetry and the classics. "We would hate to do it, hate to be bored. . . . But of course, it sunk in," Dominick admitted.

The Dunne side of the family was not shabby either. The father who gave Dominick regular whippings did well enough as chief surgeon at St. Francis Hospital to raise his family of six children with the help of three servants in a seven-bedroom stone manor that came with a six-car garage. Their neighbors were equally blessed: across the street from the Dunnes lived the family of another well-to-do man of medicine, Dr. Thomas Norval Hepburn, father of actress Katharine Hepburn. Although the Dunnes and the Hepburns lived nearby on the same street, they rarely socialized, and the reason why had everything to do with another thing Dominick did not like about himself.

"We were a strange family in that we were rich Irish Catholics in an all WASP town," he explained. "We were in the clubs. We were in the private schools. We had the summer houses, you know all this, but we were never quite there." The Dunnes were, he added, "only tolerated by the Protestants," who were very much *there*.

A friend explained Dominick's inferiority complex and its link to his family. "They weren't the Vanderbilts, the Rockefellers, the Du Ponts," said Joseph Hardy. They were not even the Kennedys, although the Dunnes worked hard to assimilate. Like most of the Protestants in their neighborhood, they voted Republican, and it took Dominick and his brother John a couple of decades to outgrow that conservative political affiliation. In 1960 Dominick headed up a group called Catholics Against Kennedy; John gave his future mother-in-law the complete works of John Birch as a Christmas present in 1963; and a year later, the newly wedded Joan Didion joined the Dunne brothers to vote for Barry Goldwater for president.

While neither of them ever voted for a Kennedy, the Kennedys nonetheless became a fixation for both Dominick and his younger brother. According to John, the Massachusetts clan held to a credo of "don't get mad, get even," where the Dunnes of Connecticut believed "get mad *and* get even." In other words, unlike the Kennedys, the Dunnes had a chip on their collective shoulder for having no political clout or connections and being merely moderately wealthy. For Dominick, it instilled in him an acute sense of inferiority, one reinforced when he fell "madly in love" at age twelve, he claimed, with a young girl who was neither Irish nor Catholic but very, very rich and socially connected. Lydia Ingersoll was the first of many heiresses whom Dominick would come to adore and rely upon for emotional, if not financial, support. The Ingersoll family just happened to be the wealthiest in West Hartford and lived in a gray stone mansion on Prospect Hill. It was quite a hill. John Gregory Dunne called Prospect Avenue "a social barricade as intimidating as the Atlantic."

Dominick, for one, did not hesitate to jump over it, but his leap up to Prospect Hill came at a price. Out of self-defense, he adopted the Ingersolls' sense of entitlement. It was a prerogative that would serve him well, and very badly, in his adult life, because unlike Lydia he did not come to it by birth. Entitlement for Dominick had to be pursued with the focused ardor of a martyr.

Compared to Lydia's life, everything else seemed "second best," Dominick declared, and that included being Irish Catholic, merely well-to-do, and having sisters who did not attend posh girls' schools like Farmington or Foxcroft. The servants in Lydia's Prospect Hill mansion were, like Dominick, Irish Catholic, and many of them he recognized as being patients of his father. "It was very upstairs-downstairs Connecticut-style," said the novelist Luanne Rice, a distant relative of the Dr. Richard Dunne family. Having grown up in the working-class neighborhood of Frog Hollow in nearby Hartford, Rice avoided daily contact with the very wealthy and the class distinctions that such intimate exposure would instill in some of her cousins living on Albany Avenue in West Hartford.

For Dominick, those class distinctions were ubiquitous, and never did they make him more uncomfortable than, at a dinner party, when Lydia served her young friends an entrée other than fish. The offending meat in question that Friday night was either lamb or chicken, depending on when in his life Dominick told the story. Whatever the meat, if he ate it he knew he would go to hell. And worse than that eternal firestorm, he worried that the servants would tell their doctor about the mortal sin his son had committed up on Prospect Hill. The good doctor would have no choice but to beat the wickedness out of him. Like a saint dispensing miracles at Lourdes, Lydia came to Dominick's rescue when she ordered her Irish Catholic servants, "Perhaps an omelette for Mr. Dunne."

When Dominick was an adult and writing a journal, even then he did not understand the "equation between" his attraction to proper young heiresses like Lydia Ingersoll and his attraction to the adult men he met in restrooms at the park and the local movie theater. But the two desires, the one exalted and the other unspeakably base, were linked and he pursued them with "the same fervor," he noted. Writing as a middle-aged man, he looked back at his difficult, conflicted youth to label himself a "park pervert," even though he was the child and his sex partners were the adults. He described himself as always the aggressor, always the active partner. Dominick claimed to have been only "nine or ten" when he first began performing acts of fellatio on anonymous men in public restrooms. Then again, Dominick tended to remember being younger than he actually was at crucial moments in his life.

He recalled seeing *Now, Voyager* when he was "twelve or thirteen," and the "movie changed my life," he said. If Bette Davis as the homely, emotionally crippled Charlotte Vale could overcome an abusive parent, so could he. Dominick saw the movie five times in as many days. The only problem with his story is that Warner Bros. released *Now, Voyager* in 1942 when Dominick was sixteen years old and attending Canterbury School, a Catholic prep school in New Milford, Connecticut. Being off a few years regarding his age is a small wrinkle in the story, which Dominick told often. Had he also been older than the "nine or ten" he claimed to be when he first performed oral sex on adult men in restrooms? More significant is that Dominick wondered if he willed himself to be a homosexual "to spite" his father.

"I was so unhappy because of the abuse I took from my father," he said. "That film showed me that it was possible to totally change your life, as Bette Davis did in that movie." He responded viscerally to *Now, Voyager*'s Cinderella story of how an ugly girl transforms herself overnight into a beautiful woman. "It made such an impression when she walks off that boat—I can still see it," he said. "She is this new person, and I thought, 'That could be me!'" Only a certain kind of man ever identified with Bette Davis. Or at least, ever admitted it.

Seeing *Now, Voyager* was not the only reason the teenage Dominick wanted to escape the lovely hilltop campus of Canterbury. In his youth, he was forever escaping something—his father, Canterbury School, and before it, Kingswood.

At that Hartford school, his brother Richard not only excelled at sports but also got accepted to Yale. Dr. Dunne knew that Dominick, with his average grade point, would never follow Richard to an Ivy League school, and so he tried to rectify the situation by enrolling his second son in a prestigious prep school away from home for his junior and senior years. There were disappointments in leaving Kingswood. Dominick would never experience the honor and privilege of walking across the school's Senior Green, a spacious lawn separating the chapel from the complex of four small stone cottages housing the classrooms. The Senior Green held an almost sacred significance for the younger students because only boys in their final year at Kingswood were allowed to walk across the carefully mowed grass there.

Canterbury School, however, had its advantages. In wartime America, the hour-long train ride to New Milford ("New England Begins Here") from West Hartford meant that Dominick would no longer be living with his father. No one at Canterbury would know to compare him to Big Dick. And best of all, the prep school appealed to his aspirations, because its alumni included children from those families that never sent their sons to the more provincial Kingswood—sons like Sargent Shriver, Rushton Skakel, and John F. Kennedy, all of whom had graduated from Canterbury in the previous decade.

Shriver, Skakel, Kennedy. Would sons from those truly wealthy, long-established Catholic families become Dominick's friends at Canterbury? The problem with being an outsider in one's own family is how a young man clings to that status, consciously or not, throughout his life. Which is why, unlike the other students at Canterbury, Dominick felt compelled in his senior year to leave the school's hilltop campus with its stupendous views of the Adirondacks and escape to visit New Milford.

"We never went to town," said Clifford McCormick, a classmate who graduated from Canterbury with Dominick in 1944. "Our whole life was up there on the hill. We were busy. It was preparing us for the Ivy League schools."

Dominick made a habit of leaving the Canterbury campus midday. "I remember risking expulsion every afternoon by sneaking into the town of New Milford, Connecticut, during sports period to read the latest accounts in the New York *Daily Mirror* and the New York *Journal-American* at the local drugstore to read all about the Wayne Lonergan murder case," Dominick recalled.

Good Catholic boys like Clifford McCormick did not read about Wayne Lonergan. Good Catholic boys at Canterbury were jocks and studied hard to get into Harvard or Yale. And they did not read about Wayne Lonergan for one very good reason: the young Canadian was a sexual pervert who brutally murdered his wealthy American wife and mother of his one-year-old child.

Dominick, on the other hand, read everything he could find on the Lonergan murder. The *Journal-American*, among other newspapers, kept him well informed. He even studied its prose, which he would one day mimic in his own writing. The newspaper both cautioned and teased its readers, "Throughout the pattern of the Lonergan murder case are woven the deep purple threads of whispered vices whose details are unprintable and whose character is generally unknown to or misunderstood by the average normal person."

Dominick wanted to emulate the handsome, Catholic, and very middle-class Wayne Lonergan, who ingratiated himself into café society by first becoming the lover of William O. Burton, heir to a brewery fortune, and then marrying his beautiful daughter, Patricia Burton, in 1941. The seventeen-year-old Dominick could only speculate about some of the "deep purple threads," but there was no misinterpreting Mrs. Wayne Lonergan's oft-published quote about her new husband, a quote that came to light only after he had murdered her. Patricia said of Wayne, "If he was good enough for my father, he's good enough for me."

In happier times, Patricia and Wayne Lonergan partied at the Stork Club and El Morocco. He looked equally smashing in swim trunks, a tuxedo, or, when the war began, his Royal Canadian Air Force uniform. The couple even had a baby together. But when they separated in July 1943 and she cut him out of her will, he wasted no time strangling and then bludgeoning her to death with not one but two candlesticks in the bedroom of her Manhattan apartment.

Despite the intrigue of such sordid details, risking expulsion from Canterbury had to compete in Dominick's mind with trying to graduate from Canterbury. When the Lonergan murder took place on October 23, 1943, Dominick was less than a week away from his eighteenth birthday, which meant he would be drafted to serve in World War II that coming February.

Clifford McCormick found himself in a similar situation. "There were four of us at Canterbury who were going to be eighteen that fall. We would have been drafted midterm. The draft was grabbing everybody they could," he recalled. To allow such men to receive their diplomas in January, Canterbury and other schools allowed those turning eighteen to study during the summer. Four Canterbury students, including Dominick and McCormick, attended summer camp on the shores of Lake Wassookeag in Maine where they took intensive courses in math and science, neither of which were Dominick's preferred subjects. "He excelled in English and social sciences," said McCormick. "I think it was difficult for him that summer."

That autumn was even more punishing: McCormick got accepted to Yale; Dominick did not. "The headmaster, Dr. Hume, had a strong relationship with all the Ivy League schools, and he recommended me highly," said McCormick. The same could not be said for Dominick. Correspondence between Dr. Nelson Hume and Dominick's father show how much Dr. Richard Dunne wanted his son to follow him into medicine and study at Yale. (He wanted the same for his son Richard, who did go to Yale but pursued a career in insurance instead.) Hume, however, did not write an enthusiastic letter of recommendation for Dominick. Instead, he pointed out in his letter to the admissions officer at Yale that while Dominick's academic performance had improved markedly at Canterbury, he ranked only in the top half of his class and he tended not to participate in extracurricular activities.

At the end of January 1944, Canterbury held a graduation ceremony in its gothic-style church for those four students going into the service. Clifford McCormick, like Richard Dunne Jr., would be accepted into a naval academy and never see combat. "Nick, however, went right off to Europe and the war," said McCormick.

In between Canterbury and the war, Dominick endured six weeks of basic training at Indiantown Gap in Harrisburg, Pennsylvania, followed by a rough Atlantic crossing on the *Mariposa*. Dominick did not make friends at Canterbury, but he met a good one in the army. He and Hank Bresky bonded over their prep-school upbringing and sense of humor, which was macabre, at least under the extreme violence to which they were soon subjected. Their first night in England they listened to buzz bombs drop, and neither of them could sleep nor stop laughing, even though both teenagers were "scared shitless," Dominick wrote a friend.

About a month after D-Day (June 6, 1944), he and Bresky arrived in Germany as part of the Ninety-Fifth Division, where they did not engage in much combat but required security clearance due to the clandestine nature of their duties. As forward observers, they routinely went behind enemy lines to search out the daily whereabouts of troops on both sides of the conflict.

Four years earlier, the Axis forces had captured Metz, France, and that autumn the Allied forces, including the Ninety-Fifth Division, received orders to take back the French garrison town. They called it the Battle of Metz. (Dominick sometimes identified it as the more famous Battle of the Bulge, which followed the Metz conflict.) In letters home, Dominick apologized for being so vague about his whereabouts, but it was army orders. He could write, however, how he had been able to pick up a Nazi helmet for his youngest brother, Stephen, despite his feelings of guilt regarding battle souvenirs. A common saying in the war was that "the English are fighting for the king. The French are fighting for their land. And the Americans are fighting for souvenirs and the hell of it." Hank Bresky told Dominick all he wanted to take home to America was a "bad memory." Dominick agreed. But he did send news of his bringing back a helmet for his kid brother.

His other younger brother, the twelve-year-old John Gregory Dunne, wrote him the latest Hollywood gossip. Among other news, John let Dominick know that the singer Dinah Shore gave birth to a "colored (nigger) baby" and George Montgomery had no choice but to sue her for divorce.

Much more meaningful were the letters from his father. Dr. Dunne wrote how much he enjoyed reading about Dominick's wartime experiences in Europe, and advised him to consider being a writer. His thoughtful words both surprised and touched Dominick, because it had always been his interest in the arts and his writing a play about Molly and Polly that the doctor criticized as being effeminate.

His father's old "sissy" comments, unfortunately, followed Dominick overseas. What he did not write to his family was the constant verbal abuse he took from a sergeant in his division. It reminded him of the names his father called him at home. Those attacks on his manhood ended abruptly, however, when Dominick and his friend risked their lives to perform a surprising act of extreme bravery.

During the Battle of Metz, Dominick and Hank Bresky received orders to retreat even though two fellow soldiers had been badly wounded in the field near the town of Felsberg. A lieutenant told them, "Sorry, my orders are to retreat. We have to leave them behind."

Dominick and Bresky ignored the command. "In the darkness, Hank and I looked at each other and we ran back toward the Germans. Some extra thing came into my being. It was black night. There was artillery over our heads," Dominick recalled. He could never forget one of the soldiers he rescued. "He bled all over me. He reached out and squeezed my hand to say thank you. I don't know if he lived."

No sergeant could ever again say he acted like a sissy after Dominick received the Bronze Star for bravery.

When the war in Europe ended on May 8, 1945, Dominick and Bresky were sent to Bavaria to await their transfer home. As would often happen throughout his life, Dominick endured the hardship in uncommonly high style and comfort. A small castle stood near the American camp, and while the other soldiers may have nicknamed Dominick and Bresky the "gold-dust twins," it was their privileged upbringing and attendant polished manners that made them fit to be cited for special duty at the royal residence. The old princess of Lippe lived in the castle, and the gold-dust twins were chosen to protect her in the aftermath of the war. It was not much of a job, but with characteristic grace and style Dominick embellished his duties by reading the princess copies of *Life* magazine sent to him from home. Dominick loved royalty, and while he understood that the prisoner labor in Nazi Germany—the Poles, the Romanians, the Lithuanians— hated their masters, he knew the princess to be a better person. To his eyes, these now-freed "slaves," as he called them, treated the old woman with genuine affection. They had been forbidden to marry, but with the war now over, the princess arranged to hold a mass outdoor wedding at her castle for any former prisoners wanting to wed. There was not much food, but Dominick and Bresky did what they could to embellish the wedding feast by bringing all the Hershey bars, eggs, and cigarettes they could gather from their rations.

Dominick enjoyed celebrating with the old princess more than he did with his own family when he returned home a decorated war hero. No one on Albany Avenue mentioned his Bronze Star until the family dined at a restaurant on Dominick's first Thursday night back home—Thursday being "the cook's night off." At the restaurant, a friend of his mother offered her congratulations, and giving Dominick a big hug, she looked at Dr. and Mrs. Dunne to say, "You must be so proud!" It was the first acknowledgement in West Hartford of his Bronze Star.

When Dr. Richard Dunne Sr. died unexpectedly two years later of a ruptured aorta, at age fifty-one, the family held a traditional Irish wake, with hundreds of townspeople paying their respects at the house on Albany Avenue. In his middle age, Dominick recalled in a letter to his brother John how he had disappeared for hours during the wake when he should have been home with his mother, two sisters, and three brothers. Instead of mourning, Dominick spent those hours with his new boyfriend, Andreas Devendorf, having sex in Dr. Dunne's black Buick near the ninth hole of the local golf course. Fortunately, hard rain pelted the car and steamed over the windows to give them a modicum of privacy. Dominick wrote of his lover, "My father had disliked him, but nothing was ever said." Nor did Dominick ever publicly reveal why Dr. Dunne hated Andreas, but he knew why.

Dominick visited his father's grave only once, for the burial, but continued to see a lot of Andreas Devendorf, an underclassman at Wesleyan University in nearby Middletown, Connecticut.

The following summer, Dominick convinced his mother he needed to brush up on his Spanish by traveling to Guatemala with his young lover. They stayed in the Spanish colonial town of Antigua, and walking down the cobblestone streets there one day with Dominick, Andreas Devendorf saw a friend from America. "Gore!" he shouted. "Andreas!" Gore Vidal shouted back. Dominick was duly impressed. Vidal's first novel, *Williwag*, about his experiences in World War II, had just been published to critical acclaim, and he was already at work on another. (That novel, *The City and the Pillar*, would make him infamous due to its homosexual theme.) Vidal was renting a house in Antigua and invited the two men to stay with him for a few days. He was not only a WASP who happened to be very handsome, wealthy, and talented; Vidal also descended from an American political dynasty that Dominick envied almost as much as the servants whom the young novelist had at his every command "to wait on him and serve meals on time." Dominick also recalled, "You cannot overestimate the amount of personal charisma Gore Vidal had at that time."

He liked to tell the story of how Devendorf and Vidal knew each other. "They met in the men's restroom at the East Hampton cinema where they fucked!" he said.

Vidal told a slightly different version. "We met in the men's restroom at the East Hampton cinema and then went back to my father's attic to fuck," he recalled.

Vidal was not living alone in Antigua, and his other guest that season gave a bisexual frisson to the young writer's mystique. Dominick knew Anaïs Nin as Henry Miller's former mistress. The Cuban memoirist, born in Paris, was already in her forties when she began her brief affair with the twenty-two-year-old Vidal. Having sex with a man so much younger made her an exotic in Dominick's eyes, as did the colored yarn Nin braided in her hair and the Isadora Duncan poses she kept striking, even when she showered or went swimming. It was there in the water—either a swimming pool or a small pond, depending on how he fashioned the story—that Dominick claimed to have unexpectedly and briefly penetrated the nymph-like Nin. "Utter nonsense!" said Vidal, who claimed that Dominick and his ex-mistress never had sex, in or out of the water. Dominick, proud of the conquest, made sure to keep proof of it. Nin's handwritten inscription to him in her book *Children of the Albatross* reads, "For Nick, Will you float me home? Anaïs, 1947."

Dominick's affair with Andreas Devendorf lasted longer than his moment with Nin (or Vidal's with her, for that matter). Vidal described Andreas as being good-looking, but "hairy like a tarantula." While Dominick and Vidal continued to see each other sporadically throughout their lives, Devendorf's life took another path. He left Wesleyan University after his sophomore year and, according to Dominick, came to resemble a character out of an Evelyn Waugh novel: a dissipated, broken youth who could never divorce himself from his family's money and control, he ended his life going in and out of mental institutions. Those character traits aside, Dominick wrote in his journal that his lovemaking with Andreas was the only time sex with another man was "innocent" and not an act of "humiliation."

His affair with Devendorf took place during Dominick's first two years at Williams College in Williamstown, Massachusetts. Having gone to war, Dominick was a little older than most students in his class. Unlike his two years at Canterbury, which had no drama department, Dominick found an extended family of like-minded young men who enjoyed performing on stage regardless of how that artistic pursuit might have compromised their masculinity in the eyes of others. Williams College suspended its theater productions during the war, but by 1947 those shows made a significant comeback, and not because of any returning soldier-professor.

That year, Dominick auditioned against a freshman for the lead in Emlyn Williams's thriller *Night Must Fall*, which had opened on Broadway to great success only a decade before. The two students tried out three times before the role of the psychopath Danny, who charms his way into a country household, was awarded to the underclassman. Stephen Sondheim got respectable reviews, but Dominick went on to receive even better reviews in the *Williams Record* for his performance later that season as the tortured mercy-killer George in John Steinbeck's *Of Mice and Men*. Whatever competition existed between the two men, it did not get in the way of their befriending each other, as well as two other theater mavens. Charles Hollerith Jr. and Howard Erskine also appeared in nearly every other production staged at Williams College in the late 1940s. Sondheim, of course, belonged in a different league—and it was not only his immense talent as a songwriter that put him there. Oscar Hammerstein II called him his protégé—Sondheim called him Okie—and the young composer would tell his college friends gossip like "Gosh, Okie's upset because Gertrude Lawrence can't reach this note and they're gonna have to . . ."

In addition to acting, Sondheim wrote musicals and revues, and after his first year at Williams, he quickly turned a Sondheim show into an annual campus event, with his three friends often on stage in the cast, beginning with the original musical revue *All That Glitters*. Except for Hollerith, whom the playwright Mart Crowley described as "the gayest straight man I've ever met," they were homosexual. Like the theater, it was a bond. And they possessed other qualities making them friends, whether it was their camp sense of humor or unbridled ambition, because unlike most college chums they never really lost touch with one another.

Hollerith's son, Chuck, recalled the four men's quarter-annual ritual, initiated as soon as a famous restaurant opened on the East Side of Manhattan in the 1950s. "At the beginning of each season of the year, they had lunch at the Four Seasons restaurant," he said. "Sometimes it would be just three of them, but that tradition continued well into the 1970s."

In their respective yearbooks at Williams College, Sondheim received the most attention in the *Gulielmensian*. His senior-year tally of accomplishments, voted on by classmates, led him to be included on lists ranging from the Most Talented to the Most Likely to Succeed. His three close friends in the theater were not mentioned in any of those categories, although Dominick did make one list. He came in sixth in his class for being among the Best Dressed on campus.

In Dominick's senior year, Sondheim took him to the final run-through of Rodgers and Hammerstein's impending hit musical, starring Mary Martin and Ezio Pinza. If acting on stage at Williams had not already done it, seeing *South Pacific* completely hooked Dominick. "This is it!" he said. "I gotta be in this kind of light!"

Dominick took extreme pride in his being the first in the Williams College gang of four to land a big job in show business. He first tried acting, but the legendary teacher Sanford Meisner, who had apparently never heard of Alan Ladd or Mickey Rooney, told Dominick that at a stocky five foot six he was too short to be a leading man. "If you're a character man, you won't make it until you're forty or something," Meisner told him. "You're so ambitious, go behind the camera."

Fortunately, television was new, and a family acquaintance had to make only a phone call to get Dominick a stage-manager position at NBC. Overnight, he became popular with friends whose children never missed an episode of *Howdy Doody*, sang "Ta-ra-ra Boom-de-ay" endlessly, and wanted nothing more in life than to sit in the show's famed Peanut Gallery to watch a wooden puppet perform live with an avuncular actor in cowboy drag named Buffalo Bob. Dominick left it to parents to explain what the TV crew in Studio 3A at Rockefeller Center did to poor Howdy's arms and legs, "these incredibly filthy things," right before air time.

Hollerith and Erskine followed Dominick with their own careers in entertainment, not into television but the theater, where they became producers. Erskine also acted, his last professional assignment being a Victorian partygoer in Martin Scorsese's 1993 movie *The Age of Innocence*.

And Sondheim? The protégé of Oscar Hammerstein II found himself on Italy's Amalfi coast in 1953, working as an assistant to producer Jack Clayton on the film *Beat the Devil*. In letters from Sondheim to Dominick, it is not quite clear what the young composer's job entailed because Sondheim himself was not quite sure, although he expressed hope he would be working on the film's score when Clayton returned to England for postproduction.

The letters, dated February 1953, can best be described as "camp," a word Sondheim used more than once to describe the starry cast. In a manner that urbane homosexuals of the period thought amusing, Sondheim often mixed up the pronouns, as well as the honorifics, to describe Humphrey Bogart, Jennifer Jones, Peter Lorre, Robert Morley, and director John

Huston. He also filled his letters with gossip about Jones being a lesbian, Lorre recovering from his drug addiction, and Morley's wife coming to visit the production in the wake of the actor's boyfriend, already ensconced in Ravello. In one letter, Sondheim introduced his new friend Truman Capote, on location in Italy to rewrite the script. No doubt, Dominick knew of Capote, who had already written one successful novel, *Other Voices, Other Rooms*, and one Broadway flop, *The Grass Harp*. Sondheim made no mention of those works. Instead, he commented on being utterly beguiled by the elfin young man despite his extreme "effeminacy." Sondheim insisted that Dominick find a way to meet Capote when the twenty-eight-year-old writer next visited New York City.

Although they are not the kinds of letters that two heterosexual men of any era would ever have written to each other, in one detail they display a very ordinary sentiment. Sondheim wrote how he wanted to return to the beautiful Italian coast one day for his "honeymoon."

# 2
## Marriage and Puppets

In autumn 1953 Dominick's mother gave the opening-night party for a new play titled *Late Love*, starring Arlene Francis and Cliff Robertson. It was Broadway-bound, and in those days, shows often held their tryout in Hartford, Connecticut, before facing the critics in New York City. Dorothy Dunne gave the party at her home in nearby West Hartford as a favor to her son's college friend Howard Erskine, an associate producer on the play. Erskine's girlfriend would be staying at the Dunne house, and Howard, busy with the show, left it to Dominick and Dorothy to take care of Ellen Beatriz Griffin, arriving from New York City. "Would you meet my girlfriend at the train station?" he asked them.

Lenny Griffin, as she was nicknamed, grew up on a 30,000-acre ranch in Nogales, Arizona, heir to herds of Santa Gertrudis cattle, as well as the Griffin Wheel Company, "which made the wheels on all the railroad trains in America in the days before air travel." Those were the words Dominick used to describe her fortune.

His words to describe Lenny were also to the point. "She was a beauty. She was an heiress," he said.

Lenny's friend Mart Crowley described her wealth as vast. "She grew up with the likes of Gloria Vanderbilt," said the playwright. "She was rich, rich, rich, an only child." She was also a dark, serene, almost melancholic beauty who considered herself attractive enough to be a model in New York City. For a brief time, she also tried to be an actress, and lived at the exclusively female Barbizon Hotel. She made the trip up from New York for Dorothy Dunne's party to celebrate her boyfriend's play, and when she stepped off the train, it would be difficult to say who was attracted to her first or more, the mother or the son. "That's the girl you'll marry," Dorothy told Dominick, and in the car ride to their house he admitted to having been "mesmerized" by Howard Erskine's pretty date.

Publicly, Dominick always said Lenny was the only person he ever really loved. In a letter written to his children in 1979 but never sent, Dominick also expressed his deep love for their mother. But it was a complicated love. In that letter of confession, he spoke of their marriage being "proof positive" he was not the homosexual his father accused him of being. And he gave another reason for loving her: Lenny "believed" in him. No one else in his family ever did, he wrote. A few months before his death in 2009, Dominick told a British reporter, "In my era, gay men were expected to get married."

Dominick did not say it at the time, but he was one of those people. So was Lenny's boyfriend Howard Erskine, who would also go on to marry and have children. Like Dominick said, gay people got married in 1954, whether or not they told their spouses about their true sexual orientation. Usually, they did not. Usually, the spouses found out the truth.

Regarding the day he met Lenny, Dominick wrote in his published memoir, "*Late Love* was a hit, and my mother's party for the stars was a smash." Three weeks later, he asked Lenny to marry him. She waited a week before she wrote a letter, telling him in the most formal terms, "Miss Ellen Beatriz Griffin accepts with pleasure the kind invitation of Mr. Dominick Dunne to be his lawful wedded wife."

They shared a love of letter-writing, and her pre-wedding letters to him during a cross-country trip, from New York to Arizona, are filled with the infectious anticipation of a young woman in love and looking forward to a life together as husband and wife. That long train trip took her through the South and exposed Lenny for the first time to the brutal treatment of blacks there. At one point in her journey, she wandered into the wrong room at a train station, and in a letter she expressed her general disorientation and horror to Dominick. She thanked him for warning her about the abuses of segregation.

Six months after they met, Lenny and Dominick married on April 24, 1954, at the Sacred Heart Church in the border town of Nogales. A huge reception, complete with mariachi band, followed at her family's vast Rancho Yerba Buena, the music a nod to the Mexican heritage of the bride's very aristocratic mother, Beatriz Sandoval Griffin.

It thrilled Dominick that the *New York Times* devoted as much copy to his nuptials as the Old Gray Lady gave to a Kennedy wedding that same day in April. MGM star Peter Lawford married Patricia Kennedy, daughter of tycoon and former UK ambassador Joseph P. Kennedy, and the two wedding announcements ran side by side on the same page. Despite the attention of the *Times*, marrying Lenny did not give Dominick everything he had hoped for in the first weeks of their marriage. The Social Register dropped Ellen Beatriz Griffin the day she took the name Mrs. Dominick Dunne; she could not have cared less, but it disappointed Dominick so much that he did not tell family or friends.

Being in the Social Register was the one thing Dominick thought he might have over the Kennedys. In his opinion, even the Kennedys were not really respected until Jack "married Jacqueline Bouvier and became the thirty-fifth president of the United States." By then, he had already begun to hate the Kennedys, but in the 1950s Dominick worshipped them despite his being a Republican.

John F. Kennedy and Jacqueline Bouvier beat the Dunnes and the Lawfords to the altar by about six months. It impressed Dominick that one of his coworkers at NBC had been invited to the Kennedy/Bouvier wedding. Sometime in 1954, the new Mrs. Kennedy came to visit Freddy Eberstadt at the network's Rockefeller Center offices in New York City. "We'd known each other since we were kids," Eberstadt said of Jackie. He introduced her to Dominick. "Nick was very protective of the Kennedys then," he noted. "He worshipped them."

Eberstadt worked as a unit manager on *Watch Mr. Wizard*, a children's science program on NBC. Also employed there was John Calley, the future chairman and CEO of Sony Pictures Entertainment, who started at the network in the mail room. Calley liked to deliver what he thought were smart remarks, and the crack he made about the new Mrs. Kennedy upset Dominick tremendously. Calley had joked, "Did you know the only reason Jackie married Jack is because Freddy threw her aside?"

Dominick recoiled at the bad wisecrack. "Nick didn't find that one bit funny," said Eberstadt.

After *Howdy Doody*, Dominick quickly climbed the NBC ladder to become stage manager for the prestigious *Robert Montgomery Presents*, one of the first TV shows to perform original hour-long dramas live on the air. Every week at 30 Rockefeller Plaza in Studio 8H, Dominick performed a ritual he loved from the moment he first said the words, "One minute, Mr. Montgomery."

Robert Montgomery called back at him from across the studio, "Thank you, Dominick," at which the actor-producer-host would look into the camera to say, "And good evening, ladies and gentleman."

Dominick knew it. "Well, I was a star!" he exclaimed.

While Eberstadt's young son, Nicholas, might have preferred that his father's friend continue working with a wooden puppet, *Robert Montgomery Presents* and other shows Dominick stage-managed at NBC introduced him to the kind of theater talent that would soon turn into movie legends. James Dean, Walter Matthau, Steve McQueen, and Joanne Woodward performed, as well as some stars no longer in demand in Hollywood—actors like Claudette Colbert, Ginger Rogers, Roddy McDowall, and Franchot Tone.

Dominick especially enjoyed taking his younger brother John, a student at nearby Princeton University, to parties in Manhattan populated by his new actor friends. The teenager did not know Grace Kelly from Geraldine Page, but those showbiz introductions would be useful to John in his future as a screenwriter, not that he ever felt obliged to return the favor.

Frank Sinatra was an exception to the star-to-be or former-star rule in live TV of the mid-1950s. Fresh off his Oscar win for *From Here to Eternity*, Sinatra headlined NBC's 1955 musical version of *Our Town*, an assignment that turned into a stage manager's worst nightmare when the star took a dislike to the crew and cast, including the very young Paul Newman and Eva Marie Saint, and refused to show up for the dress rehearsal. Sinatra and his frazzled stage manager would meet again in Hollywood, much to Dominick's grief and humiliation.

"I followed Dominick from afar at NBC. He was a big deal," said Liz Smith. In the mid-1950s, the future gossip columnist worked on the network's weekly travelogue *Wide Wide World*. "Dominick was always kidding around with me how we had started together in television, but I don't think he really remembered me from then."

After a brief stint in television, Smith began her long career in journalism, starting as an assistant to Igor Cassini, who wrote the Cholly Knickerbocker gossip column for the Hearst newspapers. Cassini was to New York's high society what Hearst's Louella Parsons was to Hollywood. Whether Dominick knew her or not at NBC, he avidly read Cassini and Smith's copy in the newspaper. No articles fascinated him more than three published under Cholly Knickerbocker's byline in 1955. That year, a chorus girl turned society lady, Ann Woodward, shot and killed her husband, Billy, heir to the Hanover National Bank fortune. The Knickerbocker column ran three in-depth stories on the deadly incident and then dropped the scandal as if it never happened. Three decades later, Dominick would speculate in his roman à clef *The Two Mrs. Grenvilles* that Hearst put a stop to Cassini writing about the scandal, even though Liz Smith, who had worked for the powerful gossip, doubted such high-level intervention ever took place. "Cassini didn't want to be ostracized at Hearst, and Hearst didn't want to be, either," said Smith, referring to the newspaper's access to New York's high society, which quickly closed ranks around the Woodward family. "I don't ever remember Hearst stopping Cassini." Dominick, for his part, saw it differently. He saw the conspiracy, the power play, the intrigue, the dark side. He often did when it came to money and murder.

If he looked like a "big deal" to Liz Smith in the 1950s, Dominick felt somewhat less so when old acquaintances like Gore Vidal came to visit him at Rockefeller Center. Vidal brought his so-called stepsister Jacqueline Kennedy (they shared the same stepfather) to NBC one day during rehearsals when Dominick, on his hands and knees, was spreading tape on the floor to simulate the boundaries of the scenery. He felt "like a mick" despite wearing his J. Press sport jacket, gray flannel slacks, Brooks Brothers shirt with button-down collar, and striped tie. Unlike most stage managers, he overdressed. He even felt like a mick when the very Irish John O'Hara came to visit the studio for all five days of rehearsals on the *Robert Montgomery Presents* adaptation of the writer's first novel, *Appointment in Samarra*, published in 1934. Everyone working on the show knew they were doing something bold for 1950s television: like the novel, the TV adaptation of O'Hara's novel would end with the suicide of its hero, Julian English, a victim of the Hangover Generation of the 1930s. Dominick admired O'Hara not only as a writer but as an Irish American who exuded total confidence with his fame, his talent, and his ethnic heritage. The novelist also wore the most beautiful tweed suits Dominick ever saw on a human being.

O'Hara and his wife watched from a viewing room while the actors performed *Appointment in Samarra* live before the cameras. Afterward, they came to the studio to greet Robert Montgomery and make their way to an uptown party to celebrate. Dominick later wrote a friend that O'Hara saw the "yearning" in his eyes and motioned for him to join them that night. Dominick felt compelled to say no. He knew his place. He was not invited. O'Hara shrugged, said it did not matter, and quickly extended an invitation to be his guest. It surprised the young stage manager when everyone at the party treated him not like a TV minion but as if he "belonged," and they were so "nice." Although he never saw O'Hara again, Dominick made it his major goal in life to get himself invited to more parties of *that* caliber. He only had to move to an even more fabulous place.

In 1957 Dominick left NBC and New York to visit Los Angeles, the city of his childhood dreams. It was not supposed to be a long stay. At seventy-five dollars a week, CBS hired him to be the assistant to Martin

Manulis, producer of the network's top-of-the-line drama series *Playhouse 90*. He had imagined himself living in Hollywood ever since Aunt Harriet Burns, a nun turned spinster, took him there back in the 1930s and they had dined at the Brown Derby to gawk at all the movie stars. In a way, those movie stars became Dominick's fantasy family, the nice family whose pictures he pinned to his bedroom wall because they were beautiful, and did not beat him or call him a sissy.

Working with stage actors on live TV in New York stirred Dominick's imagination, but it could not compare to what he would soon experience in Los Angeles on *Playhouse 90*. In bringing live television to the West Coast, CBS made possible on a regular basis what had not been in the East: week after week, major movie stars were only a short limousine ride away from their homes in Beverly Hills to the CBS studio in Los Angeles. Film production had slowed considerably, and in between the occasional movie, the biggest stars could further enhance their career with TV's easy money and vast exposure. The first *Playhouse 90* episode Dominick worked on was a remake of the play and movie *The Petrified Forest*, with Humphrey Bogart reprising his role of the gangster Duke Mantee.

Much to his surprise, it was Frank Sinatra who recommended Dominick to Bogart to be stage manager on the Robert E. Sherwood drama. "Word got around that I was good with the stars who were scared of live television," Dominick recalled. CBS put him up at the preternaturally pink Beverly Hills Hotel for the three-week rehearsal. One day, Dominick told Bogart he went to Canterbury School and Bogart revealed that he also had attended an East Coast prep school, Andover. As soon as they got beyond those minor academic preliminaries, the young man from New York confessed, "God, I love looking at movie stars!"

"What are you doing Friday night?" Bogie asked, and Dominick found himself invited to an affair that turned the John O'Hara party into something resembling a beer blast. There at Bogart and Lauren Bacall's Holmby Hills home Dominick heard Judy Garland and Frank Sinatra sing, and everyone from Spencer Tracy to Lana Turner showed up. Dominick knew how to tell a story, and when those names were not dazzling enough, he would also throw in the fact, or the fiction, that the party ended with everyone, including the dogs and "the women in their gowns," jumping into the pool. Whatever actually went on in or out of the water that night, Dominick definitely could not sleep when he returned to the palm-leafed hallways of the Beverly Hills Hotel. He phoned Lenny in New York City to tell her he thought he had died and gone to the Academy Awards, only better. "Lenny, we've got to move to Hollywood," he insisted. "It's incredible." That Bogart party was everything the little boy who ought to have been born a girl ever wanted in life.

Lenny and Dominick already had a two-year-old son, Griffin, and a newborn, Alex. "Nick went out to L.A., and Lenny was not enthusiastic about it," said Freddy Eberstadt. "The idea was it would be for a minimum of six weeks, a maximum of six months. They were not going to be Angelinos. In a sense, they never came back."

Stage managers and producer assistants who made seventy-five dollars a week could not afford to rent large houses on the beach in Santa Monica. Dominick did not care. He wanted to live in Harold Lloyd's beach "cottage" with its "seven or eight bedrooms"—Dominick could not count them all. Stunned at its immense size, Lenny got no farther than the kitchen when she turned to her husband to remark, "Were you drunk?" And there was another big plus to the humongous cottage: the famous couple whose wedding he had followed with such devotion in the *New York Times* lived down the beach in the old Louis B. Mayer house. They had been linked in print; now Dominick could call Pat and Peter Lawford his neighbors.

"We spent too much money," Dominick admitted. "Lenny was always inclined to hold back. Not me. I was of the more-more-more school." It was mostly her money he spent, and his profligacy caused problems in the Griffin family. "Lenny's mother was a gorgon," said Mart Crowley. "She not only ruined Lenny's life; she despised Nick." The Mexican dowager considered her son-in-law a gold digger, and the beach house was only the beginning. In the near future, Dominick would infuriate her further by indulging in a far more extravagant example of reckless spending.

Despite their opposing views on money, Dominick described Beatriz Sandoval Griffin in reservedly sympathetic terms, calling his mother-in-law a "strong, uncompromising woman who has never not stated exactly what was on her mind in any given situation, a trait that has made her respected if not always endearing."

Dorothy Dunne proved much less judgmental. Dominick wrote his own mother enthusiastic letters about his roseate new life in Los Angeles. For his family's first Christmas on the West Coast, Dominick mentioned the big fete at the neighbors' down the beach. The Lawfords held a premature tree-trimming party where the kids got to open their gifts two weeks ahead of time, because Pat and Peter would be spending the holidays in Palm Beach. What Dominick did not write is how sorry he felt for the son-in-law of Joe Kennedy, having seen the Brit be "humiliated" by the fierce patriarch in front of guests. Nor did he write that he found himself physically attracted to Lawford, who would be the first of his many

Hollywood infatuations. Years later, Dominick admitted to having had many such "crushes," as he called them. "I wasn't good at love. Never worked." A future boyfriend disagreed slightly. "Dominick told me he was in love with Peter," said Norman Carby. "He was very open about it."

Dominick also kept secret from his mother the whole truth about the annual Christmas parties at his boss's house. He did write Dorothy about Charlton Heston's tradition of reading "'Twas the Night Before Christmas" to all the children gathered at the Manulis home; how the Edgar Bergen family, including wife Fran and daughter Candice, joined them there, as did *Gone with the Wind* producer David O. Selznick and his movie-star wife, Jennifer Jones; and that the gossip columnist Louella Parsons got "plastered."

But reporting on who drank too much was about as controversial as Dominick got with Dorothy. There were other advantages to living among the stars and the powerbrokers of Hollywood, and Dominick shared those secrets with neither his mother nor his wife.

"I met Nick at his home when the boys were two and three," said Scotty Bowers, a well-known bartender around town. Bowers shared a couple of friends with Dominick, and it was those two out-of-town guests who took him to the home of the young TV executive and his family where he and Dominick met for the first time. While Bowers tended bar at Hollywood parties, he earned additional income by running a thriving escort service, operated from a filling station on Hollywood Boulevard. His service catered to a number of homosexuals in the entertainment business, and those illustrious clients included Martin Manulis and Ralph Levy, producer of such long-running TV series as *The Jack Benny Program* and *The George Burns and Gracie Allen Show*. "There were about six guys who were all big in television," Bowers said of his vast client list. "They were all buddies and used my service. TV was starting up then."

It was a small, powerful community of gay TV executives with wives and kids. "Dominick was shy at first," Bowers recalled. After they met at Dominick's house, Bowers later saw the young husband and father at an all-gay party. "I was bartending. Dominick was already there, and as soon as he saw me he ran to the balcony to hide. He didn't want me to see him. He spent the next four hours out on that balcony."

Dominick eventually outgrew his shyness to join Manulis and Levy as a Bowers client. "He liked it if the guy had a place of his own, so he could go there," Bowers said of Dominick's taste in call boys. "Some men liked to go out to dinner first. Dominick wasn't one of those. He was in and out quick." Hiring prostitutes, in addition to gossiping and name-dropping, was another trait Dominick shared with his brother John. But being hetero-sexual, John Gregory Dunne could boast of his sex-for-hire predilections in his memoir *Harp*. Dominick had to hide his. It was just one of many differences between being straight and being gay in mid-twentieth-century America.

Dominick's days with the Bowers service began after he and Lenny, in 1958, bought a two-story Georgian house at 714 Walden Drive in Beverly Hills. Again, much of the purchase money came from Lenny. Both he and she wanted to move. There had been too many personal tragedies in the rented house on the beach. One of the nannies died unexpectedly, and Griffin, age three, found the body. Far worse, two children born to Domi-nick and Lenny died of hyaline membrane disease within days of being born. When the first of the baby girls died, the hospital called Dominick at two thirty in the morning. He said he wanted to see his child. They said no. It was not recommended. He went to the hospital anyway and demanded to see her. They took Dominick into a kitchen where the dead baby lay under a sheet on the counter, her skin having already turned yellow. He could only look for a moment, and yet it would be "an image" he never forgot. To welcome Lenny home, Dominick planted a rose garden for her in their yard despite it being a rented house, one they would soon leave.

They had not lived long on Walden Drive when tragedy also struck there. This death, however, was not in any way personal, and Dominick could indulge in its spectacle without reservation or remorse from a couple of blocks away. It was the kind of famous murder case he had thrived on as a boy and young man, only this particular murder topped even Ann Wood-ward's when it came to sheer glamour, not to mention media coverage. Who knew? Maybe he moved to Beverly Hills as much for its movie-star parties as its movie-star scandals. This one took place "almost just around the corner" from where he now lived.

Despite the heavy rain in Beverly Hills on April 4, 1958, Dominick and Lenny heard the police sirens sometime before midnight. It was Good Friday. Their sons, Griffin and Alex, were already upstairs in bed. Earlier that night, they had all watched *The Phil Silvers Show*. Later, Dominick and Lenny tuned into Edward R. Murrow's interview with singer Anna Maria Alberghetti on *Person to Person*.

When the sirens grew louder and then came to a sudden stop nearby, Dominick grabbed an umbrella and went out to take a look. Lenny told him not to bother. Ten minutes later, when Dominick returned to tell Lenny about the police and the commotion over on North Bedford Drive, she expressed embarrassment that the neighbors might see him peering into the house where a movie star lived. For Lenny, it did not matter that the movie star was Lana Turner and someone in the house had just been stabbed to death and that someone was her gangster boyfriend.

Dominick kissed his wife goodnight and told her not to wait up. "I wouldn't miss this for the world," he said. And off he went, leaving their house a second time that night to gawk like an autograph hound at the spectacle in front of Lana Turner's rented house. Not only was the ambulance parked in front, but there were a half-dozen police cars and many more cars with reporters and photographers piling out of them.

People were pointing at a white Thunderbird parked in the curved driveway of the colonial house built by Laura Hope Crews with her earnings playing Aunt Pittypat in *Gone with the Wind*. Black shutters dressed the ten windows, and if you added pillars the place could have doubled for Tara. The white T-bird belonged to Johnny Stompanato. Or it *had* belonged to Johnny Stompanato, now dead. People were telling Dominick that Lana's daughter by her second husband, Joseph Stephen Crane, had killed the gangster. Others said Lana herself had done it. But why then was the fourteen-year-old Cheryl Crane the one led out of the house in handcuffs?

"I stood outside Lana Turner's house and watched as Jerry Geisler, the criminal lawyer, went in and out," Dominick recalled. He even claimed to have heard Lana shriek at Geisler from within the house, "Why won't they let me bring my baby home?!"

But Dominick had an alternate version of what happened that night. He imagined Lana and the lawyer concocting the whole Cheryl-stabbed-him defense, with Geisler coaxing her, "How about if Cheryl did it, trying to protect her mother from this thug who was beating the crap out of her?"

Even then, Dominick had a flair for drama, not to mention a sore spot for criminals who call their lawyers long before they phone the ambulance or the police. He called it "a rich-people thing."

Alex Dunne did not remember the night of April 4, 1958. "But my dad was obsessed with that story," he said. "His story was that the daughter took the rap, the daughter didn't really kill him."

Dominick remembered it simply as "one of the stories that most influenced me." He found it even more alluring in its intrigue and cover-up than the Woodward or the Lonergan murders. Only later, more than a quarter century later, did he realize murder could be personal, ugly, and anything but fascinating.

Dominique Dunne was born on November 23, 1959. "Dominique became our treasure," he said, referring to the two infant girls who died before her. Dominick called her Darling. "My relationship with my daughter was perfect," he said. "I adored her and she me."

The relationships with his two sons proved more complex.

"Even at age eight we knew he was flawed the way he'd get so upset and worked up about stuff," said Griffin Dunne. "He drove my mom up the wall. He was a human being in development."

"Our mother was a real free spirit," said Alex Dunne. "Dad had to have everything *just so*."

Griffin believed, "conscious or not," that their upbringing was "based on the royal family. The nanny would have meals with the kids and the adults would check in, have a little something maybe and then go out to drink and dance," he recalled. "They would think nothing of having people in black tie, and we'd be upstairs and listen to them getting hammered and having a great time."

Photographs of the two boys, and later Dominique, show them in matching outfits for a casual day at the beach or a dip in the backyard pool. "Even we were art-directed," said Griffin. Dominick's attention to the styling of his children was never more evident than when it came to the family portraits, based on Cecil Beaton's photographs of the royal family. "They were deadly serious Christmas cards, taken in the middle of summer. They weren't your happy Christmas cards. No smiling. They were 'Look how beautiful this family is.' We hated them," said Griffin.

One year, Dominick set up his Leica and then promptly tripped over the tripod. All three kids broke up laughing, their expressions of spontaneous delight over their father's unexpected tumble recorded on film. "That's the only card I kept," said Griffin.

What his sons already knew at an early age is what many people were openly saying about Dominick in the 1960s. "He's a snob," they said. Later, he would develop a sense of self-deprecating humor about his social climbing, his name-dropping, and his star-fixations, but in the early 1960s Dominick turned those avocations into a full-time career, and he nurtured them with solemn devotion. His social predilection combined with his drinking and extramarital affairs with other men made him something less than admired in Hollywood. "His reputations had holes in it," said Freddy Eberstadt. "Lenny's never did."

Lenny remained his greatest asset. It may have been why Frank Sinatra decided to unload on her, and not Dominick, that terrible night at the Bistro. The agent Irving "Swifty" Lazar was throwing a party in the upstairs room at the tony Beverly Hills restaurant, and whatever Sinatra said to Lenny there left her in tears. (A soused Sinatra also tore into Lauren Bacall,

Maureen O'Sullivan, and Lazar at the Bistro party.) Dominick would only say how Sinatra had called him a "loser," but there were implications that Sinatra also thought Lenny was being used by her husband, and not just for her money.

For a man of Sinatra's ego, humiliating a man's wife did not satiate his need to conquer and destroy. His next ploy would be to confront Dominick, albeit with somebody else's fist.

Shortly before that encounter took place, Dominick found himself seduced into making a mistake he would not be able to correct for nearly two decades. Unfortunately, it played into Sinatra's plan to further denigrate him in the eyes of Lenny and all of Hollywood.

In the early 1960s, Dominick's haircutter Jay Sebring talked him into getting a toupee to cover a growing bald spot at the crown of his head. Sebring, who introduced the blow dryer to men's hairstyling, said he could make him a small toupee that would blend in with his real hair and no one would ever know. Concerned about his appearance—"I always felt insecure about my looks"—Dominick agreed to wear it. But he hated it. He even wrote in his private journal how he would rather be exposed as a homosexual than as a rug wearer. That is doubtful; Dominick often resorted to exaggeration to make his point, even to himself. When he became a journalist, the worst thing Dominick Dunne could write about a man was that he put a rug on his head. He never wrote publicly that he used to wear one.

Dominick always believed that no one can spot a rug on a man's head faster than a fellow rug wearer. Frank Sinatra wore a toupee, and Dominick believed Sinatra knew about his own hairpiece. Long before Hollywood and the rest of America had become litigiously inclined, Sinatra used to pay the Daisy's maître d' to humiliate people he disliked. Dominick called himself and Lenny "charter members" of the Sunset Strip disco, a private club with a $500 initiation fee. "It's our own little Hollywood clique," said TV producer Aaron Spelling. "If you get bombed, it's not in the paper next day." Nor did George the maître d' punching Dominick make the paper. It was a soft punch, by all accounts, and no sooner did he throw it than George apologized, saying, "I'm awfully sorry, Mr. Dunne. Mr. Sinatra made me hit you in the *head*."

Dominick asked if he had been paid. George said Sinatra gave him fifty dollars.

Over the years, the "Frank Sinatra paid George to hit me" story was one of Dominick's most oft told. His story began, "Frank Sinatra picked on me. I was the amusement for Sinatra. My humiliation was his fun." Dominick, however, always left out one important detail in the retelling, and it was the thing that made the punch so potentially ego-bruising. There was something about the way George said "hit you in the *head*" that led Dominick to believe he meant to use the word "toupee" instead. Being hit by a fist under any circumstance is awful, but what Dominick worried about most when he took George's fist was that his rug would dislodge. Billy Wilder's wife nearly guessed the truth. She told Dominick what she thought of Sinatra's unprompted attack. "If he ever did that to me, I would pull his wig off," said Audrey Wilder.

Dominick did not pull off Sinatra's wig, but he and Lenny never returned to the Daisy, where, in the following decade, O.J. Simpson would meet the blonde waitress Nicole Brown. Otherwise, Dominick's partying, drinking, philandering, and social climbing continued unabated.

"Nick kind of lost his head in Los Angeles," said Freddy Eberstadt. "Lenny stayed level-headed. He got swept away by the grandeur and glamour. It was the only time I was not very close to him. I found him quite difficult."

Years later, Dominick repeatedly admitted, "I write assholes so well because I used to be an asshole." He did not exaggerate. In the 1960s he got into a too-public fight with Henry Fonda's third wife, Afdera Franchetti. He laughed too hard at skater Sonja Henie taking a bad fall on the ice when she came out of retirement. At very private parties, he took too many snapshots of Princess Margaret and union lawyer Sidney Korshak, "who was never photographed," Dominick noted. In some ways, Dominick Dunne turned himself into something of a joke. He got invited to important parties, but often only after the dinner had been served to the host's small, select group of truly important friends. He and Lenny soon became known as the After Dinner Dunnes.

Worst of all, his marriage to Lenny was breaking up and people knew it. He did what many Hollywood spouses do when they want to plaster over fissures in a marriage. He decided to celebrate their wedding anniversary in grand fashion. It was 1964, and they had been married ten years.

"It was strained then," Mart Crowley said of the Dunne marriage. At the time, the future playwright was the secretary of Natalie Wood, one of Lenny Dunne's closest friends. "Lenny and Nick just got through that [anniversary] party, before the marriage really did fall apart," said Crowley.

If Lenny's mother, Beatriz, ever needed more evidence that her son-in-law lived in high style thanks to her daughter's bank account, it was the $20,000 party Dominick threw on April 24, 1964. "Lenny's mother was furious," he wrote.

Dominick dubbed it the Black and White Ball. He got the idea from his dinner guest Cecil Beaton, who had been in town to design the sets and costumes for the new movie musical *My Fair Lady* at Warner Bros. "The black-and-white motif for our party was taken from the Ascot scene," Dominick noted, referring to the film's chiaroscuro visuals.

"It was gorgeous," said Mart Crowley. "Yes, the party was over the top, but not in a glitzy Hollywood way."

Dominick put his stage-manager talents into full play to redecorate the house as if it were a theater set. He put all the downstairs furniture into storage and sent his three children to spend the night at the Beverly Crest Hotel. Before they left home that evening, Griffin, Alex, and Dominique got to see the opulent magic created by a famous muralist and stage designer.

"Jack McCullagh turned the house into a stage," Alex Dunne recalled. "He built these beautiful white trellises that we had for years later. The trellises were very French, making the place look like a chateau. We had these cypress trees by the pool in the backyard and Jack painted these jungle scenes so you saw animal faces coming at you through the trees. It was a big deal and I couldn't understand why we weren't allowed to be there."

Even the invitations were special, engraved by Smythson's of Bond Street in London. It advised women to wear black or white. Men would be wearing tuxedos, of course. Dominick planned for 250 guests and absolutely no more. He even told some of his bachelor friends they could not bring a date. "I was one of the extra men that were invited," said Crowley. "We were always useful, to invite the women to dance. I could get a party going. I could dance with everybody." The Beverly Hills fire marshal put a limit on the number of guests. No more than 250. But at the last moment Truman Capote phoned to make it an illegal 252.

Capote was the guest of David O. Selznick and Jennifer Jones. *In Cold Blood* was more than a year away from being published, in 1965, but the writer had publicized it relentlessly. "So naturally we invited him," Dominick reported. "Then he called and asked if he could bring Alvin Dewey—the Kansas detective who had broken the case and arrested the killers—and his wife. I told Truman that because of fire laws we couldn't let anyone bring extra guests. But he wouldn't let it go. It was clear that he wasn't going to hang up until he had gotten the Deweys into the party, so eventually I relented."

If a party takes place in Beverly Hills and no one is there to photograph or report it, has the party really taken place? Dominick did not think so. He enlisted his soon-to-be sister-in-law to pull some strings at *Vogue*, where Joan Didion reviewed movies (until a 143-word pan of *The Sound of Music* got her fired the month before *Vogue* published its coverage of the Black and White Ball). The fashion magazine sent photographer Bob Willoughby. Dominick got his artist-friend Don Bachardy, Christopher Isherwood's partner, to sketch Lenny's gown for an item in *Women's Wear Daily*. He also had luck finding someone to report on the party, even though he would be the one providing all the copy. George Christy told Dominick that such a party was not right for his column in *Town & Country*. "I was doing interviews with Alfred Hitchcock, that kind of thing," Christy recalled. However, the columnist promised to pass on Dominick's "party details" to Aileen Mehle, who wrote as Suzy Knickerbocker for the *Journal-American*. "It'd give her column international flair rather than just New York society," said Christy.

As promised, Suzy ran Dominick's copy, reporting on a guest list featuring an eclectic roundup of movie stars, from Loretta Young to Dennis Hopper, along with top directors Billy Wilder and Vincente Minnelli, L.A. society ladies Betsy Bloomingdale and Edie Goetz, as well as a future first lady and president, Nancy and Ronald Reagan. Dominick was thrilled. Suzy even repeated verbatim some of the copy he gave her: "There were hydrangeas everywhere, two orchestras, and a late supper. The music stopped at four." Years later, Dominick repeated those words in his published memoir, *The Way We Lived Then*.

"It was an exciting launch for his social career," said Christy, who told Dominick to "send me more. I'll pass them on." Christy was just one of many columnists who began receiving Dominick's morning reports of parties he gave and the parties he attended. Lenny told him, "If all else fails, you can always write a column." She knew her husband better than he did.

Dominick's unbridled drive was part entitlement, part anxiety. Even though his marriage was falling apart, he deserved to throw himself a $20,000 party, but the sheer extravagance masked deep insecurity. "I always felt I was there on a pass," he said of life in Beverly Hills. "I wasn't going to last. I didn't belong there. I always had a feeling I wasn't a part of this. I was just watching."

Griffin Dunne saw the unhappy side of his father's obsession. "He was at the mercy of these people who he was entertaining. It was almost as if they weren't real unless they liked him and came to his house," he said. Even their presence was not enough. Dominick needed to relive the experience through the voluminous scrapbooks he kept, ordered specially from Smythson's. "Every telegram and every acceptance to his invitation were ironed into a scrapbook. He would use an iron so they would stay in," said Griffin. Dominick was creating the life of the person he had invented to replace the boy he had been born, and his fabricated life needed to be documented. He needed to believe it was real, that he was not making it up.

Dominick's career in television became a sideline, although a very successful one. He left Fox television, where he produced the hit TV series *Adventures in Paradise*, to become a vice president at Four Star Television, which had fourteen shows on the air when he arrived there in 1963. Although he partnered with the movie stars David Niven and Charles Boyer, fellow actor Dick Powell led the company, its true visionary. He and his wife, June Allyson, were close friends of Nancy and Ronald Reagan in their actor days. Powell used to tell Dominick, "See if you can find a part for Nancy on *Burke's Law*," one of Four Star's most popular series. Powell did not have to recommend Nancy. Neither did Dominick. TV executives and casting directors all wanted to meet her, and not because she was a great or even an adequate actress. Privately, Dominick told friends that Mrs. Reagan was a popular request thanks to her expertise at performing fellatio upon request. Powell, however, did not continue to support the actress's flagging career too long after Dominick's arrival at Four Star. He died of cancer at age fifty-eight, and his absence soon affected the company. Within two years of Powell's death, Four Star had only five shows on the air; two years later only one. Dominick could do nothing to stop the precipitous decline.

He tried with a TV marriage not made in heaven.

In 1965 the seminal gay-themed play *Boys in the Band* was three years away from being produced on stage, but it was already "indicative of what was on my brain," said its creator. Mart Crowley always wanted to be a writer, but after an assistant's job on the movie *Splendor in the Grass*, he ended up as Natalie Wood's secretary instead. But he was no ordinary secretary. Sometime during all the phone answering, he found time to come up with an idea for the actress's next film.

What Crowley wrote was a screenplay based on a book by Dorothy Baker, the author of several controversial books on lesbianism, as well as a similarly themed play called *Trio*, which closed on Broadway when Protestant ministers put up a picket line in 1945. Today, Baker is best known for her novel *Young Man with a Horn*, the screen version of which stars Lauren Bacall as Kirk Douglas's sophisticated, aloof, and very bisexual wife. In 1962 Baker wrote a novel called *Cassandra at the Wedding*, about twin sisters—one heterosexual, the other lesbian—and Natalie Wood, at the peak of her popularity, possessed the clout to get Twentieth Century Fox to buy the movie rights for her. The screenplay was written by her secretary, Mart Crowley, and Dominick's old boss Martin Manulis would produce.

"We were preparing *Cassandra at the Wedding*, and Nick and I met through Martin," said Crowley. The three men lunched and discovered they shared the same sense of camp humor, among a few other things. "We laughed a lot," said Crowley.

But two weeks before shooting was to begin on *Cassandra at the Wedding*, Fox pulled the plug. "Darryl Zanuck never liked the script; they knew it was a controversial film," said Crowley. "They used the sets for *What a Way to Go!* Threw some hot pink paint on them." Manulis licked his wounds and instead produced *The Days of Wine and Roses*, starring Jack Lemmon and Lee Remick, which he had originally done on TV at *Playhouse 90*. As would happen throughout their careers, Dominick and Crowley threw each other a lifeline. This time it was Dominick's turn to give Crowley a job. "I was at liberty and Nick gave me a six-month contract at Four Star Television," said Crowley.

One day, the young secretary turned writer was "sleeping on the couch in my cubby hole of an office" when Dominick ran in panic-stricken. He had just shown a veteran movie star the script, by Cy Howard, for a pilot titled *The Bette Davis Show*.

"No way!" Bette Davis told Dominick. "I'm backing out." Dominick begged her to give him the weekend to have the script rewritten. She harrumphed. What could be done in a weekend? Dominick told Crowley to do his stuff. Fast.

"I need the script back by early Monday morning," he ordered. It was Friday.

Crowley hardly slept for the next three nights and bunkered down in his office at Four Star to rewrite *The Bette Davis Show*. He even gave Davis's character, an interior decorator, a gay sidekick whom he envisioned being played by Paul Lynde. "Which was, after *Cassandra at the Wedding*, another indication of the way I was going," he said. Monday morning, before anyone arrived at the studio, Crowley slipped the script under Dominick's door and went home to crash.

Dominick hand-delivered the script to Bette Davis's home. A maid told him that the lady of the house was not there, but would he please wait in the foyer anyway. The maid then walked the script to another room, closing the door behind her. From within, Dominick soon heard Margo Channing's inimitable dry cackle of a laugh. Fifteen minutes later, Bette Davis appeared, beaming, pages in hand. "This is terrific. I've never laughed so hard," she said.

All of a sudden, the pilot was a go again. Except for Davis's gay sidekick. "Paul Lynde and Bette Davis would have been hilarious together," said Crowley. But CBS said no: the sidekick had to be played by an actress.

"Who can we get for Bette?" asked Dominick. "She's so paranoid about her looks."

In tests, Davis had demanded more flattering lighting, and even had her neck painted a dark brown to create a shadow effect to hide her wrinkles. Crowley suggested Mary Wickes, who appeared in such Davis vehicles as *Now, Voyager* and *The Man Who Came to Dinner*. "She's not intimidated by her," said Crowley.

"Wickes would be perfect," said Dominick.

And they were perfect together. Wickes did not get in the way and never tried to steal a scene. "But Bette couldn't adjust to the rapid pace of television," said Crowley, and she started acting like she was back at Warner Bros., demanding retakes and holding up production.

Four Star scheduled a typical five-day shoot for the pilot, retitled *The Decorator*. "And by Wednesday the sponsor had already pulled the plug," said Crowley. They did not want to get involved with a temperamental star. Dominick, however, had to keep the news away from Davis since they had two more days of shooting. "Bette would have freaked out if she knew," Crowley recalled. When she was told on the following Monday, Bette Davis did as everyone expected. She freaked out.

*The Decorator* did not become the big success Dominick needed at Four Star. But Crowley would not forget the favor, and it was he who would give Dominick his second act in Hollywood.

In the summer of 1965, Lenny rented a house in Malibu so she and the kids could spend less time with Dominick. She also accepted a rich cousin's invitation to vacation with him and his boyfriend on a yacht in the Greek isles. Alex Dunne recalled the day she arrived back home in Beverly Hills after being away from the family for two months. "Mom walked in the door with her sandals over her shoulder. We were all 'Mommy! Mommy! Mommy!' And she was real cool. 'Hi, kids.' And walked on. It was the first time for her to live her own life," he said. Alex told the anecdote without resentment at either parent. "We had the nanny," he explained.

Lenny wanted out of the marriage, and Dominick did not see it coming. He and Lenny were driving home from a party "she didn't want to attend" when he got the news. "She wanted to separate from me," he wrote. Dominick pulled his Mercedes-Benz convertible over to the curb on Sunset Boulevard and started to cry.

Griffin would later say that his father "lacked the substance she craved. . . . He was a very superficial guy. He needed those parties," which had become "more important than his family. He lost his way."

Alex voiced a simpler reason for the breakup. "It couldn't have been fun to be married to a gay man who couldn't quite make up his own mind. I'm sure that was hard for my mom," he said.

Friends also put the breakup at the door of Dominick's sexual orientation.

"I think she found out something concrete," said Crowley. "Because of Lenny's disdain and utter turning on him, I think she got wind of something. She was so contained and there was so much anger going on in there."

She and Crowley were close. "Every year, Mart would give my mother a movie-related gift," Alex Dunne recalled. One year, Crowley gave Lenny a sled with the name Rosebud printed on it; another year, she received a satin pillow, the name Rebecca embroidered in the slightly scorched satin. But having homosexual friends is different from being married to one.

Crowley claimed never to have discussed Dominick's sexual orientation with him. "Whatever I found out I found out from other people," he said. "And sometimes way after the fact, and I was astounded because he had lied to me."

In his private journals, Dominick was honest, at least with himself. He wrote about Lenny having dinner guests at the Beverly Hills house and his taking the men to the Chateau Marmont afterward to have sex. He liked the hotel's old Hollywood ambiance and would regale with stories about all the famous people he knew, from Gore Vidal to Paul Newman, who used to stay there on the fifth floor. But inevitably, Dominick would "regret" his infidelity as soon as he left the Chateau.

At their rented Malibu beach house, Dominick invited his call boys to stay to have lunch. He called them his "masseurs." It was a bold, repeated indiscretion that his sister-in-law Joan Didion observed and wrote about in her 1970 novel, *Play It as It Lays*, in which she based a closeted, substance-abusing movie producer on Dominick. And there were other more innocuous signs that Dominick was not a typical father with wife and kids. The family's two pet poodles answered to Oscar and Bosie, named after Oscar Wilde and his callow lover Lord Alfred Douglas.

Masseurs and curiously named poodles were not the only thing Dominick brought into his home.

"The first time I dropped acid, I dropped it with Jay," Dominick recalled. "He brought it over to my house on Walden Drive one time when

Lenny and the kids were at her mother's ranch." It was Jay Sebring who also introduced Dominick to Sharon Tate, soon to be a victim, along with the haircutter, of the Charles Manson gang.

Lenny had reason to be angry, and her sense of betrayal was evident not only to Mart Crowley. In the early days of their separation, Dominick often remarked how hurt he was that all her friends "despised" him. Lenny's going to too many Hollywood parties was the least of her problems with the marriage.

One of those "friends" met Lenny through Connie Wald, wife of the prolific film producer Jerry Wald. "Connie hated Dominick because he sold her his dog," the novelist Susanna Moore recalled. "What kind of man sells his dog?" Mrs. Wald used to ask rhetorically.

"People loved Lenny," said Moore. "She wasn't Fitzgerald-ish, but there was something lost about her, certainly in the marriage that caused her to be adrift. She had great charm and was funny and was used to people in power. Dominick had a camera with him and took pictures of everything, every meeting and party. It was intrusive. It wasn't her nature."

With the breakup of their marriage, Lenny attempted to keep her anger away from the Dunne children, and devised a quick and seemingly easy plan to make their separation less traumatic. She would take the kids to Coronado Island off the coast of San Diego, giving Dominick a few days to remove all his belongings from the Walden Drive house. Not that Lenny was the most conservative parent. During their brief respite away from home, she and Griffin planned to make a stop at her in-laws' place on Franklin Avenue in Los Feliz. It was a twenty-eight-room house, and John Gregory Dunne and Joan Didion rented out its many bedrooms to artists and other writers, including the future novelist Susanna Moore. The couple did not charge high rents because, as Didion described the place, "paint peeled inside and out, and pipes broke and window sashes crumbled and the tennis court had not been rolled since 1933." Much more significant to keeping the multiple rents low was the "senseless-killing neighborhood" in which the once-elegant mansion now stood. None of which kept Lenny away from a party where Janis Joplin promised to be a guest. Alex and Dominique were a tad young, but Griffin, recently a teenager, could handle such an adult party, she thought. Mother and son both wanted to see Janis Joplin. Joan Didion recalled the rock star being at the party, which took place about a year before Joplin died of a drug overdose. "She had just done a concert and she wanted brandy-and-Benedictine in a water tumbler. Music people never wanted ordinary drinks," Didion wrote.

Self-destructive rock stars were one thing. What Lenny did not want any of her children to witness was an emotionally fraught scene between her and Dominick. Lenny planned for them to tell their three children everything in a most civilized manner after Dominick finished moving out.

But "he totally changed the game plan," Griffin recalled. Back together with his family at Walden Drive, Dominick began well, following his wife's careful scenario, telling the children, "Your mother and I have decided . . ." Then he broke down. "Your mother wants to divorce me!" he blurted out.

Lenny could only roll her eyes.

Dominick would try to win her back, but she was not having it. "Nick forever referred to Lenny as 'my wife,'" said Crowley. "And that drove Lenny up the wall."

She told people, "We are divorced. I am not his wife." Dominick and Lenny's separation was immediate, although the couple did not finalize the divorce for three years.

In one respect, the separation left unaffected Dominick's status in Hollywood. He was equally delighted and relieved when the *Los Angeles Times'* gossip columnist kept both him and Lenny on her celebrated A-list. Joyce Haber had recently taken over for Hedda Hopper at the newspaper, where she promptly coined the term "A-list" to designate the town's top echelon of stars, power players, and society ladies. Dominick knew of Haber long before she arrived at the *Times*. His brother John used to date Haber in their *Time* magazine days together. She was the kind of woman, said John, who had two opinions of men: either they were gay or they were rapists. Dominick knew never to cross Haber, and stayed on her good side by feeding her party news and other gossip.

"There were a lot of calls from Nick Dunne in those days," said Haber's assistant Harry Clein, who later became a top Hollywood publicist. Dominick made a habit of phoning Haber the morning after a party they had both attended. Already a chronic alcoholic, she did not have a great memory, and Dominick helped her with his pointed observations, telling the gossip who arrived with whom and who left with whom. It was one way of staying on Haber's A-list, even if most people in town thought he no longer belonged there.

Feeding items to a columnist, however, could not save his job at Four Star, a company without any hits in the late 1960s. Despite his precarious position there, Dominick rented a three-bedroom apartment with maid's room at 132 South Spalding Drive in Beverly Hills. "It was marvelous," said Alex Dunne. "When we went to visit, each of us kids had our own bedroom. And there was a room for a live-in Chinese butler, but he didn't last long."

Dominick drank and dropped acid to forget that his family no longer lived with him during the week. He had once criticized actor Michael Caine for smoking marijuana in his home. Now, by his own definition, Dominick was a "real pot head." While vacationing in Acapulco, he led two lives, just as he did in Los Angeles. During the day in Mexico, Dominick purchased an ounce of marijuana from a boy selling it at a gay beach there. At night, he dined with actress Merle Oberon and went to the ballet with Mrs. Douglas Fairbanks.

On the trip back to Los Angeles, Dominick considered stashing his marijuana in the airplane seat to avoid taking it through customs. On second thought, he wanted to smoke it when he got home, even though he had plenty of grass stored there. Besides, he looked "the picture of propriety" in his gray suit made for him by Angelo in Rome. Everyone else on the Western Airlines flight looked like a tourist; Dominick looked like a business executive and, as always, he flew first class. What did he have to worry about?

No sooner did he get to customs than two men asked Dominick to follow them to another room. When he answered that he had no drugs, the undercover officers quickly searched him to find the marijuana in a suit pocket. They then stripped him and gave him an anal probe. Standing there naked, Dominick worried about his children. John Gregory Dunne and Joan Didion were bringing Alex and Dominique to the airport. What if they saw him? Two officers carried Dominick under his arms through the airport to a waiting police car, its red light flashing. Fortunately, Joan and John had taken his children back home as soon as they suspected Dominick's arrest and somehow made sure Alex and Dominique saw nothing.

The couple bailed him out of jail the next morning, and Joan suggested he spend the next few nights at their house instead of returning to his Spalding Drive apartment. She feared Dominick might be suicidal; he feared the arrest would make the papers.

Dominick received a surprise phone call from a man he barely knew, offering his help. He had met Beldon Katleman at a few Hollywood parties, but Dominick never invited him to his own home because of his ties to organized crime in Las Vegas. Worse, Lenny found him uncommonly vulgar, especially after Katleman paid her a crass compliment. Dominick also found it crass, but, unlike Lenny, he also found the remark funny, so funny he repeated it to his sister-in-law, who promptly paraphrased the line to read "What I like about your wife . . . is she's not a cunt" and put it in her novel *Play It as It Lays*. Katleman, however, did not make the "cunt" remark in reference to Lenny. He said it to her face: "What I like about *you* is . . ."

As instructed, Dominick went to Katleman's house at 200 Baroda Drive in Holmby Hills to discuss his upcoming day in court. He knew the house well. It was a modernist glass, wood, and stone treasure formerly owned by Gary Cooper, whose daughter, Maria, was Dominique's god-mother. The place had changed. Gone were the English antiques and other signs of good taste. Dominick looked around. Everything seemed to have been doused in the color orange. Katleman lived with a starlet, and as soon as Dominick arrived, Katleman told the girlfriend to "beat it."

Katleman invited Dominick to join him in the sauna room. He asked about his arrest. Dominick lied. Katleman told him he did not want to hear the "bullshit" and to tell him the name of the judge who would be hearing the case. Katleman knew the guy and told Dominick not to worry. End of sauna, end of visit.

Only Dominick's lawyer was more shocked than he when the judge threw the case out of court. Afterward, the lawyer asked Dominick, "Who do you know?"

Dominick phoned Katleman to ask him, "Why did you do that?" And Katleman explained, "Because when I went to parties and no one would speak to me, you always spoke to me."

In the following decade, Dominick would call himself "an architect of my own destruction." But even the arrest at LAX did not change his ways. The only lesson he learned from his previous drug bust was to smoke his marijuana on the plane *before* he departed it.

In 1970 the future novelist Michael M. Thomas sat on the board of Twentieth Century Fox and owned a small piece of the L.A. Rams. That year, he boarded a 747 flight from New York to Los Angeles to see his team play against the New York Giants, and he and a friend immediately broke out some cookies laced with marijuana to better enjoy the cross-country trip. "When we went for the loo to step up the cookies, and in the middle of this enormous cloud of cannabis smoke coming from the restroom was this little figure," he recalled. It was Dominick Dunne, fresh from smoking a joint. "What till you see what we've got," Thomas told this total stranger. "And we enjoyed the rest of our marijuana in the loo and went back to our seats."

Shortly before he lost his job at Four Star, Dominick ran into Mart Crowley at a party in Malibu. The Royal Ballet of England, of all things, was being honored in Lalaland. "I'm worried about you," Dominick began. "You're drinking and not working." Dominick drank as much as Crowley, but at least he had a job. At least for a few more months. "What's going on?"

"Oh, don't worry," Crowley replied. "I'm busy. I'm writing a play."

"Great. What's it about?"

"It's about a bunch of gay guys getting together at a birthday party."

That one-sentence synopsis almost knocked Dominick speechless, but he made an attempt at diplomacy. "Well, Mart, I think it's great you're writing a play. It's good for you. It's therapeutic . . ."

Therapeutic? Crowley flinched. "It's going to be terrific. It is terrific!"

Trying to be supportive, Dominick asked about the play's title. Crowley was not sure. He liked *The Birthday Party*, but Harold Pinter beat him to it. Then there was *Somebody's Children*, but it sounded maudlin. "How about *The Boys in the Band*?" he asked.

Dominick did not know what it meant. Crowley explained: it's that line in *A Star Is Born* when James Mason tells an insecure Judy Garland, "You're singing for yourself and the boys in the band."

While Dominick was not sold on the title, he knew for sure what he thought about a play with nothing but homosexual characters. "Just don't let it throw you if it doesn't get produced," he said.

What Crowley did not tell Dominick is that he based one of the play's characters on him.

Much to Dominick's surprise, less than a year after their talk on the beach in Malibu, *The Boys in the Band* opened to rave reviews in New York City and proved such a hit that Crowley could easily afford his dream of living in Manhattan's legendary Algonquin Hotel.

On the West Coast, it was now Dominick's turn to be the one out of work, having lost his job at Four Star and so hard up for money that he had to give up his live-in Chinese butler. In his journal, he wrote of receiving $80,000 dollars in "alimony" from Lenny, which he now spent to live. It was 50 percent of the estimated value on the Walden Drive house, where the rest of his family continued to live.

# 3

## Mengers and Disaster

When he had to let his butler go, Dominick feared he would also have to give up the spectacular Spalding Drive apartment. That was when Mart Crowley returned the favor of *The Decorator* and made Dominick his executive producer on the film version of *The Boys in the Band*. Crowley parlayed the play's international success into a film contract making him producer-screenwriter and retaining the original Off Broadway cast. He lost only one battle: keeping the stage director Robert Moore. CBS Films insisted on someone at the helm with film experience.

"We wouldn't have gotten Billy Friedkin without Nick," said Crowley. Dominick and Friedkin knew each other from their days at Four Star, and Friedkin had recently directed *The Night They Raided Minsky's* and the film version of *The Birthday Party*. It was the Harold Pinter play that made the powers at CBS Films believe Friedkin, a future Oscar winner, could transfer yet another play about an unusually ominous birthday celebration to the screen. Dominick, at the time, was "down and out and broke, and he needed a job," said Crowley, "and I needed someone to do all the heavy technical dirty work and be a diplomat with CBS, which I was not. I flunked out of diplomacy school. All the paperwork and money and all the phone calls with people bitching constantly—I didn't want to do that."

Dominick's duties on *Boys* included all those phone calls and paperwork but did not end there. He also took care of Crowley's problem securing a Diners Club card, and on that matter, Dominick put into play his guest list for the Black and White Ball and other parties. He went right to the top, writing to Alfred S. Bloomingdale, the department store heir who had merged his Dine and Sign charge-card business with Diners Club years ago. The formerly cash-strapped Crowley got his piece of plastic from no less a person than the so-called father of the credit card.

And there were perks, too, for being executive producer. The job put Dominick in daily contact with his most profound infatuation to date. He had met Frederick Combs the year before when the actor performed in the original Off Broadway cast of *The Boys in the Band*, and Dominick fell in love, madly in love, with the clean-cut, preppy-looking young actor, who played a clean-cut, preppy-looking young man in the play.

Howard Rosenman, a film and TV producer, knew both men. "I'd never seen that kind of obsession, one person for another, like Nick had for Freddy," said Rosenman. Dominick managed to spend a great deal of time with Combs, which did not mean the affection was entirely reciprocated.

Combs was very popular, and not only with Dominick. "Freddy couldn't go to the corner for a bottle of milk without getting a blow job," said Crowley. But whether the actor had an intimate relationship with Dominick, Crowley never knew for sure. "That's the $64,000 question. But it's very unlikely. Freddy was one of those guys who liked anonymous sex with great-looking guys." Repeatedly, Crowley overhead Combs tell other men, "I like you, but I'm just not attracted to you. I wish I was." Dominick was one of those men. "Nick was not Freddy's type at all," added Crowley.

Dominick bore the burden of his unrequited love; in fact, as he would later write in his private journal, it may have been the basis for his attraction to Combs. "I suppose it was that I disgusted him physically that made him so indispensable to my life," he admitted.

Most people working on the film did not know that Crowley based one of the play's characters on his producer-friend Dominick, but a few suspected. In *The Boys in the Band*, the all-gay birthday party is interrupted when Alan McCarthy, a college friend of the host Michael, makes an unexpected visit to the apartment. Like Dominick was at the time, the character is married but separated from his wife, and despite protestations of the men's gay behavior, McCarthy does not quickly leave the party. Peter White, the actor who originated the role, wondered if the character was gay or straight. During rehearsals, Robert Moore directed him to play the "ambivalence, so that one-half of the audience thinks he is and the other half thinks he isn't." Crowley told him, "You decide and don't tell me."

And Peter White never did. In return, Crowley never revealed to White the prototype for his character. When interviewed for this biography,

White spoke of being "flabbergasted" at the news that Crowley based the Alan McCarthy character on Dominick Dunne. "You're blowing me away with this. My understanding is it was Mart's roommate in college. I have no idea who told me that at the time. I did meet some of the prototypes for the other characters," said White.

Crowley also did not reveal the genesis of the character to Dominick. "We never talked about it," he said. "I never told him. Whether he knew it or not, I know he suspected." Some of the lines spoken by the McCarthy character—"I'm not going to put up with this!"—were in Dominick's standard repertoire of uptight retorts. "Nick got the vibe," said Crowley.

So did other friends in their theater circle. "I heard about it," said Joseph Hardy, who, at the time, was directing Woody Allen's Broadway comedy *Play It Again, Sam*.

"Everybody knew the character was based on Dominick!" claimed Howard Rosenman.

Curiously, Alan McCarthy is the only character in the play that Crowley chose to give a last name. "The character is named after two men I despised," said the playwright. "Alan J. Pakula, who was a closet case of some order, and the other is Frank McCarthy, who was General Patton's right-hand man. McCarthy was gay as a snake, and was the lover of Rupert Allan, a very famous and powerful publicist in Hollywood. They lived in separate houses in Beverly Hills that shared a common courtyard." Dominick knew Allan, and when tragedy struck his own family in the following decade, he would call the publicist to help with a major public-relations problem.

Working in New York City on *Boys*, Dominick sublet an apartment in the East 70s. To enter the building, residents faced several locks, and to boost the security an elaborate alarm system required a code to be punched in to gain entrance. More than once, Dominick entered the wrong numerals, and a security team promptly came to the rescue. In addition to the sophisticated security, the owner of the apartment also splurged on the décor. Griffin Dunne once visited his father there, and when he returned to Los Angeles he told his mother it looked like a French bordello. At least that was the story Dominick told friends. "Griffin was thirteen going on adulthood," said Rosenman, who sometimes babysat the Dunne children and claimed to have offered Dominick's oldest child his first joint.

One night, Dominick made plans to meet Tammy Grimes at nine o'clock at Elaine's restaurant, twenty blocks away from his Eastside sublet. He knew the actress from the Colony in Malibu when he and Lenny rented a beach house there and Roddy McDowall gave weekend parties starring everyone from Rock Hudson and Sean Connery to Jane Fonda and Tuesday Weld. Despite the distance to Elaine's, Dominick decided to walk but did not get very far. At the corner of Madison and East Seventy-Ninth Street, he spotted a very attractive young man on the street. He cruised Dominick. Dominick cruised back. Dominick looked forward to seeing Tammy Grimes. Not only was she a good friend from the West Coast, but she also was a star, and somebody who always dressed like one. Dominick wanted very much to be seen with her at a high-profile spot like Elaine's. But this young man on the street was so attractive and so available. "Basket, pecs, buns, you name it, this kid had it," Dominick noted.

Back at his sublet, Dominick undid all the locks. He entered the correct security code, careful not to notify a squad car. For some reason, the excessive security unnerved the young man. Inside the apartment, Dominick phoned Grimes to cancel. She was not happy, he could tell. The young man did not know Tammy Grimes from Barbara Cook. But when did Broadway trivia ever compromise hardcore lust? Dominick felt romantic. He lit candles. He poured wine. He rolled a joint and was so mesmerized by the young man's great looks that he did not notice how theirs was a one-way conversation.

Dominick, now forty-four years old, had grown a pot belly and was terribly self-conscious. Nor did it help that the pickup refused to remove so much as his shirt but proceeded to undress his host completely. Standing there naked, smoking a joint and holding a glass of wine, Dominick first felt a fist slam hard into his Adam's apple. He lost his breath; gasping, he collapsed to the floor. Before he could regain control, the stranger tied Dominick's arms behind his back with a telephone cord, put a paper bag over his head, and started throwing lit matches at him. Dominick's mind turned to his children. He prayed they did not read about him in the newspapers, another of those "sordid gay murders."

Only the constant ringing of the telephone saved his life. Or was it God answering his prayer that made his attacker leave? He had rummaged through everything, obviously looking for something to steal. Dominick did not know whom to call. He could not phone a straight friend. He thought of Howard Rosenman. He knew his phone number by heart, and with his arms still tied behind his back, Dominick used his nose to dial. Rosenman's boyfriend answered. John Norton and Dominick had never met but knew each other's names. When Dominick learned that Rosenman was out of town, he had no choice but to tell a virtual stranger about his dire predicament. Norton promised he would be right over and arrived within the hour. Blanche du Bois is not the only one who relied on the kindness of strangers.

The summer they filmed *The Boys in the Band* stood out for reasons other than Dominick's dangerous sex life. The Stonewall Riots took place, erupting in the early morning hours of June 28, 1969, and lasting six days. "This unpleasantness in the Village. It was no big deal," Mart Crowley recalled thinking at the time. In years to come, the standoff between the police and patrons of the bar would oft be cited as the start of the modern-day gay-rights movement.

Later that summer, on the other coast, there was no mistaking the impact of what happened on August 9, 1969, when followers of Charles Manson slayed five people in the home of director Roman Polanski. Joan Didion wrote, "I was sitting in the shallow end of my sister-in-law's swimming pool in Beverly Hills when [Lenny Dunne] received a telephone call from a friend who had heard about the murders at Sharon Tate Polanski's house on Cielo Drive. The phone rang twenty times during the next hour. These early reports were garbled and contradictory." With her patented casual despair, Didion added, "I remember that no one was surprised."

Dominick remembered being more than surprised at what came to be known as the Helter Skelter murders. He knew two of the victims, Jay Sebring and Sharon Tate. Frantic, he flew back to Los Angeles the day of the Beverly Hills carnage to be with his family. Lenny had received the phone call about the Manson murders from her good friend Natalie Wood, often first with the local gossip in the movie capital. "Children were sent out of town," Dominick recalled. "Ours went to my mother-in-law's ranch." It was not a long visit away from home for either him or his kids. Dominick needed to return to New York to finish *The Boys in the Band*, which had run a month over schedule and would not be completed until mid-September. The Dunne children went back to school despite fears. Everybody was traumatized, but in some ways, nothing changed for Dominick. Not even a mass murder in his family's neighborhood could shake his determination to always make a good impression. On August 14 he wrote his brother Richard in Venice, California, asking if he could take a photograph of his three children for the family's annual Christmas card. Dominick would have done it himself but needed to return to New York to finish *Boys*. In the letter, Dominick gave instructions to his older brother. He wanted Dominique to wear a long dress and the boys to be put in matching shirts and slacks but nothing too formal. He made only one unusual request: he wanted all three children to be photographed barefoot.

A façade of normalcy again descended, but not completely. The Hollywood community bunkered down out of fear, and for an entirely different reason nothing would be the same for Ellen Griffin Dunne.

When *The Boys in the Band* finished shooting, Dominick returned to his apartment at Spalding Drive. One evening, Lenny called to invite him to dinner at the Walden Drive house. With the entire family sitting around the dining room table, he could only wish that the five of them had enjoyed more times like this, rather than having the kids eat with a nanny while he made plans to run off to yet another party. Lenny finally told Dominick and her children the news. She had been diagnosed with multiple sclerosis. The disease was not curable, and her condition would only deteriorate. In the following decade, Lenny had no choice but to sell the Walden Drive house and leave it in a wheelchair.

The lavish parties that Dominick craved were unthinkable in the wake of the Manson murders. Even the West Coast premiere for *The Boys in the Band* the following winter was relatively subdued. On March 16, 1970, Natalie Wood invited the company over for drinks at her Beverly Hills home before the screening. Later, she and actress Diana Lynn hosted a small party at Scandia restaurant on Sunset Boulevard. Dominick spent the night "following Freddy around," said Neil Koenigsberg, the film's publicist. "Like a puppy dog," added another observer. Dominick did not seem to notice the gossip he left in his wake. He had never been this public about his desire for another man. Combs and he even took vacations together in Haiti, Hawaii, and Cape Cod, and Dominick, as usual, brought his camera. Combs signed one photograph of himself at the beach, professing his love to Dominick. But as Crowley suspected, it was never an intimate relationship, at least not in the way Dominick wanted.

Before *Boys* wrapped, Mart Crowley did what all screenwriters and producers do: he worried about his next project. Making one gay-themed film did not automatically lead to offers on other projects. In fact, the actors had difficulty being cast due to the suspicion that they were all homosexuals; the heterosexual Lawrence Luckinbill even lost a cigarette ad because, as he put it, "They don't think fags smoke their fags." Crowley kept fretting, "I don't know what I'm going to do next." Surprisingly, it was the formerly unemployed Dominick "who used his exec producer credit on *The Boys in the Band* to leverage *The Panic in Needle Park*, even before our film had finished," said Crowley.

Dominick looked forward to making a film with his brother John and Joan Didion, and the idea they all liked best was a film version of James Mills's novel about a couple of young drug addicts on Manhattan's rough Upper West Side. Didion summarized their film adaptation of *The Panic in Needle Park*, calling it *"Romeo and Juliet* on heroin."* It was the kind of short, snappy synopsis film executives loved and Didion delivered often in the coming years. The success of such an offbeat hit as *Easy Rider* opened the door for another low-budget drug-themed movie, and Dominick's producer credit on *Boys* made him acceptable to studios. The positive buzz on *Boys* helped, too.

Didion and the Dunne brothers' ideas for casting their film were unorthodox but right in step with what Hollywood now deemed hip. They wanted Jim Morrison of the Doors to make his screen debut as the drug addict Bobby in *The Panic in Needle Park*. The Beatles scored with *Help!* and *A Hard Day's Night*, and Mick Jagger had recently been cast in *Performance*, to be his screen debut. Casting Morrison made sense. Also, Didion and the Dunne brothers had briefly met the rock star, already notorious for his alcoholism and substance abuse. It would be brilliant type-casting, they all thought. Dominick knew Morrison from a party he threw to inaugurate his new bachelor pad on Spalding Drive. Morrison, completely stoned, became so entranced with the multimirrored walls of the apartment's oval dining room that he got lost in its refracted image. Much to his host's amazement, the rock star appeared to be fondling himself.

Joan and John met Morrison under slightly more decorous circumstances. The Doors were recording their third album, *Waiting for the Sun*, at the Two Terrible Guys Studio near Sunset and Highland in Hollywood. Morrison showed up late, belligerent, drugged, and ready to set his much-inspected crotch on fire with a match. Didion, on assignment from the *Saturday Evening Post*, hoped to get an interview with the rock star. When Morrison proved incommunicative, she instead wrote an essay about the recording session for her book *The White Album*. She noted how the Doors talked to each other "from behind some disabling aphasia. . . . There was a sense that no one was going to leave the room, ever."

Dominick, with his *Boys in the Band* producer credit in hand, secured a deal with Avco-Embassy. Although not one of the majors, the studio did have the recent distinction of having released *The Graduate*, which, together with *Bonnie and Clyde* and *Easy Rider*, revolutionized the Hollywood film industry. John Gregory Dunne had preternaturally charted that business upheaval in 1967 with his nonfiction book *The Studio*, which dissected Twentieth Century Fox's box-office disaster *Dr. Doolittle*, an absurdly overproduced musical that held no appeal for young audiences raised in the era of the Vietnam War. Didion, ever the cynic, held little hope for the alternative. She wrote how the new studio executives were "narcotized by *Easy Rider*'s grosses," and criticized them for thinking "all that was needed to get a picture off the ground was the suggestion of a $750,000 budget . . . and this terrific 22-year-old kid director."

Didion thought nothing of biting the hand that greenlit *The Panic in Needle Park*.

The movie may have boasted a budget under one million dollars, but that did not prevent Dominick from getting Avco-Embassy to put him up at the Volney Hotel, once home to Dorothy Parker, on East Seventy-Fourth Street in Manhattan. Since Joan and John were still working on the script, they took up residence at a much less desirable address, the Alamac Hotel, across Broadway and West Seventy-First Street from Sherman Square, home to more needle addicts than trees and better known as Needle Park. Living at the seedy Alamac, they thought, would be part of their research.

John and Joan were on their way to being known as the Didions in Hollywood, much to his distress. Their friend Billy Hale, a major TV director (he later directed Dominick's *People Like Us* miniseries), remembered the couple scouting Upper West Side locations for *The Panic in Needle Park*. "They went to Abercrombie & Fitch and bought all these jungle outfits. They were going into the heart of darkness. They took it very seriously," he said. But not that seriously. The couple typically lunched on the other side of town at La Côte Basque.

It was also a time, Hale believed, when the two brothers walked very different paths despite working on the same film. "Nick got more into the 1960s social scene," he said. "John was an Eastern suit. He was pretty straight."

Real panic struck when Avco-Embassy abruptly dumped the *Needle Park* project, and Dominick had to work overtime to negotiate a deal with Twentieth Century Fox and also try to hire a young director, one of those "terrific . . . kid directors" whom his sister-in-law ridiculed. He much admired Jerry Schatzberg's edgy film *Puzzle of a Downfall Child*, starring newcomer Faye Dunaway. At the time, Schatzberg was better known for his fashion photography in *Vogue*.

"I read it with one eye and not much heart," Schatzberg said of the Didions' *Needle Park* script. What did excite him was a young actor whom Dominick wanted to cast after Jim Morrison proved too debauched (and soon died from a drug overdose). The director had seen Al Pacino in the play *The Indian Wants the Bronx* and told his agent, "Boy, if ever I did a film, that's the guy I'd like to work with." Dominick also saw Pacino, but in another play, *Does a Tiger Wear a Necktie?*, and promptly thought of him to play Bobby in *Needle Park*.

"'Al Pacino' were the major words," said Schatzberg. They were not major words, however, for the executives at Fox. Richard Zanuck and David Brown wanted another actor, one who was taller, less ethnic, and better looking. They wanted a star.

"Nick was terrific; he agreed with me about Pacino," said Schatzberg, and best of all, Dominick put together a strategy for getting the studio to agree with their offbeat casting choice. "We'll set up casting," he told Schatzberg, "and if we come up with someone who's fantastic, fine. And if we don't, we'll go back and say Pacino is the only one." For a few weeks, Robert De Niro looked like a contender—although not a star, he had made one movie to Pacino's none—but Dominick's patience and political skills with the studio prevailed. Pacino got the role.

Dominick also found his female lead on the stage, in San Francisco at the American Conservatory Theater. She was playing, of all roles, George Bernard Shaw's St. Joan. "I never did ask Nick how he saw Helen in my St. Joan," said Kitty Winn.

Again, the studio was not happy. "We'd like Mia Farrow," a studio boss opined.

"Oh my God!" said Schatzberg. "Isn't that the girl who just divorced Frank Sinatra?"

After Mia Farrow turned out not to be available or too expensive or simply uninterested, Kitty Winn met with the studio chiefs, who voiced disappointment over her being all of twenty-five years old; Farrow, at the time, was twenty-six. They thought Helen should be twenty. "Nick went in and fought for me," said Winn, who, at the time, looked eighteen.

Dominick played the studio casting game a second time; again, he assuaged the executive fears, and they cast the very reserved Kitty Winn as Helen. Schatzberg recalled, "Nick and I both liked these unknowns who could have come from any place in America" to play the film's drug-addict lovers, their modern-day star-crossed and strung-out young lovers.

Schatzberg called Dominick "a terrific producer." He was also super-protective of his relatives' screenplay. "Nick got a little upset when he watched the dailies," said the director. "His brother and sister-in-law wrote the script and maybe he was anxious about their seeing [the film]. I like the actors to improvise. I actually did not see John Gregory and Joan once we started [shooting]."

Kitty Winn made one suggestion for changing the script. One long monologue did not read well. "It came from this literary place," she recalled. Winn told Schatzberg that "maybe there shouldn't be any words." Dominick overheard the conversation and asked them to keep the monologue. In the end, the actress and her director dropped it.

A couple of weeks into production, Dominick called his leading lady to his New York pied-à-terre at the Volney, the same hotel where he had recently sniffed so much amyl nitrate that he "knocked over a lit candle onto the curtains, which went up in flame," and had to quickly banish "the trashy late-night strangers of the love-for-sale variety who were my guests" before the cops and fire fighters arrived. Putting on a more professional face for his leading lady, Dominick wanted to talk to Winn about her performance. He liked her subtlety as an actress, but she was being too subtle, in his opinion.

"Al's going to steal the film from you if you don't up your game," he began.

Winn came from ACT, an extremely non-star-oriented ensemble. She did not know the first thing about upstaging. "Tell me a scene where you feel Al is stealing the scene," she asked.

Dominick did not hesitate. "You're in Blimpie and Al is eating a sandwich and it is falling out of his mouth and all you see is his being stoned with food falling out of his mouth while you're talking to him."

Winn took a deep breath. She had never made a film before but stood by her understated interpretation of Helen. "Nick, I have to be true to my character and Al has to be true to his character and I can't sit there doing what Al's doing to steal the scene back," she said. "It really is the director and the cameraman if they want to focus on me or they focus on Al. It's not up to me. It's only up to me to play my part." Winn called that afternoon at the Volney Hotel "our only contretemps."

Once shooting started in autumn 1970, the *Los Angeles Herald-Examiner* sent a reporter to do a story on the film. Bridget Byrne arrived around midnight for a shoot near the Museum of Natural History on Central Park West. Pacino told the reporter about the Method, his approach to acting. "When I have a scene in which I have to push Helen around, I push Kitty around all day," he said, then added, "Jerry doesn't pretend to know anything about acting. But he has a sure instinct for what will work and what won't, what looks right, what doesn't."

Dominick did not think such talk helped the film. Nor did John's comment about New York City being a dying city, which was why he and his wife lived in California. Most upsetting personally to Dominick, however, was Byrne's description of him. She wrote, "Dominick Dunne hovers at the end of the alley during a set-up. Despite the absence of a rattle he looks like a cheerer at a football game."

Shortly after shooting ended, Dominick and Schatzberg took their unfinished film to Paris to show it to officials from the Cannes Film Festival. They also spoke to journalists there, hoping to create some buzz. Dominick joked with the French reporters, telling them, "They put us up at the George V. I think I'm going to steal a couple of ashtrays from the hotel."

Dominick's off-hand crack caused a minor stir. The publicist for the Cannes Film Festival said something in French to the maître d'. "And five minutes later they brought a package of hotel ash trays," Schatzberg recalled.

Dominick was not happy. "No, you don't understand," he told the maître d'. "I wanted to *steal* them!"

Later, he got his chance to lift something from the five-star hotel, but even that theft was thwarted. Back in the United States, customs agents searched the two filmmakers' luggage "because we were bringing a film back," explained Schatzberg. The search did not go well for Dominick.

"Those sons of bitches!" he said as soon as he and Schatzberg cleared customs. "They took the bathrobe out of my suitcase!"

"Nick had stolen a George V bathrobe! That was Nick," said Schatzberg.

*Needle Park* played the Cannes Film Festival, where Kitty Winn won the award for best actress on May 27, 1971. Al Pacino did not make the trip, having already started production on *The Godfather*. (It always irked Dominick that Pacino never remembered him, even though he had given the actor his first big break in the movies.) Schatzberg found the experience of having a film shown at Cannes to be part excitement, part humiliation. "We were put up at the Carlton a block away from the Palace—Nick, Kitty, Joan and John, and I came down. There was a big limo waiting for us. We drove one block and got out, and as we got out we saw the press running toward us." Even before the screening, the *Needle Park* company entertained fantasies their film would be a big hit. "Then the press ran right past us. Michele Morgan, the president of the Cannes jury—her limo was right behind ours!" Dominick did not care. He had gotten *this close* to Morgan, the French film actress whose photograph had once adorned his bedroom wall back in West Hartford.

*The Panic in Needle Park* received an excellent reception from the assembled filmgoers, and their applause bathed the American team in adulation as they walked down the grand staircase at the Palais des Festivals. "Then when we got outside, there was no limo and we had to walk back to the Carlton. Nick loved it!" said Schatzberg.

After *Needle Park* won a couple of awards at Cannes, Dominick traveled to Paris to take meetings for his next film, *Play It as It Lays*, based on Joan Didion's second novel. It would be a difficult project to bring to the screen for no other reason than the executive in charge of the movie at Universal Pictures hated it. In fact, Ned Tanen only agreed to greenlight the film because he personally liked Frank Perry and Universal had done well with the director's previous movie, *Diary of a Mad Housewife*. "I always had this fear of studio heads," Dominick said. "Any male in charge brought back the father thing to me." Tanen quickly became one of those men.

No sooner did Dominick arrive in Paris to begin the preproduction process than Tanen called the novel and the script it was based on "a piece of shit."

As producer, Dominick had to take what he got—no other major studio wanted the project—and he began casting the leads. He knew Tony Perkins through their mutual friend Stephen Sondheim, and it was on his post-Cannes trip to Paris that Dominick met with the tall, lanky actor to discuss *Play It as It Lays*. In the 1950s, Perkins enjoyed great success with the bobby-soxer set but underwent a major image overhaul when he played the serial killer Norman Bates in Alfred Hitchcock's *Psycho*. In subsequent screen performances, he never quite lost that creepy edge, and his career suffered, especially with the young female moviegoers who had moved on to the more virile Warren Beatty and Steve McQueen.

Dominick's meeting with Perkins oozed subtext. He was in Paris to offer the currently out-of-work actor the role of the closeted, substance-abusing film producer BZ (short for Benzedrine), who commits suicide in the arms of the dissolute leading lady after she hands him a lethal dose of pills. Not only was Perkins a closeted homosexual, but he was being offered a role that Joan Didion had based on her closeted, substance-abusing brother-in-law producer.

The two men could not have chosen a more apropos spot in Paris to meet and talk. Perkins stayed at L'Hotel, the final home of Oscar Wilde, and it was there on the Left Bank that Dominick made his pitch, saying, "I thought you'd be terrific for this film I'm going to do." Dominick had not yet admitted to himself that he was asking Perkins to play a role he had inspired his sister-in-law to write.

Perkins mentioned reading the book. "I don't think he's like me," he said in defense to Dominick's suggestion that he would be "terrific" in such a flamboyantly gay role. Not that the actor could be choosey.

On his Paris trip, Dominick also met with Perkins's agent, Sue Mengers, who saw *Play It as It Lays* as a treasure trove of roles for her growing stable of actors. In addition to Perkins, the superaggressive, often outrageously caustic agent wanted Dominick to cast a second client in the film. She thought Ann-Margret would be perfect to play the female lead, Maria. Dominick wanted Perkins; he did not want Ann-Margret, whose brassy Las Vegas persona at that moment in her career clashed with Maria's nearly debilitating existential angst. That casting disagreement aside, Dominick later groused how his meeting with Mengers "interlocked us for a number of years." They met at Café de Flore, and it was there that the powerful agent introduced him to a Belgian man who spoke with a thick French accent. Where Mengers was overweight and blowsy, her boyfriend was tall, tan, fit, and very attractive, and also unlike her, he was not well connected in Hollywood—except for his girlfriend. One thing disturbed Dominick about the unlikely couple. She called him Jean-Claude Tramont. Dominick blanched at the name. He knew Mengers's boyfriend from his days at NBC in the 1950s when Tramont went by the name Jack Schwartz, was a Jewish guy who lived with his mother in the Bronx, and worked as a page boy at the door of the network's Studio 3. Seated across from the Hollywood couple at the historic Café de Flore, where Georges Bataille and Robert Desnos practically invented surrealism, Dominick knew what Tramont knew, and he dared not mention their common Rockefeller Center past. Finally, the agent's boyfriend acknowledged, "It has been a long time." Dominick glanced at Mengers, and he saw trouble. "It was not that she did not know that his name had been Jack Schwartz. She did. What she hated about the encounter was that I knew," he later remarked.

When Dominick expressed interest in Tuesday Weld to play the role of Maria, Mengers took note and quickly wooed the actress away from the William Morris Agency. So much for Ann-Margret.

Dominick and the Didions always agreed that Weld should play Maria, the novel's B-list actress who is trying to recover from a nervous breakdown by starring in a C-list biker movie and riding the L.A. freeways in a convertible on a road to nowhere.

Dominick knew Weld from Roddy McDowall's parties at his Malibu beach house in the summer of 1965 when the blonde sex-kittenish actress was still married to the actor's secretary, Claude Harz. He considered Weld a friend, having invited her to his Black and White Ball. But there were other reasons he wanted the actress and they could be summed up in one word, "typecasting." *Time* magazine described Weld as "Shirley Temple with a leer." By her own admission, Weld was an alcoholic by age twelve and had attempted suicide several times, imbibing a not-quite-lethal cocktail of aspirin, gin, and sleeping pills. She would not be the easiest actress to work with. "Miss Weld is not a very good representative for the motion picture industry," complained gossip crone Louella Parsons.

But Dominick adored her, even though his wicked sense of humor sometimes got the better of him on the subject of Tuesday Weld. As Joyce Haber described the situation in her *Los Angeles Times* column, guests at Dominick's parties in Beverly Hills used to engage in a macabre betting pool: "Each of them listed precisely the month and the day that Tuesday

Weld would end her life," Haber wrote. Playing outrageous games or stealing George V bathrobes, Dominick always knew how to keep people entertained. "He collected people and people liked him," said Mart Crowley.

Weld forgave Dominick's suicide watch. In addition to sharing a skewed sense of humor, they were fellow potheads, and he could always be counted on to score the best weed. "I get high on anything," Weld said.

Whatever she was feeling the actress did not make it easy for Dominick. She made him woo her for the role. As she told the press, "Well, they're after me to play the lead . . . and, I mean, I told them I could just phone it in because that's my life, I mean, it wouldn't be any real challenge."

Meanwhile, Frank Perry wooed Dominick and the Didions. Although Mike Nichols and Sam Peckinpah also expressed interest in directing, Perry made the better case. Or was willing to work within a very limited budget. He told his three collaborators that theirs was "absolutely a marriage, a marriage with no provision or divorce until the film is made. . . . You two write the screenplay, Nick and I will produce and I will direct."

Together, the four of them visited all the locations in the book—the desert, the beach, the L.A. freeways—and they screened movies like *The Pumpkin Eater* and *Petulia* that "experimented with time," said Perry. They then holed up in Dominick's Spalding Drive apartment for four days, using a bulletin board and multicolored cards to chart the sequence of scenes.

In a curious twist of fate, *Play It as It Lays* launched one career in Hollywood that eventually outshone most of the principal talent on the film.

"I stalked Dominick Dunne," said Joel Schumacher. In the early 1970s, Schumacher had "burned many bridges" in the fashion business and looked to reinvent himself as a costume designer. Dominick's friend Howard Rosenman invited Schumacher to an early screening of *The Panic in Needle Park*, in part "because I had a serious relationship with drugs" and in part "to meet Dominick." John and Joan were also present. Later, Dominick introduced Schumacher to Frank Perry, who told him, "We need a $200-a-week costume designer."

"They gave me a two-week trial," said Schumacher, who passed the test.

Even though John and Joan rarely visited the *Play It as It Lays* company during production, Schumacher made a point to know the couple. "Nick introduced me to his brother and sister-in-law. They were fantastic to me," he recalled. "They had this house on the beach in Trancas, and they had what would be called a salon. It was very international." John knew people from *Life* and *Time*; Joan had written extensively for *Vogue* and the *Saturday Evening Post*. "It wasn't just movie people. Which was unusual at that time. Back then it was such a tiny one-industry town. You didn't meet people from outside the film business," said Schumacher. "But at John and Joan's, there were a lot of great reporters, people who were covering wars. It was an incredible mix of people."

But mostly, it *was* movie people with whom Joan and John wanted to network to secure script work. Those movie people included Julia and Michael Phillips, Martin Scorsese, Paul Newman and Joanne Woodward, Steven Spielberg, and a smattering of fellow screenwriters. Paul Schrader described the soirees in Trancas as being "very heady." In addition to barbecuing, swimming, sunbathing, and talking about movies, "a lot of these writers and directors helped each other," said Schrader. "Even though we were relatively unknown, there was a real feeling that the world was our oyster."

That heady mix at the Didions' weekend salons, however, did not include Dominick.

"They invited me to their house at least once every other week. They went out of their way to invite me," said Schumacher. "Nick was never invited. Something was going on."

It had been going on since they lived together as brothers on Albany Avenue in West Hartford. Despite their seven-year age difference, Dominick resented John calling himself "Dad's favorite son," and worse, it was true. By John's own assessment, he was "allowed to get away with far more" than his older siblings. Dr. Dunne accepted John; he did not accept Dominick. He liked John's "cheekiness" and he hated Dominick's being a "sissy." John called himself "the son of a surgeon" because he was proud of his father's exalted status in the Irish-Catholic community. "I can think of no higher praise," he said. It was the kind of thing Dominick would never have said or written about his father.

Dominick later remarked how he got along great with Joan and John on *The Panic in Needle Park* but *Play It as It Lays* was another story. He felt he had made valuable suggestions for the *Needle Park* script, as well as *Play It as It Lays*. The Didions, however, were not interested in his ideas. In turn, the couple worried about Dominick's increasing substance abuse and how it adversely affected his reputation in Hollywood—and, by association, theirs.

Peter Bart was one of many Hollywood powerbrokers who sometimes offered Dominick a ride home after an industry event. "He drank a lot, was confused," said Bart, then a vice president and head of production at

Paramount Pictures. "Nick would emerge from a function and wander around looking for a car or a cab. He was always a little mystified what he was doing there. I was surprised how he figured out to get from here to there."

It was easier helping talent on their way up, like the Didions, who had great publishing credits, than helping talent on his way down, like Dominick, who had a great substance-abuse problem. Regarding his brother, Dominick felt the irony of their opposing career trajectories, which only exacerbated his humiliating downward spiral.

"Nick knew everyone in the movie business in Los Angeles, and when John came out there Nick introduced him to everybody, helped him," said Freddy Eberstadt. Later, John did not return the favor, and often used his adopted daughter as an excuse, trotting her out at industry events instead of inviting his brother. "When Quintana was still a little girl, John would take her to dinner where Nick might be expected to go. John would phone Nick to tell him that they were taking Quintana instead," Eberstadt recalled.

Regardless of Joan and John's treatment, Dominick dedicated himself to seeing his sister-in-law's novel brought to the screen in a faithful adaptation. It was an unusual project to be produced by a major studio. During the winter 1972 production, journalist Rex Reed wrote, "The filming of *Play It as It Lays* is being observed with raised eyebrows and clinched teeth in a town not famous for its liberal attitude towards movies that tell the truth about itself."

"Nick was a very good producer," said Schumacher. "He knew the world we were making the movie about. He saw the humor in everything. And his humor was ironic and it could be stinging." But it was not a fun shoot, because it was not a fun script. Also, Frank Perry had much to prove.

"It was important for Frank to be the director, and Nick let that happen. This was Frank's first film without [Eleanor]," said Schumacher, referring to Perry's ex-wife, with whom he had made such successful films as *David and Lisa* and *Diary of a Mad Housewife*.

The Perrys' divorce proved less than amicable, according to their friend Dotson Rader. "Frank thought Eleanor was trying to sabotage his career," said the journalist. Frank Perry felt especially vulnerable after their separation when his wife began having an affair with a female painter. "It left him with a sense of betrayal," said Rader, "and that suspicion and wariness fell over into his relationships with Tony Perkins and Dominick Dunne on the set of *Play It as It Lays*. Eleanor changed the way Frank looked at people. He didn't fully trust deeply closeted people." Perry also surmised that Didion had based the BZ character on her brother-in-law.

Never truly embraced by Perry and increasingly estranged from his brother and sister-in-law, Dominick soldiered on as producer. Making his job even tougher was Ned Tanen, who hated the film even more once he started seeing rushes. The Universal Pictures executive called it Didion "vomiting up her life."

Dominick, in turn, called Tanen "the most awful person."

His sense of isolation and abandonment only increased when the film's crew took to calling the leading lady Miss Paranoia, and even more difficult for Dominick, they made fun of Tony Perkins's sexual orientation by leveling gay slurs at his character, BZ. When dealing with the macho crew, Dominick protected himself by talking about his ex-wife and three children. Perkins did not have that cover, although he would soon get it when a reporter from Andy Warhol's *Interview* magazine arrived on set. In time, Berry Berenson and Tony Perkins would marry and have two sons.

Finally, *Play It as It Lays* was in the can, edited, and ready to be released. Immediately after the premiere, Dominick told Ned Tanen how much he hated him, and said telling off the executive was "marvelous."

It would have been even more marvelous if the film had been a critical and commercial success on its release in October 1972. Major critics like Vincent Canby in the *New York Times* and Charles Champlin in the *Los Angeles Times* liked it, but Stanley Kauffmann in the *New Republic* and Pauline Kael in the *New Yorker* called it a pretentious bore. Dominick described it as having "won an award at the Venice Film Festival, but only ten people saw it. It was that kind of picture."

Dominick considered himself a good producer. He had taste. He knew how things should look. And when called upon, he could spruce up the dialogue on the spot. He also had a knack for suggesting ideas to directors and making them think it was their idea. He never made a lot of money as a producer. He called it "peanuts." Then again, Dominick's idea of mere nuts was what other people lived on and lived well. Looking back at the 1970s, he would lament "the thousands of dollars" he had spent on hustlers, not to mention drugs, parties, designer clothes, and the large apartment on Spalding Drive.

After the film's release, Dominick finally confronted his sister-in-law about his being the prototype for BZ. Joan Didion told him no: the character was based on a man they both knew who, in Dominick's opinion, bore no resemblance whatsoever to a closeted, suicidal movie producer.

Dominick admitted he should have seen the similarities between himself and BZ as soon as he first read the novel. He always had a "masseur to lunch," just as BZ does. But he chose not to see.

It was a curious, singular distinction. What other man had produced two films, each of which featured a prominent character based on him that he, in turn, chose not to recognize? His vision of himself was "blurred in those days," as he would later describe it.

One good thing about Dominick's next project was that its screen-writer left him out of the picture. The bad thing was that Jean-Claude Tramont wrote the screenplay, and he could not write. Compounding the script problems was Tramont's girlfriend-agent, Sue Mengers, whose recommendation to Paramount Pictures led to Dominick being named the producer. It was a favor for his casting so many of her clients in *Play It as It Lays*. It was also a favor that would end his career in Hollywood.

Besides being a paying job, *Ash Wednesday* possessed one big plus—at least for someone as chronically star-struck as Dominick.

"An Elizabeth Taylor movie!" he gushed. "That's a big deal." He decided to forget (as did Robert Evans, head of Paramount Pictures) that the actress had not made a hit movie in more than four years, and as her box-office clout shrank, her outrageous and costly behavior on and off set exploded.

Unlike Dominick, Larry Peerce harbored few illusions about making an Elizabeth Taylor movie, and worse, he found Tramont's basic story ludicrous: a middle-aged woman (Taylor) undergoes a facelift to win back her philandering husband (Henry Fonda). "Nick and I were involved in this nightmare," Peerce recalled. "Nick was divorced; I was getting a divorce. We were two guys desperate for a job."

While Peerce had the box-office hit *Goodbye, Columbus* to his credit, his reputation took a big hit when Paramount's head of production fired him from what was to be his follow-up romantic blockbuster, *Love Story*.

"Larry wanted to add a back story about the Vietnam War," said Peter Bart, who thought Peerce was trying to "overintellectualize" Erich Segal's potboiler about a rich kid who falls in love with a poor girl dying of cancer.

Unlike his producer, Peerce never genuflected before movie stars. Dominick told people he "liked the idea" of doing a film about a woman's facelift. But then there was the script. Dominick knew writing, and he knew they could not film Tramont's script.

"Tramont wrote the first two acts of a script; that's where the film ended. It needed another act," said Peerce. Dominick agreed and started negotiations with Paramount to fly Tramont to Cortina d'Amprezzo, Italy, to do rewrites as soon as the film began shooting there.

Dominick and Peerce met Elizabeth Taylor and her husband, Richard Burton, on New Year's Eve 1972. The world's most famous couple was staying at the Grand Hotel in Rome and Burton was cleaning up dog poop on the carpet when the two men arrived. He offered his guests champagne and then poured himself a very large scotch on the rocks. "Which he downed as if it were club soda," said Peerce. Even before Taylor made her belated appearance, Burton drank three more. "And he was not a man who could hold his liquor. He must have had a liver the size of a golf ball."

Taylor finally appeared "very regal, bedecked in lavish jewelry," noted Peerce. "She told me at some point that she drank mostly what Richard drank. It soon became obvious that she could tolerate alcohol much better than he could."

On that first night in Rome, the four of them dined at La Toula, one of the Eternal City's most expensive restaurants. The Burtons traveled there in a huge limousine, so large that Peerce did not have to stoop to enter it. Dominick expected to follow him when Burton blocked his way. Without explanation, he told Dominick to take a taxi or some other mode of transportation to La Toula. The two men's relationship never recovered, presaging deep troubles to come.

Having somehow alienated Burton, Dominick nearly did the same with his famous leading lady when he suggested they dine one night with Andy Warhol. She initially scoffed at the idea. "That man made millions off me!" exclaimed Taylor, incensed at the artist's quadruple silk screens of her in *Cleopatra* getup circa 1964. (Fifty years later, the quadtych would be valued at $20 million.) Warhol's slight rip-off aside, Taylor finally agreed to meet the king of pop art.

Warhol's first mistake was showing up at the restaurant in Rome with his usual gang of hangers-on, transvestites, assorted freaks, and Paul Morrissey, the man responsible for actually writing, directing, and producing most of the Warhol movies. "You, over there!" Taylor ordered Warhol's entourage, and pointed to the opposite corner of the restaurant.

The Warhol/Taylor confab became one of Dominick's favorite anecdotes in years to come. He recalled how it began as a pleasant, chatty, alcohol-doused dinner before it turned ugly. After dessert, Taylor got up to go to the ladies room, and pushing herself off the red leather banquet she felt something hard under her sable coat. Warhol had surreptitiously placed a tape recorder there, and it was taping their every word.

"You've been recording me while I'm drunk?!" she cried.

Dominick felt "mortified and furious at Andy," since he had arranged the dinner. Warhol's pasty white skin turned Campbell's soup red as he removed the tape from the recorder and meekly handed it to the star. Dominick and Taylor left in what he called "stormy silence." Later, Paul

Morrissey told Dominick that the problem with *Ash Wednesday* was not the script. "If you called it *Elizabeth Taylor's Facelift*, everyone would go to see it!" he advised.

Shooting began in March 1973, and when the Burtons finally arrived at the ski resort of Cortina d'Ampezzo, Dominick flew from room to room at the Miramonti Majestic Grand Hotel to give everyone the big news. "The Burtons are coming! The Burtons are coming!" he announced with childlike excitement. His room overlooked the front of the hotel and its driveway, and Dominick invited everyone to witness the spectacle of the Burtons' arrival. They came chauffeured in a stretch limousine, a Mercedes-Benz, followed by a large truck hauling thirty pieces of luggage and anything else needed to camp out in a five-star hotel in the Italian Alps for a few weeks. There was also their usual entourage, which included a secretary, butler, chauffeur, hairdresser, makeup artist, maid, and two Maltese terriers. Dominick noted that the Burtons' luggage appeared to be made out of carpet emblazoned with big roses.

It was a cozy company of actors hand-picked by their producer. Dominick had seen Keith Baxter on Broadway in the hit thriller *Sleuth* and wanted the British stage actor to play the gay photographer David in *Ash Wednesday*. For the role of the gigolo Erich, Dominick indulged in type-casting, giving the part to the twenty-eight-year-old actor Helmut Berger, whose sixty-four-year-old lover had lobbied hard for his current inamorato. The Italian director Luchino Visconti even went so far as to hold a private screening for Dominick, showing him his new film, *Ludwig*, in which Berger, again typecast, played the mad, decadent king of Bavaria. After the screening, Visconti and Dominick chatted, and among other topics the legendary director launched into a complaint about today's young actors "who have everything handed to them."

Berger interrupted the old man. "You think it's easy fucking you every night?" he asked. Dominick could not resist casting such an actor.

Keith Baxter did not think the European press exaggerated when they called Helmut Berger "the most beautiful man in the world." Not that Berger let such an accolade go to his head. He never played hard to get. "Helmut and I had an affair, which I soon regretted," said Baxter, "because Helmut would stay out all night, hit the clubs, and then come banging on my door every morning at three o'clock. Dominick adored Helmut, but nothing came of it. Dominick was a very moral person, and he was very aware of his daughter and boys and Lenny."

Dominick, in fact, was simply more discreet than moral, at least when it came to the most beautiful man in the world. According to Dominick's longtime partner, Norman Carby, Berger could count Keith Baxter *and* Dominick as two of his many off-the-set conquests during the production of *Ash Wednesday*. Whenever Baxter did not answer an early morning call from Visconti's boyfriend, it was Dominick who benefited.

Into this maelstrom of male camaraderie walked Elizabeth Taylor, already well known in Hollywood for her close relationships with homosexuals like Roddy McDowall, Rock Hudson, and Montgomery Clift. She even brought her own entourage of male companions, as Larry Peerce and Dominick were soon to discover. Taylor's first scene in the film took place in the town square outside a church. Dominick could not stop telling people, "This is an Elizabeth Taylor movie!" Beyond camera range, tourists and townspeople stood in the plaza to gawk at the movie star, still notorious from *Cleopatra*, made years earlier in Italy. In the church scene, Keith Baxter plays a fashion photographer shooting a model who opens her fur coat to reveal she is wearing nothing but a bikini as churchgoers stare in shock on their way from Mass. One of those dismayed spectators, unfortunately, was not a paid extra. He was a monsignor, and he brought the production to an abrupt halt. "Scandale!" he cried upon seeing the nearly naked model. Dominick tried to explain. "No, it isn't that kind of a film."

Since the monsignor required much persuading, Taylor took the opportunity to give herself a long break and invited Baxter to her trailer.

"Do you like vodka?" Taylor asked her dark, handsome costar.

"We were there two and a half hours," Baxter recalled, while poor Dominick dealt with the priest and his anger over a near-naked model desecrating his church. "We sat there drinking and talking, and Elizabeth talked about being terribly constipated. She didn't know what to do."

"Just stick your finger up your ass," said her butler, Raymond Vignale.

"I've tried that," said Elizabeth.

"It doesn't work because you wear that big ring!" Vignale cracked. In addition to being chronically constipated, Taylor admitted that she and Burton had not had sex in months, despite her butler's best efforts to provide them with pornography.

While his actors proceeded to get smashed on vodka, Dominick dealt with the irate monsignor. He would later admit, "My drinking reached its zenith during [*Ash Wednesday*], but everyone was drunk on that movie, no one ever noticed, except possibly the village priest of Cortina d'Ampezzo." After Dominick lied and called the model's exposure a huge mistake, he graciously said good-bye to the priest and promptly fell down the church steps. "We were all drunks, except Henry Fonda, and doing [cocaine]," said Dominick, sniffing and touching his nose to suggest the drug.

Jean-Claude Tramont tried to rewrite the script to Peerce and Domi-nick's satisfaction but was not up to the job. He also turned himself into something of a joke on set when he gave everybody gifts of T. S. Eliot's poem "Ash Wednesday" and signed them "with best wishes, Jean-Claude."

Pretentiousness laced with lack of talent is never endearing, and to the amusement of his actors Dominick revealed that Tramont also qualified as a complete phony. "I'd known him when he called himself Jack Schwartz and was an usher at NBC when I was doing live TV," Dominick told them. Taylor also hated the script and thought less of the man who wrote it when her butler overheard Tramont launch into a scathing critique of the star's questionable taste in clothes. She told Dominick, "Get that ass-hole off the set!" He had two choices: alienate Sue Mengers, who helped get him the job; or alienate his star, who threatened to become even more intractable.

Dominick had no choice. He fired Tramont and hired a rewrite man. "And we got Bob Evans to OK it," said Peerce. But ill fortune struck when the Writers Guild called a strike. "And that was the end of the rewrite." Stuck with the Tramont script, the two men took satisfaction in having at least "run him off the mountain," said Peerce.

It was that rare example of producer and director wishing their star had complained earlier in the process about the script. "I don't think Elizabeth ever read *Ash Wednesday* [beforehand]," said Peerce. "She'd read a page and recite it back to you verbatim, total recall. I'd never seen anything like it. She knew the script was no good, but she never questioned it." Until it was too late.

Dominick continued to play sycophant to Elizabeth Taylor, performing little tasks to keep her happy—like dashing off telegrams to Paramount Pictures to tell them not to send her any more bouquets of carnations. She hated carnations. She thought carnations were bad luck. He suggested they send bouquets of roses on a daily basis instead.

It did not make any difference. Taylor never arrived on set on time, even though her contract stipulated a very leisurely work day, from 10:00 a.m. to 6:00 p.m. "But she never worked until after 4:00 p.m.," said Peerce. Missing hours of production time due to an incensed priest was not a typical work day on the *Ash Wednesday* set. A typical day began with Taylor showing up two or three hours late. Her tardiness continued even when Henry Fonda arrived at Cortina d'Ampezzo. For their first scene together, she showed up later than usual. Her acting assignment that day did not require much—a walk across a dining room filled with dozens of extras. Among them were Dominick's daughter, Dominique, visiting on spring break, and the Burtons' adopted daughter, Maria, another spring break visitor.

On Fonda's first day, Taylor walked on set shortly after noon. Rather than taking the time to greet her famous costar, she instead made an abrupt, puzzling announcement, "If there's going to be anything grotty, I'd better have Richard here!"

Dominick could not imagine what could be grotty (i.e., unpleasant) about her walking across a dining room. But, as usual with Taylor, he did as she told him. Dominick fetched Burton.

"Richard, what do you think?" the star asked her husband.

Burton looked around, and seeing nothing grotty told her, "Frankly, I agree with Larry and Nick."

The couple, on the verge of divorce, often used the cast and crew to wage war on each other. Upset by his wife's chronic lateness, Burton asked Henry Fonda to speak up and complain. "That's not my job. I'll have no part of it," said Fonda. Other times, Burton defended his wife and lashed out at how Dominick and Peerce treated her. In a letter to the two men, he wrote how they were dealing with a "bombe plastique" that could go off at any moment if they were not careful.

Dominick told Joel Schumacher that he felt he had a "great connection with Elizabeth." However, he also "felt the need to cater to her."

Ultimately, it fell to the director to discipline. When Taylor showed up one day with her usual male entourage, Peerce waved them away. "You go!" Then he pointed at her. "You stay." The star did not speak to the director for two full weeks. "That's some way to make a movie," said Peerce.

When Taylor was not creating problems, it was Burton's turn. He housed a volatile temper, especially when drunk, which was often. During one early morning breakfast, Dominick burst into the actors' caravan of trailers. He was frantic. "Where's Helmut?" he asked. As usual, the actor was listening to the new hit single "Alone Again, Naturally," which held some special significance for him. He played it endlessly. Baxter continued reading *Bleak House*, and Fonda went back to his hobby, painting miniatures.

"Helmut," said Dominick, "you've got to come down! Immediately! We're taking you to another hotel! Richard is on the way with a gun!"

Taylor's daughter, Liza Todd, had made the mistake of developing a schoolgirl crush on Berger, and her adoptive father did not much like it. "Richard couldn't bear the fact," said Baxter.

Dominick threw Berger into a taxi and had him chauffeured down the mountain to the Hotel de la Poste.

After Dominick succeeded in saving Berger's life, Burton did indeed arrive at the caravan of trailers. He carried no firearms but he was angry and, of course, he was drunk at ten in the morning.

"Where is he?" Burton screamed. "That queer, Helmut!"

Baxter explained that Berger had departed to another hotel. "He's queer. Doesn't it make your flesh crawl?" asked Burton.

"I'm queer," said Baxter.

"But you're Welsh!"

"You couldn't have Liza in safer hands," said Baxter. "Helmut's wonderful with her."

Liza Todd's affection for Berger also disappointed Dominick, but for an entirely different reason. His daughter and Liza were about the same age, and he hoped they would "become chums," said Baxter. It would have helped to solidify his friendship with Elizabeth Taylor. "But the two girls didn't become friends."

When Burton was not threatening Berger, he took to berating his wife. In one scene, the actors needed to improvise a game of bridge. Taylor got confused and asked, "Four of *what?* What am I supposed to be saying here?" She did not play bridge.

Burton, on the other hand, was an expert. "You stupid cow! Just show your big tits!" he yelled from behind the camera. During another altercation, Dominick watched as Burton called Taylor a "cunt" in front of her children.

Stupid cow or movie star, the actress caused the executives at Paramount Pictures to step up their complaints about the lack of footage coming from Italy. Dominick tried talking to his star about her tardiness. "Oh, what now?" she complained.

"Elizabeth, this can't go on," he told her. But, of course, it did. Taylor enjoyed boasting that she had kept the Queen of England waiting twenty minutes, Princess Margaret thirty minutes, and President Josip Broz Tito an hour. "They can damn well wait for me a few minutes!"

When Taylor was not late, it was something else. During production on *Ash Wednesday*, she came down with the measles, missing even more days of work. Obviously, MGM had protected the actress even from contracting a childhood disease.

"Elizabeth was bright," said Larry Peerce, "but her biggest problem was she was born and raised in the aegis of the big studio, the Louis B. Mayer father syndrome."

Some father.

Taylor did not just dislike being on a movie set. She hated it. Off hours with vodka in hand, she enjoyed regaling the *Ash Wednesday* cast with horror stories from her childhood days at MGM, like the time she filmed a Lassie movie with her friend Roddy McDowall and the producer used unbleached corn flakes to simulate snow. When they turned on the fans to blow the brittle pieces of corn, McDowall and Taylor flinched as a hurricane of dry breakfast cereal hit them in the eyes. MGM took care of that problem by having the two children's faces anesthetized with multiple shots of Novocain.

Dominick sympathized. "But you've got to understand, Elizabeth, this isn't MGM," he said. The old studio system, however, had controlled her life for so long that she never learned to cope with the vagaries of life like a normal person.

Taylor turned to alcohol, usually vodka or champagne, and it did not help that Dominick had made a deal with Dom Perignon to feature it prominently in the film in exchange for plenty of screen time. Larry Peerce recalled seven hundred bottles of the champagne being delivered to Cortina d'Ampezzo. When Taylor was not chronically late, she was trying to get her costars chronically drunk.

Between takes for their big bedroom scene, she asked Helmut Berger, "Do you want a little champagne?" It was not even noon yet, and she continued to ply him with the complimentary Dom Perignon until he was drunk and Peerce had to stop the work day before lunch.

Taylor's champagne days, however, were some of her more productive ones on the set. More problematic were her whisky or vodka days. On those days, she carried her own glasses—that is, Raymond Vignale carried her glasses. They were huge sixteen-ounce goblets. Her work day began with a cry to her butler, "I want a Bloody Mary, Raymond baby. I need a bloody!"

That was Vignale's cue to fill one of her sixteen-ounce glasses with vodka, a weak splash of tomato juice, and one small ice cube. At one o'clock, it was time for lunch, which entailed three or four glasses of wine and required Giancarlo to redo her makeup. An assistant would arrive to break up the two-hour lunch: "Elizabeth, we're ready."

"Yes, I'm coming," she replied, irritated, taking at least another half hour. Back on set at three o'clock, she then ordered, "Raymond baby, how about a Jack?"

Out came the jumbo glasses, one ice cube, a little soda, and a lot of Jack Daniel's. It was when Dominick knew that Peerce had about half an hour to get something of Taylor on film.

"Our careers, Nick and mine, were disappearing as Elizabeth and Richard lived out this human tragedy," said Peerce. The drinking on set was contagious. "Nick was drinking prodigiously at that time; we all were. Drinking was a way of life, but Nick could pile them on."

Dominick continued to get phone calls and telegrams from Paramount, telling him, "Get that fat pig on set!"

Meanwhile, Taylor received cables from Paramount, telling her, "You look beautiful in the rushes!" And the studio kept sending her roses as other bills piled up, including ones for Richard Burton's request that the studio serve a traditional Thanksgiving turkey dinner for the entire company in the month of May at the expensive Miramonti. Paramount was not happy and neither was the Miramonti staff, which had looked forward to departing in April for more lucrative summer jobs at the Lido in Venice.

Dominick ultimately stopped taking any telephone calls, not the best way for a producer to ingratiate himself with the studio. Cast and crew who wanted to reach him had to get on their hands and knees to whisper in his hotel-room keyhole, "It's me. I need to see you."

It was Elizabeth Taylor, ironically, who gave Dominick the bad news. "You know, this is going to be your last film," she told him.

The expenditures on *Ash Wednesday* and its low grosses were only part of the problem. Other producers have survived worst defeats. What they did not have to weather was a one-line joke "that was funny when I told it; it was not so funny when it was reprinted in the *Hollywood Reporter*," said Dominick.

After a disastrous autumn screening of the movie in Los Angeles, Dominick repeated one more time his story about Jean-Claude Tramont being Jack Schwartz from the Bronx. But in this latest retelling, he added a quip about the zaftig agent Sue Mengers, whom Tramont had recently married: "One day, if the true story of this film is ever told, it should be called *When a Fat Girl Falls in Love*," said Dominick. Even an insult about the agent's weight was not enough, so he embellished the anecdote further. He said he was writing a book about the making of *Ash Wednesday* and calling it *When a Fat Girl Falls in Love*. He was not writing such a book, but he thought it sounded funny. At the time.

On the eve of the film's premiere, Marvene Jones retold Dominick's story in the November 13, 1973, issue of the *Hollywood Reporter*. She reported his joke as if it were fact, telling her readers, "Dominick Dunne didn't just produce *Ash Wednesday* and while away his leisure hours on location. He compiled a diary which he's turning into a book titled *When a Fat Girl Falls in Love*, not so loosely based on Sue Mengers (she's becoming overexposed) and her *Ash Wednesday* writer-husband, Jean-Claude Tramont. Ohhh what he wrote down! IFA will arrange the pulishing [*sic*] contract, and also for a film. . . . Starring Cass Elliot?"

Paramount's Robert Evans read the item. He phoned Dominick to inform him, "You'll never work in this town again!" For his part, Evans did not remember the conversation but admitted, "It's possible. Sue was a great friend of mine."

In the years to come, whenever Dominick told the fat girl anecdote, he put Evans on the phone with his right-hand man at Paramount, Peter Bart—as if to add an audience to his insult and injury. "We never made calls together," Bart said of his tenure at Paramount with Evans. "I was never on the phone with him."

According to Bart, who later became *Variety*'s editor in chief, there were two potential box-office bombs in the works at Paramount in 1973: *Ash Wednesday* and John Schlesinger's film adaptation of *The Day of the Locust*. *Ash Wednesday* was Evans's baby, and *Locust* was Bart's.

"I felt *Ash Wednesday* was a ridiculous exercise," Bart recalled. "I never had a meeting on it. But Evans got his revenge. Bob stayed out of *The Day of the Locust* completely, and got his revenge on me."

Although Dominick continued to disparage Tramont whenever he told his *Ash Wednesday* story, Bart knew another man.

"Jean-Claude shouldn't have tried to be a director or screenwriter," said Bart, "but he was a substantial and brilliant financial guy. Today you'd call him a financial adviser, and good at it. I think he made Sue Mengers a lot of money." Also defending Tramont was the agent's biographer, Brian Kellow, who wrote that Jean-Claude Tramont was, indeed, born in Belgium and given that name at birth. Kellow surmised that Tramont might have later changed his name to Jack Schwartz in order to assimilate when he and his mother moved to America.

Tramont died of cancer at age sixty-six in 1996, and while he enjoyed a substantial career beyond the film business, it is also true that his girlfriend-turned-wife, Sue Mengers, did help to end Dominick's career in Hollywood.

Unwittingly, Elizabeth Taylor may have thrown the knockout punch to Dominick's career by repeating the fat girl anecdote to any number of hairdressers, makeup artists, stylists, and other fashion sycophants who, in turn, told it to Marvene Jones. The *Hollywood Reporter* columnist made a frequent habit of quoting, if not shamelessly plugging, such sources in her fawning coverage of the movie star.

Dominick was not Mengers's only victim. "She destroyed Nick, she tried to destroy me," said Larry Peerce, "and then she wanted to be my agent. She was a very complex human being. Such craziness with that woman."

# 4

## Begelman and Purgatory

Once again, he was broke, and worse, Dominick thought he would never produce again in film or television after the *Ash Wednesday* debacle. He had no choice in 1974 but to accept a midlevel position at a new division of RCA. Tom McDermott, a former boss at Four Star, got him the job "as a favor," said friends. Working at Spectavision took him several steps down from being the producer of an Elizabeth Taylor movie, but it paid the rent, if not his kids' tuition at private schools. Lenny shouldered that responsibility.

Dominick still had a few parties to attend, not as many as before, but a few. On nights with nothing better to do, Dominick put on his satin dressing gown and green velvet monogrammed slippers and got drunk. He also smoked some grass, sniffed a few lines of coke, maybe dropped a little acid, and carried on imaginary conversations with two of his favorite authors. He wrote in his journal that Noël Coward and W. Somerset Maugham encouraged him to be a writer. In Dominick's midnight imagination, never did the two ghosts arrive to visit on the same evening at Spalding Drive. Dominick knew better than to make himself the third wheel at such a party, but in separate late-night tête-à-têtes, Noël and Somerset repeatedly told him he had real talent.

Dominick's days were somewhat less fanciful than his nights. The job at Spectavision involved watching lots of old movies and making recommendations to RCA on which classic titles should be put on video. His new office could not compare to the one at Four Star; regardless, Dominick believed in making a good impression. Although not spacious, the office needed to appear sophisticated in a way that belied his real status at the company. He thought some original art on the walls might help and asked friends for recommendations of young, talented, and, most important, inexpensive painters. He interviewed several such artists, and one of those was a twenty-four-year-old named Norman Carby. Dominick bought two drawings. "They were illustrative, ink on acrylic wash," Carby recalled. "They were of buildings." Dominick liked the art. He also liked the dark, bearded, handsome, and six-foot-five young man, and invited him to dinner. Carby turned out to be as pleasant and good natured as he was tall. Despite his being very much in love with Frederick Combs, Dominick began an intimate relationship with the artist that would continue, often long distance, for the rest of his life.

"Dominick told people that I met him through Dominique, but that's not the truth," said Norman Carby. "We met that day in his office. Later, he introduced me to Dominique and she and I became very good friends. I was also very close to Lenny." Dominick thought people would be less suspicious of his relationship with the young painter if he said they met through his daughter rather than it being a chance encounter. A fringe benefit of dating Carby was that Frederick Combs also found Dominick's new boyfriend attractive, and on a couple of occasions the three of them slept together. Those were the only times Dominick enjoyed sex with Combs, who always refused a "one on one," as Dominick described it.

Although he and Carby never lived together, they became a couple at about the time that Dominick lost his mother. Dorothy Dunne passed away in December 1974. Dominick said his mother "didn't come into her own until after my father died." His brother John wrote that their mother's life "had been a tomb of secrets." At the end of Dorothy's life, she proved more forthcoming with her younger son. When John told of problems in his own marriage, she said divorce was not an option for a Roman Catholic but "drink" and "drugs" were. Dominick wanted to talk to her about his father, and why she never intervened to stop the beatings. "That didn't happen," Dorothy replied. "Why do you say these things?"

As Dominick's friends in the entertainment business abandoned him, one manager stayed loyal and never failed to invite him to his parties—of which there were many in the 1970s. Being a very successful Hollywood manager, Allan Carr made sure to keep an extremely diverse talent roster that included Ann-Margret, Dyan Cannon, Cass Elliot, Marvin Hamlisch, Rosalind Russell, and Peter Sellers. Curiously, as Dominick's status in Hollywood declined, the flamboyant Carr, who wore colorful caftans to cover his morbid obesity, turned himself into the town's major party-giver, a latter-day Elsa Maxwell in the post–Charles Manson Hollywood. To facilitate that transformation, Carr bought Ingrid Bergman's legendary Hilhaven Lodge in Beverly Hills, built an Egyptian-themed disco in the basement, and made sure to feature cutting-edge, if not downright raunchy, entertainment at his parties. With groups like the gender-bending Cycle Sluts in performance at Hilhaven, Carr turned his homosexuality into a fanciful calling card in an era when David Geffen dated Cher and Elton John took a wife. His parties were not so much A-list as they were A-to-D list with plenty of pretty, willing young men and women thrown into the drug-spiked punch.

Dominick and Carby often arrived together at Hilhaven Lodge, but even at these anything-goes affairs he kept his boyfriend at an uncomfortable distance. "He never wanted it to look like we were on a date," said Carby. Dominick continued that charade even at the party Carr gave for ballet star Rudolf Nureyev in early April 1974. Also attending were Bianca Jagger, Jack Nicholson, Anjelica Huston, Diana Ross, and Roman Polanski.

In Joyce Haber's coverage of the pre-Easter party for the *Los Angeles Times*, the gossip nearly outed the attendees: "If Bunnies were lacking, muscle-bound young men were not. Mae West would have had as much of a ball as Nureyev." As usual, Dominick made a point to be on the phone the next day to give Haber some of her juicier tidbits about the party, but he knew when to shut up. Dominick told her nothing about the subsequent party that Carr threw for the émigré danseur.

"Nureyev was sexually insatiable," said Dominick. "For one party in his honor, Allan hired a hustler for every room in his house so Nureyev could be served on the spot, if he so chose." Carr jokingly required all guests to bring a mattress to his house that night, which is why it came to be dubbed the Nureyev Mattress Party. Some revelers wondered if it was payback for all the women Nureyev had to dance with on that previous evening. At the all-male party, Allan Carr welcomed his guest of honor with an abundance of Beluga caviar, Stolichnaya vodka, and Hollywood rent boys. It is the latter dishes that Nureyev never got around to sampling, since he retired to a stone cottage on the estate—the same stone cottage where Ingrid Bergman and Roberto Rossellini consummated their adulterous affair a quarter century earlier—and quickly inspired two dozen men to offer him their bodies.

When Dominick sometimes retold the Nureyev gang-bang story, he often added a disclaimer. "I wasn't there. It's just what I heard," he would say with a smile.

"We were there," said Carby.

Otherwise, the 1970s were not a good decade for Dominick's party card. So much had changed since he arrived in Hollywood in the 1950s. His lavish Black and White Ball had been forgotten, unlike Truman Capote's copycat Black and White Ball two years later in New York City that quickly took on a resplendent aura of urban myth. Worse, Capote did not invite the Dunnes to his party, a slight Dominick never forgot.

When he was married to Lenny, Dominick received numerous invitations to parties given at Jules and Doris Stein's home. Their house, called Misty Mountain, offered awesome views of Los Angeles and beyond. They did not get more powerful in Hollywood than Jules Stein, who in the 1920s founded MCA, an agency known as the Octopus even before it acquired Decca Records and Universal Pictures. Dominick signed the Steins' guest book hundreds of times. He had been to all of their daughters' coming-out parties and considered himself such a good friend that, when Jules left parties early and his wife invariably got drunk, Dominick made it his responsibility to see tipsy Doris up the treacherous drive to Misty Mountain.

Now a midlevel executive at RCA, Dominick no longer got an invitation to the Steins' home. In a way, it gave him enormous freedom. No longer beholden to the Steins or people like them, Dominick became a receptacle not only for stories of Hollywood humiliation he witnessed but stories that he merely heard—like the one about Doris passing out drunk in her bathtub after a late-night party in London, Jules bringing a pillow to prop under her head so she would not drown, and her thinking he was trying to smother her and yelling for help. "It's really a terrible story to repeat, isn't it?" said Dominick, who repeated it a lot. He also coined a couple of great one-liners: "Sit down! You're not going to believe what I'm going to tell you." And "I never repeat gossip, so listen closely the first time." Which always got a big laugh.

What did he have to lose now? With reckless abandon, Dominick confessed to friends, as well as people he had met for the first time, about being thrown off the Hollywood merry-go-round: how the wife of the producer of Johnny Carson's talk show had disinvited him to a party at the last minute because a friend had not left for Europe after all and she could only seat an even dozen for dinner. It hurt, but not as bad as Swifty Lazar dumping him from his annual Academy Awards blow-out, which numbered two hundred guests at the Bistro Garden. Twelve guests was one thing, but when you were not in the top two hundred in Hollywood, you were worse than dead. You were the uninvited.

It especially galled Dominick that he no longer received invitations to parties where the hostesses had to replace the Steuben glass ash trays with a dime-store variety because a columnist for one of the trade newspapers kept stealing the expensive kind. "He gets invited, but not me," Dominick complained. Suddenly, Lenny's taunt "if all else fails, you can become a columnist" looked prophetic, if still not a compliment. Maybe he should be a columnist—just to get invited to parties the way kleptomaniac reporters did.

Instead, Dominick told his stories for free. Tony Kiser met him in 1974, and, among other reasons, they became good friends because "Dominick was always very honest about his problems in Hollywood. It was one of his more endearing qualities, his utter honesty on that point," said Kiser. Also, Dominick knew everyone in Hollywood, and while Kiser came from big money back East, he was new to town, "because I got a job working at Universal television." Kiser began as the producer's assistant on *McMillan & Wife* and quickly worked his way up to associate producer on TV shows like *Columbo* and *Rich Man, Poor Man.*

Fortunately for Dominick, Allan Carr could always be counted on to throw another party. At least they had pizzazz, even if there were only a smattering of A-listers. In November 1975 Dominick entertained a few of his friends at a cocktail party. His doorbell at Spalding Drive rang, and when he went to answer it, a uniformed officer greeted him with a summons. At least, Dominick thought it was a summons. His guests had to wonder what crime he had committed. "When you open the front door and someone is serving you a subpoena, your heart stops!" said Dominick.

Then he realized: it was an Allan Carr joke, and not only a joke but an invitation to a party in honor of Truman Capote, to take place on December 15, 1975, at the vacant Lincoln Heights Jail in northeast Los Angeles. Dominick got the joke, lame as it was: Capote wrote *In Cold Blood*, hence the jailhouse theme. It was the way Carr's mind worked. Who cared if the novel had been published nearly a decade earlier? At least the party would be a good plug for Capote's acting debut in Neil Simon's *Murder by Death*, which was Truman's official reason for being in town. A more apt way to honor Capote, thought Dominick, would be a party in a restaurant decorated to look like La Côte Basque, which was the title of a chapter in Capote's long-awaited and still-unfinished novel *Answered Prayers*. That chapter, excerpted in *Esquire* magazine, was the real reason the author fled New York City. "La Côte Basque 1965" totally alienated Capote's good friend Babe Paley; it was also said to have caused the suicide of chorus-girl-turned-socialite Ann Woodward, who thought her resemblance to a husband-killer in the short story hit too close to her Park Avenue apartment.

The night of Carr's Capote party, Dominick drove himself to the jail, a trek that took him past downtown L.A. and Chinatown and into forgotten Lincoln Heights, the city's dumping ground for all its street-maintenance equipment. Carr staged a faux riot at the entrance of the jail, with actors dressed as escaped prisoners directing cars to the nearest parking area. Dominick might have brought his boyfriend, but Norman Carby was working that night: a member of the costume-catering company known as the Doo Dah Gang, he donned a cop's uniform to take guests' mug shots, which wound up on a souvenir coffee cup. Carr spent the early evening, as people arrived, screaming at members of the Gang. "Do something! There are no ashtrays! They'll mutiny," he said of his guests, who included Peter Sellers, Diana Ross, and Lucille Ball. Others like David Niven, Charles Bronson, and Francesco Scavullo danced as the Link, a five-piece band, played "Jailhouse Rock" and "Killing Me Softly with His Song."

The guest of honor played along, for a while. Truman Capote wore tinted specs and a gangster mix of big-brimmed black Borsalino, a double-breasted jacket, and what he called "my Brazilian dancing shoes," which sported red leather and rubber soles. However, the experience of being one of five hundred well-dressed guests crammed into a space built for three hundred convicts left Capote oddly unnerved. People tried to have fun, but they were in a jail. It was creepy. The guest of honor retreated to a cell to be alone. It was at this moment that Dominick, standing alone in another cell, caught his eye. He also was not in a party mood—at least not this party. "There was such sadness in Truman's eyes," said Dominick. "He never recovered from that snub of Mrs. Paley's. This was not his new milieu—Hollywood, and it wasn't up to what he was used to in New York."

Ditto Dominick in Hollywood. Never had he identified more with the author of *In Cold Blood*.

The journalist Dotson Rader knew both men. In the early 1970s, Rader met Dominick at "some boy parties given by a film distributor" in Hollywood. "Dominick was just this little guy who was nice and told stories about a lot of famous people," Rader recalled. "He was very gossipy, and seemed to be using his story-telling. It was like Truman in a way, a way of getting attention, because Dominick wasn't physically prepossessing. It was the way someone who wasn't a born star could dominate a conversation or get the attention of people."

Rader did not remember Capote being fond of Dominick: "What Truman found deeply annoying is Dominick wasn't just gay and quiet. He was gay and boastful about being straight." Rader went on to admit, "We were all captive to the times."

Sometime after Allan Carr's jailhouse party, Rader met for drinks with Dominick and Capote at the Beverly Wilshire Hotel. "You used to go in there, and if you sat long enough you'd end up with four or five people you hadn't seen in a while. People drift in who you know," Rader noted.

A friend of Capote arrived unexpectedly at the hotel lounge. The woman's marriage to a movie star was not going well, and because she wanted to confide in Capote, the two of them went off to a corner to commiserate and drink. When the unhappy wife finally left, Capote returned to Dominick and Rader. "She's in one of those marriages that end up in either murder or suicide," he told them.

"There's no nice way to get out," Dominick added.

"And that's how the subject of suicide came up," said Rader, who had no idea that Dominick struggled with thoughts of ending his own life. That destructive impulse resurfaced more vigorously on Rader's subsequent trip to Los Angeles, where he had been invited to a party at Tony Kiser's house in Malibu. Rader saw Dominick there. He had been drinking heavily. "I have a car," Rader suggested. "Let me give you a lift."

"No, no," Dominick replied, drunk.

Rader insisted. "I've got a driver. I never drive in L.A. I'm giving you a lift."

Dominick carried a little black bag with him that night. "Like a doctor's bag, but it wasn't," said Rader. In their ride back to Beverly Hills, Dominick brought up his deep depression, that he did not have any money, his career had tanked. He oozed self-pity.

"There's broke and there's broke," Rader told him. "You're not broke." They talked about getting together the next day when Dominick mentioned that he would not be spending the night at his Spalding Drive apartment. "I'm checking into the Tropicana tonight," he said, and gave the motel address to the driver.

"Why the Tropicana?" asked Rader.

"I've got friends meeting me there."

"At the Tropicana?"

"Yes, I do have friends."

"I know you have friends."

"You've got to drop me off there."

Dominick refused Rader's offer to go to the motel with him. "I'll see you, darling," Dominick said, and was gone.

A few blocks later, Rader noticed Dominick's little black bag. He had left it in the car. Rader looked inside, thinking he would have the driver take the bag back to the Tropicana. "It was full of pills, four bottles of pills," said Rader. "Opiates and Quaaludes. It didn't occur to me that he was going to kill himself. He's going to take a trip on this shit, which is fine. But it's not fine if you're drunk. It will kill you."

Rather than return Dominick's bag to the Tropicana, Rader took it with him back to the Beverly Wilshire Hotel, and later phoned Dominick to say that he had given the bag to the hotel management. Dominick could pick it up there at his convenience.

Years later, Dominick admitted, "I was always with strangers doing drugs. I was in somebody's closet. We used a Turnbull & Asser tie to get the vein going and we were shooting cocaine and one of the people died and I ran."

His young journalist friend Marie Brenner said she did not know that Dominick Dunne, the one who "set the curtains on fire. I didn't see that person." To Brenner and her journalist boyfriend Jesse Kornbluth, Dominick became "a kind of father figure" in the 1970s. The three met him through Griffin Dunne, and the couple found Dominick deeply interested in their work as writers for the *New York Times Magazine*, *New York* magazine, and other major periodicals. Kornbluth also had ambitions to write screenplays. "We were known as the Young Didions," said Kornbluth, which did not do much for his ego.

"Jesse and I used to see Dominick regularly," Brenner recalled. "I always had the sense he was a reporter manqué. Whether he was reporting or not, he was acting like a reporter. He was obsessed with news, what's going on, who's doing what to whom. He also had a tremendous sense of self, or whatever it is you need to document yourself." She enjoyed looking at the detailed scrapbooks he kept of his many parties. "He was reporting his own life from such an early moment, a memoirist from the earliest moment."

More than assembling scrapbooks, Dominick loved writing letters. He wrote letters on a daily basis, and at least two of his children inherited that interest.

When Dominick produced movies, Alex and Griffin Dunne would occasionally write to congratulate their father. A typical letter began with good wishes about the fate of one of his films at the latest festival, whether it be Cannes or Venice. As with missives from most teenage boys to their parents, good wishes often led to requests for money or a new leather jacket. (In the following decade, Alex's letters to his father would become far more intimate and expansive, occupying several pages.) Dominique's letters to her father were always very personal. Dominick called her "darling," and their relationship was epitomized in one letter written to him after she had returned to Italy to continue her studies in Florence. She wrote to her father, asking that he tell no one about her being attacked by a man near the Ponte Vecchio. The incident took place one night after seeing the movie *Young Frankenstein* with school friends. Badly bruised, she told friends how she had fallen down a flight of steps. Dominique considered returning to the States but in the end decided to write her father a letter instead, only asking for his "sympathy."

Dominick's own letter writing took on a novelistic quality, especially with regard to his own reduced relationships with some of Hollywood's major powerbrokers. Fran and Ray Stark continued to invite him to the occasional dinner at Trader Vic's. On Sunday nights, the Polynesian-themed restaurant in Beverly Hills attracted not only the producer of *Funny Girl* and his wife but Nancy and Ronald Reagan sitting next to Hannah and Alan J. Pakula sitting next to Betsy and Alfred S. Bloomingdale. Afterward, Dominick wrote down what Ray and Fran said over dinner, including the producer's joke about which ethnic group hit the pavement first after jumping off a tall building. It was not a very good joke, but it startled Dominick. Stark's own son had committed suicide in the previous decade by leaping from a window.

Dominick told stories, but people also told stories about Dominick. He had never worked with Daniel Melnick, but that did not prevent the producer of *Straw Dogs* and *All That Jazz* from taking a Sinatra-level dislike to him. Shortly after Melnick had been made head of production at MGM, turning the near-dead studio around with such hits as *The Sunshine Boys* and *Network*, he told people that one of the Dunne children had caught Dominick having sex with another man in his Spalding Drive apartment. The story had legs and would continue to be told in Hollywood even after Dominick's death in 2009. When Dominick first heard the sordid tale, he panicked. He railed at the rumor, which he claimed to be totally false. But what could he say or do to resurrect his already beleaguered reputation? He called the rumor the kind of story that, in its ugliness, could cause him to commit suicide, like Truman Capote's short story in *Esquire* had destroyed Ann Woodward. All he could do was write in his journal of the pain at being held in such "low esteem" in Hollywood when he was broke, unemployed, and utterly defenseless.

His only solace was his letters and journals. And gossip. Dominick told friends that he had several outlandish vignettes involving the first families of Hollywood. "I've listened to their farts," he reported. And no Hollywood first family did he know better than the Starks. He thought their life resembled a novel. Gradually, he began to chart a plot connecting the movie producer and his family with Sue Mengers, whom he hated more than anyone in Hollywood. Mengers was so blatantly gross and the Starks were so colorfully eccentric—the way their servants wore denim outfits with the words "Camp Rastar" at the Stark ranch and the horses were named after dead movie stars who had once been their friends. ("They were named after friends, not movie stars," said the Starks' daughter, Wendy.) A novel would give him much-needed money, he thought.

Dominick could only wish he had already written such a roman à clef and been paid, because in 1977 MCA announced its own line of video cassettes. Rather than compete, RCA unceremoniously shuttered its video division, and Dominick had no choice but to apply for unemployment insurance. He no longer had a job, not even a midlevel one.

Desperate to pay his rent, Dominick did what a lot of people in Hollywood do when their back is up against the wall: he thought about writing a screenplay. It is much quicker than writing a novel; there are so many fewer words to type. The only problem: he did not have an idea for a screenplay. He spoke to his friend Tony Kiser, whose years as associate producer of the long-running Rock Hudson series *McMillan* were coming to an end. Kiser looked to segue from television to movies.

"I pitched to Dominick [a story] about a rich guy falling in love with some hooker," said the producer. "It was along the lines of that Richard Gere movie with Julia Roberts."

Apparently, what Dominick wrote was no *Pretty Woman*. Plus, he gave it the unpromising title *A Time to Smell the Roses* and made the even greater error of showing the screenplay to his brother and sister-in-law. John and Joan had just written a great box-office success, the 1976 remake of *A Star Is Born*, starring Barbra Streisand. The critics hated it, but because many moviegoers actually paid to sit through *A Star Is Born*, what the critics wrote did not matter. The Didions sat atop the screenwriter heap in Hollywood. It was not the best time for Dominick to be asking their advice, but he showed them *A Time to Smell the Roses* anyway. He thoroughly enjoyed writing it and considered his writing top-notch. The Didions did not. Joan sat quietly. Even when she did deign to speak, Dominick often complained he could not hear his very frail sister-in-law. It was why he called her Frail behind her back. John, whom Dominick nicknamed Big Time, took a much more active role when it came to analyzing the many problems with *A Time to Smell the Roses*. He read aloud some of the screenplay's dialogue, emphasizing its clichés and general clumsiness of style. Frail sat there and said nothing as Big Time proceeded to eviscerate his older brother's ego.

"It was a real stinker," Kiser said of the screenplay. Dominick did not disagree after John's critique, but he never forgot, or forgave, his brother's brutal words that day. Years later, Dominick wrote a letter to John, recalling the humiliation and "every comma" of his criticism regarding *A Time to Smell the Roses*. He even went so far as to blame John's extreme negativity for his "nearly dying of shame" three days later.

Kiser recalled the contretemps. "At that point in their relationship, which was chilly, I'm sure John would've not been in the least supportive, especially since he and Joan were enjoying a successful career as screenwriters. The toast of Hollywood, as it were at the time," he added.

Asa Maynor, another friend, also saw the intense brother rivalry and how it affected Dominick. She had been married to the *77 Sunset Strip* heartthrob Edd "Kookie" Byrnes and often ran into Dominick at parties where she and her husband were "one of the dress extras," as she ruefully described their nine-year marriage.

"Dominick always wanted to write and he hadn't because John was so famous. Dominick didn't want to look like he was hopping on John's bandwagon," said Maynor, an actress who later became her friend's financial analyst.

Alex Dunne put the competition between brothers in even stronger terms. "Dad always felt that John followed him [in the entertainment business], and when Dad got into the writing profession, John was like, 'How dare you, on my territory?' Very indignant."

Three days after his brother tore into *A Time to Smell the Roses*, Dominick checked himself into the hospital for a routine operation to have a cyst removed. Very unexpectedly, he suffered cardiac arrest, almost died, had an "out-of-body experience," and emerged from the hospital a "very different man." He even threw away his toupee, finally.

Dominick now realized he must escape Los Angeles. He thought back to the day when a neighbor moved out of the Spalding Drive building and told him she was relocating to the Cascade Mountains in Oregon. The Cascade Mountains! Those words sounded so beautiful, so tranquil. He wanted to move there, even though he had never been. Such a place sounded ideal for writing his Hollywood novel about people like Sue Mengers and Ray Stark. If only he could somehow save enough money to make the trip and live in Oregon long enough to finish the book.

Every other Wednesday in 1977, Dominick picked up his check for $108 at the unemployment office in Beverly Hills. On one of those visits, the lines stretched longer than usual, and he was already late for another Allan Carr party. Suddenly, he found himself almost dreading another Allan Carr party. They were vulgar, often silly affairs. Then again, they were the only party invitations he received, and Dominick had to admit: Carr remained a loyal friend, even after he had struck movie gold the previous year. While visiting Mexico City, the caftan-wearing manager saw a Spanish-language movie about cannibalism and immediately obtained the rights to dub and distribute *Survive!* in the United States. Having made a lot of money from such schlock, he and his coproducer, Robert Stigwood, were now trying to parlay that success by turning the mediocre Broadway musical *Grease* into a movie. Even if Stigwood could get the Bee Gees to write new songs, Dominick thought *Grease* as a movie would never work, not that anyone ever went broke underestimating the taste of the American public. Certainly not Allan Carr.

The country continued to sink into a recession, and the lines for un-employment were endless, even in Beverly Hills. Unfortunately, it was not a typical Wednesday afternoon at the unemployment office. NBC sent a TV crew to tape the long lines for a story the network was doing on the recession. Deeply ashamed, Dominick quickly grabbed a discarded news-paper and used it to cover his face, praying, "God, please don't let my picture get on the news." He dodged that blow to his pride, but it put him in a foul mood for the party, and it did not help that the party was in honor of Gladyce Begelman, who had written an absolutely shameless book.

*Beverly Hills on a Thousand Dollars a Day* could not have been a more unfortunate, ill-timed book title. Columbia Pictures had recently suspended the author's husband from his presidency at the studio for what was being called financial irregularities. In fact, David Begelman had forged a few checks.

Not yet full blown, the nascent scandal rallied the Hollywood elite—people like Ray Stark and Barbra Streisand—to show their support for Begelman by refusing to talk to reporters about it. Dominick noted, "The heavy artillery were out showing solidarity behind one of their own kind. . . . Still, no one in Hollywood wanted publicly to get so close to throw a book party for his wife and her tacky new book, which was a guide to women on how to overspend."

Allan Carr, on the verge of big success with *Grease*, wanted to be seen as a major Hollywood player and used his book party for Gladyce Begelman to help secure that status. Power brokers who had never been seen at an Allan Carr party attended this one. They wanted to show their support for Begelman without actually having to say nice things about him to the press or throw his vulgar wife a party.

Carr gave his party at Hilhaven Lodge a Christmas theme with nary a menorah in sight. As the host toasted Mrs. Begelman with a long speech, blithely ignoring the two ghostwriters who had done all the work, a group of carolers in the background sang "Money Money Money" from the musical *Cabaret*. The husband of the fake authoress stood next to Dominick at the buffet table, where both men turned the cocktail party into a much-needed lunch. As Carr lectured his guests about Gladyce's important book, David Begelman piled pate de foie gras on pieces of pumpernickel bread to fill his mouth. "And she was like an opera star receiving applause at the end of a great performance," noted Dominick. His review: "It was like a gangster's party."

And there was something else about the party Allan Carr (née Alan Solomon) threw for Gladyce Begelman. Just as Dominick felt out of place among the successful Protestants on Prospect Hill, so this Irish Catholic did not really belong among the successful Jews of Hollywood. In his private journal, he took out his tortured frustration, leaving the pages replete with the K-word to describe them.

Dominick realized how much he no longer wanted to be part of this industry scene and that the day of his departure was imminent. Perhaps he would have departed sooner, but like some mafioso trying to go straight, Hollywood kept drawing him back in.

The first setback to his leaving Los Angeles occurred when he lunched with his agent, Arnold Stiefel, at the Polo Lounge right before Christmas 1977. Dominick heard his name being paged in the restaurant. It had been a very long time since that last happened. He excused himself and went to the front desk, where he met a man he had never seen before. John Berry, a reporter from the *Washington Post*, introduced himself and told Dominick that years earlier he had been his younger brother Stephen's roommate at Georgetown University, where they were both expelled for binge drinking. When Berry saw Dominick enter the Polo Lounge, he noticed a strong resemblance to Stephen Dunne; he thought he would give it a shot and have Dominick paged.

Berry was in town to investigate the brewing Begelman scandal at Columbia Pictures and had little time to get the story. *Esquire* and the *Wall Street Journal* already had reporters on it. Those articles had not yet appeared, but Berry and co-reporter Jack Egan feared being scooped and hoped that Dominick, with all of his Hollywood contacts, could help them. As Berry explained, the owner of the *Post*, Katharine Graham, took a personal interest in the scandal because it affected her dear friend Dina Merrill and her husband, Cliff Robertson. Begelman had forged a $10,000 check made out to Robertson, who had never received the money even though it later appeared on the actor's W-2 form. Merrill complained to Graham that the *New York Times* and the *Los Angeles Times* were not covering the scandal. Could she do something about it in her newspaper?

While Dominick did not know the inside details of the case, he did know Robertson and Merrill, who had been to his home a few times when he was married to Lenny. Robertson, in fact, was Dominick's house guest in West Hartford when he and Lenny first met in 1953. Regarding the Begelman scandal, Dominick noted, "I knew every participant and their wives and their mistresses." He assured Berry that he could help him with vital telephone numbers, and before saying their good-byes, the two men made a date to talk later that day.

Back in the Polo Lounge, Dominick lied to Stiefel, a good friend of Begelman, and said he had just run into an old friend from college. He would later recall how Stiefel told him over lunch that his career as a producer was finished in Hollywood: "I can't get you a picture. Nobody wants you."

Dominick did not blanch at the bleak news. For a brief moment, he almost did not care. He wanted to be a journalist. This was his chance. He had written for the Kingswood School newspaper when he was a student there. He had always wanted to be a crusading reporter, and it stirred his moral indignation that powerful people in Los Angeles put pressure on Dorothy Chandler and her newspaper, the *Los Angeles Times*, to ignore the story. If she did not, they would refuse to donate to her beloved Music Center with its Dorothy Chandler Pavilion. "The story was being swept under the table," he complained.

John Berry's proposal rejuvenated Dominick, lifted him completely out of his funk, and overnight he turned into what he called a "crazy person." He phoned Berry as soon as he got home that afternoon and gave the reporter every vital phone number from his Rolodex. Dominick wanted nothing more than to get his revenge on a town that turned its collective back on him. He did not know the inner workings of Columbia Pictures; he could not help John Berry and Jack Egan grasp the studio politics. But he did possess important information, which not only included private telephone numbers but also where all the power players had vanished to over the year-end holidays. The Starks were in Sun Valley, Danny Melnick was in Vail, and so on.

In the following days, when Berry made his phone calls, he let Dominick listen in on another line as Melnick, Stark, and others freaked out at the reporter's pointed questions.

"I felt alive again," Dominick wrote. He knew Sue Mengers was at the heart of his obsession to get even. If he still had a great job, he would be like everybody else in Hollywood and ignore the story just to be political. But he did not have a job. He did not have to shut up.

"It's when my dad began to think he could be a journalist," said Griffin Dunne. It was not just the two *Washington Post* reporters who fascinated Dominick. Showing little loyalty to Jack Egan and John Berry, he also began feeding information about Begelman to Liz Smith at the New York *Daily News*, to Andrew Tobias at *Esquire*, and to Lucian Truscott IV at the *New York Times*. He gave reporters little anecdotes that did not expose the scandal but enlivened the story, gave it color—things like Ray Stark having once been a florist at a cemetery.

On December 20, 1977, David McClintick broke the story in the *Wall Street Journal*, followed a few days later by Egan and Berry's piece in the *Washington Post*. Andrew Tobias at *Esquire* had the story first, but due to the magazine's long lead time his article followed the others. "Marie Brenner put me in touch with Dominick," said Tobias, "but more of my information came from David Geffen."

"John Berry and I continued on the story after our first article," Jack Egan recalled. "It led to the much bigger story of Hollywood finances, and how the studios practice creative accounting, ripping off some of the biggest stars, who are guaranteed a percentage of the profits, which never materialize. We owed Dominick a lot."

At the height of the scandal, Dominick spotted David Begelman at Mortons restaurant. He said hello, shook the crook's hand, and asked how he was doing. It was a glorious moment for Dominick. Begelman had no idea how this Hollywood has-been, this industry nothing, reveled in being one of the "major instigators" behind the mogul's stupendous fall from grace and power.

Lucian Truscott repaid his debt to Dominick by recommending him to Betty Prashker, a prominent book editor at Doubleday. A lunch meeting was arranged. She asked Dominick what he wanted to write. He said he wanted to write a roman à clef about the Begelman scandal. He was not quite sure how to approach the subject but told Prashker what form he thought the novel should take. He wanted it to be part letters, part screenplay, part diary. Prashker listened and nodded, but she was not enthusiastic enough to assign such an ambitious, if inchoate, book to a novice writer.

Helping reporters bring down David Begelman satisfied Dominick's need for revenge, but he continued to dream about the lovely sounding Cascade Mountains and his escape from Hollywood. But how to get the money to make the trip and live for a few months while he wrote his novel?

An old friend came to his rescue. Dominick knew Doug Cramer from their Young Turk days together in television when Dominick was the much bigger deal at Four Star. In the 1970s, Cramer was now the much bigger shark, having partnered with Aaron Spelling to make such lucrative junk as *The Love Boat* and *Charlie's Angels*. Cramer also was married to Dominick's old phone-buddy Joyce Haber, and one night the power couple invited him to their home. For some reason Dominick never could comprehend, Mr. and Mrs. Cramer decided to tell their two children they were getting a divorce on the very night he came to dinner. Dominick would describe Haber as being drunk and looking as blousy as Bette Midler in the final reel of *The Rose*. It did not go well. In some respects, the embarrassment of this family spectacle reminded him of his Café de Flore meeting with Sue Mengers and Jean-Claude Tramont, only much more dramatic due to Haber's ever-running tears, booze, and mascara. With both these Hollywood couples, Dominick knew too much about them, too much for there ever to be a comfortable working relationship. In the end, the Cramer kids did not seem to mind much that their parents were separating and instead fought over a toy truck one of them had received as a present to soften the blow of the impending divorce. When he left their house that night, Dominick thought Doug Cramer would be the last person to offer him a job. As with Mengers and Tramont, he knew too much.

Unbeknownst to him, Doug Cramer and Aaron Spelling were looking to turn Joyce Haber's best-selling novel *The Users* into a TV movie and needed somebody to head up the project. Since the 1976 potboiler focused on the high and low life in Hollywood, Spelling said what an executive almost never says when he is looking for a producer. "We need somebody who knows about tent parties," he said.

Cramer immediately thought of Dominick and his lavish Black and White Ball with its huge outside tent for dining and covered pool for dancing. Spelling liked the idea but had to ask, "Where's he? I haven't heard about him for a long time." Cramer said that Dominick Dunne was around but not working.

Dominick got the picture. They did not want to hire him because he was a good producer. They wanted to hire him because of his social reputation. The tent-party qualification, however, did not seem out of line to the man hired to direct *The Users*. "Tent parties were all the rage," said Joseph Hardy. "The movie's big scene takes place at a tent party."

What Dominick did not know was that Spelling and Cramer wanted him for another equally critical but seemingly obscure reason. Dominick had been friendly with Haber during her gossip days at the *Los Angeles Times*. And "neither Aaron nor I wanted to deal with Joyce," said Cramer, who had recently divorced his wife.

The two executive producers sweetened the deal by also hiring Dominick to do some script rewrites. No sooner was this news relayed to Joyce Haber than she spread the rumor that the rewrites were actually being done by John Gregory Dunne and Joan Didion. On other days, she spread the rumor that Mart Crowley was doing the rewrites.

"Dominick did the rewrites with me," said Joseph Hardy. The two men bonded over the script. "The writing was medieval, really bad. We rewrote every scene, and would hand out what we'd written the day before as the actors arrived on set each morning."

Hardy thoroughly enjoyed working with Dominick and appreciated his irreverent sense of humor, but he drew the line at participating in one of his producer's quirkier habits. "Dominick loved to go to funerals of famous people," said Hardy. Dominick liked to tell stories about going to Gertrude Lawrence's funeral with Stephen Sondheim and getting kicked out. He told of going to Clifton Webb's funeral with Mart Crowley and the mortician being so nice because very few other mourners showed up. He told of going to Louis Armstrong's funeral with Howard Rosenman but having to leave because they could not stop laughing at an obscenely large floral arrangement made up to look like a big trumpet.

Hardy refused to attend celebrity funerals. "It's morbid," he said.

"I know, but it's fun," said Dominick.

"They're dead!" said Hardy. Nonetheless, the director liked and respected Dominick. "He never apologized for being a fan."

Regarding their totally revamped *Users* script, Dominick took special pride in a scene he had thought up in which the Jaclyn Smith character finds her husband, played by Tony Curtis, in the shower with another man. "Dominick told me who the real people were in Hollywood, who he'd based the characters on," said Hudson Hickman, an associate producer on the movie. "I didn't know who he was talking about." The twenty-six-year-old Hickman had recently moved from Mississippi and been hired by Doug Cramer, *The Users* being the young man's first TV credit in Los Angeles. "Dominick became a real mentor. He knew Hollywood and what it took to be a good producer."

Dominick's tales of Hollywood did not end with his behind-the-scenes scoop on the movie's same-sex shower scene. "He also told me about a sponge baby. I'd never heard that term before. It had to do with how a gay man conceived a child with a woman," said Hickman. "Again, I didn't know the people he was talking about."

When *The Users* went into production in early 1978, Dominick used his producer influence to get Frederick Combs and Norman Carby small roles in the TV movie. "Combs was the love of Nick's life," said Hardy. Unlike Mart Crowley and other gay friends in the entertainment business, Hardy did get Dominick to speak openly about his sexual orientation. "He was always very honest with me about it. We went around and around about it."

Hardy told Dominick, "The most difficult thing to live with is dishonesty."

"I know. I know. But it's such a *thing*," Dominick said of being born gay.

Not that Hardy found it easy to be out in a town like Hollywood. The stigma "still existed as far as getting hired," he noted. "I came up against it, but I had such a good agent." In Hollywood, not being married after a certain age counted as a professional liability. Aging bachelor writers and agents were the least affected. Even unmarried directors had it much easier than producers and studio executives, in other words, closeted gay men like Dominick who were expected to socialize and network with wives on their arm.

Having been a successful theater director in New York City, Hardy did not enjoy the Hollywood social scene. He found it frivolous. "Who cares about those people?" he asked Dominick.

"I care completely whether they like me or not," Dominick said without apology.

"Nick longed to be invited," said Hardy. "It was so sad when he no longer was."

Doug Cramer and Aaron Spelling expected *The Users* to be a huge ratings success. Before reality told them otherwise, they hired Dominick to write the script for the sequel. He would write as well as produce a major network TV miniseries. There was only one problem: what is the sequel to *The Users*, the story of a small-town girl who marries a has-been movie star and schemes to give him a comeback that will also launch her own career as an actress?

No one knew, and that included Dominick. Desperate to come up with a story, he told Cramer about his own Hollywood roman à clef. Cramer liked its plot and convinced him to put the brash Sue Mengers character at the center of *The Users* sequel, a creative infringement that somehow did not seem to matter in the heat of their brainstorm.

Until now, Dominick had been considering suicide. Not long before he landed the first *Users* job he found himself wanting to jump in front of a train in Santa Barbara. On another occasion, he poked himself gently with a butcher knife to feel what it would be like to plunge the blade into his flesh. He blamed it on the grass he had been smoking and vowed to stop. But he did not stop smoking grass. If not for his therapist, Dominick thought he might have gone through with his suicide attempts. Despite his finances, he never missed a weekly visit to the doctor's office on Overland Avenue. Dominick considered him and his doctor an odd couple. This Jewish man was so unstylish and square, yet he understood his patient. Dominick always found the money to pay his therapist, as well as his hustlers.

Dominick somehow managed to finish the teleplay for the sequel to *The Users* in record time. It told the story of the agent Mona Berg (Sue Mengers), who has an affair with a hitchhiker (based on Dominick and Norman Carby's friend Tom Keller), whom she turns into a TV star, only to have him marry Cecilia Lesky (Ray Stark's daughter, Wendy). Berg murders the TV star, but rather than going to prison, producer Marty Lesky (Ray Stark) makes her CEO of a major studio (David Begelman in reverse).

Before ABC aired *The Users* on October 1, 1978, Aaron Spelling Productions held a star-studded screening at MGM in Culver City. Dominick invited Joan Didion and John Gregory Dunne, and for his own date he brought Dominique, who had been working as a part-time secretary for his brother and sister-in-law.

Dominick felt the movie played well for the invited guests, but when the lights came up in the MGM screening room, he saw John and Joan make a quick exit. Later, he looked for them at the after-party in the commissary but soon realized they had left the studio lot after the screening.

"John and Joan were bad behaviorists, full of themselves," said Joseph Hardy. "They were unkind. Nick had introduced them to everybody in Hollywood, and then they wanted nothing to do with him."

Despite there being several photographers at the party, no one took Dominick's picture, which in his mind meant he had not really produced *The Users.* They instead lavished their flash bulbs on Joyce Haber, who never once congratulated him on a job well done. At one point during the party, Doug Cramer asked Dominick to introduce Tony Curtis to his ex-wife. Dominick did not know that the actor hated the erstwhile gossip columnist, and Curtis looked at Dominick like he had just passed gas when he tried to make the introduction. Curtis even called Haber a "cunt" to her face. Had Cramer set him up? Dominick called it the worst party of his life.

The next day, his brother phoned to tell him that the movie was "fun," then changed the subject. John went on to commiserate about the "blah review" that the *New York Times* gave Griffin Dunne's movie, *Head over Heels,* which had recently screened at the New York Film Festival.

Dominick had not read the reviews but was deeply disappointed for Griffin. It was the first film his son had produced. Dominick tried to bring the conversation back to *The Users* but regretted it when his brother and sister-in-law, now on the other line, gave him faint praise. The conversation left him with a bad feeling, the kind he used to get whenever his father congratulated him, "making me feel worse instead."

In the next issue of *Women's Wear Daily*, Dominick read how the Didions made "grim-faced early departures" from the screening. He also read some positive reviews of Griffin's new movie, reviews his brother avoided telling him about.

*The Users*, however, received few favorable reviews, not that reviews mean anything in television. Ratings, however, do, and they were not good enough to warrant making a sequel. Also, "Spelling and the network wanted nothing to do with Nick's script for the sequel," said Hardy. "It was too good at skewering Hollywood."

For the second year in a row, Norman Carby gave Dominick a bag of groceries for Christmas. "It's the only present I got that made any sense for what the state of my life is," he told his boyfriend.

Groceries were nice, but a bigger Christmas present arrived belatedly after the first of the year, thanks to Dominick's agent. Arnold Stiefel, a veritable miracle worker, recycled Dominick's teleplay and turned it into a proposal for a novel to be titled *Joyce Haber's "The Users," Part 2*.

Dominick loved the advance money, from Simon & Schuster no less, but hated the title. Except for a couple of characters, it was his story, not Joyce Haber's. But as Stiefel explained, Simon & Schuster was paying a hefty $75,000 advance precisely because of Joyce Haber's name being in the title. Dominick groused, "It takes a little of the kick away right from the first day when there's another writer's name in the title ahead of yours." But he needed the money. Stiefel had other good news. Dominick's editor at Simon & Schuster would be Michael Korda, a major kingpin of the book industry, as well as son of the legendary British film producer Alexander Korda. It pleased Dominick how his brother and sister-in-law greeted the Michael Korda news with pained silence.

The first Simon & Schuster check came to $30,000 dollars, and it angered Dominick that Stiefel took his 10 percent "knowing I was broke," but not so broke he could not afford a weight-loss treatment at the expensive Schick Center and something called the Advocate Experience. He heard about the est-like group therapy for gay men and lesbians from friends who had gone to sessions in Los Angeles. Dominick could not risk exposure where he lived, so traveled to San Francisco for back-to-back weekend meetings there.

"I told him not to go," said Hardy. "Nick was honest enough about his sexual orientation. Why add spice to the brew?"

Not everyone agreed with Hardy. "Dominick was never honest with himself about his sexual orientation," said Carby.

Dominick knew about mass group therapy. He had been going to AA meetings in Los Angeles for years but never spoke or shared his stories in front of fellow alcoholics. The Advocate Experience somehow forced him to be more than an observer. On the second day of the San Francisco retreat, Dominick took the mic and talked about his sexual orientation openly and honestly for the first time in his life. The response he received overwhelmed him. One-hundred twenty gay men and lesbians applauded and gave him a standing ovation. He wrote of being "uncheered" in his life, so the response left him feeling immensely gratified and wanted. He belonged. Yet, now that he had told people he was gay, he was not sure. Was his sex with men merely "revenge" on his father? He vowed to answer the question, writing in his journal that "the time of understanding is nigh."

The Advocate Experience advised closeted homosexuals to disclose their sexual orientation to close friends and relatives. Rather than tell them face to face, Dominick chose to write to his children. "He discussed the letter with me," said Hardy.

The letter began "Dear Kids." Dominick let his three children know how much he loved them and that however they reacted to his news would be fine. But he felt compelled to inform them now that he had always been gay, and the shame of his secret was "a giant cancer eating its way through my body."

Although he dated it January 21, 1979, from the Hyatt Regency Hotel in San Francisco, Dominick did not mail the letter. At the top of it, he scrawled the words "not sent."

Life back in Los Angeles continued with a veneer of normalcy. He had money. He was writing a novel, at long last, but he had to be careful. As soon as he told people his novel was about Sue Mengers, they told him horrible gossip just so he would put it in his book, even though much of it was not true. Dominick loved the story a bigtime TV producer told him about Mengers wearing a dildo and using it on Jean-Claude Tramont, but he did not believe it.

Writing a novel for Michael Korda at Simon & Schuster would put him back on the A-list. He just knew it.

A bright spot that spring were his British house guests, Henry and Claire Herbert, the earl and lady of Pembroke, who were staying with him at the Spalding Drive apartment. The Herberts held a title going back to the twelfth century, and even though Dominick could barely pay his back taxes, he threw a party in their honor, inviting seventy of his closest friends. And forty of his closest friends did not bother to show up, which was especially disappointing because in Dominick's estimation, those not attending were "all the glitter and glamour ones." The absentees included his old bosses Aaron Spelling and Doug Cramer, as well as Marisa Berenson, who had shot Stanley Kubrick's *Barry Lyndon* at Wilton, the Herbert's family estate near Salisbury, England. "I had a young, rich, and beautiful earl and countess as bait. I realized then I was a dead duck," Dominick told friends.

The night of the fiasco Dominick entertained a masochistic fantasy in which his brother John phoned to ask him why he was giving a party when he was broke. John never made such a call, but in a way Dominick almost wished he had, because his brother would have been right.

Dominick did not want the earl and lady to get the impression that he had been completely ostracized in Hollywood despite the poor turnout for the party. Desperate, Dominick asked Arnold Stiefel to take them all out to dinner at Chasen's. The plan was for his agent to pick up the check and Dominick would reimburse him later. It did not go as planned. Stiefel left an overly generous tip, in Dominick's estimation, despite knowing the state of his client's finances. "It's Chasen's!" Stiefel explained.

Leaving the restaurant, Dominick made a big deal of saying hello to Danny Melnick. He could not forgive Melnick for spreading the unfounded having-sex-with-another-man rumor about him, but maybe if he made nice Melnick would stop telling the story. Almost as important, Dominick wanted the earl and lady to know that he knew the man slated to replace David Begelman as the president of Columbia Pictures. When he said hello, Melnick failed to say hello back.

Henry and Claire soon left Spalding Drive for Palm Springs. A few days after their departure, Dominick received a letter from Doug Cramer, apologizing for not coming to his party in their honor. Cramer replied that he had never received the invitation and commiserated how he only learned of the party when Henry and Claire came to dinner at his house in Palm Springs. The letter told Dominick one very important thing: Cramer had not invited him to his dinner party.

If nothing else, there was always something going on at Hilhaven Lodge. Allan Carr, however, was not the Allan Carr of the disgraceful

Gladyce Begelman book party. During the summer of 1979, he became the man who produced *Grease*, the top-grossing movie musical of all time. Carr let the success go straight to his head. "*Grease* was the best and the worst thing that ever happened to him," said his friend David Geffen. Before he went on to produce the major disco dud *Can't Stop the Music*, starring the Village People and Bruce Jenner, Carr gave a major party that was part wedding celebration and part baby shower for Alana Hamilton and Rod Stewart.

Things happened at the party to amuse Dominick. Beyond the bride's advanced state of pregnancy were the ice sculptures, which melted in the summer heat to mix with the seafood cocktail, where it ran off the table and onto the ladies' dresses. He also enjoyed listening to Swifty Lazar's wife ask Valerie Perrine, being touted for an Oscar for her performance in *Lenny*, if she bought her colorful dress at Frederick's of Hollywood.

Dominick lived for such low encounters among the Hollywood high life. As if such fun came for free at an Allan Carr party. The manager-turned-producer approached Dominick sometime during dinner. He had always dangled the carrot of giving his unemployed friend a script to write. While no assignment had ever materialized, Carr wanted to collect prematurely on his munificence. He asked Dominick to give him an after-dinner toast to congratulate him on the beautiful party and also to break the big news: Carr would be producing the movie version of *A Chorus Line*.

Dominick said he could not give the toast; he did not feel comfortable doing it. Carr told him he could. They went back and forth on what Dominick could or could not do when a butler arrived just in time to divert the host's attention. There was a problem with the aspic stork or something. Dominick turned to his friend Wendy Stark to tell her what just happened. She wisely advised him not to give any such speech.

At least Dominick still had his Simon & Schuster novel to write. Ray Stark had recently asked him about it. "You've been working on that for an awful long time, haven't you?" said the producer. "Fran's brother is like that. He can never get anything finished."

At a luncheon at the Beverly Hills Hotel, a columnist from the *Los Angeles Times* asked Dominick about the novel. Before he could answer, Doris Stein walked by slightly less tipsy than usual and said, "No, that's his brother." Doris no longer invited Dominick to Misty Mountain, but that did not mean she had stopped spreading gossip about him.

It got worse.

Lenny phoned Dominick to say that her good friend Connie Wald had to disinvite him to her party next week in honor of socialite Marguerite

Littman. Sue Mengers requested it. Maybe she demanded it. The agent would not be in the same room with the man who called her a fat girl. It fell to Lenny to give him the bad news.

No sooner was Dominick unceremoniously disinvited to one party than an invitation arrived last-minute for another. Jack Benny's widow, Mary, had her secretary phone Dominick at four o'clock in the afternoon for a party that night. Dominick knew what that meant: someone had canceled, and Mary now had an odd number of guests at her table. Or tables. The secretary called it a "barbeque," but since it was a barbeque at Mary Benny's house Dominick knew there would be nothing casual about it. He considered taking the high road and telling the secretary no. He could not possibly attend. He was busy. But Dominick was not busy. He did not have other plans.

No sooner did he enter the Benny house that night than Dominick saw Fran Stark. He hoped he did not see Ray himself. The producer had bought Dominick's pitch about an Olivia Newton-John movie based on the Svengali/Trilby legend in which the pop singer plays a secretary at a recording studio before making it big. Stark paid him $10,000.

Wendy Stark recalled, "Nick was down and out and needed money. We were trying to help him, but also give him something to do for the money. His heart wasn't in it."

And it showed. Ray Stark hated Dominick's treatment. Fortunately, the producer skipped the Mary Benny party and let his wife attend alone.

The hostess avoided greeting Dominick. She had also invited her hairdresser at the last minute. Mary Benny managed to say hello to him. With nary a hot dog or hamburger in sight at the barbeque, the tables sat fifty each and came loaded with silver, porcelain, and crystal. Dominick saw his good friend Tita Cahn and told her of his plans to go to Oregon for three months to write his novel. The wife of lyricist Sammy Cahn listened thoughtfully and told him it was a great idea. Others listened and then changed the subject to talk about what bartender they should hire for their next party or what to do about their pet dachshund's bad breath.

Out of malice, perhaps, Mary Benny sat Dominick next to his new arch-enemy Connie Wald, fresh from asking Lenny to tell him he was no longer invited to her upcoming party in honor of Marguerite Littman. Dominick wanted to ask Connie if she had gotten her money's worth from the pooch he had sold her years ago. Instead, they kissed and did not say a word to each other the whole night. Jerry Wald's widow was busy telling people another of her Audrey Hepburn stories—Dominick often called her Connie "My Best Friend Is Audrey Hepburn" Wald—and across the table Billy Wilder's wife, Audrey, was laughing too hard at a Johnny Carson story that the late-night TV host's producer, Freddie de Cordova, was telling. (Dominick would remember that kind of over-the-top laughter when O.J. Simpson's lawyers responded in kind to jokes the accused told them in court.) The only bright spot in the conversation came when someone asked, "Who's Jerry Zipkin?" Dominick wanted to say that Zipkin was a homosexual bachelor who had done nothing with his life but escort women like Nancy Reagan and Betsy Bloomingdale to the opera when their husbands preferred staying home to get a good night's sleep. But he held his tongue. Instead, Dominick told himself he had played this scene too many times, got up from the table, and left Mary Benny's barbeque.

Outside, a parking attendant who prided himself in driving nothing but Porches, Rolls-Royces, and Mercedes-Benzes let out a loud huff when he brought up Dominick's dusty old Granada. If Dominick ever had any doubt about leaving Los Angeles and starting a new act in his life, it had been atomized.

# 5

## Capote and Suicide

The second-hardest thing about leaving L.A. would be giving up his Spalding Drive apartment. The hardest would be holding a big sale. The humiliation of having to ask friends to purchase his belongings nearly paralyzed Dominick. But he had no choice. It would pay for his trip. Maybe he would go as far north as Vancouver, where Alex now lived. His younger son had founded his own magazine, *Belle Lettres*, which made Dominick very proud. He had a journalist in the family. As a boy, Alex used to write monthly newsletters. "They were what today we'd call a blog," said Freddy Eberstadt. "Alex was the most endearing child."

Dominick dreaded the idea of friends tramping through his apartment, haggling about prices, wondering about his ignominious defeat. Just when he was about to tag everything he owned for the sale, Arnold Stiefel once again came to him with a much preferred solution. Twentieth Century Fox recently hired a new president, and coming from London, Sandy Lieberson needed a place to live in Los Angeles. He would pay $2,000 a month for the apartment, which was $1,000 more than Dominick paid in rent to his landlord. Lieberson also agreed to pay the first and last month's rent, meaning Dominick suddenly had enough money to finance his trip north without selling so much as a Steuben ashtray. Lieberson wanted a furnished apartment.

With that sublet cash in hand, Dominick took off for the California coast, and when he got to Santa Barbara he phoned a lady friend he had met at an Allan Carr party. Linda was wealthy, nice looking, and she had promised to take Dominick to some of the area's finer restaurants. She also owned a beautiful home overlooking the Pacific Ocean, and the two of them spent a few nights together there before he continued his way up the coast. They were both very lonely, Linda later noted in a letter to him.

It was a glorious trip north until Dominick arrived at the picturesque ocean-side town of Coos Bay, Oregon. The local bookstore boasted a newsstand so cosmopolitan that it carried Andy Warhol's *Interview* magazine. Dominick remembered his lunch earlier that summer at the Polo Lounge with the magazine's executive editor. He wondered if Bob Colacello had made good on his promise to mention him in his column. Dominick may have left Hollywood, but he was not immune to wanting some good publicity. He bought a copy of *Interview* and quickly turned to Colacello's article, titled "Out in California." The editor had spent twelve days that August on the West Coast, eating his way through some of the Napa Valley and L.A.'s better restaurants. Dominick saw his own name under the entry marked Friday, August 3. He read with much anticipation what Colacello had written: "Lunch at the Polo Lounge with Dominick Dunne, who produced *The Users*. Too used to describe." Dominick kept reading. Later on August 3, Colacello dined at Mortons with two editors from the *Los Angeles Times* whom Dominick had never heard of. Colacello wrote of them, "Too timely to describe."

Dominick staggered out of the bookstore. He could not believe that Colacello, who purported to be his friend and invited him to lunch, would trash him so publicly, so dismissively, in so few words. But what difference did it make? He had left Hollywood. Besides, what the *Interview* editor wrote was the truth. Nasty, but the truth. It reaffirmed for Dominick how much he needed to leave Los Angeles.

Dominick was continuing his trip up the Pacific coast when the battery on his Granada died. Years later, when he told the story, it became a flat tire that landed him near Camp Sherman, Oregon. The town did not amount to much—a post office, a bait shop, a general store, a restaurant, two filling stations, and something called Twin View Resort. It was very well named. Each of the eight red cabins offered splendid views of Black Butte on one side and Mount Jefferson on the other. In the beginning, Dominick found it peculiarly charming that the walls of his cabin were knotty pine and the floor linoleum, and the single bed had a plastic covered headboard made of imitation leather and flecked with gold. In the cupboard, he found Texas Ware cereal bowls. Could he be any farther away from Chasen's and the Bistro Garden? Best of all, he liked the equally basic but picturesque Hungarian couple who owned the place.

It is doubtful that Joyce and Nick Osika believed Dominick's story about being poverty-stricken; regardless, they let him bargain the cabin's monthly rent from $400 to $250, even though that included utilities, towels, and sheets. They liked that he would be staying for more than a month. When he saw them checking out his Gucci luggage, he told the Osikas he had bought it used. Actually, he had not bought it at all. It was Henry Fonda's Gucci luggage from *Ash Wednesday*, just as he "owned" Tuesday Weld's Sony cassette recorder from *Play It as It Lays* and Tony Curtis's terry cloth robe from *The Users*. Elizabeth Taylor gave him the gold chain around his neck. He kept those origins a secret, not wanting anyone to know his Hollywood past. Joyce and Nick could not see inside his luggage, which further stretched his penniless story. He had packed six cashmere sweaters, several tortoiseshell sunglasses, and a few tweed jackets, all of which were not castoffs from a movie set but bought at top dollar on Rodeo Drive and environs.

A mechanic named Harvey fixed the battery and got his Granada running, and, better yet, he sold him some grass to smoke. Dominick asked about the mushrooms he had seen growing near the cabins; he did not know if they were the killer kind or the "tripping kind." Harvey said he did not know anything about eating mushrooms except out of a can. The more people he met, the more enchanted Dominick became with the residents of Camp Sherman. Unlike people in Hollywood, they were not fakes. They looked him in the eye, not over his shoulder to see who else just walked into the room. They lived life from "the gut," he wrote in his journal.

Between the grass and the kindly locals, he did struggle with loneliness. Whenever he got depressed, Dominick drove his Granada to the Black Butte Ranch, a first-rate resort, and gawked at the rich Oregonians. And there were other things to do. "I began to feed the birds. Birds?" he said. "I never fed birds before." He also worried about the deer. Hunting season had begun that autumn, and the constant gun fire reminded Dominick of World War II. Oregon hunters typically carried two guns—one rifle and one pistol, to finish off the animal if the bigger weapon did not do it. Dominick found the hunters barbaric.

On one of his lonelier days, he wrote to a West Hollywood friend, asking him if he knew of any gay bars or baths in Eugene, Oregon. He might make a trip there. Meanwhile, he wrote. He did not write the Joyce Haber novel, but he did write a lot of letters. Long letters.

"The letters would be five pages," Griffin Dunne recalled. "Then ten pages and then twenty pages single-spaced. He was using them like a workshop to find his voice."

Dominick found that if he wrote a letter to a friend about the novel he was supposed to be writing for Simon & Schuster he could trick himself into actually writing a scene for the novel.

His desk in cabin number 5 featured all the usual accoutrements: a typewriter, paper, pencils, and papers clips. Dominick added one elegant touch from his very recent past: a pink vase from a breakfast tray that he pilfered from the Beverly Hills Hotel. At night, Dominick cheered up the single room by lighting a fire and putting on his satin dressing gown and velvet slippers, just like he used to do on Spalding Drive. He had stopped drinking alcohol, but he did smoke a joint. It was then that his twin fantasies, Noël Coward or W. Somerset Maugham, took turns visiting, just like they used to on Spalding Drive. They gave him invaluable advice on how to write his novel. Noël told Dominick to dump Joyce Haber's "The Users," Part 2 and write his own novel about Sue Mengers and the Stark family, to be titled A Faller by the Wayside. Somerset gave him the idea for a narrator: The story should be told from the viewpoint of a burned-out Hollywood producer who escapes to Oregon to find himself and, in the process, exposes every ugly Tinseltown secret he knows.

Dominick could not have loved Noël and Somerset's ideas more if he thought of them himself, which, of course, he had. He loved it so much that he turned down his Santa Barbara girlfriend's offer to attend Henry and Claire Herberts' ball at their Wilton estate in England on October 26, 1979. Linda told him it should not be missed, that Prince Charles might attend. She even offered him a first-class roundtrip airplane ticket to and from London. Dominick enjoyed feeling like a "gigolo," of being offered something so extravagant, especially from a lady friend. But he had his new priorities, and going to a party nine thousand miles away was not one of them.

In a letter, Linda called their nights together an "affairette." The word saddened Dominick, and he wrote back how their time together meant much more to him. He called it "a perfectly lovely love affair."

That same autumn a second offer of a free roundtrip airplane ticket arrived at Twin View Resort, this one from his son. Griffin Dunne's movie Head over Heels was about to open commercially. "The kid's done it!" Dominick exclaimed. Griffin wanted his father at the movie's premiere and offered to pay for the trip. "He wrote me a beautiful letter saying he simply could not come to New York, even though it was to celebrate me," Griffin recalled. "He was on a journey and a path that he could not take himself away from."

Nothing could deter him from the novel he was trying to write. When Linda wanted to visit him in Oregon, Dominick made it clear that his cabin was small, only one room, and the toilet did not work very well. It required at least two flushes, sometimes three. He advised her instead to

book a room at the nearby Black Butte Ranch. He would make the reservation for her, but could not. He wanted to preserve his anonymity there,
because he sometimes used the resort's Xerox machine. Linda got the hint,
never made the trip, and a few months later, she married another man.

Dominick often spent the early evenings with Joyce and Nick in their
cabin watching TV. He had begun to like her better than him. Nick indulged in this odd habit of screaming at the TV screen whenever Dan Rather
appeared. He somehow thought the newscaster was responsible for the
Iran hostage crisis, and Dominick wondered why Nick did not just watch
ABC or NBC instead.

Joyce quickly emerged as the saner of the two. She sometimes gave
Dominick hot dishes she cooked, and he ate elk for the first time in his life.
Somehow the topic of Elizabeth Taylor came up one evening—he did not
tell her he had produced *Ash Wednesday*—and Joyce mixed up the order
of the actress's husbands. Dominick's immediate instinct was to correct
her, but did not. He told himself, "Let it go. It doesn't matter." When he
said goodnight to the Osikas that night, he felt he had made a breakthrough
not mentioning that Mike Todd came *after* Michael Wilding in the trajec-
tory of Liz's men.

His old way of life, however, had a way of slapping Dominick in his
Gucci pocketbook, even in the wilds of Oregon. He hated paying for the
delivery of a package that went to the Spalding Drive apartment since he
needed every dollar. He opened the package to find monogrammed slippers
purchased that summer. They cost him $600 at a time when he railed against
his agent for taking 10 percent of the $30,000 advance from Simon &
Schuster.

Financial concerns hit him even harder when Dominick learned that
the studio executive subletting his Beverly Hills apartment had been fired
as president of Twentieth Century Fox. Mart Crowley sent him the latest
issue of the *Hollywood Reporter*, which carried the full scoop. Sandy Lieberson resigned, which was a nice way of saying he had been fired, and after
only a few weeks on the job. Lieberson had paid two months' rent with an
option for a third, and Dominick was now living on the deposit, which
had to be repaid. He considered getting drunk but forced himself to remain
on the wagon, and instead pigged out by driving fourteen miles to what
Nick and Joyce told him was the most expensive restaurant in all of central
Oregon, the Tumalo Emporium near the town of Sisters.

In most of his missives to friends, and there were many, Dominick
made them very aware of his impending fifty-fourth birthday. It worked.
Birthday cards filled his mail box on October 29, 1979. Many contained

gifts. Linda sent him a Rigaud candle. Dominique sent two Yves Saint Laurent shirts. His brother Stephen sent boots from L.L. Bean. And best of all, Aunt Harriet sent him a check for one hundred dollars. He wrote back, telling her how he had been "humbled" most of his life but was beginning "the last quarter fresh."

Griffin also wrote to say that *New York* magazine recently profiled him for his new movie. It thrilled Dominick. Then he panicked. Would his own son be referred to as John Gregory Dunne and Joan Didion's nephew? Would he, the failure of a father, even be mentioned?

One thing was for sure. A birthday greeting from John thoroughly depressed him. His brother wrote about going to Sue Mengers's house for dinner, how charming and delightfully funny she had been, and how he and Joan chatted for the longest time with their new friend Gore Vidal. The blatant name-dropping scalded Dominick's ego. John knew he hated Mengers, mocked her loser husband, and had once been friends with Vidal. Dominick vented by writing a letter to his therapist, saying how John's insensitivity reawakened in him these "he-should-have-been-a-girl feelings." What made it all so devastating was that John's rise in Hollywood was "concurrent" with his equally precipitous decline.

Dominick never outgrew hating his father. To rediscover the little boy who never was allowed to grow up, Dominick wrote to both John and his therapist to tell them about his homosexuality. Afraid these confessions might never be sent, like the one he wrote to his children, Dominick drove to the town of Sisters to mail the two letters. He made the trip despite a snowstorm and his not having the money to put snow tires or chains on his Granada. He felt the written confessions were vital to his rebirth and peace of mind.

In the letter to John, Dominick mentioned recent events like the Advocate Experience, as well as episodes from their youth, like the time he had sex with Andreas Devendorf in the Buick when the rest of the Dunne family attended their father's wake. He also mentioned *Play It as It Lays*. Dominick doubted that Joan would be surprised at the news of his sexual orientation since she had based the BZ character on him.

Unlike the letter to his brother, Dominick made the one to his therapist sexually graphic, even though the two men had never discussed his homosexuality in their sessions together. He wrote of his childhood encounters with adult men in restrooms. He wrote of sex for hire. He wrote what he liked to do and did not like to do in bed with men. Regardless, Dominick claimed that none of these encounters gave him real pleasure. The one exception was his lovemaking with Andreas Devendorf, which he considered innocent and untarnished by guilt. And he wrote about his attraction to Frederick Combs, with whom he never had sex on a "one-to-one basis, and was grateful." Dominick called such love "a sickness."

Before the year-end holidays, Dominick prepared for his return to Los Angeles, to give up his apartment and auction off his belongings. It depressed him that he had not written the novels, either of them, and the Simon & Schuster one was due the first of the year. And it depressed him that John's Christmas card made no mention of his coming out. The disclosure meant so much to Dominick. It clearly meant nothing to John.

Driving south on Highway 1 to Los Angeles, Dominick considered trying to return to his old film career there. Someone might hire him. He recalled how Bette Davis took out an ad in *Variety* asking for a job, which led to her being cast in *Whatever Happened to Baby Jane?* It sounded like a good idea. Maybe it would work for him. He would buy an ad, telling people he was available to produce movies and/or write screenplays. Just then a big bird dumped on his windshield to let him know it was a wretched idea. As much as he identified with Charlotte Vale, Dominick would never be Bette Davis.

Over Christmas 1979, Dominick visited Lenny and their children Dominique and Alex in his ex-wife's new home. It was a single-story house that made it easier for her to get around in a wheelchair, and Dominick liked that Dominique lived in a little cottage on the property. That Christmas, Griffin remained in New York City, where he performed in Wallace Shawn's new play, *Marie and Bruce.* For Dominick, the visit's best moment came when the four of them gathered around the TV set to watch his daughter's guest appearance on the TV show *Family.* Her acting career had taken off, and she had recently signed an exclusive contract with the producer Leonard Goldberg. Dominique and Griffin had inherited their mother's delicate Latin looks; Alex appeared more the strong Irishman, and in the Dunne family most closely resembled his uncle John.

Although stricken with multiple sclerosis, Lenny remained gracious and caring, and she never lost her sharp sense of humor. She and Dominick laughed a lot together, more than when they were married, and never more so than when Lenny showed him a newspaper interview with wealthy women who shared their secrets for conserving energy during the ongoing oil shortage. According to Betsy Bloomingdale, she asked her servants not to turn on the self-cleaning oven until after seven in the morning.

Lenny's humor and self-awareness, despite her money, always prevented her from turning into another Betsy Bloomingdale. But seeing her in a wheelchair, prematurely aged and felled by multiple sclerosis, Dominick felt wracked with guilt: "She loved me and believed in me, and I let her down."

Even though he said he wanted to avoid the holidays in Los Angeles, Dominick remained a social animal. He could not help but make the rounds. Together with Tony Kiser and his soon-to-be ex-wife, Kiki, he went to a New Year's Eve party at the old Dolores Del Rio mansion. He also made a quick trip back up to Santa Barbara, not to see Linda but to put in an appearance at Wendy Stark's wedding to a "penniless fellow" named Doug Gorsuch. He loved Wendy, but it amused Dominick that her father, Ray, had flown in from Vail on his jet and kept the taxi waiting during the ceremony so he could return as soon as possible to Colorado. Fran Stark did not make the trip because she was having fifty-five to dinner that night and did not like to fly in small jets, even ones owned by her husband. She had tried to persuade her daughter to have the ceremony in Las Vegas instead, so she could have flown commercial and still been back to Vail in time for her party. But Wendy wanted the wedding in Santa Barbara, so no mom. Dominick, as usual, made the mistake of telling Jack Martin about Ray Stark and the taxi, and the *Hollywood Reporter* columnist called for verification. Wendy was not pleased.

Dominick dreaded the impending sale of his furniture. And once again, Arnold Stiefel played savior, delivering more last-minute good news. "Have you sublet your apartment yet?" he wanted to know. At a party the night before, the agent met Madeline Kahn, who was in town to make another Mel Brooks movie. The actress needed a place to live for two months, maybe three. She would pay what Sandy Lieberson had been paying, $2,000 a month.

Ecstatic, Dominick showed her the apartment himself, and Kahn loved it. She had her concerns, though. She wanted the rugs cleaned, the TV in the bedroom fixed, and the Z channel hooked up. But not to worry. She would pay for everything, and did he mind if she paid him three months in advance?

Back in Oregon, Joyce and Nick Osika nailed a big sign over the door of his cabin. "Welcome Home Dominick!" It was good to be among real people again in Camp Sherman, even if Joyce had to make a rather frantic run to his cabin to tell him Madeline Kahn did not know how to drain the bathtub. There was no phone in Dominick's cabin. He apologized to Kahn, telling her he forgot to have it fixed, and gave the name and number of a good plumber.

A few days later, Joyce made a second, more frantic run to his cabin. There had been a phone call from his brother John, who said to call him back as soon as possible. Since Joyce told him it was urgent, Dominick worried: maybe Aunt Harriet had died. He thought of the money she had recently sent him for his birthday and how she had been the one who took him to Hollywood to lunch at the Brown Derby when he was a boy. As kids, Dominick and his siblings adored their spinster aunt but used to gossip quietly about her leaving the convent, something nuns just did not do in the 1920s. What sin had she committed to break her vow to God?

But Aunt Harried had not passed away. It was his youngest brother, Stephen. He committed suicide. Stephen's wife, Laure, called John at four that morning to tell him the unthinkable. When he heard the news, Dominick more than cried. He screamed. His brother would later write about that harrowing phone call in his memoir *Harp*. "When I told him what had happened, there was a cry of such bleakness that I can remember it still. He pulled himself together and said he had been contemplating suicide himself, perhaps even at the exact same moment as Stephen," John wrote.

Dominick did not have the money to attend the funeral. After being offered no fewer than two roundtrip airplane tickets in recent weeks, Dominick now had to beg his brother for one, even though he already owed him a $10,000 debt. The request did not go as expected. John explained how he was "all tapped out," having lent Stephen $35,000 for a design business he wanted to start. John added that it was not absolutely necessary for Dominick to be at the funeral. Because of their age difference, Dominick and Stephen were never close, in John's opinion. The remark incensed Dominick. Who does not go to his brother's funeral?

"I just would have stayed on and on," Dominick said of his life in Oregon. "But I had to go back for the funeral. Suicide is so utterly heartbreaking. I thought, I will never commit suicide. It had been on my mind for the last two years."

After talking to John, Dominick returned to his cabin. He looked at the typewriter and what he had written the night before. There, wrapped around the roller, was a suicide note. In a way, Stephen's suicide had prevented him from taking his own, even if it did make Dominick feel "upstaged," he wrote in his journal.

Dominick borrowed the money from Aunt Harriet to fly to the funeral in Connecticut. Everyone in the Dunne family stayed at the Holiday Inn in New Canaan, everyone but Big Time and Frail, who chose a much more upscale hotel. The whiskey flowed as the family held an old-fashioned Irish wake, and John thought it amusing when he asked their sister Virginia "which breast had been removed." She had recently undergone a mastectomy and would die a year later from the cancer.

Dominick's friends said he "never" or "only rarely" mentioned his two sisters, Harriet and Virginia, except to say that one of them married an "awful guy" and they both died of breast cancer. The intense relationships were with his brothers, especially John. During the wake in New Canaan, Dominick learned how Stephen took his life: he locked himself in his car, turned on the ignition, and then wrapped a rosary around his hands. His three children knew something was wrong even before their mother did. The exhaust fumes from the garage filled their bedroom and made the kids sick. It was their cries that woke Laure Dunne.

Very strict Roman Catholics believe suicide to be the one unforgivable mortal sin, and Dominick worried that his brother might not be given a Mass or buried in a Church-consecrated cemetery. It turned out otherwise, and he thanked the priest for being so considerate of the Dunne family.

Bad weather plagued Dominick's return to Oregon, and two flights turned into three, as well as an overnight stay in Portland, where he found himself screaming profanities at God after fog forced him to rent a car to drive the final two hundred miles back to Camp Sherman. In his cabin, he found a letter from his renter. Madeline Kahn would not be staying the extra third month as expected, and would be vacating his apartment at the end of February. Please send the deposit. Which he had already spent. He looked at the kitchen knife with the words "Twin View Resort" on it, as if the words would prevent anyone from stealing it. Dominick put down the knife, suicide no longer an option.

His brother's death compelled Dominick to look for references to suicide in *Play It as It Lays*. He reread Joan Didion's novel, looking for those lines about the "fags" who enjoyed Maria's company "because she would listen to late night monologues about how suicidal they felt." Also, he reread Maria's line about pills being "a queen's way of doing it." Despite the novel's virulent homophobia, Dominick sent John and Joan a note, telling them how much he enjoyed reading her novel again after all these years. He wrote that it was even more "exquisite" than he remembered.

Friends wrote their condolences, and among those many letters was one from Truman Capote. He did not mention Stephen's death; maybe he did not know about the suicide. In his letter, Capote told Dominick that he was doing the right thing, going to Oregon to write. But, "that is not where you belong. When you get out of it what you went there to get, you have to come back."

Dominick would later say that Capote's letter "made me cry. I had felt forgotten. He made me feel like I mattered. His letter was the impetus of my return to the fray, with my new career as a writer."

In a way, Dominick had no choice but to return to Los Angeles. He could not put off the sale of his furniture. He had to let go of the Spalding Drive apartment. Tony Kiser offered him a place to stay in Santa Monica. Mart Crowley sent him $1,000. He was broke. He was already way overdue on his novel to Simon & Schuster. But he had good friends.

On his way south on the 101 Highway, Dominick picked up a young, good-looking hitchhiker outside Santa Barbara and realized he had made a mistake as soon as the guy sat down and closed the car door. He gave off a bad vibe. Dominick begged God to protect him. He kept praying, but in Malibu his worst suspicions were realized when the hitchhiker pulled a knife and demanded that Dominick get out of the car. Dominick did as told but grabbed the car keys before he made a quick exit, which led to a chase down the middle of the road. Finally, a man in a truck told him to get in, and they watched as the police apprehended and arrested his attacker. Dominick later wrote that it was only one of three moments in his life when he was almost killed under "murky circumstances." This was one of those times.

The sale of Dominick's belongings lasted three days. Dominique helped with the tagging, and even gave him the rent money for his final month at the Spalding Drive apartment.

Dominick asked his friends to be shoppers. Those who stopped to look and buy included Mart Crowley, Arnold Stiefel, Caroline Whitman, Wendy Stark, and Jack Martin, who brought the Egyptian billionaire Mohamed Al-Fayed. They all bought something, "paying more than they were worth to help Dominick," said Stiefel. Stark overpaid for an old fireplace fender, giving her friend an $800 check.

With money from the sale, Dominick moved to New York City, unencumbered by anything except his clothes, packed into Henry Fonda's Gucci luggage from *Ash Wednesday*. Dominick also felt a renewed determination to finish his novel. Or was that novels? New York City was the place to do it, not Oregon or Los Angeles.

Dominick had a way of living in extraordinarily fine style regardless of his finances. In Manhattan, he lived for a while with an heiress named Gillian Spreckles Fuller Spencer-Churchill Pisercio Campello—or Gillian Fuller, for short. As with so many women Dominick befriended, she was not only rich but elegant. Gillian reminded Dominick of the Tracy Lord character in *The Philadelphia Story*. When he put out the word he needed a place to stay in New York, she offered him a bedroom, even though her apartment was in the process of being drastically renovated. It helped that she was not often home, working fourteen-hour days at a TV show on

ABC called *Kids Are People Too*, which, according to Dominick, made her less money than she paid her part-time secretary. Better yet, Dominick did not have to make love to her like his lady friend Linda, because Gillian was dating a younger man. It would be a perfect living arrangement, except for the renovation. He told friends the apartment looked like a Cocteau movie, and described to them the black lacquered tables, the Coromandel screens, and paintings by Hockney, Rauschenberg, and Vasarely—everything covered in cellophane tarpaulins and lit from above by a giant skylight in the two-story living room. Dominick called Gillian "Medici-like."

Also Medici-like was Tony Kiser, who, "quite by coincidence," had recently returned to New York City and now lived in Fuller's apartment building, at 131 East Sixty-Sixth Street.

Kiser took one look at the extensive renovation and asked his L.A. émigré friend, "How the hell can you write with all these workmen in here all day?" Dominick had no idea, and Kiser offered him an office in the charity foundation that his family operated nearby, at 1 East Fifty-Third Street. Dominick could walk there every day. Medici-like, indeed. Also convenient was the Church of St. Vincent Ferrer, near Fuller's apartment building, and St. Thomas Church, near the Kiser Foundation. Every morning Dominick stopped at one church or the other to pray. Statues of saints festooned both buildings and Dominick believed they kept vigil over him.

Only a couple of things were missing. For some reason, Noël Coward and W. Somerset Maugham no longer made their separate visits like they did at Spalding Drive and the Twin View Resort. Maybe the stone saints scared them away. Maybe it was St. Thomas or St. Vincent who now advised Dominick to incorporate his Simon & Schuster novel, *Joyce Haber's "The Users," Part 2*, into his own book, *A Faller by the Wayside*, which he had retitled *Portrait of a Failure*, and write one big novel. It would tell the story of Mona Berg (Sue Mengers) from the viewpoint of the Hollywood has-been Burnsy Harrison (Dominick Dunne), who meets all of these characters at a party given by Marty Lesky (Ray Stark). Even though Maugham was no longer speaking to him, Dominick borrowed the structure for his Hollywood novel from *The Razor's Edge*, wherein Maugham's character Sophie gives the low-down on all the people attending the opening-chapter party. Burnsy Harrison would be a Sophie-like guide to contemporary Los Angeles.

Dominick delivered several pages of this new novel to Michael Korda. He thought they were excellent pages. Korda did not, and promptly rejected them. According to the editor, Dominick strayed too far from the original story, and Korda ordered him to get rid of the Burnsy Harrison character completely.

Dominick rewrote in a mad panic. In his rejection letter, Korda went so far as to suggest that Simon & Schuster would take legal action to recover the advance money if Dominick did not write a novel based on the story in his unproduced teleplay. The threat of the advance money being returned made Dominick put aside any ego about being a good writer. He had wasted so much time in Oregon writing letters instead of the book. In New York, he got the new pages back to Korda in record time, before Labor Day 1980, then spent the holiday fretting in the hot, humid city. To take his mind off Korda, he visited a friend who lived on Sutton Place and, for some reason, had not escaped to the Hamptons or the country for the holiday. Seemingly everyone Dominick knew in Manhattan had a fabulous address out of a Ross Hunter movie about the metropolis. On this particular afternoon, he was not invited to check out the view of the historic Pepsi-Cola sign across the East River in Queens. The lure at Sutton Place was to meet Cal Culver. In 1980 the general public did not know Cal Culver, but among the gay cognoscenti he was famous for being a living replica of Michelangelo's David, only bleach blond. Under the name Casey Donovan, Culver starred in the most famous gay pornography film ever made, *The Boys in the Sand.* "Cheap enough?" Dominick said of his invitation to Sutton Place. The owner of the apartment apologized profusely for saying hello and then leaving the two men alone: he had to keep a pity date with one of his rich widow friends recovering from a face lift.

Cal Culver very much looked forward to meeting the producer of *The Users*, which, fortuitously, re-aired only the night before. The porn star claimed to have seen it several times, and proved especially astute in his observations about the bugle-beaded gowns that Nolan Miller designed for Jaclyn Smith, Michelle Phillips, and Joan Fontaine. Culver informed Dominick that, despite being thirty-eight years old, he continued to be hired for sex on a regular basis. He did not consider what he did hustling or prostitution. It was sex therapy. Besides, he needed the money for his new investment. Culver was in the middle of renovating a guest house he owned in Key West, Florida, where, he hoped, he would one day retire to run a bed and breakfast. Whatever sexual "guilt" Dominick had felt in the past with men evaporated that afternoon on Sutton Place. And for sixty-five dollars, he noted, "I had one of the most extraordinary afternoons of my life."

Paying sixty-five dollars for the services of a hustler or a sex therapist did not leave Dominick much money to go to the theater, one of his favorite pastimes. But unlike sex, he got to indulge that leisure for free, always on the invitation of a rich friend. In the summer of 1980, Dominick saw *Evita*, *Children of a Lesser God*, and *42nd Street*, which he found had been overrated due to the timely opening-night death of its director, Gower Champion.

The best news arrived right after Labor Day. Dominick met with Michael Korda at his office at Simon & Schuster, and the last batch of re-written pages—the ones without Burnsy Harrison—won raves from the editor. However, because so much of the novel remained to be written, Korda put his first-time novelist on a strict regimen. They would meet every Friday at the publishing house to go over the new pages. Dominick admitted he needed deadlines, many of them. What Dominick did not realize was that an editor meeting with a novelist on a weekly basis to finish writing his novel is about as typical as a doctor making a house call because somebody has come down with a bad headache. It was the kind of special treatment Dominick thought he deserved and, in the future, the kind he would get from two very important editors.

Korda gave high praise, and Dominick later told friends, "It was like the father approval I've waited my whole life to get." Korda also told him, "There's nothing the public enjoys more than the rich and the powerful in a criminal situation." Dominick heard a "boing" go off in his head. "That's my life!" he thought.

On the elevator ride down to the lobby on Sixth Avenue, he cried in great heaving sobs.

Dominick might have reserved a few of those tears for the novel that might have been. Korda wanted a best seller, and in doing so he cut the much better pages of what Dominick originally gave him. After his first novel, Dominick's most vivid characters were always his narrators, whether it be his Truman Capote doppelgänger Boris Plant in *The Two Mrs. Grenvilles* or his own alter egos: the prep-schooled Harrison Burns in *A Season in Purgatory*, the best-selling author Philip Quennelle in *An Inconvenient Woman*, or the magazine reporter Gus Bailey in *People Like Us* and *Too Much Money*. When Korda cut Burnsy Harrison from the novel, he lost forever Dominick's most exquisitely rendered portrait of failure and despair, not to mention one of the more scabrous views of the Hollywood pecking order described by Harrison in the opening-chapter party. Never again would Dominick Dunne unwrap his wounded ego and brutally offer it up for such public exposure.

Otherwise, the year ended well. Dominique got cast in a TV series called *Breaking Away*. Griffin finished a ten-week shoot in Poland on *The Wall* and landed the lead in *An American Werewolf in London*, and Alex moved his *Belle Lettres* from Vancouver to Seattle, where he now lived. Dominick made a suggestion to his son about the magazine. "You need to put your name on it," he said. But Alex rejected that suggestion. "The best magazine in the world didn't have a masthead," he said, referring to the *New Yorker*. While Dominick might want to compromise with his writing, his younger son had no such intention with *Belle Lettres*.

Michael Korda made Dominick very happy by giving the novel, finished in early 1981, a new title. In an act of mercy and less clumsy syntax, he was calling it *The Winners*. But the title came with a caveat: to honor the Simon & Schuster contract with the original author, the book would carry the unfortunate subtitle *The Sequel to Joyce Haber's "The Users."* At least when people asked him the title of his book, Dominick could say "*The Winners*" and not mention the other part about the woman he hated more than plastic luggage.

Dominick thanked his Medicis, Tony Kiser and Gillian Fuller, and said good-bye. At long last, he moved into his own Manhattan apartment to live and write. When Griffin came to see the studio at 9 Fifth Avenue in the Village, he looked out the window into an airshaft and told his father that he could not live there.

"Yes, I think I can," replied Dominick. And he did.

# 6

## Didions and Murder

Dominick dealt with the *New York Times'* pan review of *The Winners* by seeing his reputation as half full. The Old Gray Lady deemed his novel worthy of being reviewed, even if she did call it "another unsuccessful try" at someone trying to write a Hollywood novel. "It was a flop," Dominick noted, but went on to boast, "I did it! I did it!"

Despite heaping praise on Dominick's future as a writer, Michael Korda did not put Simon & Schuster's money where his mouth was. He let another publishing house pick up the option on Dominick's next book. At first, Dominick considered writing a roman à clef about the Reagans. He did not want to get political. The novel instead would be about Nancy and Ron's "thoughtless spectacle," as he described it; using the structure of the 1932 Broadway play *Dinner at Eight*, Dominick wanted to fashion a story about a president and first lady who have to cancel a party due to an international crisis. He liked the title *Edwina Calder's Brother-in-Law*. It referred to the time when Joyce Haber, speaking to *Washington Post* columnist Maxine Cheshire, referred to him as "Joan Didion's brother-in-law," as if he had no better identity. The Reagan roman à clef, however, developed no further than a few sample paragraphs and a letter to agent James Oliver Brown. Unencouraged in that endeavor, Dominick began work on something he initially titled *North Shore*. The book's editor was Betty Prashker, whom Dominick had met over lunch at the suggestion of Lucian Truscott IV during the David Begelman brouhaha. At their meeting, Prashker showed no interest in characters based on Begelman or Ray Stark, at least as presented to her by an unpublished writer. Two years later and now working at Crown Publishing, Prashker liked his new proposal for a second novel, *North Shore*, a roman à clef about the Ann and Billy Woodward marriage. That high-profile, tempestuous union ended abruptly in 1955 when she shot him with a rifle in their Long Island mansion. Was it murder or a horrible accident? Truman Capote had already created a scandal by retelling the violent death in his short story "La Côte Basque 1965," published in *Esquire* magazine and reported to be a chapter of his long-awaited novel *Answered Prayers*. Rumor had it that Ann Woodward got her hands on an advance copy of *Esquire*, read the story, and promptly imbibed a cyanide tablet. Capote wrote a short story. Dominick would write a whole novel about it.

Betty Prashker made one quick, bold decision when she assigned the novel. She wanted to call it *Mrs. Grenville*. Dominick approved the title. It had mystery. Who was the Mrs. Grenville of the title: Ann Woodward or her patrician mother-in-law, Elsie Woodward? After the homicide, that other Mrs. Woodward stood by her son's wife and killer in order to avoid a press melee. The police did not charge Ann Woodward with murdering her husband, and Dominick liked that Capote never thought to write about the lesser-known, more elusive Mrs. Woodward in "La Côte Basque 1965."

Working on the new novel, he no longer battled writer's block because he was no longer writing a book with Joyce Haber's name on it. Dominick especially enjoyed researching the story like a real reporter would investigate an unsolved murder. That fact-finding might have been more arduous if not for another possible act of high-profile homicide among the wealthy and socially prominent. In winter 1982 Claus von Bülow stood trial for attempted murder, having been accused of giving insulin injections to his diabetic wife, Sunny, now comatose in a $700-a-day suite at NewYork-Presbyterian Hospital. The smoking syringes had been found in a closet at the victim's Newport, Rhode Island, estate, called Clarendon Court. Dominick knew that the Old Guard of New York would never talk to him about the Woodward murder if they knew he was writing a novel about it. But they thoroughly enjoyed gossiping with him about the debonair von Bülow, and how Sunny turned the Danish financier into her well-kept but resentful husband. Dominick found it easy to segue from Sunny and Claus to other high-society crimes, the Woodward scandal among them. Those rich old biddies on Park Avenue and Sutton Place had no idea they were actually being pumped for information about Ann, Billy, and Elsie.

Unlike his time in Oregon, Dominick's life became extraordinarily regimented in New York City. In addition to writing and researching his new novel, he attended AA meetings in Greenwich Village. In the 1970s, Griffin Dunne moved to the Village with hopes to lead a Damon Runyon kind of life. Instead, he became a movie star, so it impressed him that his producer-father from Hollywood was the one who ended up knowing "these Bukowski characters and crossdressers with hair nets." Father and son would be having lunch or coffee at a sidewalk café and street people would call out to him, "Hey, Nick!" Griffin asked his father how he knew such colorful characters. "Oh, the rooms," Dominick said. "I know them from the rooms." He meant the AA meetings. Griffin called it his "favorite time" with his father.

It was the time that might also have been right for Dominick to come out of the closet. He was living in the ultra-liberal Village, going to AA meetings there, populated with lots of other like-minded gay men. But for him, it was not the right time. It was the onset of the AIDS crisis. It was the time that famous homosexuals in the fashion and entertainment business sold their houses in the gay resort of Fire Island Pines and gave interviews to *Playboy* magazine. It was the time that Studio 54's Steve Rubell, already infected with HIV, talked to *New York* magazine about the "empty" gay lifestyle and opened a new disco, the Palladium, which caused his good friend Bianca Jagger to comment on the club's wonderful heterosexual ambiance. It was not the time when men on the verge of stardom chose to come out of the closet. For Dominick, it was not the right time.

The phone call on Sunday, October 31, 1982, came at five in the morning. Detective Harold Johnson of the Los Angeles Homicide Bureau phoned to tell Dominick that his daughter, Dominique, had been brutally attacked and was now in a coma at Cedars-Sinai Medical Center in Beverly Hills. Dominick, in complete shock, managed to ask if Dominique's mother knew. The detective said he was phoning from her house and put Lenny on the phone. She did not have to say more than his last name, "Sweeney." Dominique's ex-boyfriend John Sweeney, a sous chef at Ma Maison, had strangled her in a jealous rage outside his daughter's house in West Hollywood.

The Dunne family never truly embraced Sweeney. Dominique thought her father's coolness toward her boyfriend was a "snob thing because he was a chef and not a kid from Hotchkiss," but it was not that. Dominick just did not like him. And now that man had strangled his daughter.

Dominick hated Los Angeles more than ever when his plane landed at noon that same day, only ten hours after he received the unimaginable news. Mart Crowley met him at LAX; Alex and Griffin would be arriving

later. Every radio and TV station in the area carried the news since Dominique's latest movie, *Poltergeist*, had been a huge hit and Sweeney worked
under celebrity chef Wolfgang Puck at Ma Maison, one of the so-called
power eateries in the city.

When Dominick and Crowley arrived at Lenny's house, several friends
had already gathered there. Years later, Dominick would write what it was
like to be in a house when someone in the family has been murdered: "No
one's total time can be accounted for. Shock prevails. People come, people
go. They hug. They whisper. They weep. Conversations are going on all
over the house—in corners, in hallways, in the kitchen, bedrooms, bath-
rooms, garage. Secrets are shared. Revelations are made. Speculation is
everywhere. News bulletins on the murder are relayed throughout the house
by those watching television."

Dominick made those observations in 1995, in the wake of what might
have taken place in O.J. Simpson's Rockingham estate the day after Nicole
Brown Simpson and Ron Goldman were found murdered outside her
condo on Bundy Drive in Brentwood. But, of course, he was really writing
about what happened in Ellen Griffin Dunne's house on Crescent Drive
in Beverly Hills the day after John Sweeney attacked Dominique.

The doctors took her off life support on November 4, 1982. When
Dominick wrote about those four days leading up to his daughter's actual
death, he thanked the "relay teams of friends" who took telephone calls,
arranged for food and coffee, and managed every other detail of the Dunne
family's life. What he did not write about in that *Vanity Fair* article,
"Justice," was the behavior of his brother and sister-in-law, which, by the
end of John Sweeney's murder trial and the ensuing ordeal, would ignite a
major feud that ended only a few months before John Gregory Dunne's
death in 2003.

After the murder trial, people would occasionally ask Dominick about
his famous sister-in-law. "You want to know what Joan is really like?" he
would say and then tell variations of the following story.

The day after the attack, John Gregory Dunne and Joan Didion arrived
at Lenny's house to offer their support before Dominique was taken off life
support. Her critical condition never improved. She showed no brain
activity and a bolt had to be placed into her skull to relieve swelling of the
brain. Due to her precarious state, the family decided early on to use one
phone line in the house to make calls and to keep the other line open in
case the doctor or police called.

Shortly after asking if there was anything she could do, Joan Didion
retired to the master bedroom to place a call on the outgoing line. She
closed the door. Later, needing to use the telephone, Dominick walked

into his ex-wife's bedroom. There, he found his sister-in-law on the bed, the phone clutched between her neck and shoulder, a pen in hand. Galleys of her next book, *Salvador*, littered the bed spread. She was on the phone with her editor in New York.

Joan looked up at Dominick. There was impatience in her expression, her voice. "Yes?" she asked.

Dominick told variations of that story to friends. Alex Dunne gave a slightly different version. "Alas, there was only one line in the house so no one else could call through to send their condolences to my mother while Joan was editing her piece," he recalled. "But it is quite possible that Joan was not aware that was the only line in the house. And yes, my father was incensed but [I] do not recall him actually asking her to get off the phone so my mother could use the line, although he very well may have eventually done so. Very tense couple of hours there for a while."

That long phone call only marked the beginning. Almost all press reports on the crime referred to Dominique as the niece of John Gregory Dunne and Joan Didion. Her parents were not mentioned, which deeply upset Dominick. Lenny took a different attitude. "Oh, what difference does it make?" she asked. Later, when her mother, Beatriz, also complained about "the niece" references, Lenny finally relented, encouraging Dominick to do something. He immediately called the publicist Rupert Allan, the longtime partner of General Frank McCarthy. "It's hurtful to us. It's as if we had not only lost her but been denied parentage as well," said Dominick. Allan turned out to be a very good publicist and took care of the problem, according to Dominick. Actually, the problem disappeared on its own as press interest in the case quickly dissipated.

Dominick would later write that Patrick Terrail, the owner of Ma Maison, "became the interim object of my growing rage." It incensed him that Terrail, a few days after the attack, told the *Los Angeles Times* that Sweeney was a "very dependable young man." Terrail went on to tell the *Santa Monica Evening Outlook* that Sweeney would receive "the best legal counsel." Dominick misinterpreted that four-word quote to write that Terrail himself "would obtain the best legal representation for [Sweeney]."

After his daughter's funeral, Dominick returned to a very different kind of life in New York City. He somehow continued to work on *Mrs. Grenville*. But he had changed because his view of Los Angeles and the world beyond had changed. Still in communication with his lady friend Linda in Santa Barbara, he learned that she was divorcing her husband, whom she married on the rebound after their "affairette." She made plans to travel to Reno, Nevada, to obtain a quick divorce, and he gave her advice on hotels and restaurants there. He also asked about her house on the beach, and if it had survived the torrential rains hitting California that winter. He told her he felt no sorrow for all the homes in Malibu being ruined, especially those belonging to "third-rate rich people from the movie business." He used to hate Los Angeles. He still did, but now he also found the place "terrifying."

Those feelings of extreme fear were compounded by the fact that he felt obligated, as Dominique's father, to travel back to Los Angeles to be present at the trial's preliminary hearings in February 1983.

He was appalled at the "public relations campaign . . . started by the owner of [Ma Maison], Patrick Terrail, trying to create a groundswell of sympathy for the killer." Terrail, for his part, denied ever seeing or speaking to Sweeney "after the night of the incident," and the only quotes he gave the press were to the *Los Angeles Times* and the *Santa Monica Evening Outlook*. Those eight words—"very dependable young man" and "the best legal counsel"—were repeated endlessly in several news stories on the case.

The preliminary hearings also incensed Dominick. In the courtroom, defense lawyer Marvin Adelson mistook Dominick for the father of the killer, not once but twice, in an attempt "to incite me to make some kind of slur on him in public," Dominick believed. He also thought that another lawyer, Joseph Shapiro, was part of the defense team and paid for by Terrail. John Sweeney, in fact, relied on a public defender, Marvin Adelson. There was, however, a great deal of disagreement regarding the other attorney. According to Terrail, Joe Shapiro never worked for him in any capacity. "He was a customer at Ma Maison," he said. Dominick insisted that Shapiro acted as the "legal counsel for Ma Maison," a statement that eventually had to pass through *Vanity Fair*'s fact-checking department, one of the most rigorous in the publishing business.

This much is certain about Joe Shapiro. He ate many meals at Ma Maison, and so admired Sweeney's cuisine that the two men became good friends. They even played on the same softball team. A member of the prestigious law firm Donovan, Leisure, Newton & Irvine, Shapiro would later be chief negotiator with the French government on the $2.3 billion Disney theme park in Paris. He died of lymphoma at age fifty-two in 1999.

In 1983 Shapiro did take a very active interest in the Sweeney murder trial but, according to Marvin Adelson, worked without pay. Whatever the truth, Shapiro's participation angered Dominick. And when Dominick hated a person, he often attacked his looks. With Adelson, he mocked his toupee. With Shapiro, he said he looked like an ICM agent.

Sometime after the preliminary hearings, Dominick told Lenny about a book he wanted to write. It was not another novel. It would be a non-fiction book about his experience of sitting through the trial of Dominique's murderer. He had never attended a trial before, but it did not matter. He was not interested in legalese or points of order in court; this book would tell of a parent's extreme anguish over having lost a child at the hands of a murderer. He could not think of another book like it. Lenny agreed and gave him her full approval to write such a book.

In early May 1983, Dominick's good friend Marie Brenner invited him to a Sunday brunch at her Manhattan apartment. Her guests included people Dominick would want to meet, like the *Wall Street Journal*'s David McClintick, one of the few reporters who did not seek Dominick's help regarding the Begelman scandal, and Tina Brown, Brenner's editor at the British magazine *Tatler*. Condé Nast had recently relaunched its *Vanity Fair* title to disastrous reviews under the editorship of a company stalwart, Leo Lerman, and Brown was in town to interview for the top job.

"Over the years, so much has been written about that brunch. It has been embroidered and embellished," said Brenner. Dominick would always refer to it as a Tex-Mex dinner. "I think I served huevos rancheros. It was very casual, just six people, maybe."

Tina Brown also recalled that early May 1983 get-together, saying, "He told me he was off the next day on a tragic mission—to attend the trial of his twenty-two-year-old daughter's murderer." When Dominick told the story, he often said he was "leaving the next day for the trial." In a Dunne profile, *New York* magazine retold his version: "The night before he left New York to attend the trial of Dominique's attacker, Dunne was introduced to Tina Brown at a dinner party. She encouraged him to keep a journal."

Dominick did not leave New York City that May for the trial in Los Angeles. He left two months later, on July 5, for the pretrial hearings, held later that month. The trial itself began in August.

Dominick remembered Tina Brown as being "this little English wren" the day they met, "not a glamorous woman as she gradually became." According to him, she advised, "Keep a journal every day and come and see me when it's over." He invariably gave her full credit, saying, "Tina Brown literally discovered me. She found inside me something I didn't know I possessed."

In future interviews, Dominick never talked about the book he originally intended to write about the trial. In their telling of it, Dominick and Brown always made him the reluctant writer, either not wanting to capitalize on his daughter's murder or too traumatized to write about the ordeal. She, in turn, was always the supportive editor who saw the light that made him shine, finally, and pushed him to write. For his own good.

Brenner, for her part, recalled telling Dominick to keep a journal during the trial. "He was very upset about it," she said. "I gave him classic writer's advice, as a way of dealing with the trauma. Tina said, 'If you write that, I'd publish it in *Vanity Fair.*'" At the time of the brunch, Brown had not yet been hired by Condé Nast.

Fortunately for Dominick's future as a writer, Condé Nast soon finalized its deal with Brown to revamp *Vanity Fair* and be its editor in chief. Although Dominick often spoke of being reluctant to write about the trial, he never had to be pushed in that endeavor by Brown or anyone else. On June 7, 1983, a full month after the Brenner brunch, he wrote a pitch letter to Brown, sending it not to the *Vanity Fair* offices but to the Surrey Hotel where she had taken up temporary residence. In the letter, Dominick reintroduced himself, reminding her how they had met at Brenner's apartment a few weeks before. He went on to reveal how he intended to write a book about the trial but thought she might consider an article on the subject before the book's publication. He made no mention of their previously talking about such a piece. In the letter, he instead recalled their discussing Henry Kissinger and how articulate and "detailed" she had been in her observations regarding the former secretary of state.

Years later, Tina Brown said, "There are writers who discover you, but the writers you love the most are those whom you discover, and I never loved any of them more than I loved Dominick."

It is debatable who discovered whom, but one thing is certain: Brown wasted no time contacting Dominick after she read his two-page, single-spaced, typewritten pitch letter. (Dominick often told the story that Brenner phoned him the day after her brunch to set up the lunch with Brown.) They met for lunch at La Goulou in mid-June and she offered him $15,000 for ten thousand words on the John Sweeney trial. She had even bigger plans. Dominick remembered her telling him, "You shouldn't be wasting your Hollywood stories at dinner parties. You should write them for the magazine. . . . It would take me ten years to train somebody who knows as many people as you know and who can tell stories the way you tell stories."

Dominick never discussed a book about the Sweeney trial with Freddy Eberstadt. They did, however, talk about the *Vanity Fair* article, and according to his close friend, Dominick expressed concern that people might find it "creepy" if he wrote about Dominique's murder and the subsequent trial.

Three weeks after lunch with Tina Brown at La Goulou, Dominick left for Los Angeles, on July 5, even though the trial would not begin for at least a month. In his *Vanity Fair* "Justice" article, he would write that he spent the plane ride speaking to a stranger seated next to him, "postponing as long as possible facing the feelings of dread within me." In his private journal, Dominick never mentioned the stranger seated next to him in first class. Instead, he wrote of using the five-hour plane ride to continue his research on the Woodward murder for *Mrs. Grenville*. That research included reading Igor Cassini's recently published novel *Pay the Price*. To Dominick's discerning eye, it was obvious that Cassini, brother of fashion designer Oleg Cassini, retold many tales based on actual events from his long tenure as the *Journal-American*'s gossip columnist. In 1955, using the nom de plume Cholly Knickerbocker, Cassini wrote three in-depth columns on the Woodward murder. Then, at the height of the scandal, the articles stopped abruptly. Had Elsie Woodward asked a Hearst executive at *Journal-American* to end the coverage on her former daughter-in-law and dead son? Dominick used that supposition as a plot point in *Mrs. Grenville*, having Alice Grenville (the Elsie Woodward character) go over the head of gossip columnist Fydor Cassati (the Igor Cassini character) to ask Millicent Hearst to place a moratorium on any more articles about her daughter-in-law, Ann Grenville.

Many people in New York City soon came to know the subject of Dominick's second novel. Not everyone looked forward to the book's publication. "Truman Capote was upset about it," said Dotson Rader. "Dominick was stealing his idea. Truman wouldn't have cared if it was an article. But Dominick was writing about the Woodwards from Truman's point of view. It was part of his book." Indeed, the narrator of Dominick's novel is a character named Basil Plant, based on Capote, whose roman à clef about the murder causes Ann Grenville to commit suicide.

In 1983 who expected Capote to finish *Answered Prayers*? Not Dominick. He had more pressing matters than Capote's wounded pride. He needed to know where he was going to stay in Los Angeles during the trial. Once again, he relied on the generosity of a wealthy lady friend, in this case, Anne McDermott, the estranged wife of TV producer Tom McDermott, his erstwhile boss at Four Star. She offered Dominick her house in the Holmby Hills free of charge but not without strings: he would have to share the house with Tom and his current girlfriend, the writer Rona Jaffe, author of *The Best of Everything* and *Mazes and Monsters*. Dominick knew Anne wanted him to keep an eye on her husband. No surprise: Jaffe took an immediate dislike to Dominick, and the feeling was mutual.

To get around in Los Angeles, Dominick drove Dominique's electric blue convertible Volkswagen. It was not his style, but at least he did not have to spend money on a rental. In the car's glove compartment, he found his daughter's sunglasses, the same pair she had called her Annie Hall glasses, the ones he had bought for her in Florence during her student days there. Putting them in his jacket pocket, he promised to carry the glasses with him as a cherished talisman throughout the trial.

No sooner did Dominick take up residence at the McDermotts' than he received a phone call from Lenny. She had major news. Vicki Morgan, the mistress of department-store heir Alfred S. Bloomingdale, had been beaten to death with a baseball bat! Morgan's schizophrenic gay roommate, Marvin Pancoast, confessed to the crime the night of the murder. Dominick immediately thought: there's another book! He also gasped. He knew the killer. Pancoast briefly worked for Allan Carr as a secretary and ran off with an extensive Rolodex, much to the manager-producer's distress. Hollywood—it's such a small town.

And poor Betsy Bloomingdale. Dominick and Lenny talked about what had to be her crippling embarrassment. Betsy had fought like a black belt to prevent the $18,000-a-month mistress from getting any of the money her husband had willed the girl. Now the Bloomingdales' close friendship with President Ronald Reagan and First Lady Nancy Reagan would be resurrected, along with Betsy's determined campaign to prevent Morgan from winning her $5-million palimony lawsuit. Betsy was no Elsie Woodward. If it meant stoking a scandal, Betsy would do it to keep Alfred's money. Poor Betsy. Dominick recalled how nice her husband had been when he petitioned him to give Mart Crowley his first credit card.

After he and Lenny finished talking about the latest L.A. scandal, they made plans that night to attend a meeting of Parents of Murdered Children (POMC) in Brentwood. It was bizarre, gossiping about the murder of a stranger and then mourning the murder of one's own daughter. That evening, at a Presbyterian church, the parents of Dominique Dunne got their first lesson on murder trials. At the POMC meeting, they learned how defense lawyers earn big money and almost always outclass the prosecutors in court. John Sweeney's defense had done extensive interviews with psychiatrists, and Dominick feared that the district attorney, Steven Barshop, would not be as prepared. Friends told him not to worry. Barshop was tough and had successfully prosecuted the killers of Sarai Ribicoff, niece of Senator Abraham Ribicoff.

In the article "Justice," Dominick would write that "friends of ours had advised us to leave town until the trial was over." He never identified those "friends," but at least two of them were actually very close relatives, John Gregory Dunne and Joan Didion. Years later, John revealed his reason for giving such advice: "Before the first preliminary hearing, I could predict that the counsel for the accused would present the standard defense strategy in cases of this sort: the victim, unable to speak for herself, would be put on trial, and presented, in effect, as a co-conspirator in her own murder."

Dominick had always intended to attend the trial. How else could he write a book or article about it? The POMC meeting in Brentwood only strengthened that resolve when the father of a murdered child told him it was his duty to be at the trial every day. He said, "It's the last business of your daughter's life."

Everywhere he went in Los Angeles people were talking about the murders of Dominique Dunne and Vicki Morgan. It caused an emotional whiplash in Dominick. He relished hearing the gossip about Morgan but recoiled at talk about his daughter. He had always loved murder stories. Now he was torn. But how could he not be fascinated by what people said about the Morgan case? Rona Jaffe speculated that someone near the Reagans might have killed Vicki Morgan because she knew all the secrets. Frederick Combs told him that Morgan's confessed killer, Marvin Pancoast, had been in AA for four years. Then Lenny phoned again to give him even more news regarding the Morgan murder. There were sex tapes.

Dominick repeated the Morgan gossip about the sex tapes to his brother and sister-in-law when he met them for lunch at Boh!, a restaurant in Santa Monica. John and Joan listened, but they were much more interested in discussing the upcoming Sweeney trial. They asked if a plea bargain had been offered by the defense team; they said it would be a way of avoiding a trial that might be unpleasant for the family. Dominick told them no, there had been no plea bargain. The three of them ate their lunch and parted on good terms.

He did not think much about the conversation until, two days later, a friend of his brother phoned. Barry Farrell had worked with John at *Time* magazine in the 1960s, and after introducing himself, the journalist said he had a message from Sweeney's lawyer, Marvin Adelson: they wanted a plea bargain, and Sweeney would be willing to go to prison for fifteen years. Farrell went on to say how Adelson saw the case as that of "a blue-collar kid who got mixed up in Beverly Hills society and couldn't handle it." Dominick knew what Adelson meant and was offended. The case would be tried "not as a crime, but as a tragedy."

The following day, John made separate phone calls to Lenny and Dominick, asking each of them to accept the plea bargain. He said he had spoken to a lawyer friend, Leslie Abramson, who told him it was not unusual for a plea bargain to be presented to the victim's family through an intermediary. Abramson herself had been approached by Adelson to perform that very duty some time ago but refused because she knew Joan and John personally. Dominick resented John's back-to-back phone calls with him and Lenny to discuss the plea bargain.

And there were worse things than phone calls being made. "We got reports that Joan and John were going to Ma Maison," said Alex Dunne. "In Los Angeles at that time, there were two restaurants that were the power places to be seen. One was Chasen's. The other was Ma Maison. And we got reports that Joan and John continued to dine at Ma Maison. Being seen there was what they cared about." What made their appearance even more galling was that many people in the entertainment business began to boycott Ma Maison to show their support of Dominick's family. In fact, the restaurant's reputation never fully recovered.

The phone calls regarding the plea bargain took place over a weekend, and neither Lenny nor Dominick had the prosecuting attorney's home phone number to discuss the issue with him. Early Monday, they phoned Steven Barshop's office to ask about a proposed plea bargain. He was furious that there had been any such talk. Besides, it was out of the Dunne family's hands, he told them. The state had taken the case to court. But what really infuriated Barshop went beyond mere talk: John and Joan had written him a letter, telling him how to try the case.

Dominick now told people he "loathed" his brother. John and Joan's secretary revealed that the couple refused to have the trial even mentioned in their home, despite their attempts to influence it. And like Alex, Dominick kept hearing that the Didions dined regularly at Ma Maison. Then he got word that John and Joan would soon be leaving for Europe with their daughter, Quintana, and would not be back until after Labor Day, at which time the trial would be over. According to friends, Joan and John had another fear beyond their dead niece's reputation being attacked in court. They worried that Quintana, a friend of Dominique, would be called to testify, and they did not want to put their daughter through such an ordeal. John called Dominique his daughter's "surrogate sister."

"Joan and John felt Quintana would be compelled to say certain things that might be used against Dominique," said their friend Susanna Moore. "They were very clear they didn't want her to testify. Nick felt they had abandoned him, that they were negligent and not caring, which wasn't the truth."

Joan and John's fear about their daughter being called to testify, however, was an empty one. "I don't think there ever was an issue that Quintana would testify," said Steven Barshop. "It would have been judged inadmissible."

With the trial only a week away, Dominick distracted himself by indulging in his two favorite pursuits, gossip and star-watching. He remained connected enough in the Hollywood community to hear news no one ever got on TV or in the newspapers. He heard that agent Freddie Fields was busted for possession of cocaine coming back from the Cannes Film Festival; Ronald Reagan would not run for a second term because he was going deaf and could no longer hide the problem; and Marvin Pancoast had not killed Vicki Morgan but took the fall. In other words, Allan Carr's erstwhile secretary would be released from a mental institution in a few years and be a million dollars richer. The case fascinated Dominick. Many amateur sleuths speculated that a killer who confesses the crime to the police would not have rubbed his fingerprints off the baseball bat; he would have been blood-splattered; and the drawers would not have been rifled through since he, Pancoast, roomed with Morgan.

While pages of *Mrs. Grenville* went unwritten, Dominick produced reams for his *Vanity Fair* article once the pretrial began. It appalled him that testimony given by Lenny and one of Sweeney's ex-girlfriends, Lillian Pierce, would not be heard by the jury. Before her murder, Dominique had been beaten by Sweeney and escaped to her mother's house. Judge Burton S. Katz ruled that such evidence was inadmissible on the grounds it was hearsay.

Two years before Dominique's murder, Pierce had been beaten repeatedly by Sweeney, causing her to be hospitalized twice. During that testimony, it startled Dominick to hear how defense attorney Marvin Adelson framed his question: "Let me remind you, Miss Pierce, when you met with Mr. Joe Shapiro and me for lunch on November third, you said . . ."

Dominick wondered why Adelson and Shapiro met with Pierce the day before Dominique's actual death. As he explained the situation, "efforts were being made to free her killer by men who knew very well this was not his first display of violence."

In the pretrial, Pierce spoke of Sweeney's violent treatment of her, and during that damaging testimony the accused lost it. He exploded and grew so enraged at what his ex-girlfriend said on the stand that he ran for the rear door of the courtroom. The bailiff grabbed the defendant and four guards wrestled him to the floor after being alerted by a secret alarm system.

Despite Sweeney's mad display, Judge Katz ruled that "the prejudicial effect outweighed the probative value" with regard to Pierce's testimony. The judge's ruling meant that her damning words would never be heard by the jury. Dominick worried, "Nearly everything Adelson requested was being granted."

He was not being paranoid. "Based on the rulings I got, almost everything was inadmissible. The case went south," Steven Barshop said years later. "The judge and I became mortal enemies, and still are. His rulings were terrible."

Dominick anguished over the fact that the jury would never see the jealous animal that lost it in court. By the time the jury appeared there, Sweeney miraculously turned himself into a Bible-toting martyr and even dressed in black to resemble a priest. Dominick told Lenny he reminded him of the religious fanatic that Robert Mitchum played in *The Night of the Hunter*. Left out of that portrayal, as well as his reporting for *Vanity Fair*, was that Sweeney, attempting suicide, slashed his wrists while in prison.

Mike Tipping covered the trial for the *Santa Monica Evening Outlook* and wrote about Sweeney's rampage in court. As soon as his article appeared in the newspaper, Judge Katz reprimanded the reporter for sensationalizing the outburst. Tipping tried to talk to the Dunne family. He knelt in front of Lenny in her wheelchair. "It was small talk. They all looked like they hated being approached," the reporter recalled. "They were royally pissed off."

In the beginning, Dominick found Steven Barshop to be brilliant. Especially effective was the dramatic moment in court when the prosecutor told the jury that it took the 170-pound Sweeney four to six minutes to strangle the 112-pound Dominique Dunne. Barshop then asked for complete silence in the courtroom and, looking at his wrist watch, said, "Ladies and gentlemen, I am going to show you how long it took for Dominique Dunne to die." Sitting there for those four grueling minutes, Dominick believed any juror would have to find Sweeney guilty of premeditated murder.

Dominick wrote about it in harrowing detail in his notes for the *Vanity Fair* article. What he did not include in the final article was a moment in court that proved equally anguishing for him—but for an entirely different reason.

In mid-August, Dominick's boyfriend took the stand. A few weeks before Dominique's murder, Norman Carby took photographs of his actress-friend. It was no ordinary photo session. She came to him late one night after being badly beaten by Sweeney. During the fight, her boyfriend had taken one of the Regency bamboo chairs that Dominick used in his Christmas card portraits and thrown it at Dominique. Sweeney threw the antique chair so hard that he reduced it to bamboo splinters. Carby, taking photographs to document her bruises, tried to buoy Dominique's spirit. He joked, "You won't need any makeup for tomorrow's shoot." She laughed, briefly, because it was true. The following day, Dominique played a battered victim on an episode of *Hill Street Blues*.

Now, almost a year later, Carby sat on the stand testifying about those photographs. Showing them to the jury, Marvin Adelson made a big deal about the one photo in which Dominique was shown laughing. If she had just been beaten by her boyfriend, why was she laughing, Adelson wanted to know? Carby explained the situation, how he had tried to make a joke, but Adelson dismissed that explanation.

Dominick grew nervous the more he watched and listened to his boyfriend testify. He felt that Carby came off very gay on the stand and worried that it would influence the jurors. When Adelson asked Carby how he knew Dominique, Carby answered that she was a friend whom he had known for many years. The attorney then asked about Carby's friendship with Dominique's father.

Dominick panicked. He reached into his jacket pocket for his daughter's Annie Hall glasses, the same ones he brought to court every day. Carby did not immediately answer Adelson's question. He paused. Suddenly, Judge Katz brought the questioning to a halt. He asked both lawyers to approach the bench. Dominick could only think about his relationship with Carby, kept secret from all but a few friends. Now it would be exposed to Lenny, his two sons, and the world beyond. Only Mike Tipping of the *Santa Monica Evening Outlook* covered the trial on a daily basis. But this bombshell could not be ignored. Now every news outlet would be eager to follow the trial.

Finally, the whispering between the judge and the two lawyers ended. When the questioning resumed, Adelson dropped any further reference to Carby's relationship with the Dunne family. Dominick could breathe again. He opened his eyes. He put his daughter's sunglasses back into the pocket of his jacket. The trial continued.

Interviewed years later, Adelson said he did not recall his line of questioning that day with Norman Carby. He denied, however, that he tried in any way to out Dominick Dunne. "That would be not only evil but foolish," he said. Carby also did not recall the exchange.

Dominick, always hypersensitive about his sexual orientation, may have exaggerated the moment. In his journal, he wrote of it being "a miracle" that his reputation had been spared.

What John Gregory Dunne and Joan Didion feared, however, did happen. When John Sweeney took the stand, he trashed Dominique's reputation, making unsubstantiated charges. When Alex Dunne began to weep, Adelson brought it to the court's attention. "Your honor, Alex Dunne has tears in his eyes," he said and asked that Dominique's brother be told to leave the courtroom.

Alex Dunne did not need to be ordered. He told his father, "I can't go back anymore. I can't be there where Sweeney is," and never returned to the courtroom.

In his article "Justice," Dominick did not repeat the exact details Sweeney gave to justify his beating Dominique. "His violent past remained sacrosanct and inviolate, but her name was allowed to be trampled upon and kicked, with unsubstantiated charges, by the man who killed her," he wrote. It marked the beginning of his victims' rights crusade.

The Associated Press had not been covering the trial, but their reporter Linda Deutsch made a special one-day visit for Sweeney's testimony. Deutsch had been covering murder cases for years, starting with the Charles Manson trial, and in the following years would become one of Dominick's closest colleagues among the courtroom press corps. They never discussed her one-day visit to cover the Sweeney trial, and she doubted that Dominick was aware she ever attended it. On the subject of victims' rights, Deutsch opined, "If you don't want your reputation dragged through the mud, don't get murdered." Regarding the Sweeney trial, she recalled finding the defendant "very pathetic. There was no question he loved Dominique to distraction and he killed her out of love. He was insane, very disturbing."

The lowest blow to the prosecution came when Judge Katz found that Sweeney committed the murder without premeditation despite the four to six minutes he had his hands wrapped around Dominique's throat. The judge's decision took out of consideration the charge of first-degree murder, leaving the jury to decide between second-degree murder and voluntary manslaughter. Although a courtroom novice, Dominick knew what that meant. If there was a split decision with the jury, they would go with the lesser charge, if for no other reason than to settle the matter and be done with it.

The jury deliberated for eight days, and in the end, as Dominick feared, the jurors leveled the lesser charge, voluntary manslaughter. As one juror explained it to a TV reporter, "A few jurors were just hot and tired and wanted to give up."

Outraged, Dominick could not accept the decision of voluntary manslaughter. He had to do something, say something. When Judge Katz thanked the jurors, he thanked them on behalf of the court, the attorneys, and the two families.

"Not for our family, Judge Katz!" Dominick yelled out in the courtroom.

Stunned, Katz said, "You will have your chance to speak at the time of the sentencing, Mr. Dunne."

"It's too late then!"

"I will have to ask the bailiff to remove you from the courtroom."

"No, I'm leaving the courtroom. It's all over here." With those words, Dominick began to wheel Lenny from the courtroom. Before he got to the hallway, he turned back to confront the judge one last time. "You have withheld important evidence from this jury about this man's history of violence against women!" he shouted.

Griffin Dunne called it his family's "proudest moment."

The court sentenced Sweeney to six and a half years in prison. Because of the time he had already spent in jail and probation, he would be free in only two and a half years.

Was Dominick's outburst in any way planned? Was he playing editor and giving his article the dramatic conclusion that the readers of *Vanity Fair* would expect?

Steven Barshop knew Dominick was writing an article on the trial for the magazine. Marvin Adelson did not. Both attorneys, however, believed Dominick's outburst to be genuine and not in any way planned or calculated. "He was obviously very upset," said Adelson.

In one important respect, the prosecutor found Lenny and Dominick typical of other parents caught in their impossible situation. "I've done cases where the guy is convicted," said Barshop. "And the parent looks at me: 'It doesn't make any difference. I want my child back.'"

Regarding the Sweeney trial, Barshop found the mother of the victim more than understanding. She even invited the attorney and his wife to dinner, Dominick not being present that evening. "I loved Ellen Griffin Dunne," said Barshop. "She was a very classy lady." His feelings about Dominick were more complicated. "I found him demanding, very self-absorbed, someone who wanted answers. Could he be vindictive? Absolutely," he said. "What goes on in the jury system and the justice system is not something lay people understand. The things that happen as they happen in a case are things that are generally out of my control, except for the presentation of evidence."

Dominick withheld his opinion of Barshop in the "Justice" article, but many years later he said he "hated" the prosecutor.

Dominick and Lenny may have been devastated by what happened in court, but unlike most parents who endured such a tragedy, they both took action. She founded a group called Justice for Homicide Victims. "It was one of the first victims' rights groups that's activist-oriented," said Alex Dunne. "Before that there were groups where you basically sat around and cried. This group was, 'Let's do something about it.'"

After the trial, Lenny took to the phone to cold-call hundreds of other parents of murdered children. She told them, "You don't know me, but we have something terrible in common. I lost my daughter the same way you lost yours." One of those parents she phoned was Marcella Leach, whose daughter Marsy had been murdered. Through the work of Leach and Justice for Homicide Victims, Marsy's Law, or the California Victims Right Law of 2008, was enacted.

Dominick also took action. When John Sweeney was released from jail two and a half years later, a friend ran into Dominick at the Beverly Hills Hotel. "Nick was ready to kill Sweeney," she said. He even went so far as to meet with Anthony Pellicano. According to Dominick, the private detective dissuaded him from ordering a hit on Sweeney. "You don't want to do that," Pellicano warned.

"I really didn't want to do it," Dominick recalled, "and I wasn't asking him to do it. I was there to see if he knew someone who could do it." Later, he did hire Pellicano to follow Sweeney, to see if he was dating other women. "My rage needed a release from the persistent plan in my mind to hire someone to kill him, an obsession I had for months," he said. "I decided I didn't want to live in a state of revenge."

In a way, Dominick had already started on another path by the time Sweeney left prison in 1985. Wracked by guilt for not having done more to protect his daughter from her ex-boyfriend, Dominick became a crusader—and not only through what he wrote. "He often went to Parents of Murdered Children meetings like a parish priest, talking to parents of other murdered children," said Marie Brenner. "I had a cousin whose child was murdered, and Dominick became obsessed with helping me with that case."

Years later, Brenner wrote the *New Yorker* article "Murder on the Border," about the homicide of an eighteen-year-old. "Dominick gave me the playbook for what to do and how to do it," she said. "His passion didn't just infuse all his writing; it was much more than a pastime. He spent from 1983 up through the 1990s going to fund-raisers and dinners, making speeches and phone calls."

To the general public, it was Dominick's writing that spoke most vividly of his commitment. The travesty of justice delivered by Judge Burton S.

Katz gave focus to everything he wrote, and that miscarriage of justice would take center stage in all the novels he wrote after *The Winners*.

But first came the private journal that he wrote during the trial and the *Vanity Fair* article it spawned. "Justice: A Father's Account of the Trial of His Daughter's Killer" did not fit perfectly into Dominick's premise that money buys justice, a premise he would expand and deepen over the years. In the John Sweeney trial, the defendant was not wealthy and it was his victim who came from money, her mother being a rich heiress. Dominick weighted the circumstances by turning Patrick Terrail, owner of Ma Maison, into the object of his hatred for allegedly helping Sweeney with his defense. In Dominick's reporting, the Ma Maison habitué Joe Shapiro became not only omnipresent but the power behind the public defender, especially with regard to the meeting between himself, Marvin Adelson, and Lillian Pierce the day before doctors took Dominique off life support.

"Justice," however, did break journalistic ground. Dominick filled it with the kind of personal, often ghastly observations that heretofore were not a part of court reporting. Just as he gave reporters covering the David Begelman scandal interesting details about Ray Stark and other movie moguls, Dominick knew how to color his coverage of the Sweeney trial to give it drama. He reported on how the defense attorney brought his children to court and lovingly taunted them, "Now don't you talk," as if to make himself beloved by the jury. He also wrote how a *People* magazine photographer had been summoned to Judge Katz's private chamber, expecting to be admonished for something he did in court. Instead, the judge wanted to know which of his eyeglasses photographed better. Dominick also revealed how it fell to Joe Shapiro to tell Sweeney's mother that her son did not want to see her even though she had endured a two-day bus trip to get to the Santa Monica courthouse. And "Justice" marked the first time Dominick described in print what he despised most about a man: his toupee. Dominick wrote that Adelson wore "a quarter pound of hair taped to his head." For Dominick, it never got worse than a rug on a man's head.

In other words, the article delivered. It was the kind of sensational material Tina Brown needed to successfully relaunch *Vanity Fair*.

"Dominick had a voice that was so personal, that spoke to you right off the page," said Brown. "He buttonholes you. It was the instantaneous arrival and debut of a writer. . . . *Vanity Fair* had found its first voice. . . . He became our first star writer. I believe the defining voice of the magazine."

For years to come, the rumor in the halls of *Vanity Fair* was that Dominick's article came to editor Wayne Lawson in the form of "scraps of paper," according to more than one source who worked for the magazine.

It was a tale embellished by Lawson's own estimation, told to people, that Dominick's prose required extremely heavy editing. There was also Lawson's reputation as a very hands-on editor even before his tenure at *Vanity Fair*. In his long career in journalism, Lawson wrote very few articles under his own byline. He was well known, however, as a ghostwriter. He had "written" Gloria Swanson's autobiography and "edited" two novels by Jerzy Kosinski, a writer infamous for employing coauthors to radically re-work his prose without giving them coauthor credit. If Dominick did in fact turn in scraps of paper to Lawson, they were pretty good scraps of writing: much of the article is verbatim from Dominick's type-written journal, completed before he delivered any copy to *Vanity Fair*.

# 7
## Bloomingdales and Videotapes

While awaiting publication of *Mrs. Grenville*, Dominick continued to follow the Vicki Morgan murder case with the rapt interest of an idle novelist in search of a terrific new story to tell. He learned that Allan Carr's ex-secretary Marvin Pancoast also confessed to the Sharon Tate murders and other crimes he could not possibly have committed. Dominick preferred writing about the wealthy upper-crust society on the East Coast, but Hollywood and its rich had their undeniable, tacky appeal. He heard about the latest status symbol for the citizens of Beverly Hills: they parked a police car in their driveway to ward off criminals. He heard stories that Aaron Spelling's driveway sported one, and as a gift the TV producer gave a patrol car to the Ray Starks. Dominick's reinvigorated hatred of L.A. would only fuel him to complete such a new novel about murder in such a "threatening" place.

After writing his "Justice" article, Dominick had to slog through a couple of celebrity fluff pieces for *Vanity Fair*, ranging from "Blonde Ambition," about such up-and-coming starlets as Daryl Hannah and Kim Basinger, to "Candy's Dynasty," about Aaron Spelling's eccentric wife. Finally, he got to cover another murder trial.

The accused killer Marvin Pancoast was not rich or famous, but his victim, Vicki Morgan, was infamous, and her mistress ties to Alfred S. Bloomingdale took the case to the highest echelons of wealth and power in America. One year into his presidency, Ronald Reagan appointed Bloomingdale to the President's Foreign Intelligence Advisory Board. It was not lost on Dominick that the scandal involved two power couples he had invited to his Black and White Ball in 1964. He never got over the

Bloomingdales, the Reagans, and their circle of friends dumping him in the 1970s. More likely they forgot him. Dominick, eager to make them remember, flew to Los Angeles in late spring 1984 to cover the trial for *Vanity Fair*.

"Dominick wasn't at the trial long," said lead defense attorney Arthur Barens. "He was in the courtroom for the Bloomingdale matter with the tapes."

The tapes were the sex tapes that reportedly showed Vicki Morgan cavorting with not only Bloomingdale but other men in President Reagan's social and political set.

Only there were no videotapes. Or no videotapes that anyone ever found, despite rumors they would be introduced as evidence in the trial. Without the tapes and without any interviews from Betsy Bloomingdale, Nancy Reagan, or anybody in their exalted social set, Dominick's article "The Woman Who Knew Too Little" for *Vanity Fair* was an inauspicious follow-up to "Justice," but not a total loss.

Covering the trial provided Dominick with research for another novel, and it led him to a memoir without which he could not have written what would ultimately be his fourth novel. Or, at least, if he had written *An Inconvenient Woman* without first reading *Alfred's Mistress*, his book would have been a far different, perhaps less convincing, roman à clef about a wealthy, politically connected woman who orders a hit on her dead husband's destitute mistress.

*Alfred's Mistress* is Vicki Morgan's memoir as ghostwritten by a screenwriter named Gordon Basichis. While she was alive, Morgan and Basichis did not get much writing done but they did become lovers, despite his being married with an eighteen-month-old son. Basichis recorded his conversations with Morgan, and after eight months of collaboration on the book and exactly one week before her murder, she fired him from the project and broke off their affair, although not necessarily in that order. Despite the split, they continued to fight. Then they made up and spent the night together, which happened to be the penultimate night of her life.

The firing, the fight, the night-before sex. It looked like Basichis did it, except he had a great alibi. He was at home with his wife watching baseball on TV when the murder occurred. And better yet, Morgan's schizophrenic gay roommate, Marvin Pancoast, confessed to the crime.

Dominick knew the ghostwriter of *Alfred's Mistress* from his Hollywood days. Gordon Basichis recalled their association with little fondness. "I had a project," he said, "a book I was going to option with another guy, and he knew Nick, and I went to his apartment, one of those older apartments in Beverly Hills south of Wilshire. He didn't look like he was doing well. This was in the mid-1970s."

A decade later, Dominick was doing very well at *Vanity Fair* and Basichis was trying to sell a memoir that publishers did not want. The two men talked, and before long Dominick got what he wanted: a copy of the unpublished *Alfred's Mistress*. Maybe he could help get it published. "I had all the information from Morgan directly. No one else had that access," said Basichis.

The book looked like the kind of smoking gun that *Vanity Fair* readers would come to expect of a Dominick Dunne article. There was only one problem: Dominick claimed that Basichis's book shot blanks, making it clear why ten publishers had rejected *Alfred's Mistress*.

Dominick delivered a full-throttle pan of the unpublished book in *Vanity Fair* but did acknowledge how one scene caught his interest: for Vicki Morgan's final meeting with a dying Alfred Bloomingdale, she spent $1,000 on her "Betsy table" of flowers and decorations. Dominick wrote that it "made crystal clear the complicated nature of their relationship."

The scene also provided Dominick with what would arguably be the most poignant moment in *An Inconvenient Woman*, published five years later.

"Nick borrowed from it freely. Under the guise of some collaborative effort. That was his MO," said Basichis.

Face to face, before "A Woman Who Knew Too Little" hit the newsstands, Dominick praised *Alfred's Mistress* to its ghostwriter. Basichis, in turn, returned the favor by taking Dominick into his confidence to reveal that there were no Vicki Morgan sex tapes. They were a ruse to throw off reporters, in his opinion. "You could write some batshit thing about sex tapes and then if you explode it out, it didn't matter that you couldn't substantiate it," said Basichis. "That's the seminal fact in terms of how journalism changed." Not to mention courtroom tactics.

Dominick and Basichis did agree on one thing: someone other than Pancoast murdered Morgan. "The blows were extremely well placed, just enough to kill somebody," said Basichis. "It wasn't where someone became extreme and lost all control, as they would in a crime of passion."

Dominick never bought the defense's theory that Basichis held down Morgan's dog while a hit man bludgeoned her, and then someone hypnotized Pancoast into taking the rap. To discredit such a scenario, Dominick reported that the courtroom erupted in "giggles" when the defense presented such speculation.

The jury deliberated only four and a half hours before finding Marvin Pancoast guilty of murder in the first degree. If Arthur Barens tried at the trial to implicate others in the crime, thirty years later he was not defending his erstwhile client, now dead. "Pancoast had confessed to another murder. Pancoast was a sick man. . . . His perception of reality was screwed. To a degree he was intoxicated with the celebrity the case gave him," said the attorney.

The trial warranted one article in *Vanity Fair*, no more. The subhead for "A Woman Who Knew Too Little" said it all: "Dominick Dunne reports from the murder trial in Southern California on a B-movie cast and a plot as trashy as her ending, the Marvin Pancoast/Vicki Morgan trial."

Dominick, however, knew there was another, better story there. All he had to do was artfully stir in soft facts, and hard suspicions, that would never get by the *Vanity Fair* lawyers and embellish the story with characters inspired by powerful people he knew in Los Angeles and Washington, DC. Years later, after he had written several best sellers, Tina Brown identified Dominick's real shrewdness as a writer of fiction. "Dominick has been quite clever to keep the novels going, actually, because in a way, very often, the frustration of nonfiction is that you can't really write what you know to be true if it isn't supported by a fact," said Brown. "So in a way, his novels are a kind of clearinghouse for all his instinctual knowledge of the subtext of all the things he's writing about—all the emotional stuff that frequently can't come out in a factual piece."

Dominick did just that with *Mrs. Grenville*. He would also do it five years later when he finally got around to writing *An Inconvenient Woman* and before it, *People Like Us*, his third novel. The only difference was his prototypes. Everybody who inspired his *Grenville* characters had passed away. The characters in his next two novels would be based on famous individuals who had the disadvantage, when it came to their good name and reputation, of being very much alive.

# 8

## Von Bülow and Comas

The disappointing commercial and critical reception of *The Winners* shook Dominick's belief in his talent. Editors like Betty Prashker and Tina Brown restored it. If he had any doubts about *Mrs. Grenville*, a third high-powered female executive took his self-confidence to a whole new level.

Even before publication of the novel, Lorimar optioned *Mrs. Grenville* for a TV miniseries. It was not feature-movie interest, but, as Dominick kept telling friends, "Novels aren't being turned into movies anymore. They're being turned into TV movies.'"

A publishing mole "sneaked" Sue Pollock the original twenty-five-page proposal of *Mrs. Grenville*. On the lookout for material to be adapted to television, the Lorimar vice president did not have to read the finished novel. "I knew with Betty Prashker being the editor that Crown would get behind it and it would be a best seller," said Pollock.

In time, Dominick would refer to it as the novel "that changed my life." But he did not know that until it happened. Before the novel hit the bookstores, Crown Publishing retitled it *The Two Mrs. Grenvilles*, and Lorimar announced it would be turned into a two-part miniseries for NBC. A veteran book publicist met Dominick at LAX to take him on a round of press interviews in Los Angeles.

"I've read a lot of books," Judy Hilsinger told him, "but this is one of my favorites. It's going to be a big best seller."

"Really?" asked Dominick.

According to Hilsinger, "He didn't know what he had in *The Two Mrs. Grenvilles*."

Dominick knew, however, what to do with the book's massive royalties. (His books would go on to sell over three million copies worldwide.) First, he bought a one-bedroom penthouse apartment with terrace at 155 East Forty-Ninth Street in Manhattan, down the block and across Third Avenue from where Stephen Sondheim and Katharine Hepburn lived next door to each other in brownstones. He also went back to using Scotty Bowers's escort service whenever he visited Los Angeles: "two or three times a week, depending on his needs," said Bowers. On the East Coast, he flew Cal Culver up from his B&B in Key West to party with him in New York City. And he set out to repurchase some of his more beloved pieces of furniture from the Spalding Drive garage sale. At the top of the list was his old fireplace fender, which Wendy Stark generously overpaid for when he needed her $800. She did not want to sell it back, but they came to an agreement: he could repurchase it for the original $800, and upon his death, she could buy it from the estate for the same $800.

Dominick did not remain humble or surprised about his literary success for long. After he recovered from the euphoria of his novel being turned into a miniseries, Dominick took an immediate and intense dislike to what Lorimar and NBC were doing to *The Two Mrs. Grenvilles*. While Ann-Margret was a good ten years too old to play the arriviste Ann Grenville, the actress made the wise choice to dine one night alongside a Lorimar executive who took an uncommon interest in her dramatic cleavage and practically promised her the role over crème brûlée. Dominick held his tongue on that casting decision. He had rejected Ann-Margret for *Play It as It Lays* but made that decision before knowing the actress's manager. He now considered Ann-Margret a friend because Allan Carr was a friend. Dominick, however, openly objected to some of the older actresses being considered for the role of Ann's contemptuous mother-in-law, Alice Grenville. Loretta Young turned it down, finding the story too unsavory for a good Roman Catholic like herself. The dueling sisters Olivia de Havilland and Joan Fontaine both wanted to play the snooty dowager. "De Havilland lobbied hard for it," said producer Preston Stephen Fischer. When Claudette Colbert emerged as the producers' clear favorite, however, Dominick said he much preferred his friend Lauren Bacall and found an easy ally in Liz Smith, who planted an item in her syndicated gossip column, saying Bogie's widow would be cast.

"Bacall didn't have the requisite class," said the film's director and supervising producer, John Erman, "and the Liz Smith item caused problems with Claudette, who'd already been approached." Dominick and Liz Smith lost that battle, as did Bacall. Erman cleverly "circumvented" the Smith item by giving journalist Robert Osborne the news that Colbert would play Alice Grenville. His exclusive scoop broke on the front page of the *Hollywood Reporter*, shaming Liz Smith and creating acrimony at the *Reporter*, where its aging Broadway Ballyhoo columnist Radie Harris thought Erman should have hand-delivered her, not the upstart Osborne, the big tip.

Dominick also hated the *Grenville* script. He wanted his friend Mart Crowley to write it, but the network wanted someone with experience writing long-format television. *The Boys in the Band* may have broken new ground in the theater, but it was not a miniseries. The TV executives wanted and got Derek Marlowe, who had written two miniseries. "Derek knew about society and being an outsider," said Sue Pollock. "He wrote a great script."

Dominick thought Marlowe wrote a terrible script and dashed off a type-written seven-page, single-spaced letter to John Erman, listing a number of problems. His complaints ran the gamut, from the use of the word "drapes" (old money never uttered the word) to spending a dime to make a phone call (it cost a nickel in the 1940s) to the word "the" in front of El Morocco (it did not belong there) to having Billy Grenville drink alcohol from a flask while driving (Dominick complained that John Sweeney had been a drunk driver, and besides, it would destroy sympathy for the character).

Erman knew Dominick's fierce determination. "We've got to fix this," he told network executives. "Nick's on everybody radar, and if he comes out against the movie, it's not a good thing."

Others involved with the production thought Dominick's real problem was not the script. Having once been a producer, Dominick desperately wanted to bring *The Two Mrs. Grenvilles* to the TV screen under his own aegis.

Fortunately for Lorimar and NBC, Dominick got somewhat side-tracked. The production of the miniseries, which shot in London, took place as the second Claus von Bülow trial convened across the Atlantic Ocean in Providence, Rhode Island. (The first trial ended on March 16, 1982, with von Bülow found guilty of attempting to murder his wife, Sunny.) Dominick briefly visited the UK production of *The Two Mrs. Grenvilles* but could not stay long, needing to fly back to the States for the trial, which began on April 25, 1985. He complained to reporters in Providence that the TV people in London "don't like rich people. They don't understand rich people."

Reporters were not the only ones who got an earful. Dominick also groused about the direction of the TV movie with an agent-friend, who, in turn, gave him a few tips on being a real journalist. "He asked me what a lede was," said Lucianne Goldberg. "The reporters at the trial kept talking about their lede, and he didn't know what they were talking about." The agent, who had represented many writers in her long career, told him it was jargon for an article's opening paragraphs. Dominick and Goldberg were not the most likely phone buddies. They met through a mutual friend "who liked to put people together. That was about the time that Tina Brown had adopted Dominick and wanted to get the story of his daughter's murder," said Goldberg. Like any good dealmaker, she needed to remain in touch socially. "But I had kids in college, I was busy with my career, and didn't have time to get out every night the way Dominick did. He was nuts about going out."

On the phone every morning, Dominick and Goldberg chatted about daily newspapers' top stories; then he would go out at night and report to her the next day. "He came back with all the dish, which I thought an enormous advantage, because I didn't have to go to the parties. He told me who left with whom and came with whom. 'Did you know so and so?' It was one of those relationships," she said.

Dominick told Goldberg everything. They shared opinions, even though the two rarely met face to face. It was not unlike his daily phone chats with Joyce Haber at the *Los Angeles Times*. Goldberg did not have a daily column but was a very plugged-in literary agent, who, in the following decade, would come to verbal blows with Dominick over her ties to the Bill Clinton/Monica Lewinsky scandal. An arch-conservative, Goldberg never thought much of Dominick's liberal politics, but they shared a similar black-and-white concept of justice. Each knew instinctively that Claus von Bülow had tried to kill his wife, and with the second trial, he was attempting to buy himself an acquittal with the expensive counsel of Alan Dershowitz, the attorney who had successfully wangled the appeal.

Dershowitz viewed Sunny von Bülow's coma not as attempted murder but the direct result of an upper-class tragedy: "these rich women who drink too much and take injections," he said. "Dominick knew that world." The two men engaged in long talks about the case, and Dershowitz laid out the medical evidence and how the incriminating bag with the insulin-crusted syringes could have been planted in a closet at Clarendon Court.

Dominick remained unconvinced. "Dominick never saw a defendant who was innocent," said Dershowitz. "He looked into Claus's eyes and saw a murderer."

Dershowitz left out the word "rich." Dominick never saw a *rich* defendant who was innocent. He considered himself an expert on the rich and, more important, he liked them, except when they were murdering people and then buying justice with overly clever lawyers. His knowledge of the wealthy not only helped him write *The Two Mrs. Grenvilles*; it gave him a distinct advantage over other reporters at the second von Bülow trial. Among the press corps, only Dominick really understood the high society world of New York and Newport, Rhode Island. Only he knew why von Bülow acted and dressed the way he did. Joyce Wadler covered both von Bülow trials for *New York* magazine, and she had never seen anything like the fustian outfits the defendant wore in court.

"There was a cuff of some sort," Wadler recalled. She asked Dominick, "What is that?" According to the *New York* reporter, "Nobody else in that crowd of reporters knew."

"It was the cuffs," explained Barbara Nevins Taylor, a reporter for WCBS. "Von Bülow wore these strange European suits with cuffs on the sleeves. That was a style that Dominick identified for all us reporters."

Those sartorial details fascinated Dominick. Other reporters considered them trivial or just did not care.

"I don't love rich people," Wadler noted. "If they want to kill each other, it's like the Mob." One trial about Claus von Bülow attempting to murder his wife was enough for her. The second trial almost sent Wadler into a coma since she had little sympathy for the victim. An heiress and socialite, Martha "Sunny" Crawford used her considerable wealth to marry a destitute prince, Alfred von Auersperg of Austria, and followed that first failed marriage with a more disastrous one to the Danish financier Claus von Bülow.

"Sunny von Bülow was this woman who had wasted her life, been born with every advantage, then had drug and drinking problems," Joyce Wadler surmised. "She just seemed to be neurotic. I didn't care for [Claus]. These two ridiculous people."

Adding to the couple's preposterousness was a very high-profile mistress. In the beginning, Andrea Reynolds watched the trial from the relative privacy of the CNN van parked outside the Providence courthouse. Charles Feldman manned the cable network's satellite station and gave von Bülow's latest girlfriend access there in turn for her giving on-air interviews on how the defendant had reacted to the day's proceedings. Feldman also got to know Dominick and what he thought of the dramatic trio. "Dominick found them to be a sordid lot, except for Sunny, whom Dominick had great sympathy for," said Feldman.

In addition to thinking von Bülow a killer who bungled the job, Dominick labeled the defendant a big phony. "He made fun of the 'von' in his name with great disdain; it made Claus sound more aristocratic than he was," said Feldman, "and he was not a fan of Andrea's, who was quite taken with Dominick."

According to the CNN correspondent, Dominick possessed a very complicated attitude toward people like von Bülow, one fraught with insecurities about his own upbringing and ancestry. "Dominick craved acceptance," said Feldman. "On the one hand, Dominick had a degree of disdain for that segment of society; on the other hand, he wanted to be accepted by them. And he enjoyed being known as someone who was kind of a priest and he could move among them and they would tell him secrets." Dominick often joked about his resemblance to a defrocked priest and thought it was why people felt comfortable confiding in him.

While there were reporters who knew more about the law, none knew more about the high society world of the accused. "Like many of the journalists there, I did come almost to consult with him about what to me was an alien world," said Feldman. "Dominick was a guide to that world."

Often it was tit for tat. "I introduced him to Rhode Island's major players at the trial," said Tracy Breton, a veteran reporter for the *Providence Journal*, "and he gave me entrée to Sunny's world in New York."

He was a generous guide and succeeded at being "one of the gang," according to several reporters. One of them, Dick Lehr, would go on to write such best-selling crime books as *Black Mass* and *Whitey: The Life of America's Most Notorious Mob Boss*. But in 1987 Lehr was a twenty-three-year-old cub reporter, on his first big assignment for the *Boston Globe*, and he instantly hit it off with the *Vanity Fair* writer, thirty years his senior.

"Dominick had the energy of someone just out of college on their first big job. It was contagious," said Lehr.

"Isn't this a blast?!" Dominick kept telling the young reporter. "Isn't this fun?!"

After a typical day in court, Dominick would invite Lehr and other journalists to hang out in his room at the Biltmore Plaza Hotel to brainstorm and run up his room-service tab courtesy of *Vanity Fair*. "Where's this trial going?" Dominick asked. "Are they going to get him? I have too much information. What am I going to use?"

Even though Dominick tried out his observations and theories on other reporters, he never turned stingy when it came to sharing his extensive knowledge of the Chippendale and chintz at Clarendon Court or the names of the designers who made the long capes that von Bülow's daughter, Cosima, wore to court.

He also entertained with stories about Liz and Dick fighting on the set of *Ash Wednesday*. Or how Peter Lawford used to play pimp for his brother-in-law and how the women complained that the president refused to be touched after sex. Dominick also did not hold back when people asked him to describe his famous sister-in-law. "Here's all you have to know about Joan," he would say and then tell the story of her tying up a phone line at his ex-wife's house in the days leading up to Dominique's death. "There was serious fallout because of that phone call," said Joyce Wadler.

Only rarely did Dominick indulge in social one-upmanship. He told reporters that Sunny's two children by Prince Alfred von Auersperg were old friends; in fact, he had only recently been introduced to Prince Alexander and Princess Annie-Laurie through his friend Freddy Eberstadt. "Dominick boasted about knowing them, Ala and Alexander, and he liked them. I didn't like them because they framed Claus," said Andrea Reynolds.

Unlike von Bülow's girlfriend, the prince and princess came late to taking an active interest in the second trial. "Sunny's family held back until they felt the trial was going badly," said Jonathan Friendly, a reporter for the *New York Times*.

They knew they also "had to fight a public relations war," said Barbara Nevins Taylor.

"It was much more controlled with the von Auersperg children," Dick Lehr said of their press conferences.

Claus von Bülow and Andrea Reynolds, on the other hand, held nightly dinners with the reporters. The defense also had another, greater advantage in the second trial. In preliminary hearings, they disposed of the prosecution's smoking gun: the black bag containing the syringes with which von Bülow allegedly injected Sunny.

Then there was the prosecution. The second time around, they failed to present a strong case. Dominick, using one of his rare sports analogies, saw it like "a football game between the New York Jets and Providence High." At one point, the judge even lectured the prosecutors "to prove their case or get out," said Jonathan Friendly. "Then I remember being contacted by Sunny's son, who told me, 'We have pictures. Mom was not a heavy drinker. She was in good health.'" The two von Auersperg children also gave Friendly a private tour of Clarendon Court.

Most reporters visited the attempted-murder scene. "The jury was taken to the house. We all went to the house," said Nevins Taylor. "One room was larger than the next, and the jurors were tittering and trying to get serious. It was a murder scene, yet Sunny's two children were in the house, living there. The whole thing was so strange."

What other reporters described in routine fashion, Dominick knew to animate, to punctuate with drama, and coming from Hollywood he possessed a natural flair for self-promotion. He fashioned his copy so that it always gave the appearance, if not the substance, of delivering something unique. He did not present his *Vanity Fair* readers with a general tour of Clarendon Court like the other reporters. He talked the two von Auersperg children into letting him "spend the night" at their Newport residence. Before bedtime on that overnight stay, he and the kids visited the neighbors. Dominick wrote, "We dined across Bellevue Avenue at the home of the Countess Elizabeth de Ramel, an American friend of Ala's titled by a former marriage, whose Newport antecedents, the Prince and Wood-Prince families, dated back for generations." When it came to name-dropping, Dominick took it to an Olympic level, and no other reporter could compete.

He also wrote about staying on the same floor of the Biltmore Plaza Hotel as von Bülow, as if he had special access. In fact, almost every out-of-town reporter stayed at that hotel, many of them on Dominick and von Bülow's floor. Only Dominick let his readers know his close day-to-day proximity to a possible murderer.

"That comes from the movies, how you create your story," said Nevins Taylor. "Dominick understood that color was important to the story."

Most significant, he knew to look beyond the witness stand for drama. Cosima von Bülow, Sunny's only child by Claus, took her father's side in the controversy. She never gave Dominick an interview, which did not stop him from lavishing copy on her. "She would show up at the courthouse sweeping down in this large cape and going to lunch with her father," Charles Feldman recalled. "It added to the theatricality of the trial. Dominick understood that: the theater happens outside the courtroom."

On the subject of Cosima, Dominick reported that von Bülow and Reynolds dined around town with her, even threw a huge birthday party populated with no one her age, because "as long as they take Cosima with them when they go out, her trust pays the bill," according to "an informed source." No other reporter bothered with such delicious gossip.

And no other reporter knew how to tell tales better than Dominick, especially when it counted most—over dinner with von Bülow and Reynolds. Those evening get-togethers with reporters took place at various restaurants around town. "There was nothing else to do in Providence," said Nevins Taylor. "Also, it was unbelievable access."

Since von Bülow had been criticized for being aloof and icy during the first trial, he tried a different tack the second time around. Not only was he accessible to the reporters, but he tried to charm them, which was not easy considering his naturally aloof and icy personality. Dominick saw through the performance. He knew rich people. He knew what they thought of reporters; at best, they considered them inferiors and, at worst, contemptible parasites. Dominick never believed von Bülow's attempts to joke with journalists. Like putting a napkin over his head to imitate Queen Victoria. Or telling stories about Winston Churchill. Or giving advice on oil stocks. Or dipping "a friendly spoon into a reporter's parfait," according to Alex S. Jones of the *New York Times*.

"Dominick enjoyed it; particularly he enjoyed Andrea," said Nevins Taylor. At least he gave the impression of enjoying it.

Where other reporters were intimidated, Dominick carried on relaxed, jovial conversations with the infamous couple. "I was just this kid from Connecticut," Dick Lehr recalled. "I didn't know what to say, but Dominick! Dominick had the social skills to just be in the conversation with Claus and Andrea, and he knew all these aristocratic people they talked about, whom I'd never heard of."

Lehr recoiled at the whole idea of having dinner with an accused murderer. It seemed very "*People* magazine" to him. "What am I doing here as a journalist?" he fretted.

Dominick never asked himself such a question. He knew instinctively what he was doing there.

One night at dinner with the reporters, von Bülow told a joke about his wife, Sunny, being in a coma. "Are you kidding me?" thought Lehr. That night he went to bed and had the worst nightmare of his life. "I attributed it to eating dinner with evil," he recalled.

According to Lehr and others, Dominick harbored similar feelings about von Bülow—"that he was evil incarnate," said Joyce Wadler.

But Dominick's acting days at Williams College served him well. "He was completely convinced of Claus's guilt," said Lehr. "This guy is on trial for murder, and they're acting like it was a night out on the town. Dominick felt genuinely disgusted, but he didn't let it show during dinner. He was working. He was a sponge. He was very smooth."

During trial recesses, Dominick and Lehr often ran into von Bülow and his entourage in the hallways of the courthouse or the hotel. "I didn't know what to say," said Lehr. "Dominick always knew how to banter."

On one such occasion, von Bülow introduced Dominick to Andrea Reynolds. "Mr. Dunne is not a friend," added the defendant.

"I'm being friendly now," said Dominick.

Dominick did not need to be introduced to Reynolds, the woman who had essentially masterminded the defense for von Bülow's second trial by contacting attorney Alan Dershowitz. (Dershowitz denied the Reynolds connection, saying retired Supreme Court Justice Abe Fortas recommended him to von Bülow.) It was definitely her idea to hold the nightly dinner parties with reporters. "I was aware of everything at that trial," said Reynolds. "Most people didn't like Claus. Maybe it was a bit of jealousy; he was very classy."

Reynolds played her role of the rehabilitator to the hilt and beyond. "Two-thirds of her ideas were bad," said Dershowitz. "One-third were good." He put the nightly dinners with reporters in the former category, saying their impact was "probably negative."

Dominick, in fact, met Andrea Reynolds years before the trial, in 1965, at the Corviglia Club in St. Moritz, where Henry Ford and his second wife, Christina, were celebrating their honeymoon. Reynolds, however, did not remember him from some alpine resort in Switzerland. She remembered Dominick from dinner parties given by her friend Alice Mason, a Manhattan socialite turned uber-realtor. Mason liked Dominick enough to invite him occasionally, but Andrea was a better friend. Or, at least, she proved more protective of Reynolds than she was loyal to Dominick.

"Alice was afraid for me; she thought Dominick would do something horrible," said Reynolds. Mason had warned her friend not to give an interview to Dominick. It was advice Reynolds refused to heed and soon regretted.

Dominick's gift as a journalist did not end with his flair for gossip and color. He also knew as an interviewer how to fill the news void when nothing happened. He knew how to create a scenario that would produce anecdotes, especially when speaking to women.

"It was obvious to me that Dominick was gay," said Joyce Wadler. If he was not physically attracted to the opposite sex, he did know how to talk to them about decor, art, fashion, hair, and makeup.

"He used those skills and those passions to make himself appealing to Andrea Reynolds in a way that other reporters could not," said Barbara Nevins Taylor. He even used that special charm on female reporters.

Nevins Taylor recalled his coming to her office at WCBS in New York City. He took one look at her coat on a hanger and immediately pointed to the Christian Dior label. "*That's* my friend!" he exclaimed. They soon became good friends.

With Andrea Reynolds, Dominick exploited that gay-friend syndrome to the max. Nevins Taylor recalled the excited conversation she and Dominick had after he interviewed von Bülow and Reynolds for *Vanity Fair*. The interview took place at the Fifth Avenue apartment owned by Sunny von Bülow that Claus and Andrea used as their residence. Dominick had been assigned by the magazine not only to cover the trial but to profile the notorious couple. That interview would turn into a spectacular cover story when photographer Helmut Newton convinced the couple to pose in matching black leather jackets. Dominick knew the photographer's sinister stylistic flourish would position his article squarely in the public's solar plexus.

After gossiping with Nevins Taylor, Dominick phoned his friend Marie Brenner to tell her all about the photo shoot, too. "You're not going to believe this!" he began. "We have gotten Claus to pose in a black leather jacket!"

Alan Dershowitz considered the cover story Reynold's worst idea. "We were just thrilled that the jurors didn't read *Vanity Fair*," he said.

Equally important to the cover story's success was Dominick's intimate tête-à-tête with Reynolds in Sunny's bedroom. He asked Claus's mistress if it was true she wore the comatose woman's jewelry.

"I have better jewels than Sunny," Reynolds shot back and then proceeded to show Dominick just how fabulous those jewels were.

"What he didn't write in *Vanity Fair* is that Andrea dumped her jewelry onto the bed," said Nevins Taylor. "They went through all the jewels together. It was delightful to him. He loved it, and he described it with such delight to me." Nevins Taylor found herself "half-appalled and amazed and astonished, and I admired him, to play both sides like that, with Andrea and her jewels. His description of Andrea and touching the jewels, it was like two girlfriends. On the one hand, he wanted to be part of this other world."

But Dominick knew he was not. He did not get sucked into their world completely. According to his friend James Duff, Dominick possessed what Thomas Mann called erotic irony—"To love something and make fun of it at the same time," said the writer-producer.

"When he was invited inside, he played. He loved the glamour and all the pretty tags," said Nevins Taylor.

"Dominick loved the jewels," Reynolds agreed. "He touched them. He did not wear them."

He came off as a fearless reporter who had no problem asking even the toughest question. The reality was somewhat different. Dominick spent hours obsessing about his interview with the couple. He did not know the right way to approach Reynolds about one story: had she shot her first husband? And how would he phrase his question to von Bülow: "Are you a necrophiliac?"

"He was very straightforward," Reynolds said of Dominick's interview technique. She also was blunt, telling him there was a "rumor" that she had shot her second husband, not her first.

Dominick proved equally direct when it came to asking von Bülow if he had sex with corpses. Von Bülow took it well. Dominick wrote of their exchange: "The necrophilia story, he says, was pinned on him in 1949, as a joke, on Capri, by Fiat owner Gianni Angelli and Prince Dado Ruspoli." Von Bülow added, "Like dirt, it stuck."

Dominick wanted more on the subject. "He was agonizing how he was going to work in the necrophilia," said Nevins Taylor. "He was convinced about the necrophilia story. He had heard that there was a funeral home on the far West Side of Manhattan where they kept bodies, and there were these parties that von Bülow attended. He was trying to get me to do a story. I tried to search it out. I could never prove it."

Other reporters on the trial got the impression that Dominick and Reynolds knew each other and were, if not close friends, good acquaintances. It was not the case.

"I was a bit scared being interviewed by Dominick. I like being scared," said Reynolds, who later remarried, and as Andrea Reynolds Plunket now runs a bed-and-breakfast in the Catskills. She never liked being made to look like "S&M people" in *Vanity Fair* and regretted falling for Dominick's charm.

"He was manipulative," said Charles Feldman. "Reporters and writers, to a large degree, are con artists. You have to convince whomever you're talking to that they're the most interesting thing in the world. You care more about their story than anybody else's. And you're their best buddy and you won't screw them over. And often you do all those things."

According to Feldman, Dominick carried a far more demanding burden than most reporters covering the trial. "If you're Tina Brown you want something that is unique," he explained. "That's a lot of pressure, to fashion something covered by so many people and come up with something that nobody else had. Dominick didn't have the rep that he had years later. This was a huge break. He was either going to succeed or fail miserably."

When the seven-week trial finally ended, the reporters had little to do while the jury deliberated. The *New York Times*' Jonathan Friendly had been more circumspect about his thoughts on the verdict than most journalists, especially Dominick, who made his choice of guilty known from the first day.

"The normal conceit in reporting is you don't take one side or another. You're skeptical about everything. Until the very end," said Friendly. He did not hang out with Dominick and the reporters for the simple fact that he did not stay at the Biltmore. The *New York Times* rented him a house for the duration of the trial. Only after the attorneys' final summations did Friendly join the press corps for a group dinner, one not hosted by Andrea and Claus. Friendly told his colleagues, "OK, here's my hat. Here are slips of paper. Guilty or not guilty?" They all agreed not to tell the results of the tally. Every reporter but one voted "guilty." The other reporter voted "not proven."

Three days later, after only eight hours of deliberation, the jury acquitted Claus von Bülow of twice trying to kill his wife with insulin injections. Von Bülow lowered his head and put his hands together. Behind him in the courtroom, Andrea Reynolds wept. The two von Auersperg children were at Clarendon Court when they heard the verdict and quickly made the trip from Newport to Providence to answer reporters' questions. The princess said, "We know and he knows that he tried to murder our mother."

Von Bülow called his stepchildren "misguided." But, he added, "I have no feeling of vindictiveness."

In his *Vanity Fair* article "Fatal Charm," Dominick pointed out how von Bülow snubbed the woman who saved his life: "He bypassed the embrace and kiss offered him by Mrs. Reynolds . . . and gave her a peck on the cheek. Then he raced to the telephone to call Cosima." Compared to the tirades Dominick would deliver to acquitted murderers in the near future, Claus von Bülow got off easy. "His dark and spacious place in social history was assured," wrote Dominick.

In 1985 David Kuhn had been hired to be an editor at *Vanity Fair*, and the first issue he worked on was the one featuring Dominick's von Bülow cover story.

"It was a huge turning point for the magazine," said Kuhn. "No one did that kind of reporting before him. It was intimate reportage of high-society, front-page crime where the writer got to know the people at the center of it. It was a new kind of storytelling. And Nick Dunne was connected enough to the subjects to get inside their world."

Seemingly overnight, Dominick emerged as real competition for John Gregory Dunne and on his brother's turf—as a writer. Dominick had a best-selling novel; he had also now written a groundbreaking article that everyone in the Didions' social set was talking about in a magazine creating considerably more buzz than *Esquire*, where John wrote. Suddenly, Dominick loomed large enough for his brother to swipe at publicly, but without mentioning his name. And John drew blood in a way that only a sibling knows how. For *Esquire*'s October 1986 issue, John wrote an essay titled "How to Write a Novel," in which he felt compelled to reveal a piece of "coincidental obscenity," as he called it. He had been working on his novel *The Red White and Blue* and six months before Dominique Dunne's murder, John wrote the following passage: "I do not understand people who attend the trials of those accused of murdering their loved ones. You see them on the local newscasts. . . . I watch them kiss the prosecutor when the guilty verdict is brought in or scream at those jurors who were convinced that the pimply-faced defendant was the buggerer of Jimmy and the dismemberer of Johnny."

John gave no reason to repeat this quote in the pages of *Esquire*, other than to show his prescience. If Dominick was already not speaking much to his brother, the time now arrived for others in the immediate Dunne family to join him. John's comments in *Esquire* so outraged Alex Dunne that the nephew played "a prank" on his uncle. "It took John ten years to figure out who did it," said Dominick's son, who kept secret the nature of that payback.

Once again, Liz Smith was asked to write something in her column, although this time Dominick did not approach her. At least, not directly. In his vast collection of correspondence, Dominick kept a letter from a man who pleaded with Smith to expose John Gregory Dunne's "cowardly blow" in *Esquire* to his brother's family. Smith, however, resisted the call. She never wrote a column about John's controversial essay.

The murder and its aftermath brought Dominick and Lenny closer together. The same was not true for Dominick and his son Alex. Years later, after he reconciled with his father, Alex spoke of having "mental health issues," which became especially acute after the loss of his sister. "The trouble started at the time of the murder," said Dominick. "I think that they were the closest brother and sister I ever saw."

Dominique's murder proved traumatic for everyone in the Dunne family circle, including Norman Carby, who moved to Hawaii to get away from bad memories in Los Angeles. Several friends noted how the ordeal affected Alex even more profoundly. Around the time that John Gregory Dunne's article "How to Write a Novel" appeared in *Esquire*, Alex met with his father at a restaurant in San Francisco where he unloaded on Dominick every abuse, real and imaginary, that he had suffered in the Dunne family. The outburst stunned Dominick and called up all the negative feelings he had for his own father. He found it incomprehensible to think that one of his own children hated him as much as Dominick hated Dr. Dunne. He asked Alex to forgive him and not do anything drastic, at least not until Lenny had passed way.

Personally, Dominick was devastated by Alex.

Professionally, he was at a very different place, having realized his most intoxicating Hollywood dream. *The Two Mrs. Grenvilles*, a best-selling novel, had been turned into a movie, even if it was a TV movie. Although the show's producers had been careful to consider some of his complaints about the script, they worried about Dominick's reaction to the finished four-hour miniseries, and wisely inoculated themselves from a bad review by giving him a special private screening, not at NBC or Lorimar but the Beverly Hills home of the movie's star. Dominick would never trash the finished product in front of Ann-Margret. And as they expected, he loved being given special treatment. "He liked the movie very much," said John Erman.

Better yet, when it aired on February 8, 1987, *The Two Mrs. Grenvilles* not only achieved spectacular ratings and boosted paperback sales of the novel; it reached the audience that Dominick cared about most. "There were screening parties up and down Park Avenue," Sue Pollock recalled.

Frank Sinatra (*far right*) on set with Dominick Dunne (*rear*), *Our Town*, 1955 (NBC/Photofest)

Lana Turner with Johnny Stompanato and daughter Cheryl Crane, two weeks before his murder, 1958 (Photofest)

Lenny and Dominick Dunne at the Black and White Ball, Beverly Hills, 1964 (Bob Willoughby /mptvimages.com)

Tuesday Weld and Truman Capote at the Black and White Ball (Bob Willoughby/mptvimages
.com)

Diana Lynn, Mart Crowley, and Natalie Wood at *The Boys in the Band* premiere, Los Angeles, 1970 (Photofest)

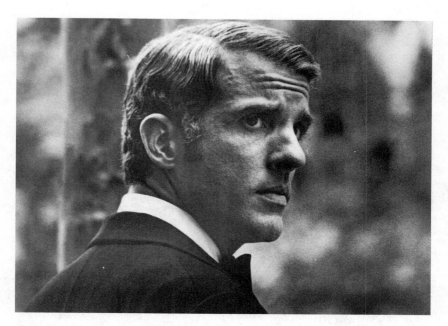

Peter White, *The Boys in the Band*, 1970 (Photofest)

Frederick Combs, *The Boys in the Band*, 1970 (National General Pictures/Photofest)

Kitty Winn and Al Pacino, *The Panic in Needle Park*, 1971 (Twentieth Century Fox/Photofest)

Tuesday Weld and Anthony Perkins, *Play It as It Lays*, 1972 (Universal Pictures/Photofest)

Elizabeth Taylor and Keith Baxter, *Ash Wednesday*, 1973 (Paramount Pictures/Photofest)

(*Top left*): Jean-Claude Tramont and Sue Mengers, New York City, 1974 (Frank Edwards/Archive Photos/Getty Images)

(*Bottom left*): John Gregory Dunne with wife Joan Didion and daughter Quintana at their Trancas beach house, 1976 ( John Bryson/The Life Images Collection/Getty Images)

Olivia Newton-John and Allan Carr at a *Grease* premiere party, New York City, 1978 (Ron Galella/ Ron Galella Collection/Getty Images)

Claudette Colbert and Ann-Margret, *The Two Mrs. Grenvilles*, 1987 (NBC/Photofest)

(*Top right*): Dominique Dunne, *Poltergeist*, 1982 (MGM/Photofest)

(*Bottom right*): Cosima and Claus von Bülow with Andrea Reynolds after his acquittal, Providence, Rhode Island, 1987 (Bettmann/Bettmann Collection/Getty Images)

Princess Diana at the Serpentine Galleries, London, 1995 (Princess Diana Archive/Hulton Royals Collection/Getty Images)

Lyle and Erik Menendez with Leslie Abramson at the Van Nuys courthouse, 1993 (Mike Nelson/AFP/ Getty Images)

Dominick Dunne with Mark Fuhrman at the Norwalk courthouse, 2002 (Shawn Baldwin/AP Photo)

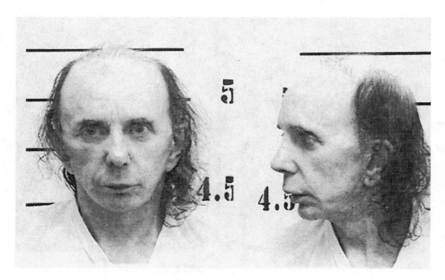

Phil Spector mug shot, 2009 (Getty Images Entertainment/Getty Images)

O.J. Simpson and Dominick Dunne at the Las Vegas courthouse, 2008 (Pool/Getty Images News/ Getty Images)

Norman Carby, Hawaii, 2013 (Robert Trickey/Norman Carby private collection)

Family at the Dominick Dunne funeral: (*clockwise from top*) Amphai, Alex, Hannah, and Griffin Dunne, New York City, 2009 (Rick Gershon/Getty Images Entertainment/Getty Images)

# 9

## Novels and Payback

If the jury acquitted Claus von Bülow, Dominick's *Vanity Fair* cover story tried to indict him. Again. But even that profile was not enough for Dominick when it came to skewering Claus and Andrea. He remembered Betsy Bloomingdale's phrase "people like us," meaning people who had a lot more money than they should and did not know it. *People Like Us* would be about those overly indulged, clueless, superrich people.

Dominick wrote the novel not once but twice. A computer person he met at an AA meeting on Perry Street in the Village turned out not to be a computer expert. After this recovering alcoholic set up Dominick's computer, it malfunctioned, completely destroying his entire manuscript, and Dominick had no choice but to rewrite it from memory. When he had finished *People Like Us* a second time and turned it in to Crown Publishing, a few observers got the impression that Dominick had written a scathing indictment of New York society in the vein of Truman Capote's "La Côte Basque 1965." *Women's Wear Daily* went so far as to suggest that Dominick used Claus von Bülow and Andrea Reynolds as prototypes for two of his most repellent characters: Yvonne Lupescu, after shooting her necrophiliac boyfriend Constantine de Rahm, quickly runs off to a high-society ball to establish a fraudulent alibi.

Griffin Dunne did not love *People Like Us* when his father first gave him the manuscript to read prepublication. Tom Wolfe's indictment of the city's financial titans, *The Bonfire of the Vanities*, had been published to great critical and commercial success the year before. Griffin warned, "Dad, this is in the same terrain. They're going to criticize you, and you're taking on these people."

*Women's Wear Daily* obtained early galleys of the book and claimed that Dominick had not ripped off Tom Wolfe; rather, he had pulled a Truman Capote and was about to "bite the hands that fed him," much as the author of *In Cold Blood* did with Babe Paley, Gloria Vanderbilt, Carol Matthau, and other lady friends, aka "the swans," whom he turned into uncomplimentary fictional caricatures in "La Côte Basque 1965."

Dominick's old *Interview* nemesis, now a colleague at *Vanity Fair*, knew he was up to something with the novel. "There we were, at a table for eight, and he didn't say a word," Bob Colacello said of Dominick. "He just listened and listened and listened. That's when I knew he was writing a book about this group."

"This group" was the new money of shopping-mall magnate Alfred Taubman and his arriviste wife, Judith Mazor Rounick, a former Israeli beauty queen, who crashed in a very Ivan Boesky way. (In *People Like Us*, Dominick presages Taubman's own fall shortly after the turn of the millennium when the Sotheby's businessman went to jail for price fixing and antitrust violations.) Dominick, for legal reasons, always insisted that his characters were fiction and neither the Taubmans nor the Boeskys nor even the Saul Steinbergs were his Elias and Ruby Renthal in *People Like Us*. Neither were Claus von Bülow and Andrea Reynolds in any way the inspiration for Constantine de Rahm and Yvonne Lupescu. So he said. Dominick did admit to basing one of his *People Like Us* characters on a real person. In the novel, a TV newscaster named Bernard Slatkin marries a woman worth billions. Dominick knew the journalist Jesse Kornbluth, who married a woman worth only one billion dollars, Katharine Anne Johnson, her mother being Anne Cox Chambers of Cox Enterprises. The Slatkin character also bears some resemblance to Chuck Scarborough, the New York City newscaster who married and quickly divorced Anne Ford of the automobile dynasty.

The inspiration for Slatkin's marriage to a wealthy debutante came to Dominick in 1987 at a lavish party held in a big white tent erected beside the Boathouse in Central Park. At the postwedding dinner, he had been seated next to Jesse Kornbluth's mother and proceeded to "pump" Pearl Kornbluth for every detail of her son's illustrious first wedding ("it cost $800,000 in 1984") and subsequent short-lived marriage. What made it a curious conversation was Dominick's interest in Jesse's previous wife, Katharine, rather than his current hours-long bride, Annette Tapert. According to Jesse Kornbluth, his mother revealed "how my former mother-in-law, Anne Cox Chambers, called her to ask if there was any chance I'd go back to Katharine Johnson, and Nick put that in *People Like Us*."

In that novel, the confluence of fiction and reality also tilts in the latter's favor with Dominick's introduction of the character Gus Bailey, who resembles the acerbic Burnsy Harrison, edited out of *The Winners* on the strong recommendation of Michael Korda. Gus Bailey is Dominick: a glossy magazine writer, divorced from an invalid wife and father of two adult sons, who hires a private detective to follow his daughter's killer upon his release from jail after receiving a prison sentence of only two and a half years. In Dominick's one fictional stretch, Bailey is heterosexual and very good in bed.

Prepublication of the novel, *Women's Wear Daily* predicted another "La Côte Basque 1965" scandal in the making, even though Dominick protested, "I didn't tell one private thing I know. There's not one betrayal in this book." Egos got manhandled nonetheless.

Annette and Oscar de la Renta were not happy with the characters of a wealthy socialite who marries a Greek shoe designer, named Loelia and Mickie Minardos. "It wasn't based on Oscar," Dominick told his publicist Judy Hilsinger. But the de la Rentas chose not to believe his denial. Their anger may have had less to do with *People Like Us* than the story Dominick told around town that the Argentinian fashion designer used to be nicknamed Darkie in his boarding-school days in Europe.

Other people were also miffed. In *People Like Us*, Dominick turned the fawning *Women's Wear Daily* columnist Aileen Mehle into the fawning columnist Dolly de Longpre. Dominick's friend Alice Mason told him that Mehle had read early galleys of the novel, and if he did not change the de Longpre character substantially there would be serious repercussions. Dominick denied making any edits, but another society columnist, David Patrick Columbia, insisted changes were made to accommodate the woman best known as Suzy in *Women's Wear Daily*. Perhaps not enough changes were made. Seated next to Mehle at a Metropolitan Museum gala hosted by actor Michael Douglas and his soon-to-be ex-wife, Diandra, Dominick overheard Suzy vow, "I will not be where this man is!" He liked Mehle when she wrote about his Black and White Ball in her *Journal-American* column. Dominick did not like Mehle when she subsequently wrote about Lenny and him, opining, "She's the cattle heiress. He's the vice president of Four Star, and that's about four more stars than you can give this marriage."

Dominick's jibes at Mehle were hardly his most pointed in *People Like Us*. He saved those poison-tipped stilettoes for Jerry Zipkin, the inspiration for the loathsome character Ezzie Fenwick, and it is doubtful he let any personality warts there get sliced in the editing process. According to Griffin Dunne, his father hated Zipkin and took delight in writing about the aging "walker" who sports "one peculiar eye, rather like a poached egg in appearance," and speaks in a "nasal voice." At heart, Dominick envied Zipkin, who had been the protégé and longtime friend of his literary idol W. Somerset Maugham. In more recent history, Zipkin had the ear, as well as the arm, of such high-profile women as Lee Radziwill, Betsy Blooming-dale, and Nancy Reagan, who called him "a great teacher." On the subject of Zipkin, Dominick tended to agree with the lady who called him "the chief eunuch of the last empress of China." Dominick put it more bluntly one night at the theater when, walking down the aisle, he accidently tripped, causing his archenemy to laugh excessively. "You cunt!" Dominick yelled back in a voice as loud as Zipkin's cackle.

Mart Crowley said the two men hated each other so much "because they were the same person."

Politically, they were not the same person. Dominick's Barry Goldwater days were long behind him when he used the C-word to describe America's best-known walker, whereas the homosexual Zipkin remained loyal to the Republican Party in an era when Ronald Reagan banned people with HIV from entering the country. Still, the Zipkin comparisons never failed to rankle Dominick. When a reporter from the *New York Times* called him a "walker" in so many words, Dominick shot back, "I never became an extra man. That ain't my role." He was a published writer, after all. What did Zipkin do but go to parties and openings?

In another respect, Dominick was also right. *People Like Us* did not alienate his friends in the way that "La Côte Basque 1965" alienated Truman Capote's. "They weren't real friends," Tita Cahn said of the "people" in *People Like Us*. "Nick was smart enough to know he was their flavor of the month. But he was enjoying it, and he would sit at their table and entertain them. Babe Paley was a true friend of Truman Capote's. That was different."

Others agreed. "Dominick would never have written about the swans the way Truman did. He was careful," said Jesse Kornbluth.

Except for the Zipkin character, Dominick kept Betsy and Alfred Bloomingdale's circle of West Coast friends out of the Manhattan milieu of *People Like Us*. Two years later, those illustrious Angelinos were not so lucky. With the 1990 publication of *An Inconvenient Woman*, it was such an easy twist of fact and fiction to have the $18,000-a-month mistress character, Flo March, murdered on a hit ordered by the billionaire's widow, Pauline Mendelson.

Dominick never believed that Marvin Pancoast acted alone in murdering Vicki Morgan. He had been looking for a way to tell his version of the story when another murder enflamed his sense of justice. It also fascinated him that the victim happened to have been a very close friend of Jerry Zipkin, Betsy Bloomingdale, and Nancy Reagan, and resembled in many ways the seventy-five-year-old Zipkin.

On September 25, 1987, someone shot and killed Alfredo de la Vega, a seventy-five-year-old realtor who had recently attended a belated birthday party for the first lady, Nancy Reagan. The homicide took place in de la Vega's apartment at 1285 North Crescent Heights Boulevard in West Hollywood. Bruce Nelson, a fellow top-of-the-line realtor, was one of the few people who knew de la Vega who, in turn, spoke to Dominick about the murder. "If it would have been anybody else, it would have been a full-page headline, and there was just one blip in the *Los Angeles Times*," said Nelson. "It was during the Iran-Contra scandal. Alfred had become friendly with the Reagans, and to save any kind of controversy they squashed the story." And that included an article Dominick wanted to write for *Vanity Fair* on the murder. "He tried to get into it," said Nelson. "He was squashed all along the way. The word [went out] that Dominick was persona non grata. 'Don't talk to him.'"

It was another hushed-up murder of yet another gay Republican bachelor with ties to the political establishment. John Gavin, a former actor and ambassador to Mexico, eulogized de la Vega, a longtime friend of his well-connected Mexican-Californian family. "We are all terribly saddened. He was an uncle figure to me. He was a person who had many friends. He loved life and enjoyed the social whirl. He was in great demand," said Gavin, née John Golenor.

His short quote was the last the *Los Angeles Times* would write about Alfredo de la Vega. Dominick wanted to correct that slight and decided to connect the de la Vega and Vicki Morgan murders, making the former crime a gay bashing in his novel *An Inconvenient Woman*. "Don't use the real names, then you can't be sued," he told Nelson.

"Dominick did believe that a friend of de la Vega knew Pancoast and may have been involved in both murders," said Norman Carby.

If people would not talk to him about Alfredo de la Vega for a non-fiction piece in *Vanity Fair*, he would recycle everything he knew about the case, put it all in *An Inconvenient Woman*, and call the homosexual victim Hector Paradiso.

The novel received Dominick's first unqualified rave from the *New York Times*. Equally gratifying, the review was written by a fellow best-selling novelist (and daughter of producer and former MGM president Dore Schary). "This is a smart novel because Dominick Dunne understands the distance between Los Angeles society and the spicy bazaars of Holly-wood," wrote Jill Robinson. "And what makes Mr. Dunne not only first-rate, but also different from other writers who write about the very rich in late twentieth-century America, is his knowledge that there's more to it than getting the labels and the street names right. He shows he knows by the way he tells you how his people feel, the way they listen, the things they cover up and the things they don't. He's lived in L.A. and gets it right, but he has the perspective you only get when you leave. He knows every story there is to tell, precisely how it happened and why it happened. He also knows there's nothing up there in society to envy."

According to Elizabeth Ashley, *An Inconvenient Woman* was spot-on, about not only L.A. society but the high-priced call girls who work the town. The actress knew Dominick from her role in *The Two Mrs. Grenvilles*; she played a character inspired by Bobo Sears, the chorus girl who married and quickly divorced Standard Oil scion Winthrop Rockefeller.

"It's awfully good," Ashley said of *An Inconvenient Woman*. A friend of the actress had been one of the most expensive call girls in Los Angeles before she married a movie star and sat on the board of an art museum there. "She was one of the smartest women. She knew a lot of the younger women in the business. They were still friends of hers and knew people involved in the whole [Vicki Morgan] thing. She knew Bloomingdale. Dominick got it!" said Ashley.

In a way, Dominick had come full circle with *An Inconvenient Woman*. Griffin Dunne summed up his father's multi-act life. "What got him in trouble in Hollywood was his big mouth, getting hammered and telling stories out of school," he said. "And what made him popular was telling the same stories and people wanting to have the stories told about them."

One of those publicity-prone people wanting to have their stories told was not Jerry Zipkin. He remained quiet about his Ezzie Fenwick character assassination in *People Like Us*. Pauline Mendelson in *An Inconvenient Woman* was another story. Zipkin lashed out after that book's publication, making sure the fabled doors of his many wealthy, influential lady friends were slammed shut. Betsy Bloomingdale and Nancy Reagan, among others, continued not to speak to Dominick, but now they did so with even more deafening silence, thanks to their favorite walker.

Dominick's novels and *Vanity Fair* articles brought him fame, as well as an innocuous notoriety. Dominick's greatest talent, however, was telling stories in private where he was unencumbered by lawyers, fact-checkers, or skittish editors.

For homosexuals living in the twentieth century, gossip became the only libel-free means to know of each other, form a community, develop an oral history, get laid. And few practiced the art better than Dominick.

When friends bought or rented a house in Los Angeles, Dominick told them the "real history" of the place—like the West Hollywood house that a golden-age movie star bought for his daughter when she married a homosexual. He told people about a decorator friend who enjoyed "full participation" sex with Gary Cooper, whom Dominick considered practically a relative because the actor's daughter, Maria, was Dominique's godmother. He told how the Dunnes' nanny used to be the Reagans' nanny, and they were "the worst parents." He told people about Nancy Reagan's expertise at fellatio, which included a story of her sitting between fellow actors Peter Lawford and Robert Walker and masturbating them both on a car trip to Palm Springs.

David Patrick Columbia and two other friends listened to Dominick repeat his standard repertoire of stories one night over dinner. Columbia was new to Manhattan, there to begin his career as a society reporter. When Dominick finally took a breath between mouthfuls of gossip, Columbia thought he would contribute to the evening's entertainment to tell a story about the recently deceased Natalie Wood. Columbia knew the producer Bonnie Weeks, who years before had been looking to replace Susan Sarandon in the Off Broadway play *A Coupla White Chicks Sitting Around Talking*. Weeks wondered if her "idol" Natalie Wood might consider the role, even though the movie star had never performed on stage before. To the producer's delight, Wood showed interest in the play and agreed to meet in Beverly Hills. "And Bonnie ended up spending the weekend and Natalie kind of seduced her," Columbia told Dominick and company.

Dominick, rather than being amused, took quick offense. "You should watch what you say!" he told Columbia. "That is not true and she was a friend of mine. And it will get you into a lot of trouble!" On the one hand, Dominick was being protective of the memory of his friend Natalie Wood. On the other, "he was telling me who I was in the order of things," said Columbia. "I was new."

# 10

## Kennedys and Cover-Ups

Was America in the middle of a golden age of crime? Or was Dominick only making it look like one? The major problem with great murders is that, once they are committed, the accused take an eternity in gumshoe time to come to trial.

Dominick occupied himself with happier but less newsworthy events in 1990. The publication of *An Inconvenient Woman*, as well as the royalties from his two other best sellers, gave him the money to buy a seven-room country house in Hadlyme, Connecticut. Even more gratifying, on April 12, 1990, he celebrated the birth of his only grandchild, Hannah, born to Griffin Dunne and his wife, actress Carey Lowell. In the years to come, Dominick would never miss an opportunity to tell close friends, as well as virtual strangers, how much he loved Hannah. "Nick repeated everything she said to me, told me about everything she wore," said one of those friends, Tita Cahn. "He got such a kick and such a joy out of her. It was the traditional joy of being a grandparent." He even took pleasure in watching how Hannah would leave home properly dressed for school. "But then she would put on a little lip gloss or add something to her outfit, once her parents were out of sight," said Cahn.

When Hannah was still a child, Dominick initiated a lovely annual ritual. Every Valentine's Day he sent his only grandchild a bouquet of flowers with the message "from a secret admirer." He never told Hannah he was that admirer.

The early 1990s were significant in other ways. Those years quickly stripped Dominick's love-hate affair with the Kennedy family of any respect or affection. "Dominick felt that the Kennedys thought they were above the law, and that burned him up," said his assistant Jack Cummings III. "He put Jackie and her children apart. He considered them separate."

Not separate was everyone else in that rich Irish clan.

His admiration of the Kennedys first took a hit shortly after he and Lenny moved to the West Coast in 1957, and Dominick watched as Joseph P. Kennedy and others in the family berated and mistreated Peter Lawford. It was Lawford who had to procure the Hollywood stars for John F. Kennedy's sexual pleasure. It was Lawford who had to tell Frank Sinatra that the president-elect would not be visiting him in Palm Springs, as promised, but would be staying at Bing Crosby's place instead. In his memoir, Dominick wrote, "Peter was ill-used by his famous and glamorous brothers-in-law. Get the girls, Peter. Get the blow, Peter. Tell Sinatra we can't come, Peter." What he did not write and what compounded the Kennedys' cruelty in Dominick's eyes was his strong physical attraction to Lawford, who died so broke in 1984 that his remains later had to be removed from the Westwood Village Memorial Park Cemetery for nonpayment of fees. It was the same cemetery where Dominick had buried Dominique.

In 1969 Dominick was not working as a journalist when Edward Kennedy drove his car over a Chappaquiddick bridge, causing the death of an intern, Mary Jo Kopechne. In 1991 he was working as a journalist for *Vanity Fair* when Patricia Bowman brought a rape charge against William Kennedy Smith, a nephew of the Massachusetts senator.

The trial against Smith in West Palm Beach, Florida, lasted only ten days, but in those few winter days of 1992 the Kennedy family flaunted everything Dominick both envied and loathed about them: he envied their money and political connections and how the American public embraced them, and he loathed how they used their every advantage to shroud themselves in dignity and familial sanctimony. Worst, for him, was how the Kennedys exploited the Church to hide their patented licentiousness. Nor was it lost on Dominick that William Kennedy Smith's "encounter" with Patricia Bowman would never have taken place if Edward Kennedy had allowed his nephew and son Patrick to remain in bed sleeping at the family compound in Palm Beach on March 30, 1991. Instead, the senator woke them because he needed a couple of drinking buddies to join him for a night of carousing, despite it being Good Friday. It was there at Au Bar, a local watering hole, where Smith met Bowman. Later, he brought her back to the family compound, where some kind of sexual encounter took place. Instead of taking any responsibility, the senator testified in court that the Kennedy family had gathered that holy weekend in Palm Beach not to party but to mourn the death of his brother Bobby and others. Dominick wrote in *Vanity Fair*, "The man who instigated the Good Friday incident by getting his son and nephew to go out drinking reversed the dynamic from a night of debauchery to one of sorrowing for dead relations."

Robert Rand, covering the trial for *Paris Match* and *Stern*, was never as sure as Dominick about Smith's guilt. He found it to be a "he said, she said" case, which is why the jury deliberated for only a few hours before finding the defendant not guilty. Dominick, however, did his research. He spoke to several women who said they had endured similar encounters with Smith, and it infuriated him that the judge did not allow these women's testimonies to be heard before the jury. Again, it brought back the crushing injustice of Judge Burton S. Katz's rulings in the murder trial of John Sweeney.

After Smith's acquittal, Dominick indulged in a bit of TV slumming. He checked out *Hard Copy*, and the episode he watched delivered a bombshell: Smith might have been in the house neighboring the backyard where the fifteen-year-old Martha Moxley had been murdered in Greenwich, Connecticut, on October 30, 1975. It was not just any old house, either. It belonged to the very wealthy Rushton Skakel, who happened to be Ethel Kennedy's cousin. Martha had been bludgeoned with a golf club. The police even found the same brand of golf clubs, Toney Penna, in the Skakel house.

The *Hard Copy* rumor about Smith turned out not to be true. He was not in the Skakel house *that* night. No matter. It gave Dominick an idea for another novel. It had everything: an unsolved murder involving rich people with political connections, as well as a big cover-up. At least, that was the way he would tell it, since the murder case remained unsolved and Skakel's two sons, Tommy and Michael, were suspects. At least, Dominick thought they should be prime suspects. In his fifth novel, *A Season in Purgatory*, the teenage scion of a powerful political family uses a baseball bat, not a golf club, to murder the girl next door when she refuses his sexual advances.

Much as he researched the Woodward case, Dominick set about reading newspaper accounts of the Moxley murder and interviewing people close to the case. The first person he contacted was Martha Moxley's mother, Dorthy, now living in Annapolis. She and her husband moved to Maryland after the murder because Dorthy could not bear to look across her lawn at the Skakel house every day. "I didn't know who did it, but I knew that in that house someone knew," said Dorthy Moxley. She never watched the infamous *Hard Copy* episode, but its erroneous story incited reports from other news outlets that she did see. "There had been a big exposé in the *National Enquirer* about Smith raping Patty Bowman in Florida," Dorthy recalled. "And at the end of the piece there was a picture of my daughter and Tommy Skakel."

Dominick met Mrs. Moxley at the airport in Annapolis in 1992. He would later write that Dorthy questioned his motives; she was "publicity shy" and did not want to talk with him in her apartment. But that was not the case. "I thought it silly to drive him all the way back to my place," she recalled. "It was easier if we just stayed at the airport for the interview." Dorthy was neither skeptical nor hesitant. "At that point, I needed to talk to everybody and anybody who was interested in the case," she said. "They had not started the reinvestigation."

Dominick told Dorthy of his own similar tragedy. Martha and Dominique were born only a year apart, and both were murdered on October 30, although in different decades. He later remarked, "Martha Moxley became a crusade for me because it reminded me of my daughter." Dominick told Dorthy that he wanted to write a novel rather than a nonfiction book about the murder of her daughter, Martha. *A Season in Purgatory* would be his next book. "It will bring attention to the case," he said. Dorthy had not read his novels, but she knew of them and readily agreed to cooperate in any way possible.

The *National Enquirer* was not the only tabloid interested in creating some fire with the *Hard Copy* rumor. At the *New York Post*, city editor John Cotter recalled how years ago a reporter at the *Stamford Advocate* and *Greenwich Time* failed to get his investigative piece on the Moxley murder published in those two Connecticut newspapers. Cotter assigned an interview with that reporter, Len Levitt, who revealed for the first time in print that the Greenwich police in 1975 had actually found the murder weapon the day after the murder. The missing Toney Penna golf club came from inside the Skakel house, yet the police failed to obtain a warrant to search the premises. One month after the *Post* ran its Levitt interview in 1991, the *Stamford Advocate* and the *Greenwich Time* published the reporter's original article, virtually untouched from what he filed years earlier.

Two months after Levitt's page 1 story appeared, the police chief of Greenwich held a press conference at the town's police headquarters. It was August 8, 1991. They were reopening their investigation of the Moxley murder.

Dominick arrived at the press event with Dorthy Moxley, who introduced him to Len Levitt. He congratulated the reporter on his belatedly published article and revealed that he, too, would now be writing about the murder. There was no competition, Dominick assured Levitt. His book would be a novel. Levitt, however, was dubious. Now that the case had been reopened, he rightfully saw himself as the most well-informed journalist on the subject and wanted to continue alone in his own investigation of the murder. Dominick, undeterred, suggested that through his own "upper-class connections" he might be able to help not only Levitt but the police.

Levitt would later write, "Did Dominick think he could waltz into a fifteen-year-old murder case and help the police solve it like Hercule Poirot? Maybe that happened in Agatha Christie mysteries, but this was real life."

Dorthy Moxley did not care who got credit. What she wanted to happen was happening. Not only did the police reopen the case but Dominick talked to dozens of sources and turned those interviews and research into the best-selling novel *A Season in Purgatory*. "It stirred interest in the case," she said, even though it diverged from the story on several points. "It paralleled the case."

For his fifth novel, Dominick resurrected the name Burnsy Harrison, cut from *The Winners*, and refashioned it into the slightly more dignified Harrison Burns, telling the story from that character's viewpoint. Harrison Burns is clearly an amalgam of Dominick and a young tutor named Ken Littleton, who began his employment with the Rushton Skakel family the day of Martha Moxley's murder. For that reason, Littleton quickly trumped the two Skakel sons as the major suspect. In the novel, the Burns character is not a tutor but a prep-school friend of Constant Bradley, being groomed for a major political career. The Bradley character kills the girl next door during rough sex play and forces Burns to help him dispose of the body. Twenty years later, a guilt-ridden Burns helps to expose Constant Bradley as the murderer.

Dorthy Moxley liked that Dominick "didn't say one thing about the Skakels" when promoting the book, even though he clearly harbored a deep hatred for the Kennedy family. During press interviews, he always tried to guide the reporter's questions away from talk of the Kennedys. "It's too easy to say that name," he said. "This is a fictional family. There are no assassinations. There is no president. There isn't a rape trial in the book." At least that is what he told reporters.

His real intentions, however, were not lost on Maureen Dowd, who reviewed *A Season in Purgatory* for the *New York Times*. She wrote, "Dominick Dunne takes all the most chilling character flaws of three generations of Kennedys and compresses them into one creepy plot line. If you can bear to read one more word, even with a gossamer veneer of fiction, about America's royal and sorrowful Irish Catholic clan, and if you like Mr. Dunne's dishy style of society vivisection, then you will probably enjoy his new tour of the toxic side of a golden American family."

Dowd was not the only one to make the Kennedy connection. In *A Season in Purgatory*, the Bradley family tries to rehabilitate the son's very tarnished image by sending him off to do charity work in Brazil. Dominick was amused when, during his book tour, a reporter pointed out that William Kennedy Smith, now a doctor, had recently returned from Somalia after doing medical missionary work there. "How amazing you should pick up on that!" Dominick noted. "It is what I said, isn't it?" Occasionally, he could not resist telling the truth about the real inspiration for his characters.

On Dominick's book tour, something far more significant happened than journalists pointing out parallels between the real Kennedys and the fictitious Bradleys. Dorthy Moxley recalled how "Dominick would go to a book signing, and then someone would come up and say, 'I know something about the Moxley case.'"

Len Levitt had to admit, "Little did I suspect that after his novel about the murder appeared people would flock to him with all sorts of tips."

Even more surprising to Levitt, Dominick never reneged on his promise to help him with his own ongoing investigation. "He was very helpful in terms of going out of his way to put me in touch with sources," said Levitt. Then again, the more Levitt wrote about the real murder, the more it promoted Dominick's fictional account.

Dominick's bookstore tour uncovered one very important piece of evidence. Dr. Kathy Morrall, a forensic pathologist, came forward at one book signing to show Dominick autopsy photos of Martha Moxley in her possession. Morrall told him, "Tommy Skakel was not the killer." And a Greenwich resident, Paul Terrien, told Dominick there had been a cover-up. That was a bombshell. Paul was the brother of George Terrien, whose house Michael Skakel said he visited at the time of the murder. Paul Terrien's version of events destroyed Michael's alibi.

Meanwhile, the police continued their own investigation. A detective, Frank Garr, looked into Michael Skakel's time at Elan, a school for troubled (and wealthy) youth in Poland, Maine. His interviews with alumni who had been in therapy sessions with Michael tied him to the murder. There was also Garr's interview with a Greenwich teenager, Andrea Shakespeare, who did not put Michael at George Terrien's house the night of the murder. And most significant, Garr linked jeans found at the Skakel house to Michael, jeans carrying Martha Moxley's long blonde hair.

Garr believed Michael guilty of the murder but did not have enough evidence to bring the case to a grand jury. Garr was also running into resistance from his own superiors, who believed either Tommy Skakel or the tutor Ken Littleton should be the primary suspect.

Garr, Levitt, Dunne. They were soon joined by a near stampede of detectives when Rushton Skakel hired a team of them to look into the 1975 murder. He wanted Sutton Associates to find the real killer and thereby clear his sons of suspicion. The report he commissioned cost $750,000, and it was everything Rushton Skakel did not want to read about Tommy and Michael.

It labeled the two Skakel sons as suspects, and in the age of DNA, Michael had been forced in his interviews with Sutton detectives to change his story slightly. He continued to place himself at the Terrien house at the time of the murder, but now revealed for the first time that he had masturbated in a tree outside Martha Moxley's bedroom window, in effect placing his DNA at the scene of the crime. The Sutton report also gave Michael a motive for the murder: jealousy over his older brother Tommy's budding relationship with Martha. Worst of all, the report cleared the tutor Ken Littleton of any wrongdoing. (DNA evidence would not be introduced at the Michael Skakel trial in 2002.)

Like any good reporter, Len Levitt got to the Sutton report but could not make a copy. Instead, he took notes and wrote an article for *New York Newsday*, which was picked up by the *Stamford Advocate*. Levitt wrote about the "masturbation," but all references to that sex act were removed from both family newspapers.

Dominick continued to receive tips, but as *A Season in Purgatory* began to fall off the best-seller lists, the stories told to him also diminished. Whenever he heard anything significant, he would phone Dorthy Moxley to share the news. "I know something about the Moxley case," he said. But those kinds of calls gradually became less frequent. More likely, he would phone Dorothy just to see how she was doing.

Dominick's interest in the case never waned, but as a reporter he became enthralled in an even grislier murder. Erik and Lyle Menendez were finally being brought to justice for killing their parents, and the murder trial would be Dominick's first for *Vanity Fair* since Tina Brown left the magazine to become editor in chief at the *New Yorker*. She had talked to Dominick about following her to the prestigious weekly, but he reluctantly chose not to. He knew the importance of having Wayne Lawson edit his copy; also, he believed his articles "needed" photographs to illustrate them. He never failed to express gratitude to Helmut Newton for his sinister portraits of Claus von Bülow and Andrea Reynolds, and how much those provocative photographs enhanced his cover story "Fatal Charm."

Brown's replacement at *Vanity Fair* surprised many people in the publishing world. Graydon Carter had cofounded *Spy* magazine, the scathing gossip sheet that on a monthly basis skewered Manhattan's sacred cows, in particular Dominick's good friend Liz Smith. And it was not just Carter who would be coming to *Vanity Fair*. The new editor planned to bring three *Spy* cohorts with him: Aimee Bell, David Kamp, and Matt Tyrnauer. Their influence would be felt.

"There was a great deal of wariness because of *Spy*," said Bell. "Matt and I were not greeted with open arms [at *Vanity Fair*]. I might as well have had leprosy." Little did it help that she, Carter, and Tyrnauer had spent the previous year at the *New York Observer* as part of what Bell described as a "cleansing process." The exceptions to their brusque treatment came not from staffers but two contributing writers: Bob Colacello, who had left *Interview* after roundly trashing Dominick in his column there; "and Dominick, who rolled out the red carpet," Bell recalled. His ebullient greeting even included an invitation for her, Kamp, and Tyrnauer to visit his house in Connecticut for a weekend brunch.

*Vanity Fair* contributor Kevin Sessums, another *Interview* alum, also remembered Dominick being a grand one-man welcoming committee when he arrived at the magazine. Better yet, according to Sessums, Dominick never indulged in the internecine warfare typical of most journalists. "Writers are competitive. Writers don't hype each other. Dominick was a real kind soul, very generous toward me" said Sessums, who likened *Vanity Fair* to an old Hollywood studio. "Everyone vying for Sam Goldwyn's attention. Who would be the golden girl or golden boy or flavor of the month? It could be a weird atmosphere in that sense. But Nick was always 'there's room for you, as well as me.'"

Despite Dominick's being a top writer at the magazine, he, too, had a new boss to impress when Graydon Carter came aboard. The upcoming Menendez trial offered him precisely the kind of sensational case he needed to reestablish himself at *Vanity Fair*. Dominick did not relish returning to Los Angeles. Dominique's murder and his professional defeat in the entertainment business there continued to loom. Neither he nor his editors knew at the time that his coverage of the Menendez trial would yield not one great article, as it had with the Claus von Bülow trial, but no fewer than four. His coverage came to represent his most comprehensive and detailed investigation for the magazine.

# 11
## Menendez and Lies

**D**ominick's research for the Menendez trial began in 1993 by phoning his most trusted real estate contact in Beverly Hills. Bruce Nelson was the place to start and the realtor took Dominick to the house at 722 North Elm Drive to inspect the crime scene. "I have heard of very few murders that were more savage," said Marvin Iannone, the city's police chief. In fact, the murders of Kitty and Jose Menendez were so savage that investigators did not believe the two sons' initial theory about it being a mob hit. Professional killers would never have been so sloppy or liberal in the number of bullets used.

The Elm Drive house, built in 1927 and completely renovated in 1974, had been rented over the years by several rock-star luminaries, ranging from Prince to Elton John. Bruce Nelson used a ruse to gain access to the house for his friend from *Vanity Fair*.

"Dominick didn't want the listing broker to know who he was. He gave some name, I forget. I took him to the house," said Nelson. "I was amazed at Dominick's powers of observation. We spent an hour there. In the *Vanity Fair* article that he wrote, he even had the names of the books in the library. I was impressed."

Dominick also memorized the layout of the house, the carpeting, the sheet music on the grand piano—"American Pie," by Don McLean—but the details that made him a favorite with *Vanity Fair* readers were those observations appealing to their snobbery. "With the exception of some reproduction Chippendale chairs in the dining room, the house is appallingly furnished with second-rate pieces," Dominick wrote.

On Nelson's one-hour tour of the Elm Drive house, Dominick retraced what he thought was Erik and Lyle's path of attack, from the lanai in the backyard to the TV room. (At the trial, a neighbor would testify that she saw two men carrying shotguns into the house through the front door.)

"We went to the patio and back to the garage area, and then we came back," Nelson recalled. "Dominick was incensed with it. He was upset— just the mere fact that the two sons were lying through their teeth. That's what got him. He hated when people were lying and he knew they were lying. It got his goat."

And that was true even before the two Menendez sons testified in court about being sexually molested by their father. Dominick "convicted" Claus von Bülow of murder when he looked into his eyes. He "convicted" Lyle Menendez of murder when he attended Jose and Kitty Menendez's memorial service, held at the Directors Guild on Sunset Boulevard in Hollywood. "There was something about the way Lyle walked, a cockiness," said Dominick. "I knew he was guilty." Six months after the memorial service, Erik and Lyle were arrested.

The two Menendez sons were not immediate suspects in the double murder, despite Dominick's suspicions. After shooting their parents on August 20, 1989, Erik and Lyle made a hysterical phone call to 911 to feign their disbelief at the carnage. They blamed the mob for the murders but did little to pursue an investigation of those imaginary hit men. Instead, Lyle bought a $60,000 Porsche and Erik hired a $50,000-a-year tennis coach. They thought they could afford it. Jose Menendez, a top executive at Live Entertainment, left an estate estimated to be worth $14 million. Neither son was charged for the murders until the following March, when they were put in jail without bail. The arrest had been delayed until a crucial piece of evidence could be secured: Judalon Smyth, a former girlfriend of the boys' therapist, tipped off the police that Dr. L. Jerome Oziel had recorded his sessions with Erik and Lyle. Those tapes contained their confessions to the murders but required much legal maneuvering to be admitted into evidence.

Despite the evidence, Erik and Lyle pleaded not guilty, saying they acted in self-defense after being sexually abused by their parents. Jill Lansing, Lyle's lawyer, told the jurors, "We are not disputing where it happened, how it happened, who did it. What we will prove to you is that it was done out of fear."

As soon as the trial started in July 1993, Dominick made friends with the chief prosecutor, Pamela Bozanich. She told the jurors in her opening statement, "This is not a prosecution trial. This is a defense trial. The defense has conceded all the prosecution charges. They have to prove that the boys were in immense danger from their parents. And they have to prove sexual molestation." It was a very unusual trial. Although Erik and Lyle Menendez shared the same courtroom and judge, they were tried before different juries and each defendant had his own defense team.

On most days, Dominick took lunch with Bozanich in the cafeteria at the Van Nuys Superior Courthouse. They ate "really crummy food," said the attorney.

Their friendship was a two-way street. "The media have sources that the prosecution can't get to," said Bozanich. "For instance, Kitty Menendez's family wouldn't speak to me about anything. A lot of people would talk to Dominick who wouldn't talk to me." One of those family members told Dominick that the sexual-abuse allegations were baloney.

In turn, Bozanich knew why Dominick wanted to lunch with her. "He used people, like most gossips, to tell their stories. I knew that was going on with me," said the attorney. "But he was genuinely motivated by a good cause. His daughter had been murdered, and the judge [on that trial] screwed over the prosecution. And it changed Dominick forever, but he decided to do something about it: to tell the side of the victims instead of the side of the defendants."

In one important respect, the Menendez case was different from any other Bozanich had prosecuted. "There was a strain of homosexuality running throughout the trial," she recalled. "We knew Erik was gay and having oral sex with the inmates." And the prosecution knew of homoerotic photographs taken of Erik. In addition, Dominick liked to gossip about a major player in the courtroom who, he claimed, was a closeted homosexual. He also speculated, as did many observers, on the exact nature of Erik's close friendship with one of the prosecution's star witnesses. It was Craig Cignarelli who, when approached by the police, told them that his good friend Erik had admitted to killing his parents. (Cignarelli said that he and Erik "double dated many girls" and his friend was not gay.)

The strain of homosexuality did not end with Dominick's suspicions about some of the trial's major participants. Early one morning, Bozanich awoke to a frantic phone call. It was Dominick. He feared he was going to be outed if he did not stop writing about the Menendez trial. Bozanich had to wonder, "Why is he telling me this at six o'clock in the morning?"

She nonetheless felt his concern. "I'd heard, and he insinuated, that when he went up north [to Oregon in 1979] he had an epiphany and became gay," said Bozanich. "I've since heard he was gay but he didn't practice. It was against his religion."

Dominick and Bozanich found it strange that Judge Stanley M. Weisberg often disallowed the word "homosexual" in the courtroom. "Leslie Abramson was panicked that people would find out or think Erik was homosexual," said Bozanich. "We had this strain all through the trial, and Dominick would whisper things people told him."

"It was really a very, very gossipy case," said Dan Abrams, the chief legal affairs anchor for ABC News. At the time of the Menendez trial, Abrams was a twenty-seven-year-old reporter for Court TV. "There's no question when it came to the trial gossip Dominick was the leader among the reporters there. He was hearing everything. Some of it wasn't true."

Dominick fixated on the possibility that, in addition to Erik, Jose Menendez might be gay. He had heard about photographs of Jose at an all-male orgy; Jose's name was rumored to be in the files of a Miami pedophile service; and there was the story, completely debunked by the crime-scene photographs, that Kitty had been shot in the vagina.

Those lurid details aside, Dominick and Dan Abrams did not disagree about much on the case. Erik and Lyle had murdered Jose and Kitty, and their sexual-abuse defense was a total sham. "And the father was not a particularly likable guy," said Abrams. The two reporters also responded viscerally to the trial's window on what Abrams called "an aspect of high society" or, at least, high society by Hollywood standards: Jose Menendez, a Cuban émigré and CEO, turned the troubled Live Entertainment into a very profitable company. In addition to the Hollywood glitter, the trial put a spotlight on the spoiled children of the Beverly Hills rich. It hit home: Dominick also raised children there.

On the von Bülow trial, Dominick made a point to get along with the attorneys on both sides. That was not the case on his third trial for *Vanity Fair*. More than any other trial he would cover, Dominick openly hated the defense, especially Erik Menendez's lawyer. And Leslie Abramson hated Dominick right back with equal fervor. Dominick's antipathy toward her, however, began sometime before the Menendez trial.

In Dominick's mind, it was bad enough that Abramson and her husband, *Los Angeles Times* reporter Tim Rutten, were friends of John Gregory Dunne and Joan Didion, and his brother had taken it upon himself to solicit the attorney's advice on a potential plea bargain for John Sweeney. As a result, he would forever link all defense attorneys to Sweeney's, but Abramson quickly came to occupy a special place in the ninth circle of complicity, according to Dominick Dunne. Abramson flaunted her maternal approach to Erik and Lyle. She called them "adorable. They're the two foundlings. You want to take them home with you." It sickened Dominick whenever she gave Erik soothing pats on the back and shoulders, and he objected to her dressing the two defendants to look like prep-school students. To Dominick, those candy-colored sweaters and button-down collars were like the Bible that Sweeney carried into the courtroom every day of his trial: nothing but courtroom theatrics.

Dominick's "therapy" approach to covering a trial, in turn, dismayed Abramson. "You don't have to be Sigmund Freud to figure out what's going on here," she wrote. "His tragic life experience would disqualify him from sitting on the jury in any murder case, but in his editors' eyes it seems to supply, if not a kind of special authority, at least a titillating twist."

In TV interviews, Abramson said of Dominick, "He comes up with false facts like Joe McCarthy." And for added effect, she would hold up documents and shake them, imitating Dominick's gestures and voice: "'I have papers here that prove . . .'"

What rumors did Dominick manufacture, in Abramson's opinion? She pointed to the story that Kitty and Jose Menendez were eating ice cream and berries at the time of the murders, and Kitty had also been working on Erik's college application. Abramson believed that these details created undue sympathy for the victims. She wrote about the berries-and-cream myth being "contradicted at trial." She also contended that Erik had been accepted at UCLA months before the murders took place. In the end, it is doubtful that what Kitty and Jose ate or did before having a few rounds of bullets pumped into them much affected either of their sons' juries.

Central to the trial was whether Jose Menendez had actually molested his two sons.

"I never ever believed for a second that he sexually abused them," said Dominick. Other reporters like Robert Rand of *Playboy* and Linda Deutsch of the Associated Press were not so sure. They tended to believe Abramson, who, in her opening statement, said that Jose Menendez "pulled Erik's hair when forcing this eleven-year-old to orally copulate him, who slapped him repeatedly when the child cried after his father ejaculated in his mouth for the first time, who forcibly sodomized him." Defense attorney Gerald Chaleff argued for Lyle Menendez, saying the older son had also been sexually abused by his father.

"Dominick and I never agreed on a trial exactly," said Linda Deutsch, a reporter whom he came to christen "the doyenne of crime reporters." Writing for the AP, Deutsch tended to see the defendants as being innocent. "Or I had no opinion," she said. It was the difference between writing for the Associated Press, which wanted just the facts, ma'am, and *Vanity Fair*, which wanted something more. The glossy magazine wanted to stoke controversy.

Deutsch and Dominick first met in 1985 when she profiled him for his novel *The Two Mrs. Grenvilles*—"because the book featured a trial," Deutsch said of the AP assignment—and they met again at the William Kennedy Smith trial in West Palm Beach. Deutsch said they became good friends on the Menendez trial despite their being in almost constant disagreement.

"We talked a lot of specifics, and if I thought Dominick was off base I told him," Deutsch recalled. "He had much stronger opinions on guilt and innocence than I ever did. I was always neutral. My impartiality became legend. He couldn't stand that."

Deutsch said it did not affect their friendship. However, shortly after the start of the Menendez trial, Dominick chose not to sit next to the AP reporter in court. It was a pattern they established for most trials to come. "He had a gaggle of people who huddled around him and listened to his every word," said Deutsch.

Shoreen Maghame, a cub reporter, sat next to Dominick most days in the Van Nuys courtroom. "I was twenty-three years old and working at the City News Service, and Dominick embraced me as if I was the biggest deal ever. Who does that?" asked Maghame.

Covering the Menendez trial, her first big murder case, Maghame focused on the motions being filed, what the various legal terms meant, who said what on the stand. But she learned something else from observing Dominick. She saw how he quickly made friends with court apparatchiks like Patti Jo Fairbanks, the senior legal assistant for the district attorney's office. "He had a connection with people, and an amazing caring, and then people opened up to him. Even the bailiffs were attracted to him. They felt he was genuinely interested in their story," Maghame said. "I was so invested in 'what are the lawyers doing?' That's important, but understanding that the people involved are affected, especially in a murder trial, I learned that from Dominick."

He made it clear to Maghame his feelings on the case. "Dominick thought the dad was a son of a bitch, an asshole, that Lyle was the ringmaster sociopath, that they went back and reloaded to kill the mother. That bothered Dominick," said Maghame.

Erik and Lyle killing their father was one thing. "But why the mother?" Dominick kept asking. "She was a victim. Why did they have to kill her? There was no threat from her."

Lyle testified that his father had repeatedly raped him, and his mother had, on occasion, inspected his testicles and put clamps on them. It was this testimony that, surprisingly, most affected Dominick.

"When Lyle testified, it was really compelling," said Maghame. After Lyle's first day on the stand, Dominick immediately turned to her to say, "I wonder if I'm wrong. Could I be wrong?" In the hallway outside the courtroom, he repeated his doubts to fellow reporter Robert Rand. Since Dominick and Rand would be appearing that evening on TV to discuss the week's events in the Menendez trial, they did not pursue an in-depth conversation then and there. Rand, however, was stunned when two hours later on Court TV's "Prime Time Justice" Dominick told moderator Terry Moran, "I didn't believe one word [Lyle] was saying from the stand this afternoon."

Rand entertained a momentary thought of "busting him right there about our conversation, but decided it would be completely unprofessional." Off-camera, Rand later asked Dominick about his abrupt change of heart. "Well, I had a moment where I thought it might have sounded true," he replied. "Then I thought it wasn't true at all."

"Dominick went back to his default position," said Rand. "I was somewhat surprised but not shocked that he was maintaining his 'brand' when we were both interviewed live on Court TV."

Ira Reiner held the office of L.A. district attorney during the Menendez trial and engaged in several conversations with Dominick about the case. "I don't recall him talking about having any doubts," said Reiner. "Dominick's view is that Leslie Abramson totally fabricated the imperfect self-defense theory. It was his point of view that this is not something the kids came up with and that she fed it to them. With the imperfect self-defense, you have to carefully [put together] the facts like pieces of a puzzle. He felt it would take a lot of spoon feeding to get them to testify right to stay within the lines of that defense."

For his *Vanity Fair* coverage, Dominick wrote about Lyle being a "great neurotic actor," in the mold of Marilyn Monroe and Judy Garland. He also observed that Lyle appeared to bask in the response he got from the courtroom, and his pride was compounded later in the trial when Erik's testimony appeared to be much less effective with the jurors.

Dominick would admit to identifying with the Menendez sons in one very significant way: he had also been verbally abused and physically beaten by his father. "But I didn't kill [my father]," he said. "I went away to college. I went away to my life." A connection that Dominick refused to make, at least publicly, was what troubled him most about being an abused child. No one in his family, including his mother, ever acknowledged the mistreatment he had suffered despite there being welts on his thighs and buttocks. In one childhood altercation, according to Dominick, his father struck him on the head so severely that his ear swelled, causing him to be hard of hearing for the remainder of his life.

Erik and Lyle Menendez also charged, in addition to the sexual abuse, that their father had stuck needles and tacks into their buttocks. After he heard those accusations in court, Dominick went back to his suite at the Chateau Marmont and stuck a tack in his buttock to see what kind of a mark it left. He reported in *Vanity Fair* that it drew blood and left a major red spot. He wondered why no one ever noticed such scars on the Menendez sons' bodies. Never in print, or in interviews, did Dominick wonder why no one ever noticed evidence of abuse on his own body when he was a child.

Shoreen Maghame, as a reporter, talked to Erik Menendez on the phone several times during the course of the trial. For obvious reasons, Leslie Abramson did not extend that phone privilege to Dominick, who circumvented the attorney by turning Maghame into one of his sources on the subject of the defendant. They discussed his supposition that Erik was a homosexual. "We debated it," said Maghame. "How could they [commit the murders] without something horrible happening [to Erik and Lyle]? I was much more naïve then."

For his secondhand access to Lyle Menendez, Dominick groomed another source, not a reporter but someone who nonetheless spoke on the phone regularly with the older brother. Norma Novelli owned a cleaning service called Grime Busters in the San Fernando Valley. She also self-published a magazine titled *Mind's Eye*, which devoted a page to prisoners who wanted to contribute to "find if they have artistic abilities." Novelli sent the magazine to various jails around the country. "And Lyle answered," she recalled. Their correspondence began with his asking for dimes to make phone calls from prison. "And it started from there," she said. "After that, I had to get permission from the judge to let Lyle listen to all the commentary said about him from the trial." After the court finished each day, Novelli would place a phone receiver alongside her TV set, making it possible for Lyle to hear what people said about him on Court TV.

Novelli's conversations with Lyle were "just casual stuff," she noted. Lyle, however, expressed keen interest in one well-known journalist covering the trial. He often asked Novelli, "What did Dominick say today?" Or, "Did you see Dominick at lunch today?" Even though Dominick rarely missed an opportunity in *Vanity Fair* or on Court TV to call the two

Menendez sons pathological liars, Lyle never developed a negative attitude toward his chief accuser in the press, and instead enjoyed the impassioned coverage.

Lyle also found a skeptic in Norma Novelli, despite their many conversations. She agreed with Dominick on the issue of sexual abuse. "We joked a lot about the trial," said Novelli. "The silly things people said, and the way Lyle cried on the stand. We both laughed. Nobody that age would act that way." She did not believe that two adult sons would kill their parents due to sexual abuse. "They just would have left home. Kids can't wait to get away from home," she surmised. Novelli looked elsewhere for their motives in murder. "Lyle wanted the money now."

Dominick did exhaustive interviews and research on the Menendez trial, enough to fill four long articles for *Vanity Fair*. Where the cover story on Claus von Bülow showed his remarkable understanding of a rarefied world of wealth and position, Dominick's articles on the Menendez trial gave full display to his talent for winning the confidence of star witnesses.

During the trial, Craig Cignarelli became known as the Snitch. Leslie Abramson also called him the Prick when she saw him in the hallways of the courthouse. Dominick, for his part, thought of him as the Conscience. Although it was rumored that Cignarelli sought out the police, he did not initiate the contact. They came to him, and after much deliberation, Cignarelli decided to tell the authorities what he knew about his best friend.

Cignarelli and Erik were in the same class at Calabasas High School and would have graduated together if not for the fact that Erik and Lyle went on a robbery spree, stealing more than $100,000 worth of possessions from homes in Calabasas, an upper-middle-class town inland from Malibu, California. Since he was underage, Erik took the rap, making it possible for Lyle to attend the Ivy League school of his father's dreams, Princeton University. As part of their probation, however, both boys were required to see a therapist. Embarrassed by his sons' crimes, Jose Menendez moved the family to Beverly Hills and into the house where he and his wife would be murdered. Before the Menendez family left Calabasas, Cignarelli and Erik cowrote several screenplays, all of them murder mysteries. In one of those screenplays, titled *Friends*, a son murders his parents in the opening scene. Two weeks before the Menendez sons shot their parents, Erik rewrote the *Friends* script without Cignarelli's participation; tellingly, Erik's handwritten notations in the margins of the document presage the extreme carnage to come.

Shortly after the murders, Erik confessed the crime to his best friend, and it was this conversation that Cignarelli repeated to the police. Wanting a taped confession, the police then wired Cignarelli for a meeting with Erik at a Malibu restaurant overlooking the Pacific Ocean. Their talk at Gladstone's did not go as planned. Instead of confessing a second time, Erik said he never should have told such a story.

Dominick admired Cignarelli, especially when he overheard Leslie Abramson call him "that fucking prick" in the courthouse hallway. "She would do anything to intimidate me," said Cignarelli, and that was before he took the stand.

For *Vanity Fair*, Dominick wrote about Erik Menendez's best friend fleetingly and not in detail. He mentioned speaking to Cignarelli only once, as if in passing outside the courtroom. Dominick asked him, "Did you know that Lyle wore a toupee?" Cignarelli answered yes. According to Dominick's reporting, that short exchange was the extent of their talk.

Dominick joked with friends that the most fascinating aspect of the case for him was Lyle's toupee. After getting rid of his own mini-rug in the late 1970s, Dominick continued to fixate on other men's fake hair, and in the case of Lyle's full hairpiece, it was not irrelevant to the two sons' defense. According to their testimony, Jose Menendez hit Lyle so hard one day over breakfast that the boy's toupee fell off, causing immense embarrassment to the teenager. In his court testimony, Erik claimed he had no idea of the rug's existence. Even in affluent Calabasas, it is very unusual for a fifteen-year-old to be wearing a toupee.

Which is why Dominick asked Cignarelli if he knew about the rug. When Erik's best friend told him yes, Dominick knew the two Menendez boys were lying. However, that one impromptu interview to discuss Lyle's premature hairpiece did not end their talks.

On occasion, the two men met at Dominick's suite at the Chateau Marmont. Dominick initially told Cignarelli, "Let's just talk as friends." And according to Cignarelli, Dominick became a good friend. "He definitely was kind of a soft shoulder during the trial, he was someone I could speak to, and nothing would be taken out of context," said Cignarelli. He found "some consistencies between Capote and Dominick in the way they wrote about trials. Nick was empathizing with my plight," he said. Dominick warned the young man that Leslie Abramson would be "aggressive and hostile" to him on the stand. Cignarelli liked that Dominick referred to Abramson as "the bitch" and "he let her know he wasn't scared of her. Leslie would yell at anyone. Nick just had a way of giving her a glance."

And Dominick was right about Abramson. She proved aggressive and hostile in her questioning. She even badgered Cignarelli for wearing a suit and tie in court, as if he were grandstanding by being well dressed.

However, the "most intimidating moment had nothing to do with Abramson," said Cignarelli, "but rather with seeing my best friend ten feet away and knowing that my words could put him in the gas chamber."

Dominick did not coach Cignarelli for his big day in court. Instead, he told him, "I respect what you're doing. You're doing the right thing and it is a difficult time and it's a difficult experience."

Other than those words, they did not talk about the trial per se. "He wanted to know about my friendship with Erik," said Cignarelli. "He wanted to know details: how I came to make the decision to turn Erik in. He treated me as a friend. He spoke about a man's place in the world and morality and justice, and that even in the face of a great trial it will serve you later on. Society said I was betraying a friend. Nick said I was a better man. He had a great way of finding the pulse to speak to you. It was a time of need for me, and he was a quiet rock that wanted information but did it in a way that was supportive and nurturing."

Judalon Smyth was another star witness whom Dominick turned into an instant confidante. It was Smyth, the erstwhile mistress of Dr. L. Jerome Oziel, who knew of the therapist's tapes in which Erik and Lyle confessed to the murders. By the time the police questioned Smyth, she had already begun to fear for her life, and friends advised her to tell a third party everything she knew about the Menendez brothers. "As protection," she explained. Mutual friends arranged for her and Dominick to meet. "They told me he was the best person to speak with."

The two immediately hit it off. She thought her life was in danger because of the stories she had to tell. Dominick identified; he thought he was going to be outed as a gay man for the stories he had to tell about the Menendez case. He shared those fears with Smyth, and they bonded.

Smyth's own personal story fascinated Dominick. "My relationship with my mother had never been good but it was on stable ground," she said. "When Oziel came into my life, every conversation turned into a battle with my mother. I became suspicious of her. You wouldn't think I'd become such a little puppet, but I did."

Dominick wondered if Dr. Oziel had also exacerbated Erik and Lyle's relationship with their parents. "Judalon, you've got to tell your story," Dominick insisted. He even paid her the ultimate compliment after reading a few chapters of her proposed memoir: "You're a better writer than I am!"

Dominick put Smyth in touch with his agent, Owen Laster. "Dominick wanted me to write my book and tell my story, to get it out there right away," she recalled. Smyth's lawyer, however, adamantly disagreed, telling her, "That will just cut your credibility [on the stand] down to zero."

As would be the case with so many troubled witnesses to come, Dominick more than interviewed Smyth; he embraced her emotionally. "Dominick and I became really good friends, and he became friends with my other friends, not just the mutual friends we already had in common," said Smyth.

Their friendship went beyond a few conversations. Smyth and Dominick watched Oziel's testimony on the stand from his suite at the Chateau Marmont. She let him listen to tapes she had "inadvertently" taped with Oziel from a self-activating answering machine. Smyth even defended Dominick in the face of Leslie Abramson's considerable wrath.

"Stop it right now!" she scolded the attorney after one verbal attack on her friend. "Dominick is one of the most decent, wonderful human beings I know. If you're going to say something bad, I'll never talk to you again."

Abramson backed away. She never made another negative comment about Dominick, at least not in front of Judalon Smyth.

Dr. Oziel's ex-girlfriend quickly emerged as one of the trial's more controversial witnesses. Smyth's initial testimony regarding the existence of the therapist's taped conversations with the Menendez brothers had been key to the prosecution's case. But during the trial, it was the defense that tried to use her to discredit Oziel, a major but reluctant witness for the prosecution. Smyth later recanted some of her early testimony, saying Oziel had "implanted" in her mind "things that didn't exist." Dominick would write in his private journal that, in the beginning, he saw Smyth as "the heroine of this story" but later developed serious doubts about her, doubts that never made their way into his reporting for *Vanity Fair*.

Getting an in-depth interview with Philip Kearney was not the coup of a Judalon Smyth or a Craig Cignarelli. In fact, among the reporters, only Dominick thought to talk to the photographer, and it showed his ingenuity at uncovering colorful but salient details.

Kearney never testified in court but almost made the witness list due to some photographs he took of Erik Menendez long before the murders were committed. Those portraits suggested a possible physical, if not romantic, relationship between the two men. Judge Weisberg found those photos inadmissible, ruling Erik's sexual orientation irrelevant to the case.

Dominick found the photos anything but. For his article "Menendez Justice," he insisted that the *Vanity Fair* photo department pay top dollar to reprint one shirtless photo of Erik, shot by Kearney. Dominick considered the photo a crucial piece of evidence, because he thought it proved Erik had lied and he might also be homosexual, a supposition that Abramson fought to keep out of court.

Like Judalon Smyth and Craig Cignarelli before him, Kearney found a friend in Dominick, even though all their conversations were conducted long distance on the phone. Dominick respected what these people said in confidence, and he wrote much, much less than what any of them revealed to him in private.

Dominick asked Kearney point blank if he had had an intimate relationship with Erik. In *Vanity Fair*, Dominick recorded Kearney's response as being "Spiritually, yes. Physically, almost."

Nearly a decade and a half after that interview with Dominick, Kearney said the relationship was actually "more physical than it was spiritual. I'd give Erik a massage and it would lead to other things." When Dominick and Kearney spoke, the year was 1993. The photographer was living in conservative New Orleans, "and I had relatives who didn't want to read about me and my life that way for the first time. Dominick respected that."

Kearney first met Erik Menendez in 1987 on a street in Beverly Hills, where he was photographing a model. "It was just a test shoot, and Erik was walking home from school," said Kearney. He remembered the teenager as being a good-looking, "not great-looking," guy who wore blue jeans and an unbuttoned denim shirt. Erik watched Kearney take pictures for a few minutes, and when the female model took a break to change her outfit, he struck up a conversation with the photographer who had just begun his career behind the camera. "We formed a friendship. Erik would come to visit and we got close and there was some physical interaction; it didn't get too particularly heavy," Kearney recalled. Erik, at that time, spoke highly of his father and how Jose Menendez wanted to be the first Cuban-born senator.

Erik claimed not to be homosexual but said, "If I was gay, Craig [Cignarelli] would be my boyfriend."

"The statement is nonsensical, but I didn't challenge it," said Kearney. One day, Erik gave Kearney a screenplay he had written. He wanted the photographer's opinion. It told the story of a teenager who kills his parents to collect the insurance money. Kearney did not read the script but knew the general outline from what Erik told him. "It's horrible enough reading your own stuff," Kearney surmised. "And I shelved it."

Kearney met Erik's brother only once. "Lyle raced over to my house one day. He came over and pressed me about my time with Erik and what he had told me, because nothing had happened. It's obvious to me now that [the double murder] was in the planning stage. Lyle was upset," said Kearney.

He also recalled a day that Erik stopped at his apartment in West Hollywood and arrived not in his usual sports car but an old clunker.

"My god, Cinderella! What happened?" asked Kearney, staring at the car.

"My car is in the shop," Erik said. Kearney asked about a small debt that Erik owed him. "I won't have your money for a while," he replied.

"You live in Beverly Hills and you don't have forty dollars?"

As soon as Kearney heard about the murders of Jose and Kitty Menendez, he contacted the LAPD. The police were not only interested in the photographs he had taken of Erik; they also wanted to see Erik's screenplay. Kearney flew back to Los Angeles from New Orleans. "A detective and I went to my storage locker to look for the script. My locker was a mess. We didn't find the script. We did find my pictures. And I made those available," he said.

It was this detective, befriended by Dominick, who told him about Kearney's photographs of Erik Menendez. "Dominick was very apologetic when he first phoned me," Kearney recalled. "He was very respectful."

In their conversations, Dominick focused on the photographs because in his testimony Erik claimed that his father forced him to pose naked over an oval mirror to obtain a more dramatic view. Dominick rejected that story. He believed Erik got the idea of the mirror from one of Kearney's photo sessions. It was this photo that Dominick insisted accompany his article in the pages of *Vanity Fair*.

Dominick and Kearney discussed at length the day Erik showed up in a beat-up car. Kearney never knew for sure if Erik and Lyle were sexually abused by Jose Menendez. "I don't know. What I do know is the father cut them off. He cut them off where it hurt the most in Beverly Hills," Kearney said of money, cars, and clothes. "And that's where it was all trailing from. The car wasn't in a shop. The father had taken it away from him. Lyle couldn't be a nobody. Erik wasn't strong enough to defy that hook Lyle had in him. Dominick saw that."

In addition to being a respectful interviewer, Dominick turned into a most entertaining phone mate. During their conversations, Dominick would often break to take another call. Back on the line, he apologized, "Oh, that was Barbara Walters." Or "Oh, that was Princess Diana." Both women wanted to hear the latest gossip on the Menendez trial. (Much to his delight, Dominick would later be introduced to the princess, and again, it would be her interest in an American murder trial that led to their face-to-face meeting.)

Dominick tried to put Kearney in touch with Barbara Walters, who wanted to interview him on ABC about Erik's sexual orientation. Kearney rejected the request. "I wasn't too interested in that," he said.

"Dominick had the aspect of an older gay man. If he had his choice, he would have been a queen," said Kearney. "He would have enjoyed holding court with all these women with the latest gossip." Like Craig Cignarelli, Kearney saw a similarity between Dominick and Truman Capote, but for a very different reason. Kearney had seen Robert Morse in the Capote bio play *Tru*, and the actor's spot-on portrayal reminded him of Dominick, "taking phone calls from these women who just wanted the latest dish. Not that I think any of that interfered with Dominick's quest for the truth," said Kearney.

He thoroughly enjoyed his conversations with the *Vanity Fair* writer. Much less comfortable were the phone calls he received from an assistant on one of the Menendez brothers' defense teams. "So Mr. Kearney, you've been with Erik. Tell me the size of his penis," the attorney wanted to know.

Kearney thought fast. "Have you measured someone's penis lately?" he asked. "If I tell you it's seven and it turns out to be six inches, you'll call me a liar."

From there, the phone conversation descended further. Obviously, Kearney handled it with aplomb. He never had to make the trip back to Los Angeles to testify in the Van Nuys Superior Courthouse.

After three weeks of deliberation, Erik Menendez's jury found itself deadlocked, unable to come to a unanimous decision on any of the charges: first-degree murder, second-degree murder, voluntary manslaughter, or involuntary manslaughter. Two weeks later, Lyle Menendez's jury was also deadlocked, and Judge Weisberg declared two mistrials. In the following month, the judge announced that the Menendez brothers would be retried but that the second trial would use only one jury.

Shortly after the judge's announcement, Leslie Abramson spoke to reporters and jurors who had been sympathetic to the defense. At the by-invitation-only meeting, she called Dominick "the little puke, the little closet queen." Robert Rand printed Abramson's slurs in a lengthy article on the trial for *Playboy* magazine. Throughout the trial, Dominick feared being outed and now a reporter he considered a friend, who called him his mentor, did the job. Mutual friends said Dominick felt "betrayed" that Rand repeated in print Abramson's smack talk.

"It was like a piece of kryptonite with Superman," Rand said of Dominick's reaction. The two men did not speak for years. "It was kind of funny. There were so many instances of his doing that to people, writing candidly about people in an uncomfortable way." Dominick's dilemma was one faced by any closeted journalist: while he expected his own privacy to be respected, he often delved into the personal lives of others, whether those confidential details related to money matters, judge-chamber negotiations, or health, like his February 1989 *Vanity Fair* article "Robert Mapplethorpe's Proud Finale," published shortly before the photographer's death from complications with AIDS.

Dominick looked forward to the next Menendez trial but would not cover it. (At that second trial, in 1994, both brothers would be convicted of first-degree murder and sentenced to life imprisonment.) On June 12, 1994, Nicole Brown Simpson and Ronald Lyle Goldman were knifed to death outside her condo at 875 South Bundy Drive in Brentwood, California. The suspect: O.J. Simpson.

Between the Menendez trial and this new double murder, Dominick found his personal life rocked again when friends leaked him a copy of his brother's new novel. Dominick, who claimed to have stopped reading John Gregory Dunne's novels years ago, intended not to read *Playland*, about a child film star gone to seed. Obviously, he did get as far as the novel's dedication page. His brother liked to splurge when it came to this publishing ritual, and *Playland* was no exception. In addition to mentioning over a half-dozen other people, John Gregory Dunne dedicated the book to Leslie Abramson and her husband, Tim Rutten, and their two children.

"It broke Dominick's heart," said Pamela Bozanich.

Dominick claimed to be "appalled" at the dedication to a woman who symbolized everything he loathed about defense attorneys. "It's a curious stand he's taken in light of what's happened to a murdered child in our family," Dominick complained of John. "If that's what he thinks is right, that's fine for him. But not for me. It's not right for me to remain friendly with him."

Dominick wrote about the feud in *Vanity Fair*: "After that my brother and I did not speak for more than six years." The two brothers were already not speaking by the time *Playland* appeared in book stores. Dominick, however, found it easier to pin their fight on a public matter, like a novel's dedication, than a private one having to do with a series of hurtful slights regarding the memory of his murdered daughter.

Dominick was not the only one who did not return for the second Menendez trial. His friend Pamela Bozanich, the prosecutor, also found herself transfixed by O.J. Simpson. Although she never visited the Los

Angeles courthouse for the so-called Trial of the Century, she did not have to show up in person. She had her own personal mole who told her everything about it, and that included what attorney was screwing what attorney and what witness was screwing what reporter. The murderers changed. Dominick did not.

# 12

## O.J. and Parties

One of the first people to phone Dominick after reports of the double murders in Brentwood made the news was a reporter friend from the Menendez trial. Shoreen Maghame needed some information. "Did you know O.J.?" she asked Dominick.

"No, not really," he said.

His reply surprised Maghame. "I thought you knew everyone in Los Angeles!" she said.

Dominick knew everyone in Los Angeles connected to the entertainment business. Sports were another story. Dominick knew more about O.J. Simpson as a bad actor than as a great football player. He often told people, he was the sissy. The three other Dunne brothers played sports, not him.

In the very beginning, Dominick knew about the murders of Nicole Brown Simpson and Ron Goldman only from TV news reports, which made it clear that they took place when O.J. Simpson had been out of town on a Hertz golf promotional. Dominick told Maghame, "Lucky for him he was in Chicago when it happened."

It disappointed Maghame that her *Vanity Fair* friend was not, as usual, a great source. "Dominick definitely thought Simpson was innocent at first," she recalled. "I believe everyone did, as we were told O.J. was in Chicago. That didn't last long. Information from the investigation quickly started leaking out. And, once the chase happened, I'm fairly positive Dominick was convinced he'd done it."

In fact, Dominick was convinced of Simpson's guilt even before the attempted escape to Mexico in the white Bronco driven by Al Cowlings on

June 17, 1994. When Simpson arrived back in Los Angeles from Chicago on the morning of June 13, the police briefly handcuffed him outside his Brentwood estate at 360 North Rockingham Drive. Dominick recalled, "For ten minutes, O.J. was in handcuffs. He let them do it. I said, 'He did it.' It's a gut feeling." It was the same gut feeling he had when he looked into Claus von Bülow's eyes. It was the same gut feeling he had when he saw Lyle Menendez's cocky walk at his parents' memorial service. These men were guilty.

There were also Dominick's daily phone calls to Lucianne Goldberg. Both of them knew it. O.J. Simpson had done it. What more proof did anyone need?

Like most of America, Dominick watched on TV as Simpson tried to escape to Mexico in the white Bronco as people along the highway held signs, "Go, Juice, Go!" That summer, he attended his fiftieth class reunion at Canterbury School in New Milford, Connecticut, and told his old class-mates how appalled he was by the highway spectacle of people cheering a man who had murdered his ex-wife and a stranger. Among his many Simpson stories, he also asked his classmate Clifford McCormick not to leave him alone in case he ran into one of Canterbury's more illustrious alums. Sargent Shriver, a Kennedy brother-in-law and founder of the Peace Corps, was there to celebrate his sixtieth class reunion, and Dominick felt he needed protection. "The Kennedys hate me!" he told McCormick. "Don't leave me!"

In January 1995 Dominick attended the pretrial hearings at which the major topics were whether Judge Lance Ito would allow TV cameras into his courtroom and if charges of domestic abuse against Simpson would be presented to the jury. Dominick had just turned sixty-nine; most reporters there were two or three decades younger. His age, however, did not prevent him from securing one of the twenty-five seats set aside for journalists at the pretrial. "Dominick was first in line every day at 6:00 a.m.," said Jeffrey Toobin, a legal analyst for CNN and the *New Yorker*. At the time, Toobin was a thirty-four-year-old reporter covering the trial for the magazine. "I was close behind him in line. I admired Dominick for that, showing up every day early." While reporters' seats would be assigned during the trial, it was strictly first come, first serve at the pretrial.

Toobin may have admired Dominick, but Dominick did not admire Toobin, and he let the reporter's boss at the *New Yorker* know it. He told Tina Brown he strongly objected to Toobin's article "An Incendiary

Defense" for her magazine; it essentially laid the groundwork for the defense's strategy that detective Mark Fuhrman was a racist rogue cop who may have planted some of the evidence, including a bloody glove, at Simpson's residence. In case anyone missed the point, Toobin asked Fuhrman point blank, "Did you plant the glove?" After responding no, Fuhrman ended their phone conversation. Toobin made sure to include that exchange in "An Incendiary Defense," published six months before the pretrial.

Tina Brown knew how easily Dominick could be swayed by small expressions of respect and deference. She wisely suggested that he meet Toobin. "You'll like Jeffrey," she said. And, of course, Brown was right. Dominick and Toobin met during the pretrial hearings in the terrazzo corridors of the courthouse. Toobin found him "standoffish" at first, but they quickly got to know each other and became friends. Much later in the trial, Dominick confessed to Toobin, "I didn't want to like you. I was mad about that piece in the *New Yorker*." The two men never agreed about Fuhrman and his motives. But they did agree about Simpson. He murdered Nicole Brown Simpson and Ron Goldman.

Dominick was not the only one who thought the defense team literally handed Toobin the police file on Fuhrman, the basis for his *New Yorker* article. Dominick's telephone friend Lucianne Goldberg went so far as to call Toobin "a turd." While he denied the charges of being given any report, Toobin did receive an important tip about Fuhrman.

Even before the preliminary hearings, the *New Yorker* reporter spoke to his old Harvard Law School professor Alan Dershowitz, who had already joined Simpson's defense, soon to be known as the Dream Team. Dershowitz said of Fuhrman, "He sounds like Oliver North, looks like Oliver North, and lies like Oliver North." With that character assassination in mind, Toobin visited the Los Angeles County Courthouse, where he found Fuhrman's file in the City of Los Angeles Fire and Police Pension System, case number C 465,544. A disability report there contained a detailed psychological portrait of the man. While the report praised Fuhrman's work as a detective, it also included a statement from a superior questioning his obsession with the "big arrest." In the file, psychologist Dr. Ronald R. Koegler wrote: "After a while [Fuhrman] began to dislike his work, especially the 'low-class people' he was dealing with. He bragged about violence he used in subduing suspects, including chokeholds, and said he would break their hands or face or arms or legs, if necessary."

Toobin knew what he had found. As he reported, "The Fuhrman disability case had the potential to thrust the specter of Rodney King into the middle of the Simpson case."

Dominick knew Toobin's tipster, having met Alan Dershowitz at the second Claus von Bülow trial. The two men decided early on to be friendly adversaries. "Dominick understood my role," said Dershowitz. "Dominick could never do what I did. But as long as I admitted to myself they were guilty, as long as I didn't distort or lie . . . He didn't like my clients, but he wasn't going to take it out on me."

According to Dershowitz, he and Dominick engaged in many long conversations during the course of both the von Bülow and the Simpson trials, conversations Dominick never wrote about. Dershowitz linked the two murder cases because, as he told Dominick, both involved evidence being either planted (the bag with the insulin-encrusted syringes in Sunny von Bülow's closet at Clarendon Court) or tampered with (a bloody sock found in O.J. Simpson's bedroom at his Rockingham estate). The lawyer and the reporter argued at length over the bloody sock. Dershowitz wanted to know why the blood contained EDTA, "which can only be found in a test tube, not in human blood." (Marcia Clark, the lead prosecutor, maintained that since EDTA is used as a food preservative, it is often found in human blood.) Also troubling for Dershowitz was the mirror pattern of blood on the sock, apparently the result of blood having been poured onto the fabric rather than splashed.

"Dominick and I talked a lot about the ends and the means," Dershowitz recalled. "Once Dominick thought someone was guilty, he didn't care what the means to get him convicted were. As a lawyer, I care a lot about the means." Dershowitz told his reporter friend, "Well, the police tampered with the evidence." And Dominick told his lawyer friend, "Look, if the police did something wrong, then the police should be prosecuted, but the guilty shouldn't go free."

Dominick's profound disappointment with defense lawyers had not changed from all the previous trials. But he had changed.

He was not the old Nick Dunne of Hollywood failure, or even the Nick Dunne who wrote a few articles and books. He returned to Los Angeles this time as Dominick Dunne. "Just call me Dominick," he said by way of introduction. He came to cover the O.J. Simpson trial as a best-selling novelist and the writer who most personified *Vanity Fair* and, in turn, the trial itself.

"Dominick was very low key during the Menendez case. He wasn't a big socializer," said Patti Jo Fairbanks, the district attorney's senior legal assistant. "But when he came back for the O.J. case, not only was he on the A-list but he was number 1 on the A-list. That guy was going everywhere! There wasn't anyone who didn't want to meet Dominick Dunne. And he loved it. It told him that he had redeemed himself from his former life in L.A."

Old Hollywood acquaintances who had snubbed him in the 1970s now invited him to parties—or, in the case of Gregory Peck's wife, Veronique— other people's parties. In his private journal, Dominick wrote of Mrs. Peck being pretentious and superior. She had dismissed him repeatedly when he was Nick Dunne, the failure.

The Simpson trial transformed him into what *New York* magazine would soon call "America's most famous journalist." More important for Mrs. Gregory Peck, Dominick was the only person she knew who held a seat (soon to be permanent) in Judge Lance Ito's courtroom for the O.J. Simpson trial. She took it upon herself to invite him to a party being given at the home of the human rights activist Stanley Sheinbaum and his wife, Betty, daughter of movie mogul Harry Warner. The party would be in honor of King Hussein and Queen Noor, whom Dominick had profiled for *Vanity Fair*. As Veronique Peck put it to Dominick, "Stanley thought you might fill the king and queen in on the trial."

Dominick did not mind gossiping for his dinner. He did not think much of Mrs. Peck, but he always admired Sheinbaum and his humanitarian projects.

More gracious were invitations from an old friend who had never turned her back on him. Tita Cahn gave a series of parties in 1995, all of which had one requirement. "You could attend only if you wanted to talk about O.J.," said the hostess. "I seat twelve, so we'd have one conversation."

Dominick was a constant at those dinners. Other guests would rotate, although Sherry Lansing and her husband, director William Friedkin, frequently attended. "Leaving those parties I had this feeling of being so special," said Lansing, then CEO of Paramount Pictures. "I'd think, 'Oh God, I have the inside track on the trial.'" But not for long. "A few days later *Vanity Fair* came out, and now the whole world knows!"

And the world eagerly anticipated Dominick's O.J. reporting in *Vanity Fair*. "People waited for those columns like they waited for the next Dickens installment in New York Harbor," said his editor Wayne Lawson. "That's how popular those things were in the course of those trials. And he knew it, and he knew that he could approach anybody and they would give him a quote."

Suddenly, it was de rigueur in Los Angeles to have Dominick Dunne as a guest at your party. It was how the town's elite got the inside scoop before the readers of *Vanity Fair* and, better yet, learned something that the magazine's lawyers might excise to avoid libel.

As with the von Bülow and Menendez trials, Dominick observed what other reporters saw but rarely put in print. Just as Dominick knew Claus von Bülow's position in New York and Newport society, he knew all about Hollywood star treatment, even if it was for an accused murderer. Only Dominick knew to report that the defendant and his dozen lawyers "had the curious look of a dinner party" in the Ito courtroom. Only Dominick knew to report how the younger lawyers laughed too much at Simpson's jokes "the way people who are not used to being in the orbit of a celebrity do." Dominick also made a specialty of giving bits of information about the never-photographed jurors, flaunting his superior sense of taste to flatter the readers of *Vanity Fair*. In one article, he noted the hairdos of two alternates, so elaborate that "they must have to get up at five every morning to prepare themselves."

In January 1995, during the pretrial hearings, every successful party list in Los Angeles included not only Dominick but one of the trial's attorneys as well, preferably from the prosecution. Ray Stark called upon his daughter, Wendy, to extend a party invitation to her good friend from *Vanity Fair*. Despite Dominick's roman à clef *The Winners*, the Stark family never took offense. That dispute would come later when he wrote about them in *Another City, Not My Own*. In winter 1995, however, all was calm between the Starks and Dominick, even if he had to tell Wendy he could not possibly attend her father's upcoming party. He was too busy. Wendy could not imagine the old Nick Dunne saying such a thing. But she knew when to bring out the big guns: Marcia Clark would be attending Daddy's fete.

Dominick suddenly was not so busy that night.

Ray Stark made only one demand. "Please don't ask Marcia about the trial or O.J.," he asked.

Dominick pitied Clark even before the trial began. Prosecutors had to be tough, and juries were sexist, he firmly believed. They did not like strong female attorneys, even if their job was to put rapists and murderers behind bars.

Dominick obeyed Ray Stark's edict, which did not mean Clark could not ask questions. She wanted to know how Betsy Bloomingdale could invite him back into her home after Dominick wrote *An Inconvenient Woman*.

Dominick demurred. He called Betsy a "classy" lady.

Classy had nothing to do with it. Nor did Betsy's explanation regarding their détente. She said they made up at Spago at one of Swifty Lazar's Oscar parties. "Everyone was looking because there he was and there I was and blah blah blah," Betsy recalled. "But I said, 'Hello.' And he said, 'Hello.' And then we were all great friends after that. A 'hello' could do it."

Saying "hello" also had nothing to do with it. In the end, the patrician Betsy Bloomingdale wanted the O.J. dirt just like everybody else in town.

"The measure of Dominick's power was that after he wrote *An Incon-venient Woman* Betsy Bloomingdale had to forgive him," said AP reporter Linda Deutsch. "Otherwise, she would have been out of the social set and wouldn't have heard all the gossip."

"Once Dominick got to be famous, people like Betsy Bloomingdale and Nancy Reagan didn't care anymore," said his book publicist Judy Hilsinger. "They wanted proximity to him because he had all the O.J. gossip. And Betsy and Nancy were so close."

Dominick topped the town's A-list. He could even entertain a notorious madam at a high-profile lunch and still curry the favor of the former first lady and her superwealthy best friend.

Heidi Fleiss first heard about Dominick wanting to meet her some-time after her 1994 arrest for attempted pandering. "It was at the Playboy mansion at one of Hugh Hefner's Tuesday night card games," she recalled. A mutual friend approached her about talking to the *Vanity Fair* writer. "Sure. Put me in touch," said Fleiss. In early 1995, she was suffering through her own trial in Los Angeles, and Dominick believed, incredulously, that she would do more time for her victimless crime than Simpson would for double murder.

Dominick arranged a proper lunch for Heidi and him to chat at the Hotel Bel-Air. "It was the most awesome day of my life!" gushed Fleiss. Excited, she even sweetened the date by bringing "a couple of my top hookers with me." Dominick did not mention the two uninvited guests in his *Vanity Fair* article, but he treated them with all due respect and kind-ness. "Dominick knew pain," said Fleiss. "He helped a lot of people, in-cluding me. He made a connection. He could have been a snobby asshole; he had achieved that. But he wasn't that way at all. He was wonderful."

To Dominick's surprise, Nancy Reagan and Betsy Bloomingdale were also dining that afternoon at the Bel-Air, and as soon as he, Fleiss, and her hooker friends stepped into the restaurant, the two doyennes sent word to join them. "We just had a lot of L.A. gossip," Fleiss said of the diverse party. After Nancy and Betsy left the hotel restaurant, she turned to Dominick. "I can't fucking believe what just happened here!" Fleiss exclaimed. Neither could he.

The Dominick-and-Betsy rapprochement did not end there. He even received a Bloomingdale invitation to a party that took place the night after the TV movie version of *An Inconvenient Woman* re-aired and a few million viewers watched again as Jill Eikenberry's wealthy widow ordered a hit on Rebecca De Mornay's out-of-work mistress.

Covering a long trial can be a grind, but stories like the first lady and her best friend dining with a madam and her girls put Dominick in good stead with the other reporters. What other journalist could corral with such tales?

"Every morning outside the courtroom, there was the bull pen of reporters," Linda Deutsch recalled. "Everybody talked about what had happened, and the highlight was always Dominick. He regaled everyone with his evening before."

Deutsch especially liked the story Dominick told about going to a rich woman's home for a party, at which the hostess announced, "I'm delaying my next facelift until after the O.J. trial is over!"

"Dominick had sort of been run out of town, and with the O.J. trial he felt he had been welcomed back," said Beth Karas, a reporter for Court TV. Her favorite stories from Dominick involved his weekly lunches with Elizabeth Taylor, another chameleon friend who forgave him the *Ash Wednesday* debacle in order to get all the O.J. news. He strongly advised the movie star not to be seen at Johnnie Cochran's tribute to her lawyer Neil Papiano in order to avoid a photo op with the murderer's biggest defender. More fun were Dominick's stories about lunch with Liz when her other guest was the king of pop. One afternoon, Michael Jackson brought his pet chimpanzee Bubbles, who sat down to eat with them. "It was the most bizarre day of my life," said Dominick. Jackson made a habit of bringing Taylor an extravagant gift, always tied up with a lavender ribbon to match her famous eyes. Inside one such package, she found a diamond and a sapphire bracelet. "For lunch! For lunch!" Dominick exclaimed, both shocked and delighted at Jackson's casual display of his mega-wealth.

"He would act out Elizabeth opening the gift," Karas recalled. "Dominick loved being the belle of the ball. He was redeemed."

*Time* magazine's James Willwerth saw something beyond mere entertainment in Dominick's morning floor show for the reporters. "Dominick milked the bull pen," said Willwerth. "If he told you great Hollywood stories and you listened to it, you want to please him, especially in L.A. And there's Dominick, 'Give me some of your inside stuff on O.J. and I'll give you some of my Hollywood stories.'"

Marie Brenner, who covered the Simpson trial for *Vogue*, put a more positive spin on her friend's relationship to the reporters. "Dominick was extra conversational and goading," she said. "He knew he got his best material from the roving reporters, who would open up to it—the minutia they couldn't use but he could use to weave these brilliant tales. Dominick was there both as sponge and commentator and parish priest and father figure. He was there having fun. He made everything fun."

"He wasn't looking to be the purveyor of sage advice," noted Dan Abrams. "He wanted information from me, too."

Dominick was especially popular with those reporters he took to dinner on the *Vanity Fair* expense account, whether the restaurant was Cicada, Eclipse, Le Dome, or Mortons. "The most defined memories were the excitement of going out to dinner with Dominick during the trial," said Abrams. "It wasn't like going out to dinner with a colleague. It was going out with a celebrity. Harry Belafonte comes up to the table; every megastar treated Dominick like he was a star."

During the trial, defense attorneys Johnnie Cochrane and Robert Shapiro, as well as prosecutors Marcia Clark and Chris Darden, emerged as some of the best-known personalities in America. "And Dominick was up there, particularly among the Hollywood elite," said Abrams. "He was the personification of the case to them." Abrams also noted how Simpson's lawyers always treated Dominick "with kid gloves," even though he was virulently antidefense. "O.J.'s lawyers all hated me," said Dominick. And it was true. Johnnie Cochran explained Dominick's reporting bias. "If you're on the defense, it's going to be an attack. That's what Dominick lives for," said the attorney. But Cochran and others on the Dream Team knew not to start a public fight with him. They had seen how Dominick tried to decimate Leslie Abramson's reputation in TV interviews and *Vanity Fair*, and they learned not to cross him.

Abrams found Dominick "very democratic" with his rotation of reporter dinner guests. One night he would be Dominick's guest; the next night it would ABC's Cynthia McFadden or the *New York Times'* David Margolick or the *New Yorker's* Jeffrey Toobin. "It was always a treat to go out with him."

Dominick relished being recognized, especially by other celebrities. "I love being famous," he said infectiously with no guile, and he took genuine pleasure when Sacha Baron Cohen and Bono introduced themselves. But he got equal joy when more obscure personalities approached him.

Shirley Perlman, a reporter for *Newsday*, remembered one evening after dinner at Mortons. When a tall man approached them in the parking lot, she stepped aside to give him and Dominick some privacy to talk. Afterward, Dominick asked Perlman, "Do you know who that was?"

Perlman had no idea. "That was John Bryan!" exclaimed Dominick. Perlman still had no idea. "He's the guy who sucked Fergie's toes!" said Dominick. Bryan, an American financial manager, had confided in

Dominick that he never really sucked the toes of the Duchess of York. He had merely kissed the instep of her foot when they were in the south of France together. Dominick said he did not believe that story for a second.

Dominick felt he owed Perlman big time during the Simpson trial. It was she, after all, who had warned him about a film crew in the courthouse. Perlman heard from another reporter that Michael Moore's people were roaming the halls. In the press room, Perlman waved to Dominick but he did not have time to talk.

"I'll be right back," he said.

"Where are you going?" she wanted to know.

"There's a film crew that wants to interview me."

"Be careful," warned Perlman. "I understand Michael Moore is in the courthouse."

Dominick nodded and then left. A few minutes later, he returned. "Oh honey, thank you."

The film crew did not identify their muckraking filmmaker when they had first approached Dominick for an interview. But later, when he asked about Moore, on Perlman's tip, they had to tell him the truth: Moore was taping his satirical newscast for NBC, *TV Nation*, and they were doing a segment on a retired U.S. Army psychological operations expert who wanted to reduce the amount of media coverage devoted to O.J. Simpson. Dominick would have been a prime target for Moore's faux exposé.

"I owe you," Dominick told Perlman.

The only real dustup Dominick had with his fellow reporters occurred just as the trial itself began. Judge Ito assigned Dominick, along with book writers Joe McGinnis and Joseph Bosco, reserved seats in the courtroom for the run of the trial. Many other reporters were given alternate-day seats or, worse, were relegated to the press rooms, where they had to watch the trial on closed-circuit TV. Bob Poole, writing for the *Los Angeles Times*, tore into Ito's decision to give a permanent reserved seat to book authors and writers with long lead times, like Dominick. For his *Times* tirade, Poole interviewed Paul Pringle of the Copley News Service, who took specific aim at Dominick, calling him "Judith Krantz in pants." Dominick later heard that Leslie Abramson took special delight in his masculinity being called into question. It was payback for his calling her kinky hair "Rastafarian."

Dominick's front-row seat in the courtroom was better than permanent. He sat between the Goldman and Brown families. Although Judge Ito let Dominick know it was very much his decision, an old friend from the Menendez trial made it happen.

"There was an issue of what reporter was going to sit next to [the victims'] family members," said Patti Jo Fairbanks. In private negotiations with Ito, the senior legal assistant told the judge, "Hey, you've got to sit Dominick there. I can trust this man explicitly." She told Ito about Dominick's own similar tragedy, and how among all the reporters he would be the most sympathetic to the families. Fairbanks knew Dominick would not "infringe on their privacy. We did it to protect the families."

The sister of Ron Goldman recalled her first impressions of the visitor seated to her immediate left. "Dominick was very much an observer in the beginning," said Kim Goldman. "We were in shell shock, and Dominick had this nervous energy about him. He'd come in all frazzled, like the Nutty Professor with all these papers, a big bag, and he'd scribbled on his pad. He was kind of a character. I didn't know anything about him."

Kim Goldman said that in time she, her father, and her stepmother began to look upon Dominick "as family." He also played the cicerone of celebrity, letting the Goldmans know whenever someone famous visited the courtroom. Kim often did not know the celebs by face or name, leaving it to Dominick to give a detailed description of why they were notable and, of course, how he knew them personally and what he thought of them.

Dominick and the Goldmans also became kindred prisoners of the courtroom. Often, he would ask, "Why are we sitting here?" The inconvenience of a long trial rankled Dominick, being called into the courtroom and then sitting there waiting, waiting. "It can be very frustrating," said Kim. "You're called into court and then nothing happens for an hour."

But that sense of unending boredom came later. When the trial began on January 24, 1995, the prosecution immediately introduced the grizzly crime-scene photographs of the two victims. The body of Nicole Brown Simpson, her arms and legs drawn up in a fetal position, rested at the bottom of the steps to her condo's front door. Marcia Clark pointed to the photographs of Ron Goldman and spoke of his being "literally backed into a cage," pushed into the corner of a fence, his shirt over his face, his bare torso punctured with several knife wounds.

A famous black man killing his white ex-wife: in America, it could not turn into anything but a media circus focused on race. It began with Jeffrey Toobin's indictment of Mark Fuhrman six months before the trial began. Less than a week into the trial, on February 1, the first African American witness was called to testify, questioned by the prosecution's only African American lawyer. The circus promptly acquired a whole new ring of action.

Chris Darden asked Ronald G. Shipp, a former police officer, to describe visiting Simpson's Brentwood estate on June 13, 1994, a day after the murders. He had gone there as O.J.'s friend, Shipp said, to commiserate with the family over the death of Nicole Brown Simpson. According to Shipp, Simpson had asked to see him alone, and in his upstairs bedroom the two men talked about DNA testing. Simpson wanted to know how long it took to get the results. Shipp did not know but guessed a few weeks. More significant, Simpson went on to reveal his most recent nightmares. In his testimony, Shipp recalled that conversation: "He jokingly said, 'To be honest, Shipp, I've had some dreams about killing [Nicole].'" (The two men also discussed the possibility of Simpson's taking a lie detector test, although Judge Ito did not allow that part of their conversation to be re-told to the jury.)

Chris Darden tried to use Shipp's testimony to counter the defense's charge that the LAPD had, in any way, framed Simpson for the murders, and, in fact, the city's police officers maintained an overly cordial relationship with the defendant. Shipp also testified that he had once been a part-time instructor at the Los Angeles Police Academy, where he taught classes on domestic abuse. O.J. and Nicole Simpson knew of his work at the academy, and years ago, the couple had separate talks with him about an altercation that took place between them on New Year's Day 1989. The couple had gotten into a physical fight after having sex and sought counseling. Shipp gave them a handbook on domestic violence, later testifying at the trial that while Nicole thought she fit some of the profiles of battered wives, O.J. admitted to identifying with only one trait of husbands who batter: obsessive jealousy.

Darden told the jury that Simpson's admission of killing his former wife in a dream was "about as relevant as any statement could be, save an outright confession."

The prosecutor was overly optimistic. Carl Douglas cross-examined Shipp, and Dominick left no doubt about what he thought of the defense attorney's interview technique. He later wrote, "I think that I have never seen a meaner face than Carl Douglas's when he went after Shipp in his cross-examination."

Douglas tried to portray Shipp as a liar, a drunk, and a part-time actor who, rather than being Simpson's friend, was searching for his brief moment in the spotlight. The "friendship" question was crucial because Douglas wanted to show that Shipp did not have the kind of close relationship with Simpson that would have allowed him to share secrets like beating his wife or having dreams of killing her.

Shipp admitted on the stand, "I guess you can say I was like everybody else, one of his servants. I did police stuff for him all the time. I ran license plates. That's what I was. I mean, like I said, I loved the guy."

Douglas also attacked Shipp for giving an interview to Sheila Weller, author of the Simpson book *Raging Heart*. Shipp replied that Weller did not pay him for the interview and had promised him anonymity. Weller identified him in the book as Leo.

Douglas asked Shipp, "Were you prepared to share intimate secrets about your friend to a total stranger without the promise of anonymity?"

"Oh, no. No," replied Shipp.

"So the promise of anonymity was the reason or the motivation for you to share intimate secrets with your friend to a total stranger?"

"Correct."

To Dominick and others, Shipp was a courageous man who spoke the truth to serve justice.

To many in the African American community, Shipp was at best a snitch. Marcia Clark reported being shocked by what happened following Shipp's testimony. "Black journalists in the newsroom below us were branding him a liar and a traitor," she wrote. The black-owned L.A.-based newspaper the *Sentinel* called Shipp a "drunk" in its article "O.J.'s Cast of 'Addicts,' 'Liars.'" In the Los Angeles neighborhood where Shipp lived, black people called him a Judas to his face, and death threats were directed not only at him but his wife and children.

Dominick joined Marcia Clark in writing about the racial divide in the journalists' reactions, but not everyone agreed with their negative assessment. John Johnson, an African American journalist, covered the trial for WABC. "First and foremost, there weren't that many black journalists covering the trial," Johnson recalled. "It was a major trial and considered a plumb assignment." Johnson said he had no problem finding Simpson guilty of the murders. Long before the trial, he had been a guest at Simpson's Rockingham estate; he danced with Nicole and discovered firsthand just how "jealous O.J. could be." Despite his own negative impressions of the defendant, Johnson felt that many white journalists were "not sensitive to the subject of a black man murdering a white woman in the American culture."

Dominick may have contributed to such insensitivity. After he attended the L.A. Opera's opening-night performance of *Otello*, Dominick remarked on how the audience recoiled when the tenor Plácido Domingo, in blackface, strangled his blonde Desdemona, soprano June Anderson. He even quoted socialite Barbara Davis as saying, "The jury should see this!"

"What did [an opera] have to do with the Simpson trial?" asked John Johnson. In an even greater leap from reality to theater, Dominick went on to cast a real-life player in the Simpson drama to essay the role of Iago. "Sometimes I think Al Cowlings fits the part," he wrote. Dominick never explained how Cowlings in any way resembled one of Shakespeare's most unmotivated villains.

The uproar surrounding Ron Shipp only increased in the following month when Simpson's mother, Eunice, and sisters, Shirley and Carmelita, testified that Shipp was never alone with O.J. on June 13. Eunice Simpson also said that Shipp looked "spaced" that night at Rockingham.

Right after his day in court, Shipp felt so ostracized that he considered seeking professional help but knew he could not trust psychiatrists. "I was afraid to see a therapist because they were selling their stories," he said. Shipp recalled how Nicole and O.J.'s respective therapists had sold their stories to the press. During his pretrial talks with the prosecutors, Shipp became friendly with Patti Jo Fairbanks and felt she was one of the few people in whom he could confide.

Fairbanks suggested he speak to Dominick. She explained how Judge Ito had seated her reporter friend next to the victims' families and how he had spoken and given comfort to Craig Cignarelli, another controversial witness, during the Menendez trial. She assured Shipp that Dominick would be equally discreet with him.

Over the weeks following his testimony, Shipp and Dominick met several times at either the Chateau Marmont or the Beverly Hills Hotel, wherever Dominick was staying at the time. "These people, at times, they were like my therapist," Shipp said of Dominick and author Sheila Weller.

He talked to Dominick about his posttestimony trauma. "In my ignorance, I truly believed in my heart that anybody, not just the African American community who loved O.J., once they knew what he did, would think he should fry. Yet there were those who didn't care, and that's what I couldn't understand."

During one conversation at the Chateau, something happened to Shipp that he did not expect: he let his pent-up anger come to the surface to explode in front of his new reporter friend. Shipp recalled, "I sat there and I went off. I went off with a bunch of my frustrations. I said, 'Dominick, I'm a victim here. Look at what has happened!' I went off on the world. I was very disappointed with what I saw in life."

Shipp's own friends tried to justify the Simpson family's behavior, telling him, "Hey, Ron, this guy is fighting for his freedom."

Shipp disagreed. "That's OK if you're not guilty. But this guy? C'mon. I can't believe they made his mom and sisters lie on the stand!" he said.

Dominick listened, but it unnerved him when Shipp lost control and started screaming in his hotel room. "I felt so bad," Shipp recalled. "Dominick looked at me, the look that he gave me! He looked at me like, 'Is this guy getting ready to completely flip out?' And another part of him was so sad for me."

Shipp spent the rest of their time together at the Chateau trying to apologize for his outburst.

"Dominick helped Ron so much," said Patti Jo Fairbanks. "Dominick was so involved with helping victims."

Dominick saw himself in the Fred Goldman family and how they never missed a day of the Simpson trial. Likewise, he came to criticize the Brown family because after the first few weeks they rarely made visits to the courtroom. One day over lunch, Dominick asked Fairbanks what compelled the Brown family to be so negligent. Fairbanks, who claimed to have a "warped sense of humor," told him, "You know, a double homicide doesn't make a dysfunctional family functional."

Dominick reached into his pocket to pull out a gold-fringed Smythson's notebook and "frantically" started writing with his Mont Blanc pen. "Dominick," Fairbanks warned, "if you ever quote me on that I'll kill you!"

He immediately put away his expensive pen and paper, and the two friends continued with their lunch. But Dominick remembered Fairbanks's quote, and he did not delete from his notebook what she said that day.

There were other witnesses Dominick also helped. "He did befriend Ron Shipp and Mark Fuhrman," said Fairbanks. "Mark owes Dominick a lot more than people know. Dominick felt so bad. He felt Mark deserved better, and Mark did deserve better."

Mark Fuhrman was supposed to be one of the prosecution's star witnesses. The Toobin article in the *New Yorker*, as well as F. Lee Bailey's cross-examination, destroyed whatever luster Fuhrman possessed pretrial. The defense team produced no fewer than four witnesses to contradict Fuhrman's testimony that he had not used the N-word in ten years. One of those witnesses, Laura Hart McKinny, was a former girlfriend who, working on a screenplay with the detective, recorded audiotapes in which Fuhrman repeatedly used the racial slur. The prosecution charged that the playing of the tape was too inflammatory, but Judge Ito ruled that a few segments could be played to the jury.

Fuhrman later pleaded guilty to perjury but always maintained that he did not remove the glove from Nicole Simpson's condo and place it at Rockingham.

"Mark was a guy who did the right thing and paid a helluva price for it," said Fairbanks. And no one agreed with her more on that point than her friend from *Vanity Fair*.

Dominick said his friendship with the detective did not begin during the trial. As Fairbanks explained, "Mark was out of the trial very quickly."

Dan Abrams agreed. "Fuhrman was under pretty tight security at the time," he recalled. "Dominick probably didn't see him apart from when Fuhrman passed us by in the hallway."

Whether they met during the trial or not, Lucianne Goldberg believed that her phone friend Dominick quickly developed a "crush" on the detective. Certainly Fuhrman's appearance and charisma were noted by many, including his major nemesis in the press. Jeffrey Toobin wrote, "In the flesh, Mark Fuhrman was an imposing figure, a muscular six foot three inches, the first man in the courtroom who appeared a physical match for the defendant."

Among the reporters, CNN's Art Harris arguably had the most contact with Fuhrman during the trial. Harris knew of the McKinny tapes but he also knew Fuhrman to be a respected, hardworking detective. Shortly after the Toobin article appeared in the *New Yorker*, Harris began work on a segment for CNN that would reveal the positive side of Fuhrman.

"I found three black women who said Mark was a great detective," Harris recalled. These women knew Fuhrman through his work on cases involving the respective murders of friends and relatives. "They said he was very compassionate with their family, that he helped solve the murders and gave them closure. They went on camera [for CNN]. It was a pretty interesting piece. The defense wasn't thrilled."

Dominick and Harris discussed the controversial detective. "Dominick was one of those who saw through the BS and the spin of what [the defense] was up to," said Harris. "Dominick knew that a good cop was a good cop, and he may have wished he had had a Mark Fuhrman with his daughter's case. Dominick and I talked about it a lot."

After the McKinny tapes surfaced late in the trial, Fuhrman returned to court. This time he took the Fifth, even to the question of whether he had planted the glove. Harris sat near Dominick that day in court. The TV camera followed the detective, and when he saw a friend in court, Fuhrman walked by Harris on his way to the stand to grab the correspondent's shoulder.

"I was not a reactionary or an ideologue," said Harris. "But when Mark squeezed my shoulder, I knew the irony. 'OK, Art Harris is going to be known as Mark Fuhrman's friend.' I saw the cutline. And the irony was not lost on Dominick."

Dominick, however, never wrote about Harris's difficult moment in court. He wrote about Fuhrman's kids instead. "What's it going to be like for them?" he worried in print.

Kim Goldman could not look at Fuhrman when he repeatedly took the Fifth, and instead she sobbed softly in court. Dominick could feel her fury but kept his own opinion of the detective to himself. Later that day, Fred Goldman held an impromptu press conference on the courthouse steps. "This is not the Mark Fuhrman trial!" he pleaded.

"Dominick became family to me during that trial. The closest and bright spot in my day," said Kim Goldman. "He loved me like a daughter. I can't express how much his role really helped me personally. My dad would say the same thing." Dominick's own daughter had been about the same age as Kim when she was murdered, and they talked about Dominique. "There was a lot of that. I never felt he was trying to get anything from me. It was a genuine fondness," said Kim.

The only real disagreements Dominick and Kim had during the long trial stemmed from his cordial relationship with Simpson's mother and sisters. "He was friendly with them, which drove me nuts," she recalled. "And they knew he thought their son was guilty."

She told Dominick she did not like his talking with Eunice, Shirley, and Carmelita. "I hate it when you do that!" she said.

"I know that," he replied.

Better than anyone, Kim Goldman knew how Dominick really felt about O.J. Simpson. "Which made it comfortable for me to talk to him," she said.

In early June, the jury finally saw the autopsy photographs of the two victims. Dominick and other reporters had to hire an attorney "to argue our right to view the photographs." The trial began with the crime-scene photos, with the victims' clothes covering much of the carnage. The autopsy photos were much more graphic. Placed on easels, they exposed every knife mark on the two corpses.

More than any of the other forty-seven reporters present, Dominick had a visceral reaction to the autopsy photographs. A few colleagues asked if he was all right. He waved away their concern but soon had to sit down. He felt faint. Shoreen Maghame sat beside him. Dominick later wrote: "What was the most haunting, what bothered me the most when I looked at these pictures was that their eyes were open. All I could think of was that she saw him. She knew. Her lips were opened. Her hair turned dark from the blood from her scalp. It just haunted me. The look on her face."

Reporters thought Dominick saw his own daughter's murder when he examined the autopsy photos. Later, Linda Deutsch asked him, "Why do you choose to do this?"

Deutsch believed that Dominick, by looking at the autopsy photographs and attending court every day, "was sentencing himself to a purgatory of reliving his daughter's killing. Other than that he was fascinated with the process."

But to her question, why he put himself through it, Dominick remained silent. "No, I didn't get an answer from him," Deutsch said.

"He went almost insane," said Griffin Dunne. "It was like a disembowelment for him, with everything that happened with Dominique. It was just churning up every ugly memory."

# 13

## Princess Diana and Breakdowns

As the Simpson trial entered its six month, everyone grew tired, became high-strung, got testy. Among the reporters, Dominick led the charge against the Nation of Islam guards who prevented anyone from entering the men's room whenever Johnnie Cochran used the facilities. Dominick expressed his fear to friends that he was "losing it." Whether or not he needed a break from his O.J. obsession, Graydon Carter gave him one: a special out-of-the-country assignment for *Vanity Fair.*

Dominick did not keep his UK visit in late June 1995 a secret. He needed to tell Judge Ito his reason for leaving the courtroom or risk losing his reserved seat. Otherwise, he enjoyed bragging about it.

"I have to leave Los Angeles for a few days," Dominick told Dan Abrams. "Graydon wants me to go to London over the weekend to cover a party *Vanity Fair* is giving at the Serpentine Galleries to honor Princess Diana." No journalist knew better how to bury the lede for maximum effect, now that he knew what the word meant.

Abrams joked, asking that Dominick set him up on a date with the suddenly single princess.

"Are you serious?" Dominick asked.

"Why not?"

"Why not?! Because . . . she's Princess fucking Di. That's why not!"

Dominick did not know if it was wise to leave Los Angeles for even a few days and possibly miss something important. Princess Diana, however, specifically requested his presence at the party. Obsessed by the Simpson case, she wanted to meet the reporter whose Menendez trial coverage she had discussed with him long-distance on the phone. His going to the party almost qualified as a command performance, and in his journal, Dominick wrote how "camp" it was, going from O.J. to Princess Di.

At the Serpentine Galleries, Dominick again received preferential seating, next to the princess. When she asked if the trial ever got boring, Dominick mentioned that Judge Ito sometimes let the lawyers speak too long. He went on to tell her that the star-struck judge gave the princess his regards.

Princess Diana dazzled that day in what was to become known as her "revenge dress," a black off-the-shoulder ensemble designed for her three years before by Greek designer Christina Stambolian. Because she considered the dress too daring, Diana never wore it. She had planned to wear a Valentino gown at the Serpentine Galleries party, but her unfaithful husband upended those plans. The day before the gala, Prince Charles admitted his infidelity, having carried on a long-term affair with Camilla Parker Bowles. At the last minute, Diana chucked the more sedate Valentino for the far sexier Stambolian. She then goosed the low-cut dress by wearing the tallest high-heel shoes ever seen on a member of the royal family. What better day to be seated next to the royal cuckquean? Dominick Dunne from West Hartford had arrived! He was finally *there*.

When he returned to Los Angeles, Dominick attended another round of dinners. One of those was to celebrate the upcoming TV movie adaptation of his novel *A Season in Purgatory*. David Brown and Aaron Spelling were the executive producers, and they had hired Robert "Buzz" Berger to produce. Or, as Berger put it, "I thought I was going to keep Spelling and Brown from killing each other."

Dominick rarely received tips anymore about who murdered Martha Moxley. The corpses of Nicole Brown Simpson and Ron Goldman replaced hers in the tabloid zeitgeist, but he wondered if a TV movie could reignite interest in the Moxley murder. Dominick, who tried to grapple for control of NBC's *The Two Mrs. Grenvilles*, kept his distance from this Spelling–Brown project. The Simpson trial occupied him full-time, but out of courtesy he accepted Buzz Berger's invitation.

"It was during the O.J. thing and Dominick was so involved," said Berger. John le Carré also attended the TV producer's party, but it was Dominick, not the famed author of *The Spy Who Came in from the Cold*, who held everyone's attention with his trial gossip. "He was singing for his supper, and everyone was tremendously interested," said Berger. At one point, the producer asked Dominick, "Why did you get out of TV and get into writing?"

"Because I couldn't get a job," he replied. "I was a drunk."

Berger held up his end of the conversation by telling Dominick stories from the front line of his battles with Spelling and Brown. The most outrageous behavior, however, came not from the two entertainment titans but actor Patrick Dempsey, who had been cast as Harrison Burns, the young friend who helps the killer move the body the night of the murder in *A Season in Purgatory*. Dempsey had indulged his ego by rewriting the script, which he presented to Berger the day before rehearsals began in Atlanta, Georgia.

Hearing the story, Dominick could only laugh and shake his head. Yes, he had made the right decision—or someone had made the right decision for him—to leave Hollywood. He absolutely hated the collaborative nature of the entertainment business. "When you write you do it yourself," he said of his books. "You produce a hit movie there are sixty people who helped you do it. But to write a book and to have your name on the spine of the book, I'm so proud of that."

Amid the talk of O.J. trivia, egomaniacal producers, and narcissistic actors, Dominick told Berger's dinner guests about a letter he had received from a woman whose daughter was dating John Sweeney, now working as a chef in Seattle. Dominick said he had recently contacted the mother, telling her, "Get your daughter out of that situation as fast as you can. She could end up dead."

"That was Nick's ongoing theme: people who get away with murder," said Berger.

And there were other dinners in Los Angeles where Dominick starred.

*Playboy* editor Lawrence Grobel threw one of the more eclectic parties of the summer. Diane Keaton and crime novelist Elmore Leonard attended, but the two bigger attractions were Dominick and the man who "wrote" O.J. Simpson's recent best seller, *I Want to Tell You*. It was quite a book and Lawrence Schiller was quite a character.

After Simpson's arrest, Schiller had to sneak into jail to interview him for the book. "They needed to raise money for his defense," Schiller recalled. Simpson's close friend Robert Kardashian had come to him, asking for ideas, and Schiller suggested a book based on Simpson's responses to the thousands of letters he received in jail. An automatic best seller, such a tome would help pay Simpson's $50,000-a-day defense bill that included not only the salaries of a dozen lawyers but an attendant team of investigators, forensic scientists, and jury experts. But the book needed to be written and published quickly, before the jury had been sequestered. "Nobody knew I was interviewing O.J. with a tape recorder in jail," said Schiller. He kept the enterprise secret by commuting from a house in the San Fernando Valley, "which nobody knew about," and driving to the jail every day in a different car.

Dominick and David Margolick "didn't know what to think of Schiller at the beginning of the trial," said the *New York Times* reporter. "He hung around" the defense team. Neither journalist knew what he was doing there, and only later did Dominick and Margolick realize Schiller's close access to many of the major players in Simpson's camp. According to Schiller, he soon became one of Dominick and Margolick's major sources.

"I wasn't interested in getting anything out of them; I didn't need anything," Schiller said of his two favorite reporters, "because I was on the inside where everyone wanted to be. The only two people I shared with were David Margolick and Dominick."

On at least one occasion, Schiller did get some payback for all the news he fed Dominick from the inside. Everyone on the defense team hated Simpson's idea to do a pay-per-view interview, rumored to be worth $20 million.

"We were all upset, which is one of the reasons I leaked it to Dominick," said Schiller. "This was a way of making it go away. Dominick could make a big issue out of it." Which he did with great moral outrage in *Vanity Fair*. He wrote how the deal would potentially pay all Simpson's legal bills so he could "restart his life. . . . But I couldn't help thinking to myself, What about Nicole? What about Ron? Do we just forget about them?" And as always, he groused about a defendant spending $50,000 a day to win his acquittal, in essence, rigging the justice system.

As Schiller and the Dream Team had hoped, the Simpson pay-per-view deal never materialized.

Schiller recalled Dominick being in top form at Lawrence Grobel's dinner party. Dominick talked about his concern for a twenty-six-year-old jurist, a flight attendant, who begged to be relieved of duty. "I knew she was flipping out because she never watched the drama that was happening and never took one note," Dominick told Grobel's guests. Judge Ito did not let her off the jury until she "ate a light bulb, she swallowed a bottle of perfume, and she slit her wrists." Even over dinner, guests could count on Dominick never to spare them the graphic details.

"Dominick held court that night," said Schiller. "Everyone wanted to hear Dominick tell his stories, because he could tell them with wit, humor, and irony."

Schiller was less enamored, however, with what Dominick wrote in *Vanity Fair* as the trial progressed. "I wouldn't use the words 'flipping out,'" he said of his friend's mental state. "I felt he was losing some objectivity. There was less clarity. I was concerned. If you look at the stuff he wrote at the beginning of the trial and then at the end, there's a difference."

Dominick and Schiller became friends. Jeffrey Toobin did not. "Schiller specialized in exploiting an arcane and odious corner of the literary marketplace: the purchase of book rights to murderers' life stories," Toobin reported, alluding to book deals Schiller had made with other killers, ranging from Jack Ruby to Gary Gilmore.

Toobin even accused Schiller of leaking "hate-filled tidbits to reporters," such as the Laura Hart McKinny tapes in which Mark Fuhrman uttered the N-word forty-two times. Schiller denied the accusation.

Late in the trial, when Dominick mulled what kind of a book he would write on O.J. Simpson, he considered doing a novel that would be to Los Angeles what *People Like Us* was to New York. He wanted to call his Schiller character Joel Zircon (an agent's name recycled from *The Winners*), someone who worked the courtroom from all angles, who had multiple inside tracks and used everyone against everyone else.

Dominick told Schiller about the Zircon character and how it would be based on him. "I want to put you in the book and I'd like your permission," he said.

"Sure," said Schiller.

"I'm going to call you a double or triple agent in the book."

"Whatever you want to do is fine with me," said Schiller, who had no intention of reading the book.

"We were close," Schiller recalled. "Dominick even came to my engagement party during the trial. That's the level we were on." Schiller may have been friends with a murderer, but when it came to getting access, Dominick never held that liability against a good source.

On August 7 Dominick got word that Alex Dunne was missing. He had been staying with his invalid mother, Lenny, and gone for a hike in the Santa Rita Mountains near her ranch in Nogales, Arizona. Because Alex took no food or water, he had been expected to return home that evening. When he did not, a friend of Lenny's phoned Dominick the next day. Griffin Dunne was already flying to Arizona to be with his mother, who had not yet been told of her younger son's disappearance.

It was not the first time Alex ran into trouble on a hike. Years earlier, he and Griffin had vacationed together in St. Barts, and when Alex wandered into a forest of poisonous manchineel trees, he broke out with a severe rash that led to his being knocked unconscious for hours. It was the last time the two brothers vacationed together.

Dominick's presence so pervaded the media during the last weeks of the Simpson trial that even the disappearance of his son turned into a major news event. CNN did hourly updates, and all major news outlets wanted interviews with Dominick. Griffin told his father to ignore the requests, but Dominick knew better. As a reporter, he felt obliged to co-operate with his colleagues in the Fourth Estate.

After four days in Nogales, Dominick gave up hope that Alex would ever be found alive. Then a severe summer storm hit the mountain range, forcing the search to be called off. Although the torrential rains appeared to be the worst news possible, they saved Alex's life and prevented him from further dehydration. The following day he walked out of the mountain range to safety.

At the hospital, Dominick found his son to be in good shape, although he continued to be dehydrated and suffered minor abrasions and bruises. Dominick was relieved. However, he worried about all the press hoopla and what people would say since his son was not badly hurt. He told friends, "If only he'd broken a leg."

That August, the trial still had a few more weeks to go. Linda Deutsch recalled her colleague's special take on everything. "Dominick looked at everything almost from a cinematic viewpoint," she said. Deutsch remembered the day prosecutor Chris Darden made the mistake of having Simpson try on one of the bloody gloves, a glove having shrunk from its original size. Dominick both marveled and recoiled at the moment when Simpson manipulated the glove so it would not fit. "Did you see that?" Dominick asked her. "He took those gloves like he was running across a football field with the football!" He threw up his hands. "This case is over!"

Dominick spoke those words on June 15, 1995. Somehow, he did not feel the case was over on September 29, when, after more than sixty objections from the defense lawyers, Chris Darden and Marcia Clark ended their rebuttal. Judge Ito ruled that the jury could not begin deliberations that Friday afternoon. They had to wait the weekend, sequestered at the Hotel Intercontinental. Like every other avid observer of the trial, Dominick spent those days pondering the lawyers' summations.

The reporters, however, were not sequestered. On the contrary. They relaxed that weekend in a major way. "We had some great parties," said James Willwerth. "Dominick didn't go to those. I went to all of them." Dominick made one exception. On September 30 he attended a party given by Joe McGinnis at the Hollywood Hills house he rented from songwriter Leslie Bricusse.

Theirs was a tight group. "During the nine months of that trial all the reporters developed the sort of friendships you generally only develop in college living together day in and day out," Dan Abrams noted.

On that final Saturday in September, the Trial of the Century spawned the reporter's Party of the Year when McGinnis and New York *Daily News* reporter Michelle Caruso celebrated the feast of San Gennaro and invited all their friends in the press. They served Italian food, played raucous music, and turned the saint's statue to the wall. Out of friendship with McGinnis, Dominick made an appearance that afternoon but did not stay long. On his way out, he warned the *Newsday* reporter Shirley Perlman, "I'm not sure you want to go in there." He intimated that a few of the forty guests had lost their inhibitions, as well as their clothes, when they jumped from the hot tub to the swimming pool and back. The *New York Post*'s Page Six column got the story, and the only person quoted was Dominick, who never could kick his habit of talking to gossip columnists. Hetero as well as lesbian goings-on were reported, and as Dominick told the *Post*, "Everyone's been to a party where they've gone too far."

No reporter at the pool party expected the jury to reach a fast decision. They could indulge in much more R&R in the coming days. The first interruption to those plans came on Monday, October 2.

At 9:15 a.m., the twelve members of the jury gathered in the deliberation room, a few steps away from Judge Ito's courtroom. The jury had deliberated for only a couple of hours when they asked to rehear the testimony of Allan Park, the chauffeur who picked up Simpson shortly after the murders took place and drove him to the airport for his flight to Chicago. Dominick found hope for a guilty verdict in that the jury asked to hear only Park's testimony. Word then arrived shortly before 3:00 p.m.: the jury had reached a verdict. Judge Ito could have called the jury into the courtroom to read the decision. Instead, he sequestered them one more day, and called for the verdict to be read Tuesday at 10:00 a.m. As Marcia Clark noted, "No one had anticipated this quick turnaround. Not the LAPD. Not the Sheriff's Department. They had to ramp up security in case the verdict lit a torch to the city."

Clark had been shopping when she got the news. Johnnie Cochran was making a speech in San Francisco. At *Vanity Fair*, Wayne Lawson and other staffers had flown to Savannah, Georgia, for a short vacation. They had just closed the November issue when Graydon Carter phoned to let Lawson know the breaking news.

"Wayne, you've got to get Dominick on the phone," Carter said. "I'm holding the issue." Lawson quickly turned the ritziest guest house in Savannah "into an office for about twelve hours."

Three thousand miles away in Los Angeles, it was not easy getting to the courthouse that Tuesday morning. The police banned cars in the vicinity. The hallway outside the courtroom itself was jammed. Jeffrey Toobin reported, "NBC had forty camera crews ready to roll. . . . ABC had assigned four producers to each juror." And when they arrived, Clark and Cochran's respective entourages included at least four guards each.

As usual, Dominick sat between the Goldman family and reporter Shoreen Maghame. He squeezed Kim Goldman's hand but knew not to try to make conversation with her or the family. They were too distraught. Instead, he spoke to Maghame, telling her how certain he was of the jury's decision. They had found Simpson guilty. It upset him, however, that not everyone agreed. That morning, he watched NBC news and listened as Ira Reiner, now a commentator for the network, predicted that Simpson would be acquitted, even though quick decisions by juries generally presage guilty verdicts. The other five talking heads on NBC disagreed with the former L.A. district attorney, and Dominick could not understand how Reiner, a respected friend from the Menendez trial, could be so willfully wrong.

Maghame admitted to Dominick that she did not know how the jury had decided. He then pointed to the reaction of Simpson's son, Jason, sitting nearby and sobbing uncontrollably. Jason knew something they did not. The jury had found his father guilty, Dominick believed.

"It's easy to say now that people knew he was going to be acquitted," said Maghame, looking back at October 3, 1995. "But I don't think that's what people thought at the time. It was really tense leading up to the verdict. Nobody knew how things were going to unfold. Thousands of people were outside the courthouse." The defense lawyers sat right in front of her and Dominick in the courtroom.

"O.J.'s son was sobbing in a puddle, and the verdict hadn't been read yet," Maghame recalled. Then the jury entered the courtroom. She noticed how juror number 6 looked at defense attorney Carl Douglas and "closed his eyes and nodded a little bit." Another defense lawyer, Shawn Chapman, was crying at the time. She and Dominick were sitting so close to Simpson's second tier of lawyers that Maghame could hear Douglas tell Chapman, "Stop crying. We won."

Maghame thought, "Oh my God, holy shit."

When the "not guilty" verdicts were read, "I literally thought Kim Goldman was going to die," said Maghame. Dominick's mouth dropped open; he looked around and then turned to Maghame. "What happened?" he asked weakly.

Maghame realized that Dominick was in a state of shock; it was not registering. She put a hand on his leg. "Dominick, I'm sorry. He was acquitted."

"No, what do you mean?"

"They said not guilty."

"No, no, that's not right."

"He got away with it. Yes, that's what it means."

"What about Fred?" Dominick asked. It was obvious to Maghame that Dominick was reliving the day in court when his daughter's killer received a lesser verdict than second-degree murder.

Dominick heard Kim Goldman say to Simpson, "Murderer." He then looked at juror number 6, Lon Cryer, as he left the jury box, his right hand raised in a fist.

Sitting in his Manhattan apartment, Griffin Dunne saw his father's stunned expression on the TV and began to weep.

Dominick did manage to say good-bye to Simpson's sisters, Carmelita and Shirley, despite his extreme discomfort. Art Harris approached as soon as Dominick left the courtroom. The CNN correspondent wanted him to appear on air to discuss the verdict, but Dominick declined. "I'm not myself," he said. Also, he wanted to go to the prosecution's press conference to hear what Marcia Clark, Chris Darden, and district attorney Gil Garcetti would say.

But Harris pursued, and after a short conversation, Dominick agreed to be interviewed on air. He would always regret the interview. Harris led him to the space reserved for CNN; it was an open-air platform, part of a four-story structure erected to accommodate the widespread international coverage in the trial's final days. Susan Rooks in Washington, DC, conducted the CNN interview and was already on the air with Roger Cossack and Greta Van Susteren. Both interviewees hosted CNN's *Burden of Proof,* a program in which she took the defense's position and he that of the prosecution.

Dominick was not happy to be sharing air time with the pro-defense Van Susteren, even if she was a few thousand miles away in another city. "Greta Van Susteren! She must be thrilled with the news!" he told Harris.

Rooks wasted no time asking Dominick his opinion of the verdict. Despite the crowd being four stories below, it was clear those gathered there agreed with the not-guilty verdict. Dominick did not care. He began the interview by calling the verdict "a disgrace. . . . They just gave the middle finger to justice. They did not even bother to deliberate."

Dominick and Cossack began to argue over the Fuhrman tapes. Dominick thought they played a crucial role in the jury's decision. Cossack did not think they mattered all that much. Van Susteren broke in to say, "The jury has spoken. The jury has given its message to the L.A.P.D."

At which Dominick lost it. "Giving a message to the L.A.P.D. was *not* what the jury's job was in this courtroom!" he shouted. Dominick heard a roar from the crowd below. At first, he thought his comments had sparked a near riot. Then he looked down to the ground to see a group of cops being jeered.

Dominick looked back into the camera. "That's what your message from the jury to the L.A.P.D. is all about," he shouted, then disconnected the mic. "I don't have to take this crap." As he left the makeshift set, a woman who had been watching the CNN program on a monitor taunted him, telling him he should die.

As with almost everyone else in America, Dominick watched the endless playback of the moment in court when the verdict was announced and Kim Goldman sobbed against her father's shoulder and Dominick sat there absolutely dumbfounded, his jaw hanging as if broken. "I look like a small-mouth bass," he later remarked. His friend Joan Ransohoff tried to commiserate. "No, you look like a big-mouth bass," she joked.

A few weeks later in New York, Griffin threw a seventieth birthday party for Dominick. In a toast, he told his father, "I beg you, let this be your last murder trial." Everyone laughed, but Griffin's wish was sincere.

Before Dominick could complete his book on the trial, other titles hit the market, including the best sellers *The Run of His Life*, by Jeffrey Toobin, and *American Tragedy*, by Lawrence Schiller and James Willwerth. Even though Joe McGinnis held a permanent seat in the courtroom, he never wrote a book on the trial "and had to give back his advance," said Schiller. "After the other books, there was nothing left to say."

Which was Dominick's dilemma. Under contract to Crown Publishing to deliver a book on the trial, he suffered more than his usual bouts of writer's block. Ultimately, he decided to resurrect his alter ego reporter from *People Like Us* and have Gus Bailey cover the Simpson trial.

*Another City, Not My Own* would be subtitled *A Novel in the Form of a Memoir*. Dominick had never written anything like it—and neither had anyone else. Dominick was Gus Bailey. He put the words he had spoken into Gus Bailey's mouth. But almost all the other "characters" in the novel, from Marcia Clark to Elizabeth Taylor, were not given fictional names. He called them Marcia Clark, Elizabeth Taylor, Jeffrey Toobin, Lawrence Schiller, and so on. Plus, he used their real quotes. Griffin Dunne said it was all true. The exceptions were his immediate family, whose names were changed to Grafton and Zander. The only major departure from reality was the novel's bizarre ending: Bailey is shot in the face by the serial killer Andrew Cunanan. Dominick said he wanted to kill off the Bailey character "as a way of ridding myself of my obsession with O.J. Simpson, whose evil was in my system." Shortly before Dominick had finished writing the novel, Cunanan murdered the designer Gianni Versace, shooting him in the face.

The reviews for *Another City* were mixed. *Time* magazine called it "thoroughly absorbing" in its name-dropping: "let's be honest: there is something fascinating about hearing Elizabeth Taylor discuss [criminologist] Dennis Fung." The *New York Times*, however, called it "numbing" and its violent finale "preposterous." Dominick suffered that review in silence, but not the pan in the *Los Angeles Times*. He lashed out at the newspaper's book review editor, Steve Wasserman, calling him a "fuckin' liar." In Dominick's opinion, Wasserman purposefully assigned a hostile detractor, Gary Indiana, to write the newspaper's review of *Another City*. The editor defended his choice of reviewers, saying, "I am not aware of any animus toward Dunne on the part of Indiana." Dominick scoffed at Wasserman's defense. Indiana had recently written *Resentment: A Comedy*, a roman à clef in which he cast Dominick as Fawbus Kennedy, John Gregory Dunne as Sean Kennedy, and Joan Didion as Cora Winchell— three famous writers who "can't get through a paragraph without telling you which famous people they know." The novel went on to speculate "what a family dinner with the three of them must be like." Considering the scabrous characters that Dominick based on Claus von Bülow, Jerry Zipkin, Alfred Taubman, and others, what Indiana wrote was mild.

Regardless, Dominick thought his brother's reporter-friend Tim Rutten at the *Times* had intervened and gotten Wasserman to assign Indiana the review, an assumption that failed to take into account how much *Resentment* also lampooned the Didions. Compounding the controversy was Liz Smith, who wrote not one but two columns on the book review, publishing excerpts from Dominick's letter to Wasserman before the editor had actually received the complaint in the mail.

More serious and long-lasting were the problems *Another City* created with Dominick's friends Wendy and Ray Stark. Despite his novel's gossipy style, Dominick had always avoided the Truman Capote curse of revealing the true secrets of good friends. In *Another City*, he did Capote one better and made up secrets about good friends, namely the Starks, and referred to them as "the Starks." In the book's fictitious finale, Gus Bailey is shot by

Andrew Cunanan, whom he first meets as a guest of Ray Stark the night the producer throws a party honoring Marcia Clark.

The fallout from Stark landed hard on Dominick. He told friends of the film producer's anger, and how he accused him, "You put a murderer at my table!" Wendy Stark joined with her father, and for the first time in their long friendship she stopped speaking to Dominick.

"Nick used real names," she recalled. "My daughter was in elementary school, and all of a sudden Nick writes that Andrew Cunanan was at our house! The school parents thought I was this racy mother sending my daughter to a conservative school. I was upset. Andrew Cunanan was never at our house, but people didn't know the difference."

Wendy Stark sympathized with Dominick's dilemma but only a little, saying, "Nick couldn't find an ending for the story so he used our house as a setting." She thought he should have titled the novel *Another Ending, Not My Own*.

Others were not happy but kept it to themselves. While Dominick contacted many people to secure their permission to use direct quotes, one of those people was not Patti Jo Fairbanks. The D.A.'s senior legal assistant was shocked to see her words about Nicole Brown Simpson's family appear in print in *Another City*: "You know, a double homicide doesn't make a dysfunctional family functional."

She thought of phoning Dominick to complain. Then she remembered his response whenever anyone got upset about one of his articles in *Vanity Fair*. Dominick used to say, "They'll have to get over it!"

Fairbanks told herself, "I'll just have to get over it."

Also voicing problems with *Another City, Not My Own* was a coauthor of *American Tragedy*. The book, written by Lawrence Schiller and James Willwerth, broke the news that the Dream Team had "staged" the Simpson estate before jurors were given a tour of the house. Photographs of blacks took the place of whites, among other ethnic embellishments of radical interior redesign. "Dominick presented that as his research," said Willwerth, who complained to Schiller, who told his coauthor he did not care.

Dominick considered *Another City, Not My Own* one of his weaker efforts. He wanted to return to writing a real novel, not a fictionalized memoir. In that endeavor he was encouraged by a visiting professor at UCLA. After the usual letter and e-mail introductions, they met at the Hamburger Hamlet on Sunset Boulevard in West Hollywood. The restaurant catered to geriatric celebrities who were no longer frequently recognized, and Dominick's choice of the Hamlet, rather than Cicada or Mortons, summed up his expectations on what would come of this meeting in academe.

Dominick never considered himself a great novelist. He always told people he was no Truman Capote. He liked to quote W. Somerset Maugham, who put himself at the top of the "second echelon" of writers. Dominick readily admitted, "I'm very aware that I'm more a popular success than a literary success."

Despite such an admission, Dr. Robert von Dassanowsky saw considerable literary value in what Dominick wrote, and his request for an interview flattered him. It was not every day that a college professor and scholar wanted to take his novels seriously as feminist tracts, of all things.

The lunch was typical of most Dominick had in one major way. He enjoyed getting up from the table to launch into celebrity greetings. That afternoon he saw Broadway star Carol Channing, and after she and Dominick finished complimenting each other, Dassanowsky set forth his proposal over hamburgers and french fries. "Someone should write a book about your novels," said the professor, who wanted to write just such a tome.

"No, it's not that kind of work," said Dominick.

"No, it's valid. It will happen soon. Your work does cross over into social chronicling."

Dominick thanked Dassanowsky for his very positive review of *A Season in Purgatory* in *LA Weekly*, in which the novel was favorably compared to Evelyn Waugh's *Brideshead Revisited*. Just as Waugh's narrator Charles Ryder goes from loving Lord Sebastian Flyte to loving his sister, Julia, so Dominick's Harrison Burns falls in love with Constant Bradley and later his sister, Kit.

The professor meant the comparison as a compliment but was not sure Dominick took it as such. "He was afraid of it," said Dassanowsky. "On one level, Dominick was happy because it gave him literary credential. On the other, he didn't want someone saying he's stealing from Waugh. I knew it was a little of both."

Dominick expected his lunch date to ask about the real identities of his fictional characters, how Jules Mendelson was based on Alfred S. Bloomingdale, and so on. Dassanowsky knew not to go there. Instead, they talked about the disappointment of his collaborations with his brother and sister-in-law on *The Panic in Needle Park* and *Play It as It Lays*.

"He had been writing with his brother, but then he was pushed back into the producer's role. There was hurt there," said Dassanowsky. "He couldn't get beyond that. In the end, he detached himself from the script; his work wasn't needed or wanted. His brother was the writer."

But mostly, the two men talked about Dominick's female characters and how they were "injured by the patriarchy; it is the only life they know and they die from it," Dassanowsky noted. "His wife, Lenny, became a model for that, this idealization he creates, these monuments to women who get crushed by society. He identified with that: someone who doesn't fit in and feels too much and trusts too much, and gets kicked in the teeth."

Dassanowsky gave no empty praise to Dominick. Eventually, he went on to write not a book but a long article, titled "The Inconvenient Women: Female Consciousness and the American Gentry in the Novels of Dominick Dunne," for *Popular Culture Review*. He did more than toss around a few feminist tropes. He used the French psychoanalyst Jacques Lacan's theories to analyze Alice and Ann Grenville, portraying them not as women "but an idealized fantasy fulfillment of masculine desire. Women internalize male desire and are thus used to adapting to roles that further the patriarchy."

Dassanowsky also used the analytical framework of Elaine Showalter, a founder of feminist literary criticism, to chart the three phases of growth in Dominick's female characters, taking Flo March and Pauline Mendelson in *An Inconvenient Woman* from their initiation into (1) the "prevailing modes of male-dominant tradition" to (2) "protest" to (3) "a search for identity."

Finally, Dominick had been taken seriously as a writer, even if he did not believe every word of the esteemed professor's praise.

# 14

## Skakels and Wills

Shortly before the publication of *Another City, Not My Own*, CBS aired its new miniseries *A Season in Purgatory*. "It aroused public interest in the case, and the paperback went back onto the best-seller list," said the show's producer Buzz Berger.

The TV adaptation of *A Season in Purgatory* in 1996 also brought to light one crucial piece of evidence that reinvigorated Dominick's interest in the case. After the show aired on CBS, he received a message at the *Vanity Fair* offices about the Moxley murder.

Dominick never shrugged off such tips, even though many of them turned out to be from cranks and crazies. In this case, he did not just return the phone call. He set up a lunch with the caller at no less a restaurant than Patroon on East Forty-Sixth Street. Jamie Bryan was not what Dominick expected when the young man arrived for their lunch meeting. He looked about eighteen years old and was not attired for such a tony boîte. Bryan wore jeans and a T-shirt, which, among other things, made it an awkward lunch for Dominick. People kept giving the odd couple questioning glances.

Bryan had in his possession the Sutton report, commissioned by Rushton Skakel to exonerate his two sons of any wrongdoing. The young man feared being exposed but took the chance with Dominick because he did not want the report to go unread. Maybe Bryan also wanted to write for *Vanity Fair*, and this was his chance. He had ambitions to be a writer. In a way, he already was one, which is why he had the Sutton report. Surprisingly, Sutton Associates never required Bryan to sign a confiden-tiality agreement even though his job as staff writer involved taking the detectives' findings and writing up a likely scenario of how the Moxley murder took place. His conclusion: Michael Skakel had committed the murder.

Dominick worried about receiving purloined material from a boy in jeans and a T-shirt. Little did he know over lunch at Patroon that the report solved the case; at least it solved it for Dominick.

Bryan thought he had made it clear to his Patroon lunch date that his superiors at Sutton Associates called it a "speculative report." Dominick, however, did not see the report as speculation; to him it was all fact. He would later send a letter of apology to Bryan, saying he did not recall any conversation about the report being anything but completely factual.

Dominick always believed he held a bombshell in his hands with the report. He phoned Dorthy Moxley. The call took place late in 1996, and it was not one of his friendly "how are you?" calls. It was urgent. "Dorthy, I know who killed Martha!" he exclaimed.

"I was dumbfounded," Dorthy Moxley recalled. Dominick told her about Jamie Bryan—"don't tell anyone his name"—and that he had given him the Sutton report, commissioned by Rushton Skakel and now suppressed by him. "I haven't read it," Dominick said, "but I'll call you as soon as I have a chance to read it. Don't tell anybody."

"OK, I won't," she promised.

But Dorthy Moxley got "antsy." She phoned Dominick the next day. Again, he told her he hadn't read the report because "I have this huge mess. I left the faucet running in the kitchen and everything is flooded. I'll have to get back to you." He said he would read it as soon as possible but would also have to return it to Bryan right away.

Dominick came to think of his solving the Martha Moxley murder as a selfless cause. "My only motivation in this has been Mrs. Moxley," he said. "No one understands the pain she's experienced like I do."

Dorthy Moxley saw the matter in a somewhat different light. Thinking back on their brief back-to-back phone conversations in late 1996, she surmised, "Dominick wasn't being nice. He did not send back the report. He had a huge ego. He wanted to help. I knew he was concerned, but it had to be Dominick first."

Dorthy reread Len Levitt's newspaper article on the case in which he mentioned Sutton Associates, but nowhere did he write anything about Michael being the killer. "Len didn't have all that in the article," she said.

A few more days passed. She did not want to phone Dominick again; instead, Dorthy called Levitt. She told him that Dominick had the Sutton report, and, according to him, it proved who killed her daughter.

"Leave it to me; I'll find out," said Levitt, who immediately phoned Dominick, who immediately phoned Dorthy to "castigate me," she said.

"We didn't talk for a couple of years," said Dorthy.

It was the same with Len Levitt. "Dominick and I didn't talk for two years," said Levitt, who, at the time, feared he might have missed something crucial in the report. Dominick, however, refused to show him the report so it could be restudied.

Detective Frank Garr was different. Garr wore a badge, and when he demanded to see the Sutton report, Dominick did as ordered. Garr later told Levitt, "I first heard about [the report] from Dorthy. She calls me at home on a Saturday and tells me Dominick has it and Len Levitt knows about it. It was one of the few times I was upset with her. No, I was furious. I mean, what good does Dominick Dunne or Len Levitt having the report do? Are they going to make an arrest? Why hasn't anyone told me? So I called Dominick and he gave it to me. But there was nothing in it. It was all theories and speculation."

Dominick vehemently disagreed with Garr on that point and, feeling dismissed by the detective, he toyed with giving the report to another reporter. He had recently met with Timothy Dumas, who planned to write a nonfiction book on the murder. Dumas grew up in Greenwich, born only a year after Martha Moxley. Dominick told the young reporter he would help him with his book in any way possible. Except one. In the end, Dominick had other plans for the Sutton report, plans that would not only incense Frank Garr but punish the detective for having chastised him.

It was not difficult finding Mark Fuhrman. The disgraced detective had signed with the agent Lucianne Goldberg, who sold Fuhrman's first book, *Murder in Brentwood*. He was now looking to solve another murder for his follow-up book. "Nick always thought Mark got a raw deal on the O.J. trial," said Goldberg. It was only natural for the agent to ask her *Vanity Fair* friend, who specialized in notable murders, if he knew of any good unsolved cases for her client to investigate.

Even before *Murder in Brentwood* hit the best-seller lists in late 1997, Goldberg arranged for the two men to meet at perhaps the most conspicuous spot in all of New York City. The timing could not have been better for a high-profile lunch at the Four Seasons. Crushed by his round of phone calls with Len Levitt and Frank Garr, Dominick decided to side with Fuhrman to tell him all he knew about the Moxley murder. "Hey,

Mark, I've got just the one for you, and I have a private detective report that's going to knock you on your ass," he said.

Levitt tried to remain in touch, but at this point Dominick responded to the newspaper reporter only by fax. Among other disputes, he believed Levitt had exposed Jamie Bryan to his superiors at Sutton Associates. Dominick sent a fax to the reporter: "After you heard from Dorthy Moxley that I had a copy of the Sutton Report, you called your friend at Sutton Associates to tell him that a young man working for him had given a copy of the report to me. The young man had performed a decent act and your call to his boss put him into a state of abject fear for which I felt a responsibility. I knew then I would never give the report to you."

Dominick's fax also revealed his deep disappointment with the Connecticut detective on the case: "In time I gave a copy to Frank Garr. . . . That was a total waste of time." In the fax, Dominick went on to reveal why he had given the Sutton report to Fuhrman: "To give this report to Mark was a calculated decision and a brilliant one if I say so myself. It has nothing to do with the fact that I knew him from the O.J. Simpson case. It had everything to do with the fact that he is both famous and infamous, and I knew that he would get on every television show on network and cable and tell the story of Martha Moxley over and over and over, until it finally began to sink in. . . . Whatever you think of Mark, he's a star. . . . By the way, his publisher would only make the deal on the condition that I write the introduction. . . . I was paid nothing and I'm a very high-priced author."

Levitt described how he felt reading Dominick's fax: "I felt as though a giant wave had knocked us down then rolled over us."

Garr put it more succinctly: "Writers, they're all the same."

Dominick enjoyed the hurly-burly of putting himself at the center of a murder investigation. He also needed the work more than ever—not for the money but the distraction. In the previous decade, Lenny Dunne had sold her house in Beverly Hills and was now living on her family ranch in Arizona. Alex often stayed with his mother, since her condition had continued to deteriorate seriously. "Griffin took care of my father like I took care of our mother," said Alex. Years earlier, he had asked a neurologist, "What is the best thing I can do for my mother right now?" The doctor leaned back in his chair and said, "If I had Dr. Kervorkian's phone number, I'd give it to you."

Dominick visited Lenny at Christmastime in 1996. Bedridden, she could no longer speak without great difficulty and required six nurses to care for her around the clock. Sitting beside her, he thought about all the lies he had told. "I'm sorry, Lenny," Dominick said. "You know, Lenny, I always loved you no matter what." He believed he was not good enough, he was not worthy. She was the real thing; he was a fake. To keep her company, he reminisced about their old friends in Los Angeles and gave her the latest news. "Do you remember the Starks? Now they've moved," he said.

Griffin remembered his father being by his mother's side near the end. She enjoyed listening to his news and gossip, which had not always been the case when they were husband and wife. Ellen Griffin Dunne passed away at the nearby Holy Cross Hospital on January 9, 1997. The family asked in lieu of flowers for donations to be made to Justice for Homicide Victims, the organization she founded in the previous decade.

Dominick always asked Alex to do nothing rash until Lenny passed away. Father and son never spoke the name of the man who had murdered Dominique, and Alex observed that moratorium even in the latest fight with his father. Suffering from what he described as "mental health issues," Alex berated Dominick, much as he had in a San Francisco restaurant more than ten years ago. This time was different, however. He put his thoughts in a letter. Dominick believed what triggered the new confrontation was an article on depression that he had clipped from the *Wall Street Journal* and mailed to his son. Faced with this new flare-up, Dominick could only wonder again what he had done as a father to provoke such anger. He could not, however, overlook Alex's demand to be disinherited. If he were not written out of his father's will, Alex vowed to give any money Dominick left him to the man who had murdered Dominique. Dominick did as ordered and wrote up a new will. He disinherited his younger son but made sure to attach his son's written demand to the new will. He did not want anyone ever to think he had made such a decision on his own volition.

# 15

## Fuhrman and Libel

With Dominick's full support, Mark Fuhrman came to Greenwich, Connecticut, to start research on his next book. It did not begin well.

He met with Len Levitt, who lost no time telling him he would write a damning article for *Newsday* about Dominick giving Fuhrman the Sutton report. End of conversation. Fuhrman next phoned Frank Garr, offering to take him to lunch. When Garr refused to meet, Fuhrman said, "I never heard of a cop who turned down a free meal." End of conversation.

Before Fuhrman tried to contact Dorthy Moxley, Dominick thought it best that he place a call to the victim's mother. The detective, obviously, needed some help.

Dominick's phone call came "out of the blue," said Dorthy. It was as if they had never stopped talking, even though they had not spoken for several months. He sounded very upbeat, telling her, "Somebody wants to write a book and solve the case. Would you be willing to solve the case?"

Dorthy did not hold grudges. "I'll talk to anyone," she said.

"You'll be surprised who it is. It's Mark Fuhrman."

Dorthy Moxley took a deep breath before saying she would cooperate with the infamous detective. But later, when speaking to Fuhrman, she put forth one major request: "Please contact the police." Fuhrman's lousy relationship with the police would come to haunt her, "because it made it awkward for me," she recalled.

Dominick was not the only one who found Fuhrman an extremely attractive man. Dorthy Moxley called him "very handsome, a charismatic person, and he was definitely a wonderful detective." He impressed her as soon as they met. But when Fuhrman pressed Dorthy to phone Frank Garr to help facilitate a rapprochement, Garr was not happy. He told her, "Mrs. Moxley, don't ever do that to me again."

Finally, it came down to Dominick to make the introductions at a cocktail party he hosted. As he wrote in *Vanity Fair*, "I invited several local cops and their wives, as well as some O.J. junkies among the weekenders who wanted to meet the famous—or infamous—Mark Fuhrman. I also called to invite Frank Garr, thinking he would be thrilled that another book on the case was in the works. He wasn't thrilled at all."

Len Levitt understood Frank Garr's position. "Why would Garr want to talk to a convicted perjurer?" asked Levitt. At the time, Garr had already heard the rumor, emanating from Dominick, that Fuhrman would name Michael Skakel as the killer. Garr did not need the pressure, even though he came to the same conclusion back in 1992. Unlike Fuhrman, he must put together a case that would convince a grand jury to indict, not just sell a few thousand books.

Fuhrman cultivated a loyal supporter in Dominick, and through him the L.A. detective got to an assistant state's attorney who would eventually be a prosecutor at the Skakel trial.

Chris Morano received frequent phone calls from Dominick during the O.J. Simpson trial. They knew each other through mutual friends in Hartford, Connecticut, and Dominick wanted Morano's opinion of Dr. Henry Lee, a forensics expert testifying for the Simpson defense. "Dr. Lee was running the crime lab in Connecticut at the time," Morano recalled, "and Nick would bounce ideas off me. After the O.J. trial, he was not a fan of Lee." (Lee, in his testimony, cast doubt on the splash pattern of droplets of Simpson's blood at his Rockingham estate. Lee also raised the possibility of there being a second shoe print at the crime scene, a pattern later verified to be trowel marks left in the cement walkway leading to Nicole Brown Simpson's condo.)

While Levitt and Garr refused to see him, Fuhrman had better luck with Dominick's friend Chris Morano. The two men met in a parking lot in Essex, Connecticut. They were not alone. Fuhrman brought his cowriter, Steven Weeks, and Morano "brought a person I trusted. We both had echo people there." Morano was skeptical, but after three hours of interviewing Fuhrman, he realized the detective was a good one and "he'd done a lot to look into" the Moxley murder.

Sometime during their first meeting, Fuhrman asked, "Where can we get a beer around here?" Morano took him to a local watering hole, where the bartender asked the obligatory "What can I get you?"

"I'll have a rum and coke," replied Morano, "and this guy will have a glass of O.J." For a moment, Morano thought he had crossed a line, and probably he did. But, not wanting to alienate one of the few law enforcers in Connecticut who would talk to him, Fuhrman laughed at the joke—after a brief pause. "Humility is the opiate of the mediocre," Morano surmised. "Mark had a big ego. He knew he was good." But he was also eager to get along with Morano; he even answered questions about the N-word controversy. "They spent a quarter-million dollars to get dirt on me from this [film] script," Fuhrman explained, referring to Laura Hart McKinny's tapes.

The conversation between Fuhrman and Morano eventually got around to the Sutton report. Fuhrman had studied it and connected the dots: Michael Skakel murdered Martha Moxley, he believed. The two men agreed to stay in touch but may not have spoken again if not for Dominick and "his relationships with people" in New England, said Morano.

One morning, Michael Skakel made the mistake of being a good Connecticut citizen. Finding a pocketbook by the side of the road, he walked it into a state trooper's office to give the lost item to the authorities. "I have to fill out a report," a trooper told him. "What's your name?"

"Michael Skakel."

Skakel did not leave it there. He went on to reveal not only his Kennedy lineage but his plans to write a tell-all book about the famous clan. The trooper listened, filled out the report, and waited for Skakel to leave the station. Then he phoned his friend in Hadlyme, Connecticut.

"Dominick could really sit down and talk to anybody and make friends," said Morano, and one of his unlikely friends was this state trooper.

The trooper told Dominick, "Nick, Michael Skakel's writing a book!"

Dominick, in turn, phoned Morano, who phoned Fuhrman, who already had in his possession the Skakel book proposal. The two men met again, this time in New York City. The book proposal was only five pages, but it contained a section titled "Murder Most Foul," in which Skakel wrote about the murder of Martha Moxley. Morano knew not to take the proposal from Fuhrman.

"With the O.J. trial, there's a whole perjury thing with Fuhrman, and the last thing I want is for Mark Fuhrman on the stand in our case," said Morano. Instead, he wrote down the name of Skakel's ghostwriter, Richard Hoffman, and immediately contacted him. He used a ruse to lure Hoffman: "Hi, this is Joe Schmoe with the Rotary Club, and we'd like you to talk about your book."

Hoffman fell for it, and investigators were able to secure a taped interview the writer did with Skakel, conducted for their book proposal, which included a thirty-minute talk on the murder. Skakel did not admit to the crime, but the story he told Hoffman was a little different from what he had said previously. "The story now has changed three times, which is very helpful," said Morano. "Dominick and Fuhrman were instrumental in getting [us] that key piece of evidence."

In the taped interview with Hoffman, Skakel tried to cast suspicions on the tutor Ken Littleton, but, more significant, his story about what happened the night of the murder changed yet again. In this third version, Michael revealed not only his masturbating but another telling detail: after the peeping-tom scene outside Martha's bedroom window, Michael returned to the Skakel house, where he walked by his sister's bedroom. Julie Skakel was asleep, but Michael somehow knew that her friend Andrea Shakespeare had been there and left to go home. "But how would he have known that?" asked Morano. "[Shakespeare] had gone home when he was not there. He knew something that he should not have known."

The night of the Moxley murder, when Julie Skakel walked Andrea Shakespeare to her car, a figure in the shadows ran in front of them. "Michael, what are you doing?" asked Shakespeare. Her question was damning: Michael's alibi had always been that he was not there, that he had spent the evening at a friend's house, the Terriens'.

Shakespeare's "Michael, what are you doing?" became so crucial to the prosecution's case that Morano and the other prosecutors kept it secret until their final rebuttal before the jury.

Dominick continued to show an uncommon dedication to Mark Fuhrman, especially when Timothy Dumas asked for a copy of the Sutton report "to even the playing field." Dominick had no interest in helping a competitor. The Sutton report, he believed, belonged to his good friend Fuhrman.

When Dominick traveled to London, he even lent the detective his New York apartment so he could work on *Murder in Greenwich*. Friends could only imagine the hyperbutch Fuhrman ensconced in Dominick's chintz-laden abode with its French antiques and mint green walls.

Lucianne Goldberg observed her phone mate's infatuation. "Nick was crazy about Fuhrman," she said, "wild about Fuhrman," to the point of obsession, not unlike his attraction to Frederick Combs. In London, Dominick made repeated transatlantic phone calls to Goldberg about his new apartment guest. Even long distance, taking care of Mark Fuhrman's every need became a top priority for Dominick, and that included what deli in the neighborhood would deliver the best food to his East Forty-Ninth Street apartment.

"The guy's name at the deli is Harry," Dominick told Goldberg. "And tell Mark to say he's Dominick Dunne's friend and he's a personal friend."

Two days later, Goldberg got another call from Dominick. "Did you tell Mark about the guy at the deli, Harry?"

"Yeah, I told him," she replied. The agent could only wonder how much more pastrami Harry would pack in a sandwich if Fuhrman mentioned the name Dominick Dunne.

Goldberg called the two men "tight friends for a long time, and Nick wanted to defend Fuhrman anyway he could. He was always Mark's defender." Dominick's care, however, went far beyond supporting the detective. "Nick had a death-like crush on Mark," said Goldberg.

The agent was not the only one who noted Dominick's new, deep infatuation. Leading up to the Michael Skakel trial, Norman Carby saw how photographs of Fuhrman began appearing all over his boyfriend's Manhattan apartment.

The "Harry at the deli" phone calls were some of Dominick and Goldberg's last friendly chats. In autumn 1997 she confided in him about an intern having oral sex with Bill Clinton in the Oval Office. "Nick knew about Monica Lewinsky three months before the story broke," said Goldberg, who knew all about it. She had advised Lewinsky's friend Linda Tripp to tape phone conversations with the intern, tapes that Tripp eventually turned over to Kenneth Starr, the independent counsel investigating Clinton on Whitewater and other controversies. Dominick was on his way back from London when, instead of a phone call, he sent a fax to Goldberg. It read: "You're so famous I'm afraid to talk to you." Later, they did speak on the phone. A staunch Bill Clinton supporter, Dominick could not believe the Lewinsky scandal. "Is there anything I ever told you that wasn't true?" Goldberg replied. Dominick told her he had seen Vernon Jordan a few weeks ago at the Four Seasons and was going to mention something about Monica Lewinsky to the Clinton adviser. "Now I'm glad I didn't," said Dominick. "I don't want to get involved with it." (To head off the scandal, Jordan had tried to get Lewinsky a job outside the White House.)

William Morrow and Company published Mark Fuhrman's *Murder in Greenwich: Who Killed Martha Moxley* in May 1998, after the detective had spent less than a year investigating the case. He named Michael Skakel the killer and Frank Garr the chief bungler of the investigation. Fuhrman wrote, "Dominick Dunne gave Frank Garr a copy of the Sutton Associates files in the winter of 1997. Yet apparently Frank had talked to hardly any of the people I interviewed whose names I got from the files."

Writing for *Vanity Fair*, Dominick gave Fuhrman full credit for solving the murder: "I firmly believe that his book, *Murder in Greenwich*, for which I wrote the introduction, is what caused a grand jury to be called after twenty-five years."

The timeline supported Dominick's assumption but only superficially. Although Fuhrman's book was not officially published until May 1998, advance copies had been available weeks before as Fuhrman hit the TV circuit to do prepublication publicity. Since the grand jury was called in May, it appeared that the chief state's attorney, Jonathan Benedict, was playing catch up. Writing a book is one thing; trying a case before the grand jury is another. In the Moxley case, the grand jury stayed in session for eight months, with over fifty witnesses called. In January 2000 Benedict held a news conference to announce that the grand jury had probable cause to indict Michael Skakel in the murder of Martha Moxley.

Before the trial began, Dominick saw Michael Skakel's attorney at the coffee shop in the Beverly Hills Hotel. Despite his belief in Skakel's guilt, he gave Mickey Sherman a tip. "It was helpful for the Skakel trial," Sherman recalled. "Dominick told me one of the investigators had a book deal, which [Frank Garr] denied on the stand. He wrote it with ghostwriter Len Levitt."

Dominick's tip to Sherman was nearly as inaccurate as the big scoop he had for Laura Ingraham. He told the conservative radio host about what he believed was Congressman Gary Condit's involvement with the disappearance of a twenty-five-year-old intern named Chandra Levy. Those revelations to Ingraham and Sherman made Dominick two for two and wrong on both counts: no Arab threw Chandra Levy out of an airplane over the Atlantic Ocean, and Frank Garr never coauthored a book with Len Levitt. Because Levitt's book *Conviction: Solving the Martha Moxley Murder* came out two years after Mickey Sherman's confrontation with Frank Garr on the witness stand, people had forgotten the courtroom exchange. While Garr was quoted in the book, Levitt wrote *Conviction* alone.

The inaccurate story regarding Chandra Levy was much more exposed, not to mention even more preposterously false. People remembered what Dominick said, and those people included Gary Condit. Dominick told his tale on *Larry King Live*, as well as at various lunches and dinner parties. But he reserved his most detailed account for the *Laura Ingraham Show*. Ingraham was an odd choice. Dominick did not care for the radio host's conservative politics, but they had met recently at the Ritz Hotel in Paris and he found her engaging. "We always have a few laughs together," he noted. When they saw each other again in New York at the Carlyle and she took him to lunch at Patroon, he could not help but share some political dirt: a man who claimed to be a "horse whisperer" had phoned him with an incredible story. Ingraham thought it such a great story she wanted Dominick to repeat it on her radio program. He agreed, even though he wondered, Who listened to Laura Ingraham, anyway?

"Now, some of this I can't explain, and I don't want to get into any trouble," Dominick's radio interview began, "but according to what the procurer told the horse whisperer who told me, is that Gary Condit was often a guest at some of the Middle Eastern embassies in Washington where all these ladies were, and that he had let it be known that he was in a relationship with a woman that was over, but she was a clinger. He couldn't get rid of her. And he had made promises to her that he couldn't keep and apparently she knew things about him and had threatened to go public. And at one point, he said, 'This woman is driving me crazy,' or words to that effect. And I wrote all this down at the time. And what the horse whisperer said the procurer said is, by saying that, [Condit] created the environment that led to her disappearance. And she shortly thereafter vanished."

Dominick told less elaborate versions of his Condit/Levy story at dinner parties where the guests included his close friends Casey Ribikoff, Liz Smith, Cynthia McFadden, and Henry Grunwald. It was Grunwald, a former *Time* magazine editor, who told him he must contact the FBI, which Dominick did.

"He had much to say at dinner parties," said Liz Smith. "I think he sort of went around the bend after the O.J. trial. I thought he took a lot of chances."

Dominick told the Condit/Levy story overseas as well. Edmund White, author of *The Farewell Symphony* and other autobiographical novels, met Dominick in London through a mutual friend. At the time, Marguerite Littman was working with the Elton John and Princess Diana foundations to consolidate their various AIDS charities. The American socialite had many stories to tell about the two famous Brits, and White wanted to hear every tidbit. "Dominick, however, wasn't interested," White recalled. "He kept telling us he had this big scoop. But the names Chandra Levy and Gary Condit didn't mean anything to us. Marguerite and I didn't care. Dominick got upset."

Even before police found Chandra Levy's skeletal remains in a Washington, DC, park, Gary Condit hit Dominick with a lawsuit for libel.

Dominick apologized publicly and profusely, admitting he had fallen for the story "hook, line, and sinker. I sounded like a fool. A horse whisperer? The laughs they got over the horse whisperer," he said.

His reputation as a journalist took a serious hit. "He was totally freaked out by it. It made him crazy," said Dan Abrams. "He knew he made a mistake. He felt ashamed."

Condit, of course, wanted more than an apology from Dominick. "He went on the air and called me a murderer and said I had something to do with the kidnapping, that I plotted the kidnapping," said the congressman from California.

Before the Condit controversy broke, filmmaker Barry Avrich had just finished making a documentary on Dominick's career. At the beginning of their collaboration, Dominick loved the idea of having his story put on film. To get acquainted, he invited Avrich to his Connecticut house. "I have something to show you," he said and took the filmmaker to his office. Dominick removed some files of photographs from a cabinet.

Avrich tried not to appear shocked or sickened. "They were the autopsy and crime scene photos of Ron Goldman and Nicole Brown Simpson. They were ghastly, like nothing I'd ever seen," Avrich remembered. If Dominick nearly fainted in 1995 when he first saw these photographs in the Los Angeles courthouse, he had fully recovered from any trauma by the time he showed them to Avrich in the safety of his office. (Other guests to his Connecticut house, including producer Martin Ransohoff and his wife, Joan, were also shown the Goldman/Simpson photographs.) Dominick kept a collection of other notable photographs as well. They included the shirtless photo of a young Erik Menendez taken by Philip Kearney. "He could be a Calvin Klein model," said Dominick, who went on to tell the filmmaker that he had recently written a letter to Erik in prison requesting an interview. He had read Erik's many unproduced screenplays, written before the two sons committed parricide, and praised his talent as a writer. In the letter, he also confessed to Erik "how often you come to my mind." Dominick told Avrich, "I don't know why, but I was captivated by him."

After their photo-viewing session, the two men began to hit some bumps in their working relationship. "Dominick complained about all sorts of little things," said Avrich. "He complained about someone being in his line of sight. The food we catered he didn't like. Then he ate everything." Much more upsetting to Dominick was Avrich's wish to interview Mark Fuhrman for the film. "He had some issue with Fuhrman," said Avrich. Dominick also hated the documentary's title, *Guilty Pleasure*, which he found tacky. Finally, he demanded that Avrich not include an interview with defense attorney Edward Greenspan, who voiced strong objections to Dominick's brand of advocacy journalism. "Remove it or I'm not coming to the screening!" said Dominick. Since a celebrity-filled preview had been planned for later in the week, it was not a mild threat. When Avrich refused to re-edit the film, Dominick showed up at the screening two days later as if never having voiced any objection.

On one major point, however, Dominick got his way. To promote the film, he had been booked to appear on *Larry King Live*, but just then Gary Condit filed his lawsuit. "I can't do it," said Dominick, who broke out in hives from the stress.

Avrich needed the publicity for his film. He told Dominick that he would talk to King and get him to agree not to ask about Condit. Dominick knew better. "Larry wouldn't be doing his job if he didn't ask about it," said Dominick.

Almost worse than the lawsuit was the rupture it created for Dominick at *Vanity Fair*. Confusion immediately arose over what Graydon Carter did or did not tell Dominick regarding the lawsuit. Even though he had not made the false claim about Condit in the pages of *Vanity Fair*, Dominick believed that Carter had assured him his legal costs would be covered by the magazine. In the immediate wake of the lawsuit, there had been a phone conversation between the editor and S. I. Newhouse, who owned Condé Nast, the magazine's publisher. In many conversations and letters with his friends, Dominick repeated what he firmly believed Carter told him: "We're going to take care of your legal bills. I talked to Si in Vienna this morning and he said he'd take care of it." According to Dominick, Carter went on to say that because Condé Nast was not being sued, the company could not pay for the legal expenses or the possible settlement, if there was one. However, Dominick would receive a bonus at the end of the year.

Owen Laster, Dominick's agent, wrote letters to Carter asking him to put in writing that *Vanity Fair* would "indemnify" his client. Carter refused to comply and soon became incensed with Laster's badgering. Later, Dominick went around Laster to write a letter to the head of the William Morris Agency, asking Jim Wiatt to intervene. That ploy did not sit well with Carter or Laster. Dominick never was the most discreet negotiator. Angered at *Vanity Fair*, he even went so far as to write a pitch letter offering his writing services to editor Anna Wintour at *Vogue*, also published by Condé Nast.

"Later, Graydon said he hadn't said it," Dominick recalled. He wanted to settle with Condit. He feared being poor again. Dominick told friends that Carter told him not to settle. In covering the controversy, *New York* magazine featured an interview with the *Vanity Fair* editor. Chris Smith wrote how Graydon Carter "shrugs off the Condit case." Carter went on to tell Smith, "We've had huge lawsuits. We fought Mohamed Al-Fayed for three years and beat him. I told Nick, 'Let's take this to court, let's fight it all the way. It will be like a scene out of a Frank Capra movie, in the end. Grow your beard long and you'll look like Saint Nicholas when you get into the courtroom, like Edmund Gwenn in *Miracle on 34th Street*. There'll be bags of mail.' Gary Condit has got a nerve to do this."

Dominick's friends and family took his side in the controversy when they saw the effect of *Vanity Fair*'s "let's fight it all the way" stance. "Dominick Dunne made *Vanity Fair*," said Jesse Kornbluth, who left the magazine shortly after Graydon Carter replaced Tina Brown.

Another Brown acolyte also empathized with Dominick's predicament. "When you get mad at a family member, there was that kind of hurt Dominick felt," said Kevin Sessums. "He and I identified as *Vanity Fair* writers; our names were on the cover all the time. We were in the office, at the parties. You began to think of it as the *Mary Tyler Moore Show*. It's this ersatz family that takes over your life. It's hard to cop to it when you realize it ain't your family. It's a job. He was slowly being pushed aside. The cancer also scared him."

Dominick's recent ill-health indeed exacerbated the ordeal. "I've had prostate cancer," he said. "I don't want to tie up my creative period; the days are getting thin." Dominick later wrote, "Rudolph Giuliani had better luck with his radiation than I did. Mine turned out to be a disaster. I got over-radiated in a private area and suffered terrible pain—three weeks of it. They don't warn you about the pain."

Regardless of the extreme physical suffering, the treatments worked. They rid him of the cancer. But Kevin Sessums was right. The cancer scared him, and it also scared him that the Condit lawsuit could decimate his hard-earned reputation and wealth. A couple of years earlier, before the cancer and Condit, Dominick met with his financial adviser for lunch. Asa Maynor asked him, "Are you happy your account has appreciated?" His reply surprised her. "Not really," he said. "When people come up to me on the street and ask for my autograph, that's what I like." He went on to tell her how silly and irresponsible he had been in his old Hollywood days, spending all that money on lavish parties. "I'll never do that again."

Now, with the cancer and the Condit lawsuit and the trouble at *Vanity Fair*, he told his friends and assistants, "I can't go back to being poor." He especially wanted to leave a large estate for his granddaughter, Hannah.

That was Dominick's side of things. Not lost on editors at *Vanity Fair* were Dominick's earlier complaints that they had rejected his many requests to write in depth about the Chandra Levy/Gary Condit story. Then, after getting sued about those same false stories, he complained that *Vanity Fair* was not paying his legal expenses. He also construed that the magazine was somehow complicit because Condit's lawyer had requested all drafts of his articles mentioning Condit. Rather than showing collusion, any deletions or changes made by the magazine's fact checkers and lawyers would prove the opposite: Dominick, in fact, had been protected by the magazine. And there were other problems with *Vanity Fair*'s star writer.

As the American public began to receive more of its news from the Internet, there were cutbacks in spending at magazines, even at *Vanity Fair*. The photo department there assigned top photographers, from Wayne Maser to Harry Benson, to shoot a portrait of Dominick every month to illustrate his column. Dominick adamantly refused the request ever to use outtakes. Much more costly were his expense reports, the dollar amounts of which dazzled. He thought nothing of spending $3,500 for two nights at Claridge's in London or $5,000 for a weekend at the Ritz in Paris. Editorial assistants at the magazine knew to book those hotels, as well as the Chateau Marmont in Los Angeles. Sometimes they were less certain about other cities and occasionally made the grievous error of putting Dominick in what he considered substandard lodgings. "Do you know who I am?" he'd scream on the phone. "I'm a star at this fucking magazine!"

Another standard retort around the magazine's offices was Dominick's other pointed question to staffers, "Where is my special treatment?!"

Four of Dominick's personal assistants worked for a very different man over the years he employed them at the East Forty-Ninth Street apartment. What they did was less a job, more a fun gossip fest.

"Dominick didn't need an assistant. He just needed company," said Jack Donahue. "I'd sit there for three hours, type a schedule, and listen to fun stories, laughing all the time."

"This was the ideal job," said Laura Nappi Connolly. "Dominick was like more of a friend than a boss. We used to have coffee every morning and read Page Six together. And we'd dish."

"No one was funnier and more generous," said Jack Cummings III. "The flip side is Dominick was Irish Catholic like me: chip on our shoulder, easily offended."

"Dominick knew he name-dropped and reveled in it, and part of his charm was his acknowledging that he did it," said William Baldwin Young, another assistant. "He would dish but hated to be dished about." Young recalled when *Out* magazine columnist Michelangelo Signorile wrote about Dominick's sexual orientation and how "upset Dominick got."

The assistants knew he liked to be called Dominick. "Nick" was only acceptable from friends who knew him *before* his New York renaissance. Like most secretaries, they kept schedules, answered phones, made reservations. More unusual duties included sending out monthly checks to a few of Dominick's needier friends, among them, Frederick Combs, who died of AIDS in 1992. Otherwise, their jobs ran the gamut, whether it was listening to Dominick's complaints about going to any dinner hosted by Barbara Walters ("She moderates") or buying him the latest gay porn video. "He'd heard that Ryan Idol was the flavor of the moment. He heard he was the boy the gay execs were hiring," said William Baldwin Young.

Jack Cummings ran a small theater company, the Transport Group, and when the *New York Times* gave one of his shows a bad review, Dominick was the first to call him. "Fuck 'em!" he said. "And take the day off!"

If any of his personal assistants ever made a mistake, Dominick lightly dismissed it and soon forgot. He was much, much less forgiving of the people at *Vanity Fair*. A bad seat at the magazine's annual Oscar party required not one but multiple apologies from the magazine's flunkies, as well as Graydon Carter. Most upsetting to Dominick was the 1995 fete when his tablemates Denise Brown and Madonna canceled at the last minute and a couple of nobodies, in his opinion, appeared in their place. "Dominick could take offense easily," said Graydon Carter. "Especially during his star period in the 1990s."

When it became clear to Dominick that a $25,000 year-end bonus was all *Vanity Fair* would "contribute" to his legal fees, he argued that the page of advertising opposite his column was the highest priced in the magazine. He said he had spoken to an advertising executive at *Vanity Fair* who told him his articles were responsible for $500,000 a year in ad sales. He said the William Morris Agency got him speaking fees of $25,000 per engagement but he often spoke to *Vanity Fair* advertisers for free. Graydon Carter disputed Dominick's ad-sales figures, as well as his speaking engagements for the magazine. "I do not recall Dominick speaking to advertisers," the editor said. "I do recall one or two in-store cocktail events where Dominick would have appeared in conjunction with promotion for one of his books."

Dominick learned from the best when it came to expecting grand treatment. He had been taught by Elizabeth Taylor, but *Vanity Fair* staffers did not call him Liz. They nicknamed him "Lear on the heath" and said he had gone completely "haywire."

A great storyteller, Dominick knew how to embellish, claiming his legal bills were costing him $90,000 a month. Rich Bernstein, *Vanity Fair*'s counsel, suggested a top lawyer in Washington, DC, who could handle the Condit libel lawsuit for him. Dominick interpreted that recommendation as meaning Condé Nast would pay for the new lawyer. Again, it escalated into another huge misunderstanding. Bernstein merely made a recommendation, not an offer to pay for the attorney's services. In the beginning, Dominick said he liked the DC attorney. Later, he found it impossible to work with her, given that she lived two hundred miles away in the nation's capital. On good days, he called the situation a "major misalliance." On other days, he called it "a fucking disaster." If ever Dominick needed a moment to prove to his *Vanity Fair* editors how much the magazine needed him, it was the Michael Skakel trial.

# 16

## Apologies and Memoirs

Finally, more than a quarter century after Martha Moxley's murder, the trial began in May 2002. Dominick never missed an opportunity on TV or in his *Vanity Fair* column to take credit for bringing Michael Skakel, the Kennedy cousin, to justice in the murder of the fifteen-year-old girl from Greenwich, Connecticut.

At the trial, Dominick met a young reporter from Court TV, and he and Beth Karas became good friends, often sitting side by side to do live interviews for her cable network. It surprised Karas, after all his TV exposure, how nervous Dominick became before each live interview. "He would take out of his shirt pocket a little wallet photo of Dominique, and he kissed it and put it back in his pocket just before we went on," said Karas. "It was a ritual."

In the courtroom, Dominick sat near Dorthy Moxley. The lead defense attorney complained about the duo. "The jury isn't looking at me—they're looking at Dominick Dunne, they're looking at Dorthy Moxley. It was like arguing against apple pie," Mickey Sherman groused.

Dorthy Moxley, with her quick smile and homespun charm, embodied the prototypical all-American mom; and after the Simpson trial, Dominick emerged as the face of outraged, jaw-dropping injustice. Also, "Dominick became, after his daughter's murder, a one-man crusade against people who got away with murder. Dominick was always a presence," said Sherman.

Left out of Sherman's all-American "apple-pie" dish was Mark Fuhrman, who covered the Skakel trial for Court TV. Moxley often invited him to sit behind her. She remained loyal to the detective for his help but realized it put her in an awkward position with the Greenwich police. She had no choice but to comply when Frank Garr invited her to the witness room but stopped Fuhrman from joining them there in the courthouse basement. "Mark, you can't come down here," said Garr. "This isn't for you. Go back to the courtroom. You're only a spectator."

Dominick, as usual, proved more than adept at working both sides of the courtroom. He and Dorthy Moxley were friends again, although she always observed a polite distance. "I had a team of angels, and it was a culmination of all these things," she said, careful to credit not only Dominick but also Frank Garr, Len Levitt, and Mark Fuhrman. "It was a joint effort. I'm adamant about that."

Dominick also befriended Skakel's lead attorney, Mickey Sherman. Aware of the flamboyant attorney's fondness for the TV cameras, Dominick used his influence to get Sherman booked on *Larry King Live* and publicized his pull with the popular suspenders-wearing CNN host by arriving at the Norwalk, Connecticut, courthouse in the same white stretch limousine with the defense attorney.

When Robert F. Kennedy Jr. criticized Sherman for being buddies with one of his family's fiercest detractors, the attorney explained his relationship with Dominick to the aggrieved cousin. "We're friends. What can I say? I'm a kiss-ass," Mickey Sherman told Kennedy. Years later, he softened that description. "It was perceived by the Skakel family that I was trumpeting the enemy. But I had known Dominick before the trial. We were on many TV shows regarding criminal issues," said Sherman.

Dominick's relationship with Fuhrman proved equally controversial. It "shocked" the AP's Linda Deutsch that her colleague had given the notorious detective the Sutton report. Also surprised was Ron Shipp, who, after his explosive testimony at the Simpson trial, stayed in touch with his reporter friend.

"Dominick phoned me specifically to talk about Mark. He was so pissed off," said Shipp. Dominick told him, "Ron, I gave this stuff to Mark Fuhrman to do his book. Do you realize that son of a bitch never thanked me? I can't believe it! You need to say something to him." Especially galling to Dominick was how loyal he had been to the detective, even refusing to give the Sutton report to a rival reporter like Timothy Dumas.

Shipp was "never great friends" with Fuhrman when they worked in the LAPD together, and they had not talked in years. He did not make the call to the detective, despite Dominick being "livid."

Two weeks later, Dominick phoned Shipp again. "Everything is good," he said. "I talked to Mark. He apologized. Mark apologized."

Dominick took personal interest in the trial, and not just as a reporter. He became distraught with the prosecution, especially the day attorney Chris Morano played the tape of Richard Hoffman's interview with Michael Skakel, conducted for their book proposal. Dominick confronted Morano outside the courtroom afterward, asking, "Chris, why did you play that tape? It made me like Michael." Morano did not explain but knew he made the right choice.

Dominick instead agreed with the press corps. The prosecution was losing the case. To make it worse, the defense team held a constant stream of press conferences, which usually ended with some reporter telling the TV cameras of the prosecutors' incompetence.

"If we had tipped our hand earlier in the trial, any defense would come up with a way to explain it," Morano explained. "A prosecutor's job is to complete the dots in the final argument."

Lead prosecutor Jonathan Benedict did just that in his final summation. Using Michael's own words, he revealed that Skakel could not have known of Andrea Shakespeare's whereabouts the night of the murder unless he was in the Skakel house—and not at the Terriens'. And it was Andrea who asked outside the Moxley house, "Michael, what are you doing?" It destroyed Michael's alibi.

According to Morano, "The jury went 'Oh my God!' It was our final rebuttal."

Skakel's cousin Robert Kennedy Jr. made an hour-long visit to the court that day, his only appearance at the trial. He walked arm in arm with his aunt Ann Skakel McCooey, and when they passed Dominick, she whispered, "Jerk."

Kennedy soon offered a somewhat lengthier critique of Dominick. He went on *Larry King Live* to call him "irresponsible," and what he did as a journalist "almost criminal." He told *New York* magazine, "The formula that Dominick Dunne has employed to fulfill his dreams has done damage to a lot of people. Dunne wants to write about two things, both of which are easy to sell: high-profile crimes and famous people. So he's forced to try to make connections between his high-profile protagonists and the crimes." Most significant, Kennedy wrote a fourteen-thousand-word defense of Michael Skakel titled "A Miscarriage of Justice" and got it published in the *Atlantic Monthly*. "I do not know that Ken Littleton killed Martha Moxley," Kennedy opined in print. "I do know . . . that the state's case against

Littleton was much stronger than any case against Michael Skakel."
Kennedy went on to cite Dominick as being "the driving force" behind
the prosecution, citing his creation of a "*Lord of the Flies* frenzy to lynch the
fat kid." He also called Dominick a "gossip."

Dominick always said, "'Gossip' is an icky, bad word." But he respected
the practice. "It also means the complications that people have that they
don't let the public see. And I have the ability to get that information," he
boasted.

If Kennedy called him "a gossip," Dominick called Kennedy "a little
shit," and he could not have been happier about the guilty verdict, which
nonetheless left him stunned. He had been predicting for weeks that
Michael Skakel would walk. (Dominick never could predict with any
accuracy how a jury would decide.) A juror told him, "If Michael had kept
his mouth shut all these years, this trial would never have happened."

Dominick may have been surprised by the verdict but not caught off
guard enough to refuse press interviews. Unlike his post–Simpson trial
performance on CNN, he relished being the go-to man for most news
outlets that day. While Timothy Dumas never succeeded in getting
Dominick to give him the Sutton report, he nonetheless wrote *Greentown:
Murder and Mystery in Greenwich, America's Wealthiest Community*. In
that book, he described the press scene outside the courthouse the day of
the verdict, and how reporters mobbed the impeccably tailored writer
from *Vanity Fair*. Dumas also observed that Len Levitt, the reporter who
had been on the case the longest and done most of the heavy lifting, stood
alone, virtually ignored by the press corps. Once again, Dominick emerged
a star. "I'm more a worker bee," Levitt admitted.

Dominick made efforts to mend fences. In an article for *Vanity Fair*, he
wrote that Levitt found the "time to go to his son's baseball games" during
the hectic days of the trial. The mention touched the reporter. Dominick
also gave Levitt a copy of his recently published memoir, *The Way We
Lived Then*. "I want you to know about me," he said.

Levitt thanked Dominick. He read the book. Amid the gossip, the
beautiful party photographs, and its lexicon of Hollywood politics
(Dominick subtitled the book *Recollections of a Well-Known Name Dropper*),
Levitt found a curious subtext. Dominick wrote about a couple of very
compromising incidents: one in which he did drugs with a stranger, who
died unexpectedly from an overdose, and another in which Dominick was
physically brutalized by a stranger during a drug binge. *The Way We Lived
Then* also featured a photo of Dominick with the actor Frederick Combs;

both men are shirtless on a beach and the caption reads "tripping on acid in Haiti." After reading the book, Levitt asked its author, "I didn't realize, but you're making like you're gay."

Dominick smiled. "That's true," he said, then quickly changed the subject. Levitt recalled, "He pushed me to ask that question, that's the feeling I got."

With *The Way We Lived Then*, published in 1999, Dominick both sanitized and spiced up what he had written in his unpublished journals in the years from 1979 to 1983. In essence, he toned down the gay sex and amped up his drug use in the published memoir: The "psychopath" who bound his wrists, put a paper bag over his head, and threw lit matches at him was not invited into his Eastside sublet apartment to have sex, which is what Dominick first wrote in his private journal. In *The Way We Lived Then*, he wrote that his assailant was there only to share some cocaine, not have sex. Dominick also changed his prayer at that near-death moment. In *The Way We Lived Then*, Dominick implored, "God, help this man who is killing me." In his journal, Dominick prayed to God to spare his children from having to read about another "sordid gay murder" in tomorrow's newspaper.

Beyond the sex and drugs, there were other editorial changes. In his published memoir, "friends" disparaged his screenplay *A Time to Smell the Roses* in a way "that made me cringe with shame at my own lines." In the private journal, they are not friends but rather close relatives. It was John Gregory Dunne who offered the scalding criticism, while Joan Didion listened in silence.

# 17
## Safra and Paranoia

The cover of *New York* magazine called Dominick Dunne "America's most famous journalist." Television pushed him to the top. In 2002, signing with Court TV to host *Dominick Dunne's Power, Privilege, and Justice*, he led a weekly investigative report on a famous crime, occasionally touching on ones he had already covered in *Vanity Fair*. He very much knew what he wanted the TV show to be. Joe Danisi, a Court TV producer, met with him at Patroon to discuss one of the first episodes, about Ann Woodward shooting her husband, Billy. Dominick knew every detail of the story, having written *The Two Mrs. Grenvilles*. The lunch went well until, much to Danisi's surprise, Dominick pounded the table to shout across his charred haricots verts, "This show better be about my book, goddammit, or I'm not doing it!"

Shortly after the Skakel trial, Court TV chairman Henry Schleiff launched the network's new show with a gala party. Dominick had been outraged when O.J. Simpson threw himself a welcome-home party after being acquitted. Dominick, a few years later, did not mind toasting the Skakel guilty verdict at his Court TV party for *Power, Privilege, and Justice*. He even pricked the controversy by inviting Mickey Sherman, who, despite losing the case, had no intention of staying away. "And they were celebrating the verdict, which was obscene," the lawyer said.

Michael Skakel spent eleven years in prison, but after launching several appeals he was released on $1.2 million bail in 2013 to await a possible re-trial. A judge ruled that Skakel had received an unfair trial due to his not being adequately represented.

Fortunately for Dominick, the Skakel trial ended in 2002 just as another major murder trial began. At least, Dominick considered it major. It is possible he might have been only mildly interested in the mysterious fire that took Edmond Safra's life, if not for the fact that the Lebanese Brazilian Jewish banking billionaire had a most fascinating wife. Over the next two years, Dominick returned to the Safra saga repeatedly in the pages of *Vanity Fair*, and would have written about it up to his death in 2009 if Graydon Carter had not put a stop to the articles. Or had influential people told the editor to stop publishing Dominick's articles on the Safras?

Carter denied any outside pressure or interference. Dominick refused to believe the editor's denial for the simple reason that Lily Safra made the story absolutely irresistible, in his expert opinion.

The fire in the Safras' penthouse apartment in Monaco was set on December 3, 1999. There was never any doubt who started it. Edmond Safra, afflicted with Parkinson's disease, employed no fewer than seven nurses, the most recently hired one being a former Green Beret named Ted Maher. When the Monaco police first arrested Maher, he claimed he had been attacked by two men, sustained serious knife wounds to his abdomen, and started the fire to set off the alarm system, which, for some reason, had been disconnected that evening despite his boss being a total security freak. Equally mysterious, no guards were on duty.

Dominick never met a victim he did not like, and just as he thought Marvin Pancoast had taken the rap for killing Alfred Bloomingdale's mistress, he thought Maher innocent of deliberately killing his boss. So what if Maher signed a confession? It was "a confession in a language the American nurse didn't speak, without an interpreter present," he wrote in *Vanity Fair*. Also, Maher's wife, Heidi, claimed to have been "kidnapped" by Monaco authorities, her passport taken and withheld. Maher signed the confession to free his wife so she could go home to America to care for their three children. And even more bizarre, Safra's Republic Bank of New York had collaborated with "the FBI to expose the Russian Mafia's international money-laundering operation." Safra boasted far more powerful enemies than a former Green Beret soldier looking to play hero by starting a fire so he could "save" Safra's life and maybe get a big bonus at the end of the year. That was the way Dominick saw it. Besides, Safra paid well. Maher received an annual salary of $170,000 for being one of seven nurses.

Dominick liked the international intrigue, as well as Ted Maher's hard-luck story. But he absolutely loved Lily Safra's good-luck story. Born Lily Watkins, she came to be worth over $1 billion through the course of four marriages. It fascinated Dominick how Lily's second husband, Alfredo Monteverde, happened to die. He reportedly committed suicide in 1969 by shooting himself twice in the heart. As Dominick was quick to point out, when a person kills himself by gunshot there typically are not two bullet holes found in the heart of the corpse. Regarding husband number four, Edmond Safra rewrote his will only two weeks before his death, and Dominick had it on good authority that the deceased's brothers were less than happy with the rewrite job.

"The damnation of Ted Maher, the low man on the nursing staff's totem pole, had begun," Dominick wrote in *Vanity Fair*. In his coverage, he begged Amnesty International to get involved. Unfortunately, Dominick alienated Maher's Monegasque lawyer by writing about what he considered Donald Manasse's weak defense of the accused.

Dominick made sure to get along better with Maher's American lawyer, Michael Griffith, but failed to ingratiate himself with the citizens of Monaco when he quoted W. Somerset Maugham's cryptic swipe at the principality, calling it "a sunny place for shady people."

The trial at the Palais de Justice lasted only ten days, but in that time Dominick met and quickly befriended a wealthy American woman who was a self-described "sucker for a murder case." As Mia Certic explained her interest, "The trial was a huge deal in Monaco. This place supposedly had no crime."

Certic's two teenage children were attending a Monaco school with ties to Edmond Safra, and she knew the principality like a second home. Her family divided the year between living in France and the United States, and she often read Dominick's *Vanity Fair* articles, in particular, his pretrial coverage on Maher and Safra. "I was so shocked by the position taken before he came to Monaco. It was so out there, and on the wrong track," she recalled. Certic recognized Dominick the moment he appeared in the courtroom and was not favorably inclined toward him. "Until I met him, and then I loved him," said Certic, who fit the Dominick mold of stylish, vivacious, rich lady friends.

Donald Manasse experienced a similar quick change of heart. After objecting to Dominick's negative portrait of him in *Vanity Fair*, the lawyer accepted his invitation to lunch in Monaco. Dominick gave tips on courtroom strategy. "I listened, not just because he was a famous writer who had experience in criminal cases," said Manasse. "His natural instinct was to go to the side of the underdog."

But Dominick was a cat swimming upstream in the Monaco court. "It's a civil law system, the judges take a more active role in questioning people, it is very different," said Manasse. "It was foreign to him. Who were the Johnnie Cochrans in the case? Who were the F. Lee Baileys?"

Even defendants can ask questions of a witness in the Monaco court, which led Dominick to become completely flummoxed when the chief rabbi of France arrived to testify. Manasse asked Rabbi Joseph Haim Sitruk if Edmond Safra would not have forgiven Ted Maher, who, according to his defense, never had any intention of inflicting harm on his employer.

After the rabbi answered in the affirmative, Ted Maher stood up to ask his own questions of the holy man. Maher was not an easy client and indulged in a few controversial moves unhelpful to his cause. Among other things, he asked the rabbi to say a prayer for Safra. Rabbi Sitruk nodded, and facing the larger-than-life crucifix nailed to the courtroom wall in this Roman Catholic country, he began to pray out loud in Hebrew.

Manasse remembered it as being a "very emotional moment. People were crying." He noticed that Dominick ran from the courtroom during the rabbi's prayer. Afterward, Manasse asked Dominick if he, too, had found himself overcome with emotion. Dominick told him no, at least not *that* kind of emotion. "I ran out of the courtroom because I couldn't stop laughing!" he said. Dominick never fell for courtroom theatrics.

In the beginning, Mia Certic observed a studied caution around Dominick for the simple reason that she refused to accept Maher's version of events. After the nurse testified in court, Dominick turned to Certic. "What do you think?" he asked.

"He seems a pretty unreliable witness," she replied.

"To say nothing of unlikable," he added.

Certic believed that "the scales had fallen from Dominick's eyes. Ted Maher had clearly lied to everyone." He was guilty of killing Safra, although it was probably not his intention.

Michael Griffith, for his part, found the *Vanity Fair* writer to be a willing student. The American defense attorney spoon-fed the case to Dominick, careful to emphasize how Edmond Safra's life could have been saved if the police had not taken more than two hours to break into the apartment after being notified of the fire. Also, the autopsy report indicated a severe altercation had taken place between Safra and another nurse, Vivian Torrente, who also died in the fire. Safra had reason to be paranoid of the Russian Mafia, but adding to that sense of insecurity was a drug he took for Parkinson's disease. The autopsy reports showed Safra and Torrente's DNA under each other's fingernails, and there was a combat-type injury to her trachea. Obviously, a struggle between the two had taken place.

The American attorney was also useful to Dominick in other ways. On the first day of the trial, there were hundreds of reporters trying to gain entrance to the Palais de Justice. Dominick feared he would not get a seat. "You stay close to me," Griffith told him. "If you have to sit on my lap, I'll get you in."

Once inside, Dominick thanked him but added, "Mike, I better move to another location. It looks like I'm part of the defense team."

Which is when he sat down next to Mia Certic. At the end of the trial, he told her, "I don't know what to do." Maher was not the total innocent he had written about in *Vanity Fair*, and he wanted to talk to someone about his new doubts. She invited him to her villa for lunch but made the major mistake of not informing Dominick that her residence was in France, a ten-minute drive outside the principality. Shortly after her driver picked him up at the Hotel de Paris in Monaco, the sedan approached the border. "Where are we going?!" Dominick demanded to know.

"He flipped," said Certic. "Did he think he was being kidnapped and taken away? He was very nervous. It took him a while to relax." It also did not help that Dominick's hostess that day played the wrong kind of music when he arrived at her French villa. "We had Frank Sinatra on, and he looks at me like I'd put it on to taunt him," said Certic. How could she have known that old Blue Eyes had once paid a maître d' fifty dollars to punch him in the face?

Over lunch, Dominick told Certic about his deep concerns for his safety. He thought his phone at the Hotel de Paris was tapped. "Everyone's phone in Monaco is tapped, seriously," said Certic. He also worried about blackmail and firmly believed someone had tried to set him up with an underage boy at the hotel. "He was genuinely spooked by Safra, which is not to suggest she was behind any of his fears," said Certic.

There were also his very considerable concerns about how to cover the trial for *Vanity Fair*. Having now sat in the Monaco court, he realized some of his suppositions were incorrect or misleading. Certic told him, "You should say, 'It looked like that to me, but now that I've been here I was wrong.'"

"I just don't know what to do," Dominick said again and again.

*People Like Us* was not Dominick's Truman Capote moment, according to Liz Smith. His Safra reporting was that moment. "Mrs. Safra was so generous and giving so much money to Israel, and Dominick kept carrying on about the murder investigation after the fire," said Smith. "He wasn't so popular in New York after that."

Dominick even believed that someone in the Safra camp might have been behind the horse whisperer giving him the Condit/Levy story. He said as much in a memo to Graydon Carter, dated October 7, 2001: "Maybe I was being set up by Lily Safra, who has sworn to get even with me. . . . Martha Stewart got an e-mail from your friend Jean Pigozzi, telling her that he and Joel Silver had just been with Lily at La Leopolda, and he said tell your friend Dominick Dunne to be careful, something's going to happen to him."

When Carter put a moratorium on any more mentions of the Monaco trial in *Vanity Fair*, Dominick railed that Lily Safra and Alfred Taubman were behind the decision, having met and spoken to the editor at a dinner party. The wealthy real estate developer harbored his own solid reason for hating Dominick, one that could be summed up in three words: *People Like Us*, with its boorish Taubman-esque character Elias Renthal. Distraught, Dominick asked Liz Smith to write about such a deal being made among Safra, Taubman, and Carter. She wrote him a note to decline his appeal. After having endured monthly attacks ("The Liz Smith Tote Board") in Graydon Carter's *Spy* magazine, Smith was not about to relive bad times by using her syndicated column to expose a three-headed cabal as imagined by her possibly paranoid friend.

Carter denied being pressured. "At a certain point, after Ted Maher, the male nurse, confessed to setting the fire, we all felt that [Dominick] had pretty much exhausted the topic," the editor explained.

Two months after being sentenced to ten years in prison, Maher escaped from the Monaco jail and was apprehended seven hours later in Nice, France. He would not be released until October 2007, when Dominick wasted no time getting him booked for an interview on *Dominick Dunne's Power, Privilege, and Justice*. On an episode titled "Murder in Monaco," Maher maintained his innocence, as well as his story that he had been attacked by two assailants the night of Edmond Safra's death. While people working on the TV series said their host's confidence in Maher had been deeply shaken, Dominick took the middle ground for his on-air interview. He concluded, "The truth went to the grave with Edmond Safra."

# 18
## Editors and E-mails

Dominick groomed a reputation for taking offense and cutting off old friends. Just as capriciously, he often renewed those severed relationships overnight. "I hate that person. We're friends again," he would tell his assistant William Baldwin Young. When asked how his change of heart came about, Dominick said, "I have no idea. It just happened."

Young explained, "That's the way he preferred to deal with conflicts. 'Let's not make a big deal out of it, let's move on.'"

Dominick was no less forgiving with his immediate family. After not speaking for years, Dominick and his brother John met "by happenstance" in the hematology department at NewYork-Presbyterian Hospital. In 2002 Dominick was recovering from prostate cancer and doing well. John was battling a bad heart but not doing well. John tended to be "dismissive" of his problems, but, according to Griffin Dunne, who stayed in touch with his uncle, Dominick's younger brother always thought he could have a heart attack and die at any moment.

In the past, whenever the two brothers happened to be at the same party or event, Joan Didion might say a few polite words to Dominick and then go to her husband in the other room. But Joan was not there at NewYork-Presbyterian. Alone together, Dominick and John chatted as they waited to see their respective doctors. "And then John called me on the phone to wish me well," Dominick recalled. "All the hostility that had built up simply vanished. . . . We never tried to clear up what had gone so wrong."

As he did with many close friends, Dominick began having daily phone conversations with John. The brothers shared an interest in politics, fine literature, gossip, and name-dropping, and if the story was worthy, John would call for Joan to pick up the other line to listen and comment.

The reconciliation of the Dunne brothers did not last long. John's daughter, Quintana, suffered poor health, and shortly before Christmas 2003, she went into the hospital with a serious case of what was thought to be either Avian flu or walking pneumonia. When Dominick received a phone call from his sister-in-law late on December 30, he feared Joan was calling to say Quintana had passed away. Instead, Joan told him it was John. He suffered a massive heart attack in their apartment after coming home from the hospital to see their daughter, and he died there. Dominick was the first person she called that night with the news.

John's body was cremated and the funeral delayed until March 23, 2004, making it possible for Quintana to attend. Dominick sat with Joan and her daughter in the Cathedral of St. John the Divine on the Upper West Side of Manhattan. Before taking his seat, he saw his brother's good friends Leslie Abramson and Tim Rutten in the church. He thought it best to ignore them but then thought again. "Hi, Leslie. Thank you for coming," he said. It made sense considering the circumstances. Abramson smiled and returned his greeting. Quintana Roo Dunne, having briefly recovered, passed away a year after her father.

Sometime after the Michael Skakel trial, Graydon Carter quipped, "The wealthy people just aren't shooting each other at the rate we'd like them to for Dominick's purposes." It was a joke, but it was also the truth. If O.J. Simpson and the Menendez brothers had not committed double murders, would Dominick Dunne ever have become the most famous journalist in America? When it came to celebrity crime, the 1990s had it all over the 2000s.

In spring 2003 Dominick's reporting on the Martha Stewart trial lacked its usual lethal punch. The American businesswoman would be found guilty on all four counts of obstructing justice and lying to investigators about an extremely well-timed stock sale. Jeffrey Toobin, covering the Stewart trial for the *New Yorker*, reconnected with Dominick in the lower Manhattan courthouse. "Anyone who sat in that courtroom, as we both did, had to be convinced she lied," said Toobin.

Dominick was not convinced. Instead of pointing out little details to skewer Stewart, like the $12,000 Hermes Birkin bag she carried to court each day, he arduously defended her choice of expensive accessories. "Nobody mentioned it was twelve years old," he reported on the handbag.

Regarding the guilty verdict, Dominick wrote, "There was an audible gasp in the courtroom, and I was part of it." Even more embarrassing, he went on to write that after the verdict he made his first-ever visit to a

Kmart, where he bought some Martha Stewart merchandise. "I just wanted her to stay in business," he insisted.

His reporting on Robert Blake also limped. The actor went to trial in December 2004, accused of having had his wife, Bonnie Lee Bakley, shot to death outside a restaurant in Studio City, California, on the night of May 4, 2001. But the homicide never caught fire with the public's imagination. The victim, people said, was a horrible person who deserved to die, and the defendant, never a huge star, had not enjoyed a hit movie or TV show in decades. Neither was Blake good-looking in the mold of O.J. Simpson or even Erik Menendez. In other words, it was not a sexy murder, and, worse for Dominick's purposes, he knew and liked Blake. "I suspect that I would have disliked [Bakley] as much as Blake apparently did," he wrote in *Vanity Fair*. "I am almost always pro-prosecution in murder cases, but I cannot help feeling sad about the untenable position Robert Blake is in."

Dominick, not to mention his editors at *Vanity Fair*, could only hope for the Phil Spector murder trial to begin as soon as possible. Spector was a guy Dominick knew, hated, and could not wait to squish under his Gucci gumshoe. The famous and very eccentric record producer had been charged with shooting the actress-waitress Lana Clarkson to death on the morning of February 3, 2003. Dominick needed the trial now, not three years from now.

Instead, the Condit lawsuit slogged on, and he could not write about the imperious Lily Safra anymore.

The year 2005 was not a good one for Dominick or his estranged son, Alex. Dominick looked forward to *Vanity Fair*'s party to celebrate his eightieth birthday on October 29, 2005. A big bash at P. J. Clarke's was in the offing when Griffin Dunne told his father to call it off. It looked bad; the Condit lawsuit and his wrangling with the magazine had not been resolved. Various gossip columns reported that he was about to be fired, or would quit; and Dominick made no secret that he was writing an article titled "I Talked to Si in Vienna This Morning." Obviously, he was not writing such an exposé for *Vanity Fair*, even though he still held a contract with the magazine. For his part, Graydon Carter did not recall planning a birthday celebration for Dominick, and if he had "we would probably have done it upstairs at La Grenouille," not at the rowdy P. J. Clarke's, said the editor.

In the end, Dominick threw his own birthday party for eighty of his closest friends, and, not wanting "any ick," he invited Graydon Carter. Reaching the numeral eighty forced Dominick to stretch the definition of the word "friend," and his voluminous invitation list included such guests as Marisa Berenson and Bob Colacello, people who had either snubbed or trashed him in the past. When real friends asked how he could hobnob with such turncoats, Dominick always said, "Believe me, I'll never forget it, but that's not going to stop me.'" In a way, it was now his turn to use them, either as sources or mere glitter to add luster to his life.

Not invited to Dominick's birthday party was his "other" son. When reporters asked about Alex, Dominick used to say that he was the shy one who vanished. "He became bipolar and wouldn't take his medication," Dominick said of their estrangement. Occasionally, he would hear that Alex had been seen in Cairo or the Philippines.

In 2005 Alex Dunne suffered two strokes at the age of forty-eight. Now living in Portland, Oregon, he had been taking classes to be a court reporter, but the back-to-back strokes made such a career change impossible. He could no longer type or write and entered a long period of arduous rehabilitation.

Cardiac arrest and stroke are very different medical conditions, but their respective effects on Dominick and Alex produced similar results in the two men. In 1978, after suffering cardiac arrest, Dominick totally reevaluated his life and left Los Angeles for Oregon. Regarding his recovery from stroke, Alex said, "It was like coming out of a fog. I have had my own mental health issues over the years."

His much-regretted request to be disinherited, Alex said, had nothing to do with his father sending him an article on depression from the *Wall Street Journal*, as Dominick believed. Alex did not recall such an article. The reason for his wanting to be disinherited, he said, stemmed from "my own internal struggles . . . which I inexplicably projected onto my dad, [which] were responsible for me doing such a horrible thing to him."

On one of his many travels overseas, Alex met a Thai woman in Singapore. Amphai Kayongwaen worked as a waitress at a restaurant he frequented. They talked. They dated. They fell in love.

"Once I got engaged, I called my dad out of the blue. I hadn't spoken to him in several years," Alex recalled.

Their conversation in 2006 began in the simplest way possible. "Hi, Dad," said Alex.

Dominick gasped, "Oh my God!"

"I'm so sorry," said Alex. "I realize what an idiot I've been. It's totally my fault and my deepest apologies. I want you to know I'm getting married. I'd love for you to come to the wedding in Thailand."

Alex remembered there being total silence on the other end of the phone for about two minutes.

"Dad," he began again, "I just said I'm getting married and you haven't said anything."

"What do you want me to say?" asked Dominick. "You haven't called me in years!"

"How about 'great'? Something!"

Alex arranged for a travel companion to escort his father to the remote Thai village for the 2007 wedding, but Dominick refused the invitation. He did not feel well enough to make the trip. "I don't want to die in Thailand," he told his son. "When I meet her, I want her to speak English."

"Oh, you do?" said Alex. "Well, I'd love that, too, Dad . . . but you know . . ."

Soon after the wedding, Alex and Amphai Dunne moved to the United States to live in Los Angeles and Portland. "When my dad finally did meet her, he just adored her," said Alex. Regarding his long estrangement from his father, he explained, "It crushed me every day."

Dominick's rapprochement with his son turned out to be easier than the one with his magazine. By now, Dominick had severed ties with the DC lawyer recommended to him by *Vanity Fair* and was on a path to make an out-of-court settlement with Gary Condit through a new lawyer, Paul LiCalsi. He did not want to attend a *Vanity Fair* staff party in January 2006, but LiCalsi advised Dominick to go for appearances' sake. Fortunately, Wendy Stark was in town and agreed to be his date. Dominick never liked to attend parties or funerals alone, and the *Vanity Fair* event was no exception.

The first few moments at the party did not go well. Dominick thought Graydon Carter gave him a cool reception. Then again, "After the fallout, Dominick was hypersensitive to anything Graydon said or e-mailed him," said Jack Cummings. Dominick used to tell his assistant, "Jack, I guess in the end I'm just a mick who needs to get even."

He said he identified with Bette Davis, at her noblest, in *Now, Voyager*, but Dominick more resembled Olivia de Havilland in *The Heiress*: the injured mouse who learned hard, questionable lessons about self-defense from a circling father hawk.

At the *Vanity Fair* party, Dominick did feel embraced by other editors, employees, and contributors. Several told him how much they missed seeing his byline in the magazine. The last four issues of 2005 went to press with no Dominick Dunne article. There had been offers from other magazines to contribute, but Dominick wanted to continue writing for *Vanity Fair*. It was his home. He had been a professional writer for more than twenty years, and almost all of his work had appeared under the imprimatur of either *Vanity Fair* or Crown Publishing. Despite his thinking he had received a cool reception from Graydon Carter, the editor phoned to chat two days later. Dominick was touched. So much of his life had been spent searching for acceptance. He just wanted to belong and be appreciated, very appreciated.

His short phone talk with Carter produced immediate results. In 2006 there were more articles from Dominick Dunne published in *Vanity Fair*. Few, apparently, met with the editor's approval. This time there was no phone call to talk over their differences. Near the end of the year, Dominick met with Carter in his office at 4 Times Square in midtown Manhattan. To his surprise, the magazine's chief attorney, Rich Bernstein, was also present. Dominick repeated to family and friends what happened that day: When he walked into Carter's office, seven recent issues of *Vanity Fair* were spread across a table, each of them opened to one of his columns. According to Dominick, Carter did not like any of them, except for one, which, in the editor's estimation, was all right. Not great, but all right.

Dominick felt like he had just been whipped by his father. Carter's critique nearly shattered him. He thought of himself as the magazine's most popular writer, its greatest asset, even if he had heard reports that certain people on the staff said he was only read by "old people."

Dominick left Carter's office humiliated but unbowed. There in the hallway he saw Wayne Lawson. Dominick later told people that his editor was smiling, as if complicit, as if he knew the meeting's discussion points. Dominick would go on to call Lawson the magazine's Uriah Heep, a reference to the character in *David Copperfield* that Charles Dickens used to epitomize obsequiousness.

Dominick fully expected Lawson to defend him against Carter. Dominick somehow forgot that Lawson, in addition to being second-in-command on the editorial staff, was also a company man who had learned long ago not to side with a reporter against his boss. Smart editors' allegiance is never with the freelancer, especially with a loose-cannon writer who might repeat at a moment's notice something said in confidence. Dominick accused Lawson of being disloyal and put those sentiments in an e-mail. Greatly compounding the offense was his decision to send the e-mail not to Lawson but to Carter.

"There were unfriendly e-mails," said Jack Cummings. "He let me read one with bad language. It was brutal. When Dominick got the zinger right, no one got it more right."

Cummings advised Dominick not to send the e-mail.

"I already sent it," said Dominick.

"I thought you were showing me to ask my opinion."

According to Cummings, Dominick and Lawson never sat down to talk about the e-mail explosion. "And under all this hurt was deep respect and love, and it never got resolved," he said. Instead of apologizing, Dominick took the contretemps even one step further. He made it well known that Wayne Lawson's name had been removed from his hallowed list of honorary pallbearers.

Dominick and Lawson, who had worked together for more than twenty years on dozens of articles, as well as his books, never spoke again. "Dominick's close relationships at the magazine were with Tina and Wayne," said a *Vanity Fair* employee, "not with Graydon." Regardless, Dominick possessed the clout to demand and get a new editor. Anne Fulenwider was precisely the kind of young, stylish, and attractive woman on whom Dominick doted, in the vein of such trial reporters as Barbara Nevins Taylor, Shoreen Maghame, and Beth Karas. After working with her on one assignment, Dominick told his assistants that Fulenwider as an editor was "just fantastic."

Wayne Lawson had his detractors. Most of them were writers who had seen his mercurial side, who had been on good terms with him then suddenly banished over a disagreement or, more likely, a less-than-stellar piece of writing.

Working on the inside at *Vanity Fair*, Matt Tyrnauer knew a different man. "Wayne Lawson saved everybody's ass," said the contributing editor. "He had the magic touch. Wayne was the master of making those people's reporting into really great journalism. He could take all the information and fragments and synthesize it into something coherent, this shiny *Vanity Fair* package. Dominick was lucky to have him."

Lawson was not the only important editor with whom Dominick parted ways. For more than five years, Crown's Betty Prashker patiently waited for Dominick to finish his novel *A Solo Act*. In February 2006 she wrote him a note, saying that the novel read well, but not to be depressed, and please, do not think of killing off Gus Bailey again. All he needed to do was finish the last few chapters. When they disagreed over how to end the book, Dominick told his assistants and others that Prashker was "too old" and asked Crown for another editor. The publishing house gave him two, Tina Constable and Suzanne O'Neill. They, however, could not speed up his writing process. Dominick, who wrote six novels in fifteen years, had completed only one book in the last ten, the short picture-laden memoir *The Way We Lived Then*.

*A Solo Act* would bring the Gus Bailey character back to life after Dominick had him murdered by Andrew Cunanan in *Another City, Not My Own*. But Dominick struggled finishing the new novel because it was "so personal," said his assistant Jack Donahue. He intended to have the Gus Bailey character come out as a gay man. Donahue asked why he wanted to expose something about himself that he spent his whole life hiding. "So people don't talk about me when I cool," Dominick replied.

Bailey's sexual orientation was not the only homosexual theme Dominick planned for *A Solo Act*. Wrapped around his alter ego's own journey is the circuitous story of two other gay men, one of them an old "walker" who passes on his contacts with wealthy widows to a young callous protégé, who abuses the calling. Otherwise, Dominick envisioned *A Solo Act* as another roman à clef, about the mysterious death of a billionairess's husband in the tiny European principality of Andorra. The tempestuous widow, Perla Zacharias, tries to expose Bailey as being homosexual to stop him from writing about her nefarious activities, hence his confession. Not even Graydon Carter's edict would prevent Dominick from writing about what he wanted to write about. As Dominick often put it, "Don't use the real names, then you can't be sued."

In addition to getting new editors, Dominick also reached out to a new agent after Owen Laster retired. He knew David Kuhn from the young man's editor days at *Vanity Fair*, and Kuhn had recently set up his own agency, Kuhn Projects. Even though Dominick could not finish *A Solo Act*, Kuhn thought it time for his new client to begin work on another book.

The agent wrote a one-page outline for the proposed autobiography and, regarding the 1960s, asked Dominick in the memo if he had been "out" in his Hollywood heyday.

Dominick told his new agent, "I'm ready to tell the story. I don't have anything to lose and a lot to gain by telling my story." Kuhn believed Dominick was going to be "totally frank with himself" in the book.

Dominick thought his new agent and his new editors would resolve his problems. Indeed, the new lawyer Paul LiCalsi did make the Condit lawsuit go away, although not miraculously. While both parties never disclosed the sum Dominick agreed to pay in 2006, it came to $1 million, according to his correspondence and assistants.

Despite the huge sum, Dominick felt relief. He did not have to sell his house in Connecticut, and there would be enough money to leave an estate for his granddaughter. All the new people around Dominick, however, could not resolve his biggest fear. For the last decade, he had been obsessed with his own death. Often, before he boarded an airplane, he would send his son Griffin notes on changes he wanted to make in his funeral arrangements—who would speak, who would be the pallbearers, what music would be played. On a trip to London, he attended the funeral of *Daily Mail* diarist Nigel Dempster and heard a one-hundred-member chorus singing "Anything Goes." The Cole Porter tune immediately went on Dominick's funeral list of must-dos. It would be just the way he wanted to kick off his own final rites.

As he aged, he had only more reason to be obsessed by death. While he had won the battle with prostate cancer, he experienced a heart-attack scare in July 2006, necessitating an overnight stay at the hospital, and found himself deeply paranoid at two in the morning. Panicking, he tore the IV needles out of his body and, dripping blood all the way, made his way back to 155 East Forty-Ninth Street. "What the fuck have I done?" he thought as soon as he walked into his apartment. He quickly phoned Norman Carby at his home in Hawaii. "You're the only person I could call," he said, referring to the six-hour time difference. That early-morning phone call was followed by a far more frantic one from his son after the hospital notified Griffin that his father had escaped.

Dominick was not an easy parent to control. Neither his weakened heart nor his paranoia prevented him from leaving for Europe only three days after the hospital getaway. On a whirlwind tour, he visited his actress granddaughter, Hannah Dunne, at the Edinburgh International Festival in Scotland, where she was performing. He then attended the seventieth birthday party of the *Spectator* columnist Taki in London. And from there, he flew to Monaco to attend Ted Maher's latest trial, regarding his imminent release from prison. Again, he stayed at the Hotel de Paris, this time on his own dime, since Graydon Carter had no interest in the trial and *Vanity Fair* was not covering his expenses.

Dominick also did not stop when doctors told him he had been diagnosed with bladder cancer. He started on yet another regimen of chemotherapy but soon disbanded that treatment to try a more experimental kind. When people lied to him to say he looked great, Dominick quipped, "It's the stem cells." He harbored horrible memories of being burned in the groin by the radiation treatments for prostate cancer. He did not want to go through ten weeks of vomiting after taking chemo. "I'm too old for this," he said. "I don't have enough time left. They say they'd give me anti-nausea pills, but I'm already taking too many pills. I hate pills."

That was what he said publicly. To friends, he was scared. He had beaten cancer once; it was unlikely he would beat it a second time, not at his age. Dominick told Michael Griffith, "I never thought it would end like this. I always thought I'd be assassinated by Lily Safra."

# 19

## Spector and Sons

What Dominick needed more than anything except a new bladder was a good, lurid murder trial. Phil Spector gave him that gift in late winter 2007. The legendary record producer, better known at the millennium for his wild outfits and big wigs than his 1960s pop hits, had been charged with shooting Lana Clarkson in the Alhambra, California, estate he called his Pyrenees Castle. The mansion's name was the least of Spector's peculiarities, and Dominick looked forward to exposing every foible and eccentricity, which included the defendant's violent history of brandishing firearms in front of unsuspecting females. All those women survived, except one: Lana Clarkson met Spector on February 2, 2003, at the House of Blues on Sunset Boulevard, where she worked as a hostess. She died early the next morning, a gaping gunshot wound to her face. Clarkson had made the fatal mistake of accepting a famous stranger's invitation to visit his Castle. Spector denied any responsibility, calling it an "accidental suicide" in which the victim "kissed the gun" before shooting herself.

Dominick fully expected his coverage of the Spector trial to be his last for *Vanity Fair*. He wanted to write three installments and then go out in a "classy" way with the last article, in which he would thank everyone at the magazine for his quarter century of work there. Graydon Carter may no longer want him, he believed, but it gratified Dominick that yet another team of filmmakers, Kirsty de Garis and Timothy Jolley, were interested in his life. Their documentary would tell his story but focus on the upcoming Spector trial.

Dominick took an immediate liking to de Garis, a former model. She fit the mold. "Dominick doted on young, very attractive, and stylish women," said Jack Cummings. He also liked her title for the film, *Dominick Dunne: After the Party*, which he considered much more appropriate than the previous documentary's title, *Guilty Pleasure*.

At the Spector trial, held in the Superior Courthouse in downtown Los Angeles, Dominick reconnected with a young Court TV reporter. He and Harriet Ryan had met briefly at the Skakel trial but did not become friends. When Dominick had asked about her previous assignment for the cable network, Ryan mentioned having covered another trial. No one rich or famous was involved, she told Dominick.

"Oh, I don't do poor-people crime," he said.

She thought, "What a snob!"

"But I later learned that wasn't the case at all," said Ryan. Her time with Dominick on the Spector trial exposed another, kinder side of the man.

Several homeless people spent their days in those hallways at the Superior Courthouse in downtown Los Angeles. Ryan found herself constantly washing her hands. "It's a rough and tumble place," she said. One day, she noticed an old man beelining his way toward her and Dominick. His suit was threadbare, his mustache untrimmed, his toupee on backward. "I just wanted to move to the elevator," Ryan recalled. Dominick, however, did not shy away.

"Excuse me, Mr. Dunne," said the man, introducing himself. "I just want to tell you I'm a big admirer of yours. Do you have a second? I have some information."

It surprised Ryan how much time Dominick spent with the man. Later, in the elevator ride down to the street, he told her, "We're going to meet up later. He has all kinds of great information about Spector."

"Dominick got a lot of calls from powerful people," said Ryan. "But he was also open to speaking to the maid's sister down the street or the second cousin who was no longer in touch with the family of the killer. He didn't see them as losers or hangers-on. He saw them as sources, and he treated them all with respect."

The Spector trial began on March 19, 2007, and continued for the next five months. "It went on longer than anyone expected," said the media-relations person Allan Parachini, or, as he called himself, "the court flack."

In the beginning, there was the usual hoopla of a big celebrity trial. Phil Spector was not O.J. Simpson. But it also was not just another murder trial. Spector gave it a freaky pizzazz. "There were a number of reporters from all around the world," said Steven Mikulan, a reporter for *LA Weekly*. And then there was the writer from *Vanity Fair*. "He was the gray eminence there, and it was 'Oh, Dominick Dunne is going to be covering this!'" His mere presence certified it being an important trial.

As usual, Dominick entertained the other reporters with firsthand Hollywood gossip. Griffin Dunne and his first wife, Carey Lowell, had divorced, and his granddaughter, Hannah, now lived with her mother and new stepfather, actor Richard Gere. Dominick told the story that the *Pretty Woman* star asked Hannah not to leave her cans of Coke on his Buddhist altar. Dominick enjoyed saying, "Hannah's mother is now married to Richard Gere, so I was talking to Richard Gere . . ." Peter Hong, a reporter for the *Los Angeles Times*, noted, "For most people that kind of fascination wears off, but with Dominick it was like he was proud of his son for having married a woman who went on to marry Richard Gere."

Dominick thought the Spector trial got off to a good start. In a pretrial motion, he cheered when the judge ruled that four women who claimed "Spector had threatened them with guns in the past" would be allowed to testify before the jury. Spector's repeated gun-wielding showed a pattern of behavior, and Dominick never forgot how John Sweeney's repeated physical abuse of women was not allowed as evidence in that trial.

But there were also major disappointments. Dominick may have been the most famous reporter at the trial, but his status did not gain him entry to Spector's Castle, where the lethal shooting took place. When the jury went to the mansion in Alhambra, every reporter on the case, including Dominick, wanted to be on the guest list, but only one received an invitation: the AP's Linda Deutsch, who had been very partial to the defense, unlike most of the press corps.

"The *L.A. Times* threw a temper tantrum about it," said Ciaran McEvoy, who wrote for the City News Service. The editors at the *Los Angeles Times*, angry that their reporter had not been allowed access, published an article that liberally quoted Dominick. "The idea that the defense and the defendant are deciding which of the media can go to the house is absolutely outrageous to me," he said. It made no difference. Dominick and others had to wait outside the Castle for Deutsch to exit to give them her observations. According to the AP reporter, the jurors wanted to know the volume of the water's splash in the courtyard fountain. Could Spector's driver,

Adriano Desouza, have heard the gunshot with all that splashing noise as he sat waiting in his boss's Mercedes-Benz, the windows rolled up, the car radio blaring?

Despite there being nineteen phones in the Castle, only Desouza thought to call 911 on his cell phone when Spector came out of the house, holding a .38-calibre Colt Cobra and shouting, "I think I shot somebody."

In addition to being refused access to the Castle, Dominick endured other letdowns. He always prided himself on his access to the families on both sides of a murder trial. In his *Vanity Fair* column, he wrote of wanting to talk to Lana Clarkson's mother, Donna. She never missed a day in court, and he admired her dedication. But the major sit-down interview with the mother failed to materialize. He approached her outside the courtroom one day and quickly got her to refute the defense's claim, voiced by Jennifer Hayes and other so-called friends, that Lana committed suicide at the Castle. "I had never heard the name of Jennifer Hayes until this trial," she told Dominick.

But that one-sentence quote was it. He never secured an in-depth interview with the victim's mother, in part because his wicked sense of humor may have offended the woman. It happened the day the prosecutor read from Lana Clarkson's journals and diaries. Dominick proved to be a less than sympathetic audience and grew tired of the "endless woe-is-me" entries. At one point, he turned to the other reporters. "You know, it sounds like she could be a real pain in the ass," Dominick said. Only then did he realize that Donna Clarkson sat near enough to hear his wisecrack. Dominick did a comic double take. "Sorry, Mom!" he whispered.

There were other moments of levity. Everyone in court, including Dominick, had a good laugh when it was revealed how Clarkson first greeted the big-haired, Edwardian-attired Phil Spector. When he asked to be seated in the VIP section at the House of Blues, Clarkson put on her best hostess voice to say, "I'll seat you here, ma'am."

There was also the day Jody Gibson came to court. Better known as Babydol or the Hollywood Madam, she testified about Clarkson being one of her top call girls. That revelation aside, Babydol received a major reprimand from the judge when she used her moment on the stand to shamelessly plug her book, *Secrets of a Hollywood Super Madam*.

Dominick and Babydol spoke cordially and at length in the hallway afterward, an encounter that shocked Linda Deutsch. "How in the world do you know that woman?" she asked. Dominick shrugged. He was not averse to letting the AP reporter think he was a Babydol customer. In fact, he had previously met the Hollywood Madam in the makeup room at

CNN when they were both going to be interviewed for a *Larry King Live* segment on Paris Hilton.

Dominick's encounter with Spector's current wife proved equally noteworthy. When he ran into Rachelle Spector outside the men's room, she joked, "Did you wash your hands in the toilet?" Her wisecrack referenced the prosecution's claim that Phil Spector might have cleaned his hands in a toilet, hence there being no blood deposits in the sink's drainage pipe.

Dominick identified with high-profile "broads" like Babydol, Heidi Fleiss, Faye Resnick, Rachelle Spector, and even Elizabeth Taylor, who, decades earlier, rocked the world with her extramarital affairs and rapid-fire marriages. These women reflected Dominick's own often racy walks on the wild side.

Despite his cancer, despite his age, despite his hurt feelings about *Vanity Fair*, Dominick worked tirelessly and around the clock. While most out-of-town reporters stayed at the Westin Bonaventure, an easy walk to the Superior Court House in downtown Los Angeles, *Vanity Fair* continued to provide a car service to ferry Dominick back and forth to the Chateau Marmont, a ten-mile trip that could take an hour in rush-hour traffic. Unlike previous trials, however, Dominick could no longer keep the driver waiting. There were cost cutbacks at the magazine, and Dominick needed to be prompt after a day in court. Sometimes he missed the scheduled pick-up time.

Late one afternoon, defense attorney Bruce Cutler heard Dominick on his cell phone, trying to call a driver to take him back to the Chateau Marmont from the courthouse.

"Come with me," said Cutler. "I'll take you."

The offer surprised Dominick. In his first *Vanity Fair* article on the Spector trial, he exposed his initial dislike of Cutler, calling him that "John Gotti lawyer," and later said he had "a Mafia-type reputation."

Then Dominick met Cutler, and Cutler offered him a ride. It rarely took much to get on Dominick's good side. Later, the two men enjoyed several meals together, every lunch arranged by reporter Peter Hong. The *Los Angeles Times* maintained its own press office, complete with kitchenette, in the downtown courthouse. Bruce Cutler did not ask the *Times* reporter for a favor. Rather, he ordered Hong, "You need to make me lunch every day. I don't want to go to the cafeteria. Ham sandwich, wheat bread, cheese. Can you do that for me?"

Cutler knew reporters and the lengths they would go to get a story. "It gave me great access," said Hong, and since he filed on a daily basis and

Dominick filed long-lead stories, he invited *Vanity Fair*'s writer to attend his office-prepared lunches with Cutler. Dominick asked for only one addition to the menu. "Fritos," he said.

"He really liked Fritos," said Hong.

In the beginning, Dominick saw Cutler as the man who kept guilty Mafia people out of jail, and threw him into the pit with defense attorneys representing murderers like John Sweeney and Claus von Bülow. But they found common ground.

"Bruce Cutler was a military groupie the way Dominick was a celebrity groupie," said Hong. Dominick often introduced himself by speaking of his abusive father and how Dr. Richard Dunne only came to respect him when he won the Bronze Star during World War II. "And Bruce would just be rapt when Dominick talked about that."

Dominick, in turn, genuinely began to identify and worry about Cutler's position on the defense team. "The trial wasn't going well for Cutler," Hong recalled. "There was this rift in the defense team and they'd shut Bruce out." Dominick considered the Spector trial a low point for Cutler and began to see his own past downfall in Los Angeles reflected in the attorney's present-day failure there. "When Dominick was at that age, that's when he had his real crash and he was very concerned about Bruce," said Hong.

Dominick often remarked, "Bruce must feel like a real failure. He's really failed, hasn't he?"

Cutler's big problem was his disagreement over the defense team's major strategy. "They wanted me to argue things I didn't believe in," he recalled. "I didn't think Lana committed suicide. They went off on a tangent. I wouldn't be a part of it."

He and Dominick concurred on that point. "I do not believe that a beautiful woman commits suicide by shooting herself in the face," said Dominick.

Cutler left the defense team in August, about a month before the trial ended. Dominick no longer used the words "John Gotti" or "Mafia" to describe him. They had shared too many lunches, too many laughs and confidences. Dominick wrote in one of his follow-up articles on the trial, "Beneath Cutler's boisterousness, there is the heart and soul of a very gentle man." And he included in his softer, newly revised portrait an anecdote about the attorney helping a "terribly crippled older woman" down the stairs of the courthouse.

"Dominick got to know me and realized I was more than an underworld lawyer," said Cutler.

Peter Hong and Dominick also bonded, over what the reporter described as "a midlife crisis." Dominick talked a lot about his own fraught middle-age, when he switched from producing to writing. Hong was forty-three years old at the time of the Spector trial and "frustrated" with his own career at the *Los Angeles Times*.

"I'd spend five minutes on the phone in some pretty heated exchanges with editors," Hong recalled. "Dominick, on the other hand, would ask to use the phone to call his editor, and he'd close the door and be in there for thirty, forty minutes." When Dominick emerged from the *Times* office, Hong remembered his looking "quite shaken." Things were not going well at *Vanity Fair*. He told reporters that Graydon Carter was jealous of him. At the most recent Cannes Film Festival, Dominick reveled in how everyone greeted him with kisses, but noted that few celebrities recognized the magazine's top editor. He had heard that Carter approached Tina Brown about writing a regular column for *Vanity Fair*, and Dominick made it clear he would not continue writing for the magazine if that ever happened. He and Brown might be friends, but this was his career. He and she shared too many of the same sources, Dominick believed. Carter denied every approaching Brown about writing such a column. "I thought of it, though," he acknowledged.

Dominick looked to prove his worth at the magazine by being more than a reporter at the Spector trial, and, in fact, made a serious attempt to be a sleuth-like participant. He had heard from one of Spector's girlfriends that she taped a conversation with the defendant in which he admitted to the murder. The confession reportedly took place in a bungalow at the Beverly Hills Hotel. Dominick waited for the tape's delivery and was joined by two undercover cops at his suite in the Chateau Marmont. But the woman with the tape never showed up.

Dominick did manage another kind of coup, much more in keeping with his famed behind-the-scenes access. During the trial, he spoke to Phil Spector's adopted sons Gary and Louis. Judge Larry Paul Fidler had placed a gag order on the family, but that did not prevent Dominick from following the two sons on a trip back to their childhood home in Beverly Hills.

A caretaker there greeted them. At the time, HBO was renting the house for its series *Entourage*. It looked the part: a historic Beverly Hills manse with seven bedrooms and a sixty-foot living room that, as the Spector sons recalled, their boyhood friends were never allowed to visit. Dominick may have had an abusive father, but compared to Phil Spector, Dr. Richard Dunne was a veritable Ward Cleaver. The two sons were often locked in their rooms. "We didn't have free roam of the house," said

Gary Spector. They did get to eat in the kitchen, that is, until Phil began an affair with Nicole Zavala, with whom he had twins, Nicole and Phillip Jr. "They ate in the kitchen," said Gary. "We ate in the pantry. We were treated like guests in the house.

It deeply upset Dominick that Phil Spector had "started to shut down," according to Gary, when the younger adopted son was about eight years old. During the tour, Dominick mentioned his own long estrangement from Alex and how much he regretted it.

He admired the two brothers' faces of neutrality at the trial, and how careful they were not to influence the jurors. However, they did discuss off-the-record Phil Spector's claim that he was not in the room at the time of Clarkson's death. Gary had to ask, "How do you know she was standing up if you weren't in the room?" There were also discrepancies in the angle of the gun shot, whether Clarkson was seated or not, since she was considerably taller than Spector. The shadow effect of the blood spray also raised doubts. Gary thought they could have been created by his father's hand. "It was hard to remain neutral. I was watching both sides," he said.

Speaking to Gary and Louis Spector helped Dominick complete his portrait of the killer, but more important for him was the often-forgotten face of Lana Clarkson. Beth Karas, also covering the trial, drove him to the cottage that Clarkson rented on the canals of Venice, California, and they spoke to the landlady. "Dominick was upset by the defense's position that it was a suicide," said Karas. "In Lana's cottage, her taxes were spread out; she was in the midst of doing her taxes. She had bought seven pairs of Mary Jane shoes so she could stand on her feet for eight hours at the House of Blues." Dominick also abhorred the defense team's declarations that, as an actress, she was "a failure, as if she deserved to die," he said.

Dominick convinced himself the jury would find Spector guilty. He said so during the trial. Spector used the C-word a lot, and whenever it was spoken Dominick could see the jury recoil. He also really liked the foreman, called him "brilliant," and noted with admiration how the man "filled thirteen notebooks" during the trial.

To Dominick's shock, it turned out to be a hung jury, and on September 26, 2007, Judge Fidler declared a mistrial. Upset over there being no conviction, Dominick leveled most of his anger at the jury's foreman, and went on a rampage against the man on TV and in print. And it did not stop there.

He and Linda Deutsch occasionally received invitations to soirees at the Los Angeles home of actress Helen Mirren and director Taylor Hackford. Journalists and film people populated the convivial get-togethers, and after the Spector trial, the famous movie couple asked Dominick and Deutsch to speak to their guests about the nonverdict. Basically, according to Deutsch, "it was Nick railing on" about the foreman who had bought the defense's suicide theory. At one point during their talk, Deutsch joked, "Nick, don't hold back!"

"I think the wrong guy was the foreman," Dominick continued undeterred. "He had an agenda, this guy. He was picky. The whole trial he was writing. You can't go on the science of it. You've also got to go on the emotion."

During the trial, Dominick was caught on tape, saying, "I think the foreman is really smart. He takes lots of notes." After that same foreman led to a hung jury, Dominick wrote, "I'm quite proud that my own opinion of Juror No. 10, the foreman in the deliberations, altered much earlier than when he became by far the most disliked member of the jury, having personally forged the hung jury that ended this trial." As with Ted Maher at the Safra trial, Dominick was not about to admit he had been wrong.

Included in his *Vanity Fair* condemnation was an apocryphal story about the foreman's son and how much the boy hated broccoli. Dominick wrote that the son could not leave the dinner table until he ate all the loathed vegetables on his plate. Reportedly, another juror stopped trying to bring the foreman around to the majority opinion to convict Spector when he heard the tale of the uneaten veggies. As Dominick saw it, a foreman incapable of changing his mind about his son's broccoli was also incapable of changing his mind about a murder conviction. It was vintage Dominick Dunne reporting.

# 20
## Clinics and Sondheim

Dominick enjoyed working with Kirsty de Garis and Timothy Jolley on their documentary. He refused them only one major request. His son Alex had been visiting him in Los Angeles during the trial. Just as the Spector sons revisited their home in Beverly Hills, so Alex and Dominick made a trip back to the Georgian house on Walden Drive. The filmmakers wanted to interview Alex on camera, but Dominick would not allow it. "It's too raw," he said of their newly reestablished relationship.

For the *After the Party* documentary, Graydon Carter graciously consented to give an interview to de Garis and Jolley despite his differences with Dominick. On camera, he dismissed the Gary Condit brouhaha, saying, "If over fifteen years you have one spat, I don't think it's that bad."

Carter later explained the contretemps in greater detail. "Dominick knew that *Vanity Fair* bore no responsibility. But Si [Newhouse] wanted to support him in the case. He told me he wanted to cover any shortfall if he had to settle with Condit. But he didn't want to be obligated because the story had nothing to do with the magazine," noted the editor.

Dominick always said he would be fine if Carter would only apologize for reneging on his promise, in his opinion. A friend who took Dominick's side in the controversy had to wonder, "If *Vanity Fair* didn't promise to cover his legal fees and Nick had simply lied about it, why would the magazine continue to employ such an unreliable reporter?"

Dominick's interview on the subject in *After the Party* was not as forgiving as Carter's blithe "I don't think it's that bad." He repeated his "I talked to Si in Vienna" line and went on to add, "That was the end between me and *Vanity Fair*."

Kirsty de Garis interpreted Dominick's "the end" remark as referring to his friendly working relationship with Graydon Carter, not the end of his writing for the magazine. Indeed, in 2007, the year of the documentary's release, Dominick signed a *Vanity Fair* contract for six articles, earning him $300,000, with another $75,000 for each additional article of between 4,500 and 5,000 words. Few writers would consider such a lucrative contract "the end" of his relationship with a magazine.

The documentary *After the Party* was not without its flubs. In his on-camera interview, Griffin Dunne said the Christmas cards from the 1960s were based on Lord Snowdon's portraits of the royal family. After viewing the finished film, his father corrected him, saying they were based on Cecil Beaton's portraits of the royal family. It was the kind of mistake Dominick prided himself in not correcting when, earlier in the documentary, he repeats the Oregon anecdote about a woman mixing up the order of Elizabeth Taylor's husbands. "Let it go, let it go," Dominick says on camera, thinking he had made a major personality breakthrough on his retreat to Oregon in 1979. A quarter century later, in an atavistic urge to be precise, he chose not to overlook his own son's mistake regarding the two British photographers.

The documentary, when released, also provoked an angry phone call from Sue Mengers, who asked Griffin Dunne, "Is your father dead yet? . . . I wish he was dead. I hate that fucking asshole." The agent resented the scene in which Jean-Claude Tramont was again held up to ridicule for having called himself Jack Schwartz once upon a time. In telling his fat-girl story, Dominick always forgot to add that Mengers's dead husband's mother's maiden name was Schwartz!

And no, Dominick was not dead yet. The producers of the TV show *Dominick Dunne's Power, Privilege, and Justice* often filmed him at his Connecticut home, where he was shown from above the waist in his signature Turnbull & Asser shirts and ties. Below the waist, off screen, he often wore pajamas, slippers, and a catheter. With his health now in serious decline, he preferred life in Hadlyme. When he bought the saltbox/Colonial house in 1990, he immediately covered its "shitty brown" exterior with white paint and named the place Clouds, after the hilltop mansion owned by the fictitious billionaire couple Pauline and Jules Mendelson in *An Inconvenient Woman*. He also bought a racing-green Jaguar XJS convertible, which he affectionately named Audrey after Connie Wald's best friend, Audrey Hepburn. People considered him a notoriously bad driver, and they much preferred eschewing trips in Audrey to having drinks in the spacious backyard at Clouds. A white Victorian gazebo rested on a stretch of land cutting dramatically into the wetlands of the Connecticut River on Whalebone Cove. The previous owner created the promontory before environmental restrictions were imposed, and in the process destroyed the nesting grounds of many snapping turtles. Dominick always feared the reptiles would take their revenge to stage a march one day across the sprawling five acres of his property. "But it never happened," said Tim Lovejoy, a neighbor.

Dominick enjoyed the Hadlyme house more than ever, and, now seriously ill, he preferred repairing old injuries to starting new fights. It continued to sadden him that Annette and Oscar de la Renta thought he had based his Mickie Minardos character in *People Like Us* on the fashion designer. As an olive branch, he took up Mrs. de la Renta's cause to defend a young gallery owner, James Sansum, who had been accused of stealing from his mentor.

"Dominick saw it as a rapprochement with Annette," said Sansum. Dominick wrote two items on the lawsuit for *Vanity Fair*, taking Sansum's side in the controversy, despite it not being a particularly compelling story. It was a small, cozy world of Manhattan gallery owners and high-society folk. Sansum's boyfriend, Markham Roberts, roomed at Brown University with Alex Bolen, who married Annette de la Renta's daughter Eliza Reed. As gallery owners, Sansum and Roberts also knew Dominick's gallery-owner friend Angus Wilkie, another Hadlyme neighbor, who made the introductions. As he so often did, Dominick turned his *Vanity Fair* profile subject into a personal friend and invited Sansum and Roberts to his Connecticut house to see the unveiling of his new Absolute Dunne vodka ad, framed and placed in his powder room (aptly named for the owner's near addiction to talcum powder). The three of them also indulged in a weekend-long Luchino Visconti film festival, which included a screening of the director's *Death in Venice*. Dominick laughed longest at Dirk Bogarde being "pinked up" to play the aging, obsessed admirer of an adolescent boy. Soon, he was telling the young couple about Visconti's lover, Helmut Berger, and the *Ash Wednesday* debacle, as well as Elizabeth Taylor's bizarre friendship with Michael Jackson. "Scared by fame, they had sympathy for each other," said Dominick.

"We became fast friends," Sansum said. "Obviously, it began with his helping me." There was also their homosexuality; it was the other thing they shared, although Dominick did not write about their same-sex attractions in his *Vanity Fair* articles on Sansum. Instead, he wrote how they were both stutterers and had suffered murders in their immediate families. Publicly, Dominick always said his father called him a sissy. He felt more comfortable speaking in private to Sansum and Roberts and expanded on the sissy remarks, telling them that his father "saw it in me and it made him sick. He wanted to beat it out of me." There was no doubt that the "it" was his sexual orientation.

Dominick told Roberts and Sansum that he "envied" their relationship. According to Roberts, coming out for Dominick was "a big deal. He was dancing around that topic. It was something he was trying to express." Dominick explained his reluctance to leave the closet. "When you have children, it is difficult," he said. "It negates your earlier life." He feared being viewed as a liar, or for people to think he never truly loved Lenny.

Dominick's friendship with Roberts and Sansum was not atypical. He also revealed his true sexual orientation to other young gay men.

When *Vanity Fair*'s Matt Tyrnauer visited the Connecticut house, Dominick brought out his many photo albums for a show-and-tell session. "Picture by picture he pointed out all the guys he had affairs with," Tyrnauer recalled. Pointing to each of those photos, Dominick tended to repeat himself: "I hate to tell you, but I had a little number with that one." Most of the men he singled out were ballet dancers or little-known actors. "The 'little numbers' were enormous," said Tyrnauer. "He really was in the closet at *Vanity Fair*."

The albums contained many photos of Lenny. Whenever Dominick saw one of her, he rubbed his finger over the image. "Isn't she beautiful?" he asked.

"There was this push-pull," said Tyrnauer.

William Mann also found Dominick to be open about his sexuality when he visited him in Connecticut. Mann had written two biographies on homosexuals, film director John Schlesinger and interior designer William Haines. The journalist's credits also include the book *Behind the Screen: How Gays and Lesbians Shaped Hollywood, 1910–1969*. At work on a Katharine Hepburn biography, Mann contacted Dominick to see if he would be interviewed about the legendary actress who used to live across the street from the Dunne family in West Hartford. That book, *Kate: The Woman Who Was Hepburn*, would be the first ever to include interviews with Scotty Bowers about his Hollywood escort service, which Hepburn and Spencer Tracy both used. Mann asked about Bowers, and Dominick told him that Scotty was a very reliable source, one whose word could be trusted without reservation. Dominick did not reveal his own professional relationship with Bowers.

As usual when being interviewed by reporters, Dominick enjoyed asking his own questions, and wanted to know about Mann's personal life. The biographer replied that he had been in a committed relationship with another man for several years. Dominick then offered his own disclosure, saying, "I'm a closeted homosexual."

Mann puzzled over how to react to Dominick's remark. He did not want to lie and say he had no idea about his host's homosexuality. Also, Mann thought Dominick would be offended if he said he already knew. And there was the greater question. "Who calls himself a *closeted* homosexual?" Mann thought. It was a first for a journalist who had conducted hundreds of interviews in his career.

For Dominick, being open about his sexual orientation was more difficult when talking to old friends, gay or straight. Dominick never discussed his sexual orientation with Mart Crowley, not even when they would be at a small dinner party at Roddy McDowall's house in Studio City and the only other guest was the very out writer Gavin Lambert, author of *Inside Daisy Clover*. It was the same with heterosexuals he had known since the 1950s and earlier. "When he was with Mary Rodgers and Chuck Hollerith, Dominick would talk about Lenny being the love of his life," said Jack Cummings. "They would roll their eyes."

Near the end of his life, Dominick took his first public step outside the closet. For a routine phone interview, the English reporter Tim Teeman sat at his office desk at the *Times* of London to speak long-distance to Dominick about his life and career. At one point in their transatlantic talk, Dominick asked Teeman, "Are you married?" Teeman replied, "No, I'm gay." Completely unprompted, Dominick said, "I'm a closeted bisexual celibate." The comment led to Teeman's asking Dominick about his marriage to Lenny. The question did not receive an answer, at least, not a direct one. "In my era, gay men were expected to get married," said Dominick.

The "closeted" remark to Tim Teeman replicated Dominick's admission to William Mann. Only it was different. When someone calls himself "closeted" to a reporter who is going to print that remark, the person is no longer, in essence, in the closet. But even with Teeman, Dominick took a step many homosexuals had before him, first claiming to be bisexual and saving full disclosure for later. The next step would be his upcoming novel, *A Solo Act*. Norman Carby denied that his partner ever expressed any sexual interest in women, and as for being celibate for twenty years, Carby said their relationship was intimate until the last year of Dominick's life. Scotty Bowers also revealed that Dominick used his escort service up to

2009. Saying he had been celibate for twenty years may have been peremp-
tory on Dominick's part; it put a halt to questions about his current
romantic life.

Dominick's claim to being celibate did not surprise reporters or cause
them to pursue the topic. In the *After the Party* documentary, Dominick
takes obvious pleasure in telling the story that, after being diagnosed with
prostate cancer, his doctor told him he could no longer have sex. "Oh, I
don't care about *that!*" Dominick replied—as if erectile dysfunction ruled
out every sex act known to man. One thing was certain: Dominick had
bladder cancer, and it caused him excruciating pain. He controlled it when
around people, but alone in his apartment he said he screamed in agony.
There was also the almost constant need to urinate. He wrote to his new
*Vanity Fair* editor Anne Fulenwider that he knew every restroom in midtown Manhattan. Doctors recommended having the bladder removed,
but Dominick decided against it after talking to Buck Henry, who had
undergone the operation. The screenwriter's horror stories left Dominick
in "a state of terror."

Late in 2007 Dominick's scheduled chemotherapy treatments in New
York City forced him to leave London and miss Mohamed Al-Fayed's big
day in court at the Princess Diana inquest. The Egyptian billionaire had
leveled accusations of a conspiracy in the automobile death of the princess
and his son, Dodi, in 1997. It "sickened" Dominick that he had to rely on
friends' reports from the London courtroom to complete his story for
*Vanity Fair*.

He vowed not to let cancer control his life a second time. In 2008
Dominick made his last visits to the Academy Awards and the Cannes
Film Festival. To make the trips, he stopped the chemotherapy treatments,
much to his friends' and family's dismay. Dominick did not care. He told
Tita Cahn, "I'd rather be kissed by Nicole Kidman in front of the Carlton
than stay here and finish my chemo."

The cancer, however, did force him to slow down and reflect. He not
only repaired his friendship with Annette and Oscar de la Renta but with
journalists Greta Van Susteren and Robert Rand. That summer he also
made friends with a Kennedy, even though it was a rapprochement conducted long-distance and in private. It thrilled Dominick how Edward
Kennedy put his political muscle behind the presidential candidacy of
Barack Obama. Dominick considered the junior senator from Illinois to
be "like God" and stood up and applauded in the TV room of his Connecticut house when Kennedy introduced Obama at the 2008 National
Democratic Convention in Denver.

Dominick's forgiveness, however, did not extend to everyone. When an old friend, Gary Pudney, threw him a party in Los Angeles for his eighty-third birthday, the CBS executive gave Dominick the guest list beforehand to approve. More than four decades after Frank Sinatra paid to have him punched at the Daisy, Dominick was not going to forgive the singer or, by association, his daughter. "The only name he crossed off the list was that of Tina Sinatra," said Pudney.

At the time, Dominick sincerely believed he would never cover another trial for *Vanity Fair*, that the Phil Spector trial had been his last. He was wrong. And again, it was O.J. Simpson who got him back into the courtroom. It was their third go-round.

During the criminal trial in 1995, armed guards separated Dominick from Simpson. They saw each other every day of the trial but never met. During Simpson's civil trial in 1996–97, there were no guards present, and the defendant frequently wandered the hallways of the Santa Monica courthouse, looking to schmooze with reporters whom he could charm with the Juice. Although Simpson tried, Dominick made sure never to shake the hand of the murderer. He did not want *that* photograph to appear anywhere.

In late 2008 Dominick walked into the Las Vegas courtroom a far frailer man, there to cover the O.J. Simpson trial for armed robbery, kidnapping, and theft of the athlete's sports memorabilia. Linda Deutsch found Dominick to be so ill it "astonished" her that he wanted to attend the trial. Besides, he appeared uninspired. "What is this?" Dominick asked her. "This is the stupidest trial. Who cares about stolen footballs?"

In some ways, Dominick was now almost the bigger news. The *New York Times* even sent a reporter, there to cover the trial as well as interview America's most famous journalist. Dominick relished being profiled. "I had a literary following before," he told the *Times*, "but because of O.J. I became a name and a public person, which I love. I think it would be a fitting way to end."

At one point in the trial, a Simpson fan entered the courtroom to get the defendant's autograph. Then she noticed another famous person sitting there. "It's Dominick Dunne!" she exclaimed and ran over to kiss him before being promptly removed from the courtroom. "Hey, she's after Dominick!" O.J. Simpson said with a laugh. "She's not after me."

During one recess in the trial, Linda Deutsch introduced Simpson to his major journalist-nemesis. This time, Dominick did shake the hand of the defendant, who promptly launched his charm offensive. "Mr. Dunne, it is so wonderful to meet you. I watch your TV show all the time. I love it," said Simpson.

Dominick melted. He later told Deutsch, "I hate to admit it, but I like the guy." The following day, he and the AP reporter were sitting on a bench in the hallway. Again, Simpson approached to say hello. "O.J., I really hope you beat this," said Dominick.

"It was such a turnaround," Deutsch recalled. "You could have knocked me over with a feather."

In Las Vegas, Dominick renewed his always cordial relationship with Simpson's mother and two sisters, and they expressed deep concern when one day in court he collapsed from fatigue. When it happened, Dominick told his fellow reporter Beth Karas, "Call Griffin. He'll know what to do."

Two hours later, Griffin Dunne arrived in Las Vegas to find his father not in a hospital but ensconced in his hotel suite, where he was "getting flowers and watching the news about himself, which he loved," said his son. The following day, Griffin accompanied his father to the courthouse. He found it a much less heady experience from Dominick's previous go-rounds with Simpson. "The first O.J. trial, compared to a movie, would have been a top-drawer, big Hollywood production," Griffin opined. "The [third] one was like going on the set of a porno."

Even pornography has its thrills. One day during the trial, Simpson approached Griffin to ask, "Are you Dominick's son?" The two men shook hands even before Griffin realized to whom he was speaking, and just as Simpson had plied the father with compliments about his on-camera career, so he massaged the ego of the son. "I didn't know what to do. I just let the hand go up and down, up and down," Griffin recalled. "It was the most surreal moment of my life."

After the jury delivered Simpson's guilty verdict on December 5, Dominick did not feel well enough to travel even farther west for Amphai and Alex Dunne's second wedding, on December 14, held at the Hollywood Hills home of Adam Belanoff, a producer-writer on *The Closer*. His non-appearance did not surprise most guests. The year before, Dominick played himself on the detective TV series in two episodes, and the show's creator, James Duff, recalled his old friend being charming and upbeat on the set. "But he had lost weight and clothes weren't fitting him properly, and he was so tailored," said Duff.

During the last few months of his life, Dominick would try stem-cell treatments instead of chemo to rid himself of cancer. He made three separate trips to a clinic in the Dominican Republic and two trips to one in Germany. The first trip to the Caribbean cost him nothing because he had agreed to write about the treatment. He traveled there alone, but on the four other trips abroad Norman Carby accompanied him.

Dominick knew he was dying. "He was very angry about it," said Carby. Dominick had worked too hard for his resurrection and incredible success, and felt that all those many years of compromise and failure followed by only twenty-five years of good times were not enough. "He wanted to live."

Dominick's last two articles for *Vanity Fair* were his coverage of the Simpson civil trial in Las Vegas and an obituary for Sunny von Bülow, who died on December 6, 2008, at Columbia-Presbyterian Hospital, where she had lived in a coma for twenty-eight years. After her funeral, the reception at the Georgian Suite proved poignant for Dominick. He saw an old colleague from the second Claus von Bülow trial, the *Providence Journal*'s Tracy Breton; in the years after the trail he helped launch her publishing career in New York. "He introduced me to all these people! Dominick was so generous," said the writer. Sunny's postfuneral event reminded Dominick of the Duchess of Guermantes ball from *Remembrance of Things Past*, one of his favorite novels. Marcel Proust's characters reunite years later only to discover that they have all grown old and are about to die.

One of his major disappointments was being too ill to cover the second Phil Spector trial, which lasted only a few days and ended with a conviction for second-degree murder. On May 29, 2009, Spector received a sentence of nineteen years to life.

That summer, Dominick and Norman Carby made their last visit to the German clinic, and the two men took car trips to find the castle in Bavaria where the princess of Lippe had once lived. Wanting to look back at his youth and relive memories of postwar Germany, Dominick wrote a letter to "Your Majesty," the princess's granddaughter. He wanted to find the castle where he had read *Life* magazine articles to the old woman and witnessed the mass wedding of former Nazi prisoners. "But we never found the castle," said Carby.

The stem-cell treatments that summer were not successful, and when Carby knew it was hopeless he sent for Griffin. At the German clinic, Dominick's son met Carby, not as his late sister's good friend but his father's longtime partner. "Norman was looking after him," Griffin recalled. "I saw this history, a long affectionate, real history between these two men. For the week it was like getting to know a stepbrother I didn't know."

At the clinic, Dominick spent time not only with Griffin and Carby but Allan Carr's good friend Alana Hamilton. They talked about the flamboyant producer's party for her and Rod Stewart when she was pregnant and recently married to the rock star. Hamilton had traveled to the Bavarian clinic to care for her friend Farrah Fawcett, a patient there.

Dominick never got to meet the *Charlie's Angels* star, who would soon die at the clinic, but he nonetheless left her a gift: his rolls of imported American toilet paper. Dominick could not tolerate the roughness of European brands.

Finally, it was time to go home. On August 14, Carby and Dominick boarded a Lufthansa flight to New York City and were about to take their first-class seats when a flight attendant approached. She apologized but had to inform them that the captain would not allow such an obviously sick person to remain on the plane for what would be a seven-hour flight. They would have to depart the aircraft immediately. Carby did not flinch as he lied as he had never lied before, and insisted with utmost calm and confidence that he had everything under control. There would be no problem during the flight across the Atlantic, he said repeatedly. In the end, Dominick's six-foot-five companion succeeded in convincing the pilot and the flight attendant that everything would be fine. On the contrary, Dominick suffered from severe diarrhea, and before boarding the plane Carby had ordered an ambulance to meet them at JFK International Airport to take his partner directly to Roosevelt Hospital in Manhattan. "Norman was a fucking saint," said Mart Crowley.

At the hospital, Jack Cummings found that Dominick, despite being gravely ill, responded positively to having people around him, and the assistant asked old friends to come visit. "Tina Brown sat on the hospital bed and they dished for three hours. It brought him right back to life," said Alex Dunne. Dominick told his former editor, "I wish I could do Conrad Murray's trial." He firmly believed Michael Jackson's doctor was responsible for the pop singer's death; Dr. Murray would later be found guilty of involuntary manslaughter. After her visit, Brown told Cummings, "He seems in great shape."

Another good day for him at the hospital was when his new editors at Crown Publishing, Tina Constable and Suzanne O'Neill, came to show Dominick mock-ups for the cover of his new novel, *A Solo Act*, retitled *Too Much Money*. They planned to publish it that autumn and were doing some last-minute editing. Dominick told another visitor, actor Frank Langella, "I did it. I finished my book."

Even old enemies like Andrea Reynolds Plunket showed up to wish him well. "I was the last person to see him alive in the hospital," said the former mistress of Claus von Bülow.

She was not the last visitor. After a few days in the hospital, Dominick moved back into his apartment on East Forty-Ninth Street, where a hospital bed had been set up in the living room. The attorney Michael Griffith inquired if Ted Maher might want to be Dominick's nurse. The offer surprised Dominick. "Edmond Safra's nurse?!" he asked in total astonishment.

Again, Jack Cummings made sure to keep the visitors coming. If Dominick happened to be sleeping when people arrived at the apartment, his assistant took the guests to the temporary waiting room. "I sat there with Reinaldo and Carolina Herrera in the bedroom, waiting for Dominick to wake up," Cummings recalled. He thought, "My life is so bizarre." Dominick had not spoken to Betty Prashker for two years, but when Cummings phoned her, she came to visit. A request to visit was not made to Dominick's other estranged editor, Wayne Lawson.

Freddy Eberstadt, who had known Dominick since their days at NBC, made his final trip to 155 East Forty-Ninth Street to see his old friend. It always amazed him that the men running the elevator never failed to comment on what a nice man Mr. Dunne was. "How many times does that happen?" thought Eberstadt. "And I've ridden in a lot of elevators." When he walked into the living room, Dominick was sleeping, but after a few moments he opened his eyes to ask his friend, "Am I still alive?"

Griffin Dunne phoned Jesse Kornbluth to ask if he could bring some medicinal marijuana for his father to smoke to ease the pain. When Kornbluth arrived, Alex Dunne thought he was a drug dealer and sent him away. Griffin had to make apologies and quickly retrieve the grass. When Kornbluth returned to give Dominick the marijuana, he warned, "It's strong stuff. It might kill you." They shared a similar macabre sense of humor. "Life amused Dominick in the way that it amuses people who are really, really sad," said Kornbluth.

Mart Crowley was another regular visitor at the end. One afternoon he arrived to find a journalist friend reading the obituary he had written, to be published in a newspaper as soon as Dominick passed way. The obit's subject, as usual, was sleeping—or appeared to be. "Don't stop reading," Crowley insisted. He wanted to hear the obit. Besides, "Dominick likes to hear about himself," Crowley added.

Dominick opened his eyes. "That's true," he whispered.

On another visit, Crowley looked across his friend's bed to see Stephen Sondheim. Even though the two Williams College men had not seen each other much in recent years, Jack Cummings knew Dominick wanted to see his friend and phoned Sondheim to request a visit. The two men used to enjoy their postcollege quarter-annual ritual lunch at the Four Seasons, but classmates Howard Erskine and Chuck Hollerith had passed away and they had not kept up their restaurant tradition. Dominick said of Sondheim, "We almost never see each other, except at large parties. We hug and say we should get together, but we never seem to." Despite those words, Sondheim remained one of the few constants on Dominick's ever-changing list of honorary pallbearers.

Dominick made one last-minute change to his funeral arrangements. He put Graydon Carter's name back on that list of pallbearers. "I don't want any ick at the funeral," he explained to Jack Cummings.

Dominick Dunne died on August 26, 2009. The family did not immediately release the news. Edward Kennedy had passed away the day before, and it seemed better not to compete for obit space against such an American icon. When Griffin Dunne finally contacted the funeral home, he was asked if the family wanted special security, to keep away what undertakers call "professional mourners." Griffin's immediate thought was to call his father to tell him they now had a name for one of his favorite pastimes, being a professional mourner.

The next point of duty was to phone all the people Dominick had requested to be honorary pallbearers and speakers at his funeral. Jack Cummings phoned Dominick's composer friend.

"But I don't have a suit," Stephen Sondheim replied.

"Can you buy one?" asked Cummings.

The phone call to Graydon Carter proved much more time-consuming. After putting in the initial request, Cummings received multiple calls from the editor's office. The questions asked ran the gamut from what were the names of the other pallbearers to what order would the pallbearers file into the church. It was so very *Vanity Fair*.

Dominick wanted to begin the funeral with Cole Porter's "Anything Goes" and end it with "The Battle Hymn of the Republic." Those songs, however, posed a problem. Father Daniel Morrisey told the family that no secular music could be sung during the Mass itself, but friends and relatives would be allowed to speak then. A compromise was reached regarding Dominick's music. "Anything Goes" could be sung before the Mass began and "The Battle Hymn of the Republic" could be sung after it had finished. The priest's edict, however, created a dilemma for Dominick's granddaughter. Hannah Dunne wanted to finish her eulogy by singing "My Funny Valentine." The song held special significance because it referenced Dominick's Valentine's Day tradition of sending his granddaughter flowers with a note signed "Your secret admirer." It fell to Griffin to tell Hannah that the priest would not allow her to sing the Rodgers and Hart show tune during High Mass.

"I don't care," she insisted. "They'll have to drag me off the stage. The priest will have to drag me off."

Griffin cautioned, "Honey, first of all, it is called an altar." Fortunately, he came up with an easy, slightly devious solution. "I have you listed as a speaker and you speak about the flowers and then you just start to sing," he advised.

Long before Dominick died, he had sent Jesse Kornbluth a letter asking him to be a pallbearer at his funeral. Kornbluth wrote back, "I'm honored. Not soon, please." He did not give Dominick's request much thought until September 10 when he arrived at the Church of St. Vincent Ferrer on Lexington Avenue. At the funeral, he saw the lineup of honorary pallbearers and found it "fucking amusing" that Graydon Carter was among them.

Stephen Sondheim, in the end, did buy a suit to wear to the funeral but caused something of a ruckus when he began to complain loudly about the singing of "Anything Goes." During the Mass, Dominick's two sons spoke, as did Liz Smith, Tina Brown, and Joan Didion, who, true to form as the person Dominick used to call Frail, could not be heard beyond the first row of pews. And Hannah Dunne defied the priest to sing "My Funny Valentine" a cappella. She created what her father called "an incredible moment. I'm sure Poppy heard it no matter where he is."

Dominick was buried in Cove Cemetery, only a quarter mile from his house in Hadlyme, Connecticut. It is a tiny cemetery, and he had purchased the last available plot from a friend who chose to have his remains buried elsewhere. Dominick's dark marble tombstone reads "Father—Writer—Advocate for Justice."

Griffin Dunne found it too difficult to go through his father's belongings at the house called Clouds, so he asked Mart Crowley and Jack Cummings if they would make the trip to Hadlyme. Dominick's papers needed to be assembled and sent to the Dolph Briscoe Center for American History. Dominick took it as a great honor that the prestigious library at the University of Texas at Austin sought permission to include his manuscripts, letters, diaries, and other correspondence in their vast collection. Over fifty boxes of his papers were to be archived there along with those of Walter Cronkite, Harry Reasoner, and other great figures in the media. While clearing out one closet, Cummings found a dusty white plastic bag filled with old documents. It had been placed in the back on the floor. Cummings opened it to find the police report on Dominique Dunne's attack. "That brought home what he went through," said Cummings.

Sometime after her friend's death, Wendy Stark made a phone call to inquire about repurchasing the old fireplace fender. As agreed upon with Dominick, she wanted to buy back the antique for $800, the price she had paid in 1980 and the price Dominick had paid to buy it back a few years later. She was informed of the item's new price: $3,000. It later sold at a Stair Galleries auction for $2,900.

In November 2009 Dominick's last book, *Too Much Money*, was published. And as promised, Gus Bailey comes out of the closet. In the novel, Bailey believes a billionaire widow has planted a young boy in his hotel room to blackmail him into not writing about the mysterious death of her banker husband. Rather than submitting to her threat, Bailey admits to being homosexual. "But I've been celibate for almost twenty years," says the character, who goes on to reveal his true sexual orientation. Bailey explains, "Can't die with a secret, you know. I'm nervous about the kids, even though they're middle-aged men now. Not that they don't already know. I just never talk about it. It's been a lifelong problem."

Griffin Dunne helped promote the novel. Two of his more high-profile interviews were with George Stephanopoulos on *Good Morning America* and Terry Gross on *Fresh Air*. Both Stephanopoulos and Gross asked an innocuous first question and then got right to it with their second one, which included a reading of the above quote from Gus Bailey about his children.

Both interviewers asked Dominick's son how he felt reading that passage.

"It is so typical for him to come out and then leave," Griffin Dunne replied. "And here I am being asked and answering the question. It's just perfect."

When told of the interview, Alex Dunne had to agree with his brother. "So true," he said. "So true."

# Acknowledgments

This book began with an e-mail to Griffin Dunne, asking if he had any objections to my writing a biography of his father. He responded that, for various reasons, he did not want to authorize such a biography. I wrote back that I did not want to write an authorized biography, which in essence would give the estate the right to edit the book. Griffin and I met briefly to discuss the book. He answered a number of questions I had about his father and then wished me well. In the following year, we exchanged a few e-mails. Sometimes he answered my questions; sometimes he did not. I talked to more than 180 people for this book. Interviewees would often tell me, "I talked to Griffin first, and he said it was OK to talk to you." I thank Griffin Dunne for that support.

At the heart of any good biography are the people who speak to you. I wish to thank the following for talking to me in person, on the phone, or via e-mail. They include Dan Abrams, Marvin Adelson, Elizabeth Ashley, Barry Avrich, Don Bachardy, Shawn Baldwin, Arthur Barens, Steven Barshop, Peter Bart, Gordon Basichis, Keith Baxter, Adam Belanoff, Aimee Bell, Robert Berger, Patricia Bosworth, Scotty Bowers, Pamela Bozanich, Marie Brenner, Tracy Breton, Tita Cahn, Norman Carby, Mia Certic, George Christy, Craig Cignarelli, Harry Clein, Eden Collingsworth, David Patrick Columbia, Laura Nappi Connolly, Doug Cramer, Mart Crowley, Jack Cummings III, Bruce Cutler, Joe Danisi, Robert von Dassanowsky, Kirsty de Garis, Alan Dershowitz, Linda Deutsch, Jack Donahue, Tom Downey, James Duff, Timothy Dumas, Alex Dunne, Freddy Eberstadt, Henry Edwards, Jack Egan, John Erman, Patti Jo Fairbanks, Charles Feldman, Preston Stephen Fischer, Heidi Fleiss, David

Friend, Jonathan Friendly, Gil Garcetti, Lucianne Goldberg, Kim Goldman, Michael Griffith, Lawrence Grobel, Anthony Haden-Guest, Billy Hale, Joseph Hardy, Art Harris, Hudson Hickman, Judy Hilsinger, Michael Hogan, Chuck Hollerith, Peter Hong, Anthony Horn, John Johnson, Richard Johnson, Beth Karas, Philip Kearney, Tom Keller, Brian Kellow, Brad Kelly, Tony Kiser, Neil Koenigsberg, Jesse Kornbluth, Jill Krementz, David Kuhn, Sherry Lansing, Moira Lasch, Dr. Henry C. Lee, Dick Lehr, Leonard Levitt, Paul LiCalsi, Tim A. Lovejoy, Shoreen Maghame, Susan Magrino, Donald Manasse, William Mann, David Margolick, Asa Maynor, Clifford McCormick, Ciaran McEvoy, Steven Mikulan, Susanna Moore, Chris Morano, Paul Morrissey, Dorthy Moxley, Bruce Nelson, Barbara Nevins Taylor, Norma Novelli, Robert Osborne, Allan Parachini, Larry Peerce, Shirley Perlman, Andrea Reynolds Plunket, Sue Pollock, Gary L. Pudney, Dotson Rader, Robert Rand, Joan Ransohoff, Ira Reiner, Luanne Rice, Markham Roberts, Howard Rosenman, Betsy A. Ross, Bonnie Russell, Harriet Ryan, James Sansum, Jerry Schatzberg, Lawrence Schiller, Henry Schleiff, Joel Schumacher, Jessica Seigel, Kevin Sessums, Mickey Sherman, Ronald G. Shipp, John Simon, Chris Smith, Liz Smith, Valerie Smith, Judalon Smyth, Gary Spector, Wendy Stark, Arnold Stiefel, Sheila Sullivan, Patrick Taulere, Tim Teeman, Michael P. Thomas, Mike Tipping, Andrew Tobias, Jeffrey Toobin, Philip Truelove, Richard Turley, Matt Tyrnauer, Marc Vanasse, E. Duke Vincent, Joyce Wadler, Marc Watts, Edmund White, Peter White, Caroline Whitman, Angus Wilkie, Jim Willwerth, Kitty Winn, William Baldwin Young, Bobby Zarem, Dr. Harvey Zarem, and a few anonymous sources. My most special thanks go to Alex Dunne. Not everyone on this list is quoted in the book or referenced in the notes. Several people gave me information that, in fact, led me to delete errors or avoid misconceptions.

I wrote this book, but I did not build the libraries that helped make it possible. I am proud to pay taxes that support the Library for the Performing Arts at Lincoln Center, the Los Angeles Public Library, and the New York Public Library. The work of their librarians is essential to any reporter. Also crucial to the research for this biography is the Margaret Herrick Library in Beverly Hills and the Dolph Briscoe Center for American History at the University of Texas at Austin. Margaret L. Schankley at the Briscoe Center provided invaluable help, as did the Austin-based researcher Anne Gaines Rodriguez.

In November 2015 I traveled to Connecticut and Massachusetts to visit the schools Dominick Dunne attended in his youth. It was an invaluable research trip and one that turned into a minivacation thanks to Meghan

Kurtich at the Kingswood School, Katie Nash at Williams College, and Samuel Register at the Canterbury School.

Peter Bloch, Stephen M. Silverman, and Nanette Varian are friends who read early versions of the book. They offered great suggestions and corrected many errors.

Barbara Carroll, Ginny de Liagre, Holly Millea, Sue Pollock, Jordan Rodman, and Laurence Sutter are also friends who delivered amazing advice, help, info, and tips.

Last and foremost, I thank Raphael Kadushin, Sheila McMahon, and Amber Rose at the University of Wisconsin Press; my agent, Eric Myers at Dystel & Goderich Literary Management; and my photo guru, Howard Mandelbaum at Photofest.

# Notes

Dominick Dunne's papers are archived at the Dolph Briscoe Center for American History at the University of Texas at Austin. For the purposes of these notes, the Dunne papers are referenced in two ways, as quotes/facts taken from either a "Briscoe journal" or a "Briscoe letter." Where possible, the date of the material is given.

A number of people were interviewed multiple times for this book. The date given is that of the first interview, whether it was conducted in person, on the phone, or via e-mail.

## Chapter 1

Quotes from Norman Carby (May 23, 2015), Mart Crowley (February 5, 2015), James Duff (March 4, 2015), Alex Dunne (May 21, 2016), Joseph Hardy (January 19, 2016), Chuck Hollerith (January 11, 2016), Meghan Kurtich (November 15, 2015), Shoreen Maghame (April 29, 2015), Clifford McCormick (December 1, 2015), Robert Rand (October 20, 2015), Luanne Rice (April 7, 2016), and Matt Tyrnauer (January 9, 2016) are from interviews with the author. Dominick Dunne quotes are from the documentary *Dominick Dunne: After the Party*, except where noted.

4   pet-ferret/"dummy"/"We're not talking": Seth Mydans, "Stories of Sexual Abuse Transform Trial," *New York Times*, September 12, 1993.

—   Menendez and Lansing quotes: Court transcript, September 11, 1993.

5   "I wonder if I'm wrong": Maghame to author; Rand to author.

6   "Dad, I knew lots": Linda Deutsch, "Trial Resembles Dominick Dunne Novel," Associated Press, July 24, 1993.

—   both his sons later denied: A. Dunne to author; Griffin Dunne (March 11, 2016) to author.

6 "fascinated": D. Dunne letter, September 7, 2001, Robert Rand collection.

7 "ought to have been a girl"/"rescue": Briscoe letter, March 7, 1980.

— "Your dress is awfully cute": James H. Hyde, "Dominick Dunne," New EnglandTimes.com, 2009.

8 verse/"physical chill": Didion, *The White Album*, 19.

— "incipient fairyism": Briscoe letter, November 6, 1979.

— interrupt his thrashing: Griffin Dunne, *Fresh Air* interview, December 15, 2009.

— "invent"/"perfect Christ child": Briscoe letter, October 30, 1979.

9 "steerage to suburbia"/"Poppa": J. G. Dunne, *Harp*, 34.

— "Papa": Hyde, "Dominick Dunne."

— "He had an enormous influence": Dominick Dunne, "A Death in the Family," *Vanity Fair*, March 2004.

— "We would hate": Hyde, "Dominick Dunne."

10 "We were a strange family": Ibid.

— "only tolerated by": D. Dunne, *The Way We Lived Then*, 4.

— Catholics Against Kennedy: Mulcahy, *Why I'm a Democrat*, 55.

— Birch as a Christmas present: Didion, *Where I Was From*, 205.

— "don't get mad": J. G. Dunne, *Harp*, 26.

— Lydia Ingersoll anecdote: D. Dunne, *The Way We Lived Then*, 5.

— "social barricade": J. G. Dunne, *Harp*, 43.

11 "second best"/girls' schools: Briscoe letter, September 11, 1979.

— "Perhaps an omelette": D. Dunne, *The Way We Lived Then*, 5.

— "equation between"/"same fervor"/restroom episodes: Briscoe letter, 1979; Carby to author.

— "twelve or thirteen"/"I was so unhappy": Dominick Dunne to author for *Variety's* "The Movie That Changed My Life."

12 Senior Green tradition: Kurtich to author.

13 "I remember risking": Dominick Dunne, "The Talented Mr. Lonergan," *Vanity Fair*, July 2000.

— "Throughout the pattern": "Slain Beauty's Father Noted Playboy," *Journal-American*, October 29, 1943.

— "If he was good enough": D. Dunne, "The Talented Mr. Lonergan."

14 correspondence between Hume and Richard Dunne: Canterbury letters, October 1, 1943, and November 18, 1943.

15 Indiantown Gap and *Mariposa*: D. Dunne, *The Way We Lived Then*, 6.

— "scared shitless": Briscoe letter, August 30, 1986.

— Nazi helmet/"bad memory": Briscoe letter, January 4, 1945.

— "colored (nigger) baby": Briscoe letter, October 12, 1944.

— R. Dunne's letters to D. Dunne: Briscoe letter, October 11, 1979.

16 constant verbal abuse: Briscoe letter, August 30, 1986.

— "gold-dust twins": D. Dunne, *The Way We Lived Then*, 6.

— princess of Lippe episode: Briscoe letter, May 25, 2009.

17 "cook's night off"/"You must be so proud": Hyde, "Dominick Dunne."

— Devendorf, having sex: Briscoe letter, October 20, 1979.

— "My father had disliked": D. Dunne, *The Way We Lived Then*, 11.

— Dominick, Vidal, and Devendorf in Guatemala: Tyrnauer to author.

18 "You cannot overestimate": Duff to author; Tyrnauer to author.

— "They met"/Vidal's "We met"/"Utter nonsense!": Tyrnauer to author.

— "For Nick, Will you float": D. Dunne, *The Way We Lived Then*, 11.

— "hairy like a tarantula": Tyrnauer to author.

— "innocent"/"humiliation": Briscoe journal, 1979–80.

19 "Gosh, Okie's upset": Hyde, "Dominick Dunne."

20 "I gotta be in": Ibid.

— "If you're a character man": Ibid.

— "these incredibly filthy things": G. Dunne, *Fresh Air* interview.

— Sondheim correspondence: Briscoe letters, February 9, 1953, and February 24, 1953.

## Chapter 2

Quotes from Barry Avrich (March 25, 2015), Scotty Bowers (January 11, 2016), Norman Carby (May 23, 2015), George Christy (September 2, 2015), Harry Clein (February 20, 2015), Mart Crowley (February 5, 2015), Alex Dunne (May 21, 2015), Freddy Eberstadt (May 6, 2015), Susanna Moore (May 4, 2015), Howard Rosenman (January 30, 2015), Liz Smith (November 4, 2015), and Michael M. Thomas (February 9, 2015) are from interviews with the author, except where noted. Quotes from Dominick Dunne and Griffin Dunne are from the documentary *Dominick Dunne: After the Party*, except where noted.

22 "Would you meet my girlfriend": *Dominick Dunne: After the Party*.

— "which made the wheels": D. Dunne, *The Way We Lived Then*, 20.

23 "That's the girl you'll marry": *Dominick Dunne: After the Party*.

— "proof positive": Briscoe letter, December 7, 1979.

— "In my era, gay men": Tim Teeman, "Dominick Dunne," *Times* (London), February 19, 2009.

— "*Late Love* was a hit"/"Miss Ellen Beatriz Griffin accepts": D. Dunne, *The Way We Lived Then*, 19.

— Ellen Griffin letter: Briscoe letter, February 11, 1954.

24 "married Jacqueline Bouvier": D. Dunne, *The Way We Lived Then*, 5.

— "Did you know": Eberstadt to author.

25 his younger brother John: Daugherty, *The Last Love Song*, 355.

— stage manager's worst nightmare: Summers and Swan, *Sinatra*, 111.

26 "like a mick"/O'Hara and *Appointment in Samarra*: Briscoe letter, undated.

27 "What are you doing Friday night": *Dominick Dunne: After the Party*.

28   "seven or eight bedrooms"/"We spent": D. Dunne, *The Way We Lived Then*, 37.

—   "Were you drunk?": Carby to author.

—   "strong, uncompromising woman": Dominick Dunne, "Justice," *Vanity Fair*, March 1984.

—   tree-trimming party/"humiliated"/"plastered": Briscoe letter, December 16, 1958.

29   clients included Martin Manulis and Ralph Levy: Bowers to author.

30   death of infant girls/"an image": Briscoe letter, November 2, 1979.

—   Stompanato murder: Dominick Dunne to author for *Party Animals*; D. Dunne, *The Way We Lived Then*, 32.

32   "He's a snob": Several sources to author.

—   Sinatra decided to unload: Summers and Swan, *Sinatra*, 325.

33   a "loser": *Dominick Dunne: After the Party*.

—   Jay Sebring toupee and Daisy anecdote: Briscoe journal, 1979–80.

—   "It's our own little Hollywood": Gene Handsaker, "The Daisy," *The Gazette*, June 6, 1967.

—   "I'm awfully sorry": *Dominick Dunne: After the Party*.

—   "hit you in the *head*"/"If he ever did that": Briscoe journal, 1979–80.

34   Sonja Henie/Princess Margaret anecdotes: D. Dunne, *The Way We Lived Then*, 139–40.

—   "who was never photographed": *Dominick Dunne: In Search of Justice*.

—   After Dinner Dunnes: Avrich to author; Rosenman to author.

—   $20,000 party/"Lenny's mother"/"black-and-white motif": D. Dunne, *The Way We Lived Then*, 115.

35   "So naturally we invited him": Dominick Dunne, "Surviving the Darkness," *Vanity Fair*, December 2005.

36   143-word pan: Charles Gandee, "The Plot Thickens," *Vogue*, September 1996.

—   Bachardy sketched Lenny's gown: Don Bachardy (March 21, 2015) to author.

—   "There were hydrangeas": D. Dunne, *The Way We Lived Then*, 116.

—   "If all else fails": James H. Hyde, "Dominick Dunne," NewEnglandTimes.com, 2009.

—   "I always felt I was there": *Dominick Dunne: In Search of Justice*.

—   "He was at the mercy": Griffin Dunne, *Fresh Air* interview, December 15, 2009.

37   "See if you can find a part": D. Dunne, *The Way We Lived Then*, 179.

—   Mrs. Reagan was a popular: Several sources to author.

38   Davis and Dunne quotes regarding *The Decorator*: Crowley to author.

39   "she didn't want to attend": D. Dunne, *The Way We Lived Then*, 143.

40   "lacked the substance": G. Dunne, *Fresh Air* interview.

—   "regret" his infidelity: Briscoe journal, 1979–80.

—   "first time I dropped acid": Dominick Dunne, "Murder Most Unforgettable," *Vanity Fair*, April 2001.

41 her friends "despised" him: Briscoe journal, 1979–80.

—— "What kind of man": Moore to author.

—— kids to Coronado Island: A. Dunne to author.

—— "paint peeled inside and out": Didion, *The White Album*, 15.

—— "She had just done a concert": Ibid., 25.

42 "he totally changed the game": G. Dunne, *Fresh Air* interview.

—— Joyce Haber: Briscoe journal, 1979–80.

43 "real pot head": Ibid.

—— "picture of propriety" and LAX arrest: Briscoe letter, November 27, 1979; D. Dunne, *The Way We Lived Then*, 175–77.

—— "cunt" remark: Briscoe letter, November 27, 1979.

44 "beat it": D. Dunne, *The Way We Lived Then*, 176.

—— "Who do you know"/"Because when I went to parties": *Dominick Dunne: After the Party*.

—— "architect of my own destruction": Hyde, "Dominick Dunne."

45 Dunne and Crowley encounter: *Making the Boys*; Crowley to author for *Sexplosion*.

—— $80,000 dollars in "alimony": Briscoe journal, 1979–80.

### Chapter 3

Quotes from Peter Bart (February 11, 2015), Keith Baxter (May 17, 2015), Norman Carby (May 23, 2015), Mart Crowley (February 5, 2015), Alex Dunne (May 21, 2015), Freddy Eberstadt (May 6, 2015), Billy Hale (February 13, 2015), Joseph Hardy (January 19, 2016), Tony Kiser (July 28, 2015), Neil Koenigsberg (March 11, 2015), Paul Morrissey (March 24, 2015), Larry Peerce (February 9, 2015), Dotson Rader (September 26, 2015), Markham Roberts (March 30, 2015), Howard Rosenman (January 30, 2015), James Samsun (March 25, 2015), Jerry Schatzberg (February 12, 2015), Joel Schumacher (July 14, 2015), Peter White (January 11, 2016), and Kitty Winn (February 13, 2015) are from interviews with the author, except where noted. Dominick Dunne quotes are from the documentary *Dominick Dunne: After the Party*, except where noted.

46 Diners Club card: Briscoe letter, March 18, 1969.

47 "I suppose it was that I disgusted": Briscoe journal, 1979–80.

49 Eastside apartment episode: Briscoe journal, 1979–80; D. Dunne, *The Way We Lived Then*, 184–85; George Rush and Joanna Molloy, "Chateau Tales," *Daily News*, October 9, 1996; Rosenman to author.

50 "I was sitting in the shallow": Didion, *The White Album*, 42.

—— "Children were sent": D. Dunne, *The Way We Lived Then*, 193.

—— photo instructions: Briscoe letter, August 14, 1969.

51 "They don't think fags": *Making the Boys*.

52 Morrison became so entranced: D. Dunne, *The Way We Lived Then*, 185.

—— "from behind some disabling aphasia": Didion, *The White Album*, 25.

52  "narcotized by *Easy Rider*'s grosses": Ibid., 159.

54  "knocked over a lit candle": D. Dunne, *The Way We Lived Then*, 183–84.

55  "Al's going to steal the film": Winn to author.

——  *Herald-Examiner* visit to set: Bridget Byrne, "Controlled Panic on Set of 'Needle Park,'" *Los Angeles Herald-Examiner*, December 20, 1970.

——  "They put us up" and other Dunne quotes relating to *Needle Park*: Schatzberg to author.

56  "I always had this fear": James H. Hyde, "Dominick Dunne," NewEngland Times.com, 2009.

57  "piece of shit": Briscoe journal, 1979–80.

——  "I thought you'd be"/"I don't think he's like me": Lois Winebaum Perschetz, "Tony Perkins," *Women's Wear Daily*, October 2, 1972.

——  Ann-Margret: Briscoe journal, 1979–80.

58  Tramont/Mengers episode: Briscoe letter, November 26, 1979; *Dominick Dunne: After the Party*.

——  "Shirley Temple with a leer": "Show Business," *Time*, May 15, 1972.

——  Weld was an alcoholic: C. Robert Jennings, "This Must Be Bedlam," *Cosmopolitan*, October 1971.

——  "Miss Weld is not a very good": "Show Business."

——  "Each of them listed": Joyce Haber, "The Evolution of a Hollywood Brat," *Los Angeles Times*, October 22, 1971.

59  "He collected people": *Dominick Dunne: After the Party*.

——  "I get high on anything": "Show Business."

——  "Well, they're after me": Ann Guerin, "Frank Perry," *Show*, November 1979.

——  "absolutely a marriage"/"experimented with time": Ibid.

60  "very heady": Daugherty, *The Last Love Song*, 320.

——  "allowed to get away with": J. G. Dunne, *Harp*, 218.

——  "I can think of no higher praise": Ibid., 235.

——  Dominick's ideas for the scripts: Robert von Dassanowsky (August 26, 2015) to author.

61  "The filming of *Play It as It Lays*": Rex Reed, "'Play It as It Lays' Sees Hollywood in Harsh Light," *Daily News*, January 23, 1972.

62  "vomiting up her life"/"marvelous": Briscoe journal, 1979–80; anonymous source to author.

——  Miss Paranoia: Haber, "The Evolution of a Hollywood Brat."

——  "won an award at the Venice Film": Hyde, "Dominick Dunne."

——  "peanuts": Briscoe journal, 1979–80.

——  "thousands of dollars": Briscoe letter, October 25, 1979.

——  "masseur to lunch"/"blurred in those days": Briscoe journal, 1979–80.

64  "very regal, bedecked": Heymann, *Liz*, 313.

——  limo episode: Peerce to author.

——  Taylor/Warhol encounter: Morrissey to author; Roberts to author; Samsun to author; Briscoe letter, January 3, 2009.

65 "The Burtons are coming!" Baxter to author.

—— "You think it's easy": Amy Collins, "The Lure of Visconti," *Vanity Fair*, December 2001; Roberts to author.

66 Berger could count Keith: Carby to author.

—— monsignor episode: Briscoe journal, 1979–80; Baxter to author.

—— Taylor and Vignale episode: Baxter to author.

—— provide them with pornography: Heymann, *Liz*, 316.

—— "My drinking reached": *Dominick Dunne: In Search of Justice*.

67 gave everybody gifts: Peerce to author.

—— launch into a scathing critique: D. Dunne, *The Way We Lived Then*, 162.

—— "Get that asshole": Anonymous source to author.

68 "If there's going to be anything grotty": Peerce to author.

—— "Frankly, I agree": Peerce to author.

—— "That's not my job": Baxter to author.

—— "bombe plastique": Briscoe letter, undated.

—— Berger and Burton encounter: Baxter to author.

69 "You stupid cow": Baxter to author.

—— "They can damn well": Heymann, *Liz*, 315.

70 Lassie movie anecdote: Peerce to author.

—— "I want a Bloody": Peerce to author.

71 Thanksgiving dinner anecdote: Baxter to author.

—— "this is going to be your last film": *Dominick Dunne: After the Party*.

—— fat girl anecdote: Briscoe journal, 1979–80; *Dominick Dunne: After the Party*.

72 "It's possible. Sue was a great friend": *Dominick Dunne: After the Party*.

—— Kellow on Tramont: Brian Kellow (February 15, 2016) to author; Kellow, *Can I Go Now?*, 201.

## Chapter 4

Quotes from Marie Brenner (October 19, 2015), Norman Carby (May 23, 2015), Douglas Cramer (July 13, 2015), Alex Dunne (May 21, 2015), Jack Egan (June 2, 2015), Joseph Hardy (January 19, 2016), Hudson Hickman (January 13, 2016), Tony Kiser (July 28, 2015), Jesse Kornbluth (April 23, 2015), Asa Maynor (October 6, 2015), Dotson Rader (September 26, 2015), Wendy Stark (April 8, 2016), Arnold Stiefel (January 29, 2015), and Andrew Tobias (August 10, 2015) are from interviews with the author, except where noted. Dominick Dunne quotes are from the documentary *Dominick Dunne: After the Party*, except where noted.

74 McDermott got him the job: Carby to author.

—— Coward and Maugham: Briscoe letter, September 26, 1979.

75 "one on one": Briscoe letter, November 19, 1979.

—— "didn't come into her own": James H. Hyde, "Dominick Dunne," New EnglandTimes.com, 2009.

—— "tomb of secrets": J. G. Dunne, *Harp*, 31–32.

75 "That didn't happen": Hyde, "Dominick Dunne."

—— Carr parties: Hofler, *Party Animals*, 28–31.

76 "If Bunnies were lacking": Joyce Haber, "The Evolution of a Hollywood Brat," *Los Angeles Times*, October 22, 1971.

—— "Nureyev was sexually": Hofler, *Party Animals*, 13.

77 Stein anecdote: Briscoe letter, December 1, 1979.

—— "I never repeat gossip": A. Dunne to author.

—— Irving Lazar party: Briscoe letter, December 7, 1979.

78 "He gets invited": Briscoe journal, 1979–80.

—— Carr/Capote party: Hofler, *Party Animals*, 32–37; Carby to author; Carol Whitman (October 5, 2015) to author.

80 Capote and Dunne quotes at Beverly Wilshire: Rader to author.

81 Dominique Dunne letter: Briscoe letter, undated.

82 Stark joke: Briscoe journal, 1979–80; anonymous sources to author.

—— Melnick anecdote/"low esteem": Briscoe journal, 1979–80.

83 John Gregory Dunne critique of script: Briscoe journal, 1979–80; D. Dunne, *The Way We Lived Then*, 188; Kiser to author.

84 "out-of-body experience": Briscoe journal, 1979–80; D. Dunne, *The Way We Lived Then*, 188.

85 unemployment anecdote: Christopher Bagley, "Party Time," *W*, October 1999.

—— Carr/Begelman party: Dominick Dunne interview with author for *Party Animals*; D. Dunne, *The Way We Lived Then*, 187.

86 Polo Lounge episode: Egan to author; Briscoe journal, 1979–80; Briscoe letters, November 6, 1979, November 26, 1979, and March 11, 1980; D. Dunne, *The Way We Lived Then*, 208.

88 Prashker lunch: Briscoe journal, March 15, 1980; anonymous source to author.

89 Cramer dinner: Briscoe journal, 1979–80.

—— "We need somebody who knows": Cramer to author; Briscoe journal, 1979–80.

—— "Where's he?": Cramer to author.

—— Haber rumors: Briscoe journal, 1979–80.

90 Dominick's funeral attendance: Hardy to author; Rosenman to author; Griffin Dunne, *Fresh Air* interview, December 15, 2009.

91 "I know. I know"/"I care completely": Hardy to author.

—— suicide attempts and sex for hire: Briscoe letter, November 30, 1979.

92 *The Users* screening: Hardy to author; Briscoe journal, 1979–80; Briscoe letters, November 1, 1979, and December 10, 1979.

—— "fun"/"blah review": Briscoe letter, November 1, 1979.

93 "grim-faced": "Eye," *Women's Wear Daily*, September 20, 1978.

—— "It's the only present": Carby to author.

—— Simon & Schuster book deal: Stiefel to author; Briscoe journal, 1979–80.

—— "knowing I was broke": Briscoe journal, 1979–80.

—— Advocate Experience/"uncheered"/"revenge": Carby to author; Hardy to author; Briscoe letter, November 10, 1979.

94 "Dear Kids" letter: Briscoe letter, January 21, 1979; Hardy to author.

—— Mengers wearing a dildo: Briscoe letter, December 5, 1979.

95 "I had a young, rich": Briscoe letter, November 4, 1979.

—— "It's Chasen's": Stiefel to author.

96 "*Grease* was the best thing": Hofler, *Party Animals*, 119.

—— Carr/Stewart/Hamilton party: Dominick Dunne interview, unpublished, with author for *Party Animals*.

—— Stark, Stein, and Wald encounters: Briscoe letter, November 12, 1979; Stark to author.

97 Benny party: Briscoe letters, October 8, 1979, and October 13, 1979; *Dominick Dunne: After the Party*; D. Dunne, *The Way We Lived Then*, 197.

## Chapter 5

Quotes from Norman Carby (May 23, 2015), Mart Crowley (February 5, 2015), Alex Dunne (May 21, 2015), Freddy Eberstadt (May 6, 2015), Tony Kiser (July 28, 2015), Ciaran McEvoy (April 16, 2015), Wendy Stark (April 8, 2016), and Arnold Stiefel (January 29, 2015) are from interviews with the author, except where noted. Griffin Dunne quotes are from *Dominick Dunne: After the Party*.

100 "Lunch at the Polo Lounge": Briscoe letter, November 7, 1979; D. Dunne, *The Way We Lived Then*, 202.

—— Twin View Resort details, anecdotes, and quotes: Carby to author; A. Dunne to author; Tom Keller (October 5, 2015) to author; "Local Woman Remembers Dominick Dunne," *The Nugget*, September 1, 2009; David Jasper, "Champ Sherman Gets a Visit," *The Bulletin*, November 23, 2007; D. Dunne, *The Way We Lived Then*, 202–3; *Dominic Dunne: After the Party*; Briscoe journal, 1979–80; Briscoe letters, September 26, 1979, October 1, 1979, October 10, 1979, October 28, 1979, and November 30, 1979.

102 Linda correspondence: Briscoe letters, September 26, 1979, October 10, 1979, and November 30, 1979.

—— John Gregory Dunne correspondence: Briscoe letters, November 11, 1979, and November 29, 1979.

104 therapist correspondence: Briscoe letter, November 29, 1979.

105 Driving south on Highway 1: Dunne interview with author for *Variety's* "The Movie That Changed My Life."

—— Bloomingdale energy tips: Briscoe journal, 1979–80.

106 "She loved me": *Dominick Dunne: After the Party*.

—— Stark wedding: Briscoe journal, 1979–80; Briscoe letter, January 28, 1980; Stark to author.

—— Madeline Kahn episode: Briscoe letters, January 28, 1980, and January 30, 1980; Stiefel to author.

107 Stephen Dunne's suicide: J. G. Dunne, *Harp*, 19 and 21; D. Dunne, *The Way We Lived Then*, 210–11; *Dominick Dunne: After the Party*; Briscoe letters, March 5, 1980, March 9, 1980, March 19, 1980, and August 30, 1986; Briscoe journal, 1979–80.

—— "all tapped out": McEvoy to author.

108 Capote correspondence and Dunne's reaction: Dan Shaw, "On the Inside, Looking Out," *New York Times*, April 11, 1993.

109 hitchhiker episode: Briscoe journal, 1979–80; Caroline Whitman (October 5, 2015) to author.

—— "murky circumstances": Briscoe letter, November 19, 1979; Briscoe journal, 1979–80.

—— Spalding Drive sale: Stark to author; Stiefel to author; Whitman to author.

110 "Medici-like" and Fuller apartment: Carby to author; Kiser to author; Briscoe journal, 1979–80; Briscoe letter, July 14, 1980.

—— *The Razor's Edge* structure: Carby to author; Briscoe letter, November 5, 1979.

—— Korda's rejection: Briscoe letters, September 2, 1980, and October 18, 1980; anonymous source to author.

111 Cal Culver episode: Briscoe letter, August 8, 1980; anonymous source to author.

112 Korda's acceptance: Briscoe letters, September 2, 1980, September 23, 1980, and October 18, 1980; anonymous source to author.

—— "There's nothing the public": *Dominick Dunne: In Search of Justice*.

113 "You need to put": A. Dunne to author.

—— "Yes, I think I can": *Dominick Dunne: After the Party*.

## Chapter 6

Quotes from Marvin Adelson (September 17, 2015), Stephen Barshop (July 28, 2015), Marie Brenner (October 19, 2015), Norman Carby (May 23, 2015), Linda Deutsch (February 23, 2015), Alex Dunne (May 21, 2015), Susanna Moore (May 4, 2015), Dotson Rader (September 26, 2015), Chris Smith (May 9, 2015), Patrick Terrail (April 21, 2016), Mike Tipping (October 15, 2015), and Joyce Wadler (September 28, 2015) are from interviews with the author, except where noted.

114 "It was a flop": *Dominick Dunne: In Search of Justice*.

—— "thoughtless spectacle": Christopher Bagley, "Party Time," *W*, October 1999.

—— "Joan Didion's brother-in-law": D. Dunne, *The Way We Lived Then*, 188.

—— Brown letter: Briscoe letter, January 15, 1981.

116 "these Bukowski characters": Griffin Dunne, *Fresh Air* interview, December 15, 2009.

—— "Sweeney": Dominick Dunne, "Justice," *Vanity Fair*, March 1984.

—— "snob thing because": James H. Hyde, "Dominick Dunne," NewEngland Times.com, 2009.

117 "No one's total time": Dominick Dunne, "Was O.J. Simpson a Loving Father and Brother, or a Cold-Blooded Killer?," *Vanity Fair*, September 1995.

—— "relay teams": D. Dunne, "Justice."

—— "You want to know"/Didion phone call: Carby to author; Wadler to author; Eden Collinsworth (April 24, 2015) to author.

118 "Oh, what difference"/"It's hurtful to us"/"interim object": D. Dunne, "Justice."

—— "very dependable young man": "Dominique Dunne Dies in Coma," *Los Angeles Times*, November 5, 1982.

—— "the best legal counsel": "'Poltergeist' Actress Attacked; Ex-Boyfriend Held," *Santa Monica Evening Outlook*, November 3, 1982.

—— "would obtain the best": D. Dunne, "Justice."

119 "third-rate rich people": Briscoe letter, January 30, 1983.

—— "public relations campaign"/"to incite me": D. Dunne, "Justice."

—— He died of lymphoma: "Joe Shapiro," *Los Angeles Times*, September 25, 1999.

—— ICM agent: Briscoe letter, August 30, 1983.

120 "He told me he was off": Tina Brown, "The Unforgettable Dominick Dunne," *Huffington Post*, August 27, 2009.

—— "The night before": Chris Smith, "Dominick Dunne v. Robert Kennedy," *New York*, June 23, 2003.

—— "this little English wren": Hyde, "Dominick Dunne."

—— "Tina Brown literally discovered": *Dominick Dunne: After the Party.*

—— reluctant writer: William Norwich, "Dominick Dunne," *Tatler*, September 1992; C. Smith to author.

121 "There are writers who discover": Brown, "The Unforgettable Dominick Dunne."

—— offered him $15,000: Briscoe letter, June 12, 1983.

—— "You shouldn't be wasting": Hyde, "Dominick Dunne."

122 Igor Cassini research: Briscoe journal, July 6, 1983; Liz Smith (November 4, 2015) to author.

123 Annie Hall glasses: D. Dunne, "Justice."

—— Lenny and Dominick's phone calls: Briscoe journal, 1983.

—— POMC: D. Dunne, "Justice"; Briscoe journal, 1983.

124 "Before the first preliminary hearing": J. G. Dunne, *Harp*, 107.

—— "It's the last business": D. Dunne, "Justice."

—— Boh! lunch/Barry Farrell offer: Ibid.; anonymous source to author.

125 Leslie Abramson: Briscoe journal, July 9, 1983; anonymous source to author.

—— John and Joan's secretary: Briscoe letter, July 22, 1983.

—— "surrogate sister": J. G. Dunne, *Quintana & Friends*, 98.

126 "Let me remind you, Miss Pierce": D. Dunne, "Justice."

127 Robert Mitchum: Briscoe letter, July 13, 1983.

—— "Ladies and gentlemen, I am going": D. Dunne, "Justice."

128 Carby on witness stand/"a miracle": Briscoe letter, August 13, 1983; Adelson to author; Carby to author.
129 "Your honor, Alex Dunne"/"I can't go back"/"His violent past"/"A few jurors": D. Dunne, "Justice."
130 Katz and Dunne exchange: Ibid.
—— "proudest moment": G. Dunne, *Fresh Air* interview.
131 "You don't know me": A. Dunne to author.
—— "Nick was ready to kill": Anonymous source to author.
—— "I really didn't want to": Tony Castro, "Celebrity Crime Reporter Inspired by Own Tragedy," *Daily News*, September 27, 2007.
—— "My rage needed a release": *Dominick Dunne: In Search of Justice.*
132 "Now don't you talk": D. Dunne, "Justice."
—— "Dominick had a voice": *Dominick Dunne: After the Party.*
—— "scraps of paper": Anonymous sources to author.

## Chapter 7

Quotes from Arthur Barens (October 28, 2015) and Gordon Basichis (June 1, 2015) are from interviews with the author, except where noted.
134 police car status symbol: Dominick Dunne, "The Woman Who Knew Too Little," *Vanity Fair*, September 1984.
136 "Betsy table": Ibid.
—— giggles in the courtroom: Ibid.
137 "Dominick has been quite clever": *Dominick Dunne: After the Party.*

## Chapter 8

Quotes from Scotty Bowers (January 11, 2016), Marie Brenner (October 19, 2015), Tracy Breton (September 19, 2016), Alan Dershowitz (February 25, 2016), James Duff (March 4, 2015), John Erman (January 30, 2015), Charles Feldman (July 30, 2015), Preston Stephen Fischer (September 17, 2015), Jonathan Friendly (October 12, 2015), Lucianne Goldberg (February 21, 2015), Judy Hilsinger (January 29, 2015), David Kuhn (August 25, 2015), Dick Lehr (October 19, 2015), Barbara Nevins Taylor (September 16, 2015), Andrea Reynolds Plunket (September 30, 2015), Sue Pollock (February 10, 2015), and Joyce Wadler (September 28, 2015) are from interviews with the author, except where noted.
138 "Novels aren't being": *Guilty Pleasure.*
—— "that changed my life": *Dominick Dunne: After the Party.*
139 three million copies: G. Dunne to author.
—— Young, Bacall, Smith, Osborne: Erman to author.
140 Radie Harris: Robert Osborne (May 12, 2016) to author.
—— type-written seven-page: Briscoe letter, July 8, 1986; Erman to author.
141 "don't like rich people": Nevins Taylor to author.

143 "Isn't this a blast": Lehr to author.

144 "a football game": Dominick Dunne, "Fatal Charm," *Vanity Fair*, August 1985.

145 "We dined across Bellevue": Ibid.

—— "as long as they take Cosima": Ibid.

146 "friendly spoon into a reporter's parfait": Alex S. Jones, "Coma Trial: After Hoopla," *New York Times*, June 12, 1985.

147 "Mr. Dunne is not a friend": D. Dunne, "Fatal Charm."

—— Corviglia Club: D. Dunne, *The Way We Lived Then*, 110.

148 "You're not going to": Brenner to author.

—— "I have better jewels": D. Dunne, "Fatal Charm."

—— "to love something": Duff to author.

149 obsessing about his interview: Nevins Taylor to author.

—— "The necrophilia story": D. Dunne, "Fatal Charm."

—— "S&M people": Mike Hogan, "What Drove Dominick Dunne's Quest for Justice," *Vanity Fair*, November 2009.

150 "misguided. . . . I have no feeling": Jonathan Friendly, "Von Bulow Jury Issues Acquittal on All Charges," *New York Times*, June 11, 1985.

151 "Coincidental obscenity"/"I do not understand": John Gregory Dunne, "How to Write a Novel," *Esquire*, October 1986.

—— "cowardly blow": Briscoe letter, undated.

—— "The trouble started"/Alex and Dominick Dunne fight: James H. Hyde, "Dominick Dunne," NewEnglandTimes.com, 2009; Briscoe letter, August 15, 1987; A. Dunne (May 21, 2016) to author.

## Chapter 9

Quotes from Elizabeth Ashley (February 6, 2015), Tita Cahn (March 5, 2015), David Patrick Columbia (February 15, 2015), Mart Crowley (February 5, 2015), Freddy Eberstadt (May 6, 2015), Judy Hilsinger ( January 29, 2015), Jesse Kornbluth (April 23, 2015), Bruce Nelson (March 30, 2015), Markham Roberts (March 30, 2015), James Sansum (March 25, 2015), and William Baldwin Young (March 18, 2015) are from interviews with the author, except where noted.

168 A computer person: Kornbluth to author.

—— "Dad, this is in the same": Griffin Dunne, *Fresh Air* interview, December 15, 2009.

169 "bite the hands that fed": "Nick Dunne Takes on the Clarence's Set," *Women's Wear Daily*, January 4, 1988.

—— "There we were, at a table": Stephanie Mansfield, "Social Butterfly Dunne," *Washington Post*, April 5, 1988.

170 "I didn't tell one private thing": Ibid.

—— "It wasn't based on Oscar": Hilsinger to author.

—— nicknamed Darkie: Eberstadt to author.

—— Mehle had read early galleys: Columbia to author.

170 "I will not be where": "Nick Dunne Takes on the Clarence's Set."
— "She's the cattle heiress": D. Dunne, *The Way We Lived Then*, 172.
171 Dominick hated Jerry Zipkin: G. Dunne ( January 21, 2015) to author.
— "a great teacher"/"chief eunuch": Bob Colacello, "A Walker on the Wild Side," *Vanity Fair*, September 1995.
— "cunt" remark: Roberts to author; Sansum to author.
— "I never became an extra": Dan Shaw, "On the Inside, Looking Out," *New York Times*, April 11, 1993.
172 "We are all terribly saddened": Jack Jones and Carol McGraw, "Fatal Shooting of Real Estate Man Probed," *Los Angeles Times*, September 27, 1987.
— "Don't use the real names": Nelson to author.
173 "This is a smart novel": Jill Robinson, "Up to No Good in Hollywood," *New York Times*, June 10, 1990.
— "What got him in trouble": Mike Hogan, "What Drove Dominick Dunne's Quest for Justice," *Vanity Fair*, November 2009.
174 "full participation" sex/"the worst parents": Young to author.

## Chapter 10

Quotes from Aimee Bell (August 3, 2015), Tita Cahn (March 5, 2015), Jack Cummings III (February 8, 2015), Len Levitt (March 4, 2015), Chris Morano ( July 28, 2015), Dorthy Moxley (March 3, 2015), Robert Rand (October 20, 2015), and Kevin Sessums (March 26, 2015) are from interviews with the author, except where noted.
176 "Peter was ill-used": D. Dunne, *The Way We Lived Then*, 198.
177 "The man who instigated": Dominick Dunne, "The Verdict," *Vanity Fair*, March 1992.
— "I didn't know who did it": Dominick Dunne, "Triumph by Jury," *Vanity Fair*, August 2002.
178 "Martha Moxley became a crusade": *Dominick Dunne: In Search of Justice*.
— "It will bring attention": Moxley to author.
— editor John Cotter: Levitt, *Conviction*, 90.
179 "Did Dominick think": Ibid., 198.
— "It's too easy to say": Dan Shaw, "On the Inside, Looking Out," *New York Times*, April 11, 1993.
— "Dominick Dunne takes all": Maureen Dowd, "The Circus of Constant Bradley," *New York Times*, June 6, 1993.
180 "How amazing you": Shaw, "On the Inside."
— "Little did I suspect": Levitt, *Conviction*, 198.
— Morrall and Terrien quotes: Ibid., 203–4.
181 Sutton report episode: Levitt to author; Morano to author; Moxley to author.
— "I know something about": Moxley to author.

## Chapter 11

Quotes from Dan Abrams (August 7, 2015), Pamela Bozanich (October 19, 2015), Norman Carby (May 23, 2015), Craig Cignarelli (July 27, 2015), Linda Deutsch (February 23, 2015), Philip Kearney (October 19, 2015), Shoreen Maghame (April 29, 2015), Bruce Nelson (March 30, 2015), Norma Novelli (November 4, 2015), Robert Rand (October 20, 2015), Ira Reiner (February 20, 2016), and Judalon Smyth (October 20, 2015) are from interviews with the author, except where noted.

183  "I have heard of very few": Dominick Dunne, "Nightmare on Elm Drive," *Vanity Fair*, October 1990.

——  "With the exception of some": Ibid.

184  "There was something about": *Dominick Dunne: In Search of Justice*.

——  Menendez murder: D. Dunne, "Nightmare on Elm Drive"; Soble and Johnson, *Blood Brothers*, 4–12.

——  "We are not disputing": Court transcript.

——  "This is not a prosecution trial": Ibid.

186  Jose Menendez might be gay: Dominick Dunne, "Menendez Justice," *Vanity Fair*, March 1994.

——  "adorable. They're the two": D. Dunne, "Nightmare on Elm Drive."

187  "You don't have to be Sigmund": Abramson, *The Defense Is Ready*, 288.

——  "He comes up with false": *Guilty Pleasure*.

——  "doyenne of crime reporters": Dominick Dunne, "Three Faces of Evil," *Vanity Fair*, June 1996.

——  "contradicted at trial": Abramson, *The Defense Is Ready*, 289.

——  "I never ever believed": *Dominick Dunne: After the Party*.

——  "pulled Erik's hair when": Court transcript.

188  "But why the mother"/"I wonder if": Maghame to author.

189  "Well, I had a moment": Rand to author.

——  "great neurotic actor": D. Dunne, "Menendez Justice."

——  "But I didn't kill": Ibid.

192  "Did you know that Lyle": Ibid.

193  "Judalon, you've got to tell": Smyth to author.

194  "implanted": Alan Abrahamson, "Psychologist's Ex-Lover Testifies He Brainwashed Her," *Los Angeles Times*, November 17, 1993.

——  "the heroine of this story": Briscoe journal, 1994.

195  "Spiritually, yes": D. Dunne, "Menendez Justice."

——  "If I was gay": Kearney to author.

196  "My car is in the shop": Kearney to author.

——  "Oh, that was Barbara": Kearney to author.

197  "So Mr. Kearney, you've been": Kearney to author.

——  "the little puke": Robert Rand, "Menendez Confidential," *Playboy*, July 1995.

198 "It's a curious stand": George Rush and Joanna Molloy, "Contempt Citation Refuels Dunne-ybrook," *Daily News*, March 5, 1997.

—— "After that my brother and I": Dominick Dunne, "Death in the Family," *Vanity Fair*, May 2003.

## Chapter 12

Quotes from Dan Abrams (August 7, 2015), Marie Brenner (October 19, 2015), Tita Cahn (March 5, 2015), Robert von Dassanowsky (August 26, 2015), Alan Dershowitz (February 25, 2016), Linda Deutsch (February 23, 2015), Patti Jo Fairbanks (March 12, 2015), Heidi Fleiss (March 18, 2015), Lucianne Goldberg (February 21, 2015), Kim Goldman (August 12, 2015), Art Harris (April 3, 2015), Judy Hilsinger (January 29, 2015), Peter Hong (May 2, 2015), John Johnson (November 30, 2015), Beth Karas (February 26, 2015), Sherry Lansing (April 30, 2015), Shoreen Maghame (April 29, 2015), David Margolick (November 9, 2015), Clifford McCormick (December 1, 2015), Shirley Perlman (March 31, 2015), Joan Ransohoff (March 22, 2016), Ira Reiner (February 20, 2016), Lawrence Schiller (March 18, 2015), Ronald G. Shipp (February 23, 2015), Wendy Stark (April 8, 2016), Jeffrey Toobin (April 23, 2015), and James Willwerth (March 13, 2015) are from interviews with the author, except where noted. Because *Another City, Not My Own* is a novel, author checked the accuracy of quotes with those people "interviewed" for the book.

200 "No, not really": Maghame to author.

—— "Lucky for him": D. Dunne, *Another City, Not My Own*, 11.

201 "For ten minutes, O.J.": *Dominic Dunne: In Search of Justice*.

—— "The Kennedys hate me": McCormick to author.

202 "Did you plant the glove": Jeffrey Toobin, "An Incendiary Defense," *New Yorker*, July 25, 1994.

—— "You'll like Jeffrey": D. Dunne, *Another City, Not My Own*, 35.

—— "He sounds like Oliver North": Toobin, *The Run of His Life*, 146.

—— "After a while [Fuhrman] began": Ibid., 147.

—— "The Fuhrman disability case": Ibid., 149.

203 Clark on EDTA: *O.J.: Made in America*.

—— "Look, if the police did something": Dershowitz to author.

204 Mrs. Peck being pretentious and superior: Briscoe journal, 1979–80.

—— "America's most famous journalist": *New York* cover, June 23, 2003.

—— "Stanley thought you": D. Dunne, *Another City, Not My Own*, 191–92.

—— "People waited for those": Mike Hogan, "How *Vanity Fair*'s Dominick Dunne Relentlessly Pursued the O.J. Simpson Story," *Vanity Fair* online, March 1, 2016.

205 "had the curious look": Dominick Dunne, "L.A. in the Age of O.J.," *Vanity Fair*, February 1995.

—— "Please don't ask Marcia": D. Dunne, *Another City, Not My Own*, 54.

—— strong female attorneys: Dominick Dunne, "Justice," *Vanity Fair*, March 1984.

—— "Everyone was looking": Mike Hogan, "What Drove Dominick Dunne's Quest for Justice," *Vanity Fair*, November 2009.

207 Neil Papiano: D. Dunne, *Another City, Not My Own*, 133.

—— "It was the most bizarre": Karas to author.

208 "He wasn't looking to be": Dan Abrams, "Dominick Dunne," *Huffington Post*, September 26, 2009.

—— "O.J.'s lawyers"/"If you're on the defense": *Guilty Pleasure*.

—— "I love being famous": Several sources to author.

—— John Bryan and Michael Moore episodes: Perlman to author.

209 "Judith Krantz in pants": D. Dunne, *Another City, Not My Own*, 71.

—— "Rastafarian": Hong to author.

210 "Why are we sitting": Goldman to author.

211 "To be honest, Shipp": Shipp to author.

—— "about as relevant": Court transcript.

—— "I think that I have never": D. Dunne, *Justice*, 173.

212 "I guess you can say": Court transcript.

—— "Were you prepared": Ibid.

—— "Black journalists in the newsroom": Clark, *Without a Doubt*, 289.

—— "The jury should see": Dominick Dunne, "Follow the Blood," *Vanity Fair*, July 1995.

213 "Sometimes I think Al Cowlings": Dominick Dunne, "Was O.J. Simpson a Loving Father and Brother, or a Cold-Blooded Killer?," *Vanity Fair*, September 1995.

215 "In the flesh, Mark Fuhrman": Toobin, *The Run of His Life*, 312.

216 "What's it going to be like": Dominick Dunne, "The 'N' Word," *Vanity Fair*, November 1995.

—— "I know that": Goldman to author.

—— "to argue our right to view": Dominick Dunne, "If the Gloves Fit . . . ," *Vanity Fair*, August 1995.

—— "What was the most haunting": Ibid.

217 "He went almost insane": Hogan, "How *Vanity Fair*'s Dominick Dunne."

## Chapter 13

Quotes from Dan Abrams (August 7, 2015), Robert "Buzz" Berger (February 16, 2015), Tita Cahn (March 5, 2015), Robert von Dassanowsky (August 26, 2015), Linda Deutsch (February 23, 2015), Alex Dunne (May 21, 2015), Patti Jo Fairbanks (March 12, 2015), Art Harris (April 3, 2015), Shoreen Maghame (April 29, 2015), David Margolick (November 9, 2015), Shirley Perlman (March 31, 2015), Joan Ransohoff (March 22, 2016), Lawrence Schiller (March 18, 2015), Wendy Stark (April 8, 2016), and James Willwerth (March 13, 2015) are from interviews with the author, except where noted.

218   Nation of Islam guards: Dominick Dunne, "London Calling (and Dishing)," *Vanity Fair*, June 2005.

——   "I have to leave Los Angeles": Abrams to author.

219   "camp": Briscoe journal, 1995.

——   Diana's revenge dress: Rebecca Adams, "Princess Di's Black Dress," *Huffington Post*, July 1, 2013.

220   "Because I couldn't get a job": Berger to author.

——   "When you write you do": *Dominick Dunne: After the Party.*

——   "Get your daughter": Berger to author; Grobel, *Signing In*, 422.

——   $50,000 a day: *O.J.: Made in America.*

221   "restart his life. . . . But I couldn't help thinking": Dominick Dunne, "O.J. Simpson: Life after the Murder Trial," *Vanity Fair*, December 1995; D. Dunne, *Justice*, 205.

——   "I knew she was flipping": Grobel, *Signing In*, 423.

222   "Schiller specialized in": Toobin, *The Run of His Life*, 253–54.

——   "hate-filled tidbits": Ibid., 400.

——   "I want to put you": Schiller to author.

223   "If only he'd broken": A. Dunne to author.

——   "Did you see that?": Deutsch to author.

224   "During the nine months": Dan Abrams, "Dominick Dunne," *Huffington Post*, September 26, 2009.

——   "I'm not sure you want": Perlman to author.

——   "Everyone's been to a party": "O.J. Reporters Romp in Hot Tub," *New York Post*, September 28, 1995.

——   "No one had anticipated": Clark, *Without a Doubt*, 276.

——   Lawson in Savannah: Mike Hogan, "How *Vanity Fair*'s Dominick Dunne Relentlessly Pursued the O.J. Simpson Story," *Vanity Fair* online, March 1, 2016.

225   "NBC had forty cameras": Toobin, *The Run of His Life*, 429.

——   "Stop crying"/"What happened": Maghame to author.

226   Griffin Dunne saw his father's: Hogan, "How *Vanity Fair*'s Dominick Dunne."

——   "I'm not myself": Harris to author.

——   CNN interview: D. Dunne, *Another City, Not My Own*, 310.

227   "I look like a small-mouth": Ransohoff to author.

——   "I beg you, let": Hogan, "How *Vanity Fair*'s Dominick Dunne."

——   Griffin Dunne on *Another City*: Griffin Dunne (January 21, 2015) to author.

228   "way of ridding myself": Briscoe letter, July 20, 1998.

——   "thoroughly absorbing": James Collins, "L.A. Confidential," *Time*, November 17, 1997.

——   "numbing": Laura Miller, "O.J. the Novel," *New York Times*, November 30, 1997.

——   "fuckin' liar": Celia McGee, "Dunne In," *New York Observer*, January 26, 1998.

— "I am not aware of any": Ibid.

229 "You put a murderer": Cahn to author; Stark to author.

— "They'll have to get": Fairbanks to author.

— "staged": Willwerth to author.

230 "I'm very aware that": *Dominick Dunne: After the Party.*

— "No, it's not that kind": Dassanowsky to author.

231 "but an idealized fantasy fulfillment": Robert von Dassanowsky, "The Inconvenient Women: Female Consciousness and the American Gentry in the Novels of Dominick Dunne," *Popular Culture Review* 8, no. 1 (February 1997): 35–47 (38).

— "prevailing modes of male-dominant": Ibid., 44–45.

## Chapter 14

Quotes from Robert "Buzz" Berger (February 16, 2015), Alex Dunne (May 21, 2015), Lucianne Goldberg (February 21, 2015), Len Levitt (March 4, 2015), and Dorthy Moxley (March 3, 2015) are from interviews with the author, except where noted.

233 "speculative report": Briscoe letter, undated; Moxley to author.

— "Dorthy, I know who"/"I haven't read it"/"this huge mess": Moxley to author.

— "My only motivation": Chris Smith, "Dominick Dunne vs. Robert Kennedy," *New York*, June 23, 2003.

234 "I first heard about": Levitt, *Conviction*, 204.

— Goldberg arranged: Dominick Dunne, "Triumph by Jury," *Vanity Fair*, August 2002.

— "Hey, Mark, I've got": Fuhrman, *Murder in Greenwich*, xiv.

235 "After you heard from Dorthy": Levitt, *Conviction*, 204.

— "In time I gave"/"I felt as though a giant"/"Writers, they're all": Ibid.

— "If I had Dr. Kervorkian's": A. Dunne to author.

236 "I'm sorry, Lenny": *Dominick Dunne: After the Party.*

— Lenny and Dominick Dunne's final meeting/"Do you remember": Griffin Dunne, *Fresh Air* interview, December 15, 2009.

— Alex and Dominick Dunne altercation: Briscoe letter, October 2, 1999; A. Dunne to author.

## Chapter 15

Quotes from Dan Abrams (August 7, 2015), Barry Avrich (March 25, 2015), Graydon Carter (March 9, 2016), Laura Nappi Connolly (February 26, 2015), Jack Cummings III (February 8, 2015), Jack Donahue (March 2, 2015), Timothy Dumas (April 7, 2015), Lucianne Goldberg (February 21, 2015), Jesse Kornbluth (April 23, 2015), Len Levitt (March 4, 2015), Asa Maynor (October 6, 2015), Chris

Morano ( July 28, 2015), Dorthy Moxley (March 3, 2015), Kevin Sessums (March 26, 2015), Mickey Sherman (August 12, 2015), Liz Smith (November 4, 2015), Edmund White (February 17, 2016), and William Baldwin Young (March 18, 2015) are from interviews with the author, except where noted.

237 Fuhrman conversations with Garr and Levitt: Levitt, *Conviction*, 101.

—— "Somebody wants to write": Moxley to author.

238 "Mrs. Moxley, don't ever do": Levitt, *Conviction*, 208.

—— "I invited several local cops": Dominick Dunne, "Trial of Guilt," *Vanity Fair*, October 2000.

—— Fuhrman would name Michael: Levitt, *Conviction*, 206.

—— "Where can we get a beer": Morano to author.

239 "They spent a quarter-million": Morano to author.

—— "I have to fill out a report": Morano to author.

—— "Nick, Michael Skakel's writing"/"Michael, what are you": Morano to author.

241 "The guy's name at the deli": Goldberg to author.

—— "You're so famous I'm afraid": Goldberg to author.

—— "Dunne gave Frank Garr": Fuhrman, *Murder in Greenwich*, 63.

242 "I firmly believe that his": D. Dunne, "Trial of Guilt."

—— grand jury stayed in session: Levitt, *Conviction*, 231.

—— "We always have a few laughs": Dominick Dunne, "Tabloid Trouble," *Vanity Fair*, March 2002.

243 "Now, some of this I can't": *Laura Ingraham Show*, radio transcript, December 20, 2001.

—— "hook, line, and sinker": *Dominick Dunne: After the Party*.

244 "He went on the air": Ibid.

—— "I have something to show" and other direct quotes to Avrich from D. Dunne: Avrich to author.

—— "how often you come": D. Dunne letter, September 7, 2001, Robert Rand collection.

245 "I can't do it"/"Larry wouldn't be": Avrich to author.

—— "We're going to take care": *Dominick Dunne: After the Party*.

—— "indemnify" his client: Briscoe letter, July 1, 2004.

—— Jim Wiatt intervene: Briscoe letter, January 26, 2005.

—— Anna Wintour at *Vogue*: Briscoe letter, undated.

—— "Later, Graydon said": *Dominick Dunne: After the Party*.

—— "shrugs off the Condit case"/"We've had huge lawsuits": Chris Smith, "Dominick Dunne vs. Robert Kennedy," *New York*, June 23, 2003.

246 "I've had prostate cancer": Ibid.

—— "Rudolph Giuliani had better": Dominick Dunne, "Murder Most Unforgettable," *Vanity Fair*, April 2001.

—— "Not really": Maynor to author.

—— "I can't go back": Anonymous sources to author.

247 $3,500 for two nights: Briscoe journal, 2005.

—— "I'm a star at this": Mike Hogan, "What Drove Dominick Dunne's Quest for Justice," *Vanity Fair*, November 2009.

—— "Where is my special treatment?!": Anonymous sources to author.

248 "Fuck 'em": Cummings to author.

—— Brown and Madonna canceled: Briscoe letters, undated.

—— year-end bonus: Briscoe journal, 2005.

—— $500,000/speaking fees of $25,000: Briscoe letter, January 26, 2005.

—— "Lear on the heath"/"haywire": Anonymous sources to author.

—— $90,000 a month: Briscoe letter, January 26, 2005.

249 "major misalliance": Ibid.

## Chapter 16

Quotes from Linda Deutsch (February 23, 2015), Timothy Dumas (April 7, 2015), Beth Karas (February 26, 2015), Len Levitt (March 4, 2015), Chris Morano (July 28, 2015), Dorthy Moxley (March 3, 2015), Mickey Sherman (August 12, 2015), and Ronald G. Shipp (February 23, 2015) are from interviews with the author, except where noted.

250 "The jury isn't looking": Mike Hogan, "Michael Skakel Retrial Order Would Have Infuriated Dominick Dunne," *Vanity Fair* online, October 24, 2013.

251 "Mark, you can't": Levitt, *Conviction*, 226.

—— white stretch limousine: Kennedy, *Framed*, 225.

—— "We're friends": Ibid.

—— "Ron, I gave this stuff"/"Everything is good": Shipp to author.

252 "Chris, why did you": Morano to author.

—— "Jerk": Dominick Dunne, "Triumph by Jury," *Vanity Fair*, August 2002.

—— "irresponsible": *Dominick Dunne: After the Party*.

—— "The formula that Dominick": Chris Smith, "Dominick Dunne v. Robert Kennedy," *New York*, June 23, 2003.

—— "I do not know that Ken": Robert F. Kennedy Jr., "A Miscarriage of Justice," *Atlantic Monthly*, January 2003.

253 "'Gossip' is an icky": *Dominick Dunne: In Search of Justice*.

—— "a gossip": C. Smith, "Dominick Dunne v. Robert Kennedy."

—— "little shit": *Dominick Dunne: After the Party*.

—— "If Michael had kept": D. Dunne, "Triumph by Jury."

—— Dunne and Levitt outside courthouse: Dumas, *Greentown*, 312.

—— "time to go to his son's": Levitt, *Conviction*, 243.

—— "I want you to know"/"That's true": Levitt to author.

254 "tripping on acid": Dunne, *The Way We Lived Then*, 183.

—— "God, help this man": Ibid., 186.

—— "sordid gay murder": Briscoe journal, 1979–80.

254 "friends" disparaged: Ibid., 207.
—— "that made me cringe": Dunne, *The Way We Lived Then*, 207.
—— scalding criticism, while Joan: Briscoe letter, November 29, 1979.

## Chapter 17

Quotes from Graydon Carter (March 9, 2016), Mia Certic (August 11, 2015), Joe Danisi (April 15, 2015), Michael Griffith (February 1, 2016), Jesse Kornbluth (April 23, 2015), Donald Manasse (August 24, 2015), Mickey Sherman (August 12, 2015), and Liz Smith (November 4, 2015) are from interviews with the author, except where noted.

255 "This show better be": Danisi to author.
—— Michael Skakel spent eleven: Mike Hogan, "Michael Skakel Retrial Order Would Have Infuriated Dominick Dunne," *Vanity Fair* online, October 24, 2013.
256 end of Safra articles: Briscoe journal, 2005; several sources to author.
—— "confession in a language": Dominick Dunne, "Another Party, Another Clue," *Vanity Fair*, March 2001.
—— "FBI to expose the Russian": Dominick Dunne, "A Playboy's Last Act," *Vanity Fair*, September 2001.
257 Alfredo Monteverde died: D. Dunne, "Another Party, Another Clue."
—— Safra had rewritten his will: Dominick Dunne, "Crime after Crime," *Vanity Fair*, October 2001.
—— "The damnation of Ted Maher": Dominick Dunne, "Death in Monaco," *Vanity Fair*, December 2000.
—— "a sunny place": Ibid.
258 chief rabbi episode: Certic to author; Griffith to author; Manasse to author.
—— "I ran out of the courtroom": Manasse to author.
—— "What do you think": Certic to author.
259 "Mike, I better move": Griffith to author.
—— "Where are we"/"I just don't know": Certic to author.
260 "Maybe I was being": Chris Smith, "Dominick Dunne vs. Robert F. Kennedy," *New York*, June 23, 2003.
—— Dominick asked Liz Smith: Briscoe letter, October 20, 2006; L. Smith to author.
—— "truth went to the grave": "Murder in Monaco," *Dominick Dunne's Power, Privilege, and Justice*, February 8, 2008.

## Chapter 18

Quotes from Norman Carby (May 23, 2015), Graydon Carter (March 9, 2016), Jack Cummings III (February 8, 2015), Jack Donahue (March 2, 2015), Alex Dunne (May 21, 2015), Michael Griffith (February 1, 2016), David Kuhn (August

25, 2015), Jeffrey Toobin (April 23, 2015), Matt Tyrnauer ( January 9, 2016), and William Baldwin Young (March 18, 2015) are from interviews with the author, except where noted.

261 "I hate that person": Young to author.

— "by happenstance": Dominick Dunne, "Death in the Family," *Vanity Fair*, March 2004.

— Griffin Dunne, who stayed: Ibid.

— "And then John called": Ibid.

262 "Hi, Leslie. Thank you": Dominick Dunne, "Runaway Jurors," *Vanity Fair*, June 2004.

— "The wealthy people just aren't shooting": *Dominick Dunne: After the Party*.

— "Nobody mentioned it was twelve": Dominick Dunne, "Going after Martha," *Vanity Fair*, April 2004.

— "There was an audible gasp": Ibid.

263 "I suspect that I would have disliked": Dominick Dunne, "Killing Me Fictionally," *Vanity Fair*, April 2005.

— P. J. Clarke party: Briscoe letter, May 5, 2005.

— "I Talked to Si": Briscoe letter, November 5, 2005; anonymous source to author.

264 Berenson and Colacello: Briscoe guest list, undated.

— "Believe me, I'll never forget": Mike Hogan, "What Drove Dominick Dunne's Quest for Justice," *Vanity Fair*, November 2009.

— "He became bipolar": Tim Teeman, "Dominick Dunne," *Times* (London), February 2, 2009.

— Dominick gasped, "Oh my God!": A. Dunne to author.

265 LiCalsi advised Dominick: Paul LiCalsi (February 20, 2016) to author.

— "Jack, I guess in the end": Cummings to author.

266 Carter office/seven recent issues/"old people"/Uriah Heep: Briscoe letter, February 1, 2007; anonymous source to author.

— "I already sent it": Cummings to author.

267 Lawson as honorary pallbearer: Briscoe letter, February 1, 2007; Cummings to author.

— Fuhlenwider was "just fantastic": Cummings to author.

— Lawson had his detractors: Anonymous sources to author.

— finish the last few chapters: Briscoe letter, February 6, 2008.

268 "So people don't talk": Donahue to author.

— "Don't use the real names": Bruce Nelson (March 30, 2015) to author.

— "out": Briscoe letter, December 1, 2007.

— "I'm ready to tell the story": Kuhn to author.

— it came to $1 million: Briscoe letter, undated; anonymous sources to author.

269 Porter tune went on Dominick's: Teeman, "Dominick Dunne."

— hospital escape/"What the fuck": Carby to author.

— "It's the stem cells": Ibid.

## Chapter 19

Quotes from Graydon Carter (March 9, 2016), Jack Cummings III (February 8, 2015), Bruce Cutler (May 4, 2015), Linda Deutsch (February 23, 2015), Peter Hong (May 2, 2015), Beth Karas (February 26, 2015), Ciaran McEvoy (April 16, 2015), Steven Mikulan (April 20, 2015), Allan Parachini (April 3, 2015), Harriet Ryan (March 27, 2015), and Gary Spector (April 16, 2015) are from interviews with the author, except where noted.

270 "accidental suicide": Scott Raab, "Be My, Be My Baby: The Phil Spector Story," *Esquire*, July 2003.

271 "Oh, I don't do poor-people"/"We're going to meet up": Ryan to author.

272 "Hannah's mother": Hong to author.

— Coke on his Buddhist: Karas to author.

— "Spector had threatened": Dominick Dunne, "Dominick Dunne's Diary," *Vanity Fair*, August 2005.

— "The idea that the defense": Dominick Dunne, "Phil Spector's Cheap Shots," *Vanity Fair*, October 2007.

273 "I had never heard the name": Dominick Dunne, "Guilty Feelings," *Vanity Fair*, November 2007.

— "endless woe-is-me"/"You know, it sounds": Mikulan to author.

274 "Did you wash": Dominick Dunne, "Cheating on Phil," *Vanity Fair*, September 2007.

— "John Gotti lawyer": Dominick Dunne, "Legend with a Bullet," *Vanity Fair*, August 2007.

— "a Mafia-type reputation": D. Dunne, "Guilty Feelings."

— "You need to make me lunch": Hong to author.

275 "Bruce must feel": Hong to author.

— "I do not believe that a beautiful": *Dominick Dunne: After the Party*.

— "Beneath Cutler's boisterousness": D. Dunne, "Guilty Feelings."

276 no one recognized the editor: Betsy A. Ross (March 2, 2015) to author.

— Tina Brown *Vanity Fair* column: Briscoe letter, March 28, 2002; Carter to author.

— the woman with the tape: Karas to author.

277 "failure, as if": *Dominick Dunne: After the Party*.

— "filled thirteen notebooks": *Dominick Dunne: After the Party*.

278 "I think the wrong guy": Ibid.

— "I'm quite proud that": Dominick Dunne, "The Verdict Is Missing," *Vanity Fair*, October 2007.

## Chapter 20

Quotes from Tracy Breton (September 19, 2016), Tita Cahn (March 5, 2015), Norman Carby (May 23, 2015), Graydon Carter (March 9, 2016), Mart Crowley

(February 5, 2015), Jack Cummings III (February 8, 2015), Kirsty de Garis (March 6, 2015), Linda Deutsch (February 23, 2015), James Duff (March 4, 2015), Alex Dunne (May 21, 2015), Freddy Eberstadt (May 6, 2015), Michael Griffith (February 1, 2016), Jesse Kornbluth (April 23, 2015), Tim A. Lovejoy (February 22, 2016), William Mann (August 4, 2015), Andrea Reynolds Plunket (September 30, 2015), Gary Pudney (May 21, 2015), Markham Roberts (March 30, 2015), James Sansum (March 25, 2015), Tim Teeman (November 16, 2015), Matt Tyrnauer (January 9, 2016), Edmund White (February 17, 2016), and Angus Wilkie (April 30, 2015) are from interviews with the author, except where noted. Griffin Dunne quotes are from *Fresh Air* interview (December 15, 2009), except where noted.

279 "It's too raw": De Garis to author.
—— "If over fifteen years": *Dominick Dunne: After the Party*.
—— "If *Vanity Fair* didn't promise": Anonymous source to author.
—— "That was the end": *Dominick Dunne: After the Party*.
280 Dominick signed a contract: Briscoe letter, March 28, 2007.
—— "Let it go": *Dominick Dunne: After the Party*.
—— "Is your father": Kellow, *Can I Go Now?*, 272.
—— slippers, and a catheter: Crowley to author.
—— "shitty brown": Lovejoy to author.
281 "pinked up"/"Scared by fame"/"saw it in me"/"When you have children": Roberts to author.
—— "I hate to tell you"/"Isn't she beautiful?": Tyrnauer to author.
283 "I'm a closeted homosexual": Mann to author.
—— "Are you married": Teeman to author.
—— "closeted bisexual celibate": Tim Teeman, "Dominick Dunne," *Times*, February 12, 2009.
—— "In my era, gay men": Teeman, "Dominick Dunne."
284 "Oh, I don't care": *Dominick Dunne: After the Party*.
—— he knew every restroom: Briscoe letter, undated.
—— "a state of terror": Briscoe letter, undated.
—— "I'd rather be kissed": Cahn to author.
—— "like God" and stood up: McEvoy to author.
285 "This is the stupidest": Deutsch to author.
—— "I had a literary following": Steve Friess, "The Final O.J. Story for Dominick Dunne," *New York Times*, September 19, 2008.
—— "Hey, she's after Dominick": Ibid.
—— "Mr. Dunne, it is so wonderful"/"I hate to admit it": Deutsch to author.
286 "Call Griffin": Karas to author.
—— "getting flowers"/"Are you Dominick's": Mike Hogan, "How *Vanity Fair*'s Dominick Dunne Relentlessly Pursued the O.J. Simpson Story," *Vanity Fair* online, March 1, 2016.
—— second wedding: A. Dunne to author; Adam Belanoff (March 5, 2015) to author.

286  stem-cell treatments instead: Carby to author.

287  "Your Majesty"/castle anecdote: Briscoe letter, May 25, 2009; Carby to author.

288  toilet paper as a gift: Karas to author.

——  Lufthansa flight home: Carby to author.

——  "I wish I could do Conrad": Tina Brown, "The Unforgettable Dominick Dunne," *Huffington Post*, August 27, 2009.

——  "He seems in great shape": Cummings to author.

——  "I did it": Langella, *Dropped Names*, 205.

289  "Edmond Safra's nurse": Griffith to author.

——  "Am I still alive": Eberstadt to author.

——  Griffin Dunne phoned Jesse: Kornbluth to author.

——  "That's true": Crowley to author.

——  "We almost never see": Cummings to author; Dominick Dunne interview, unpublished, with author for *Party Animals*.

290  "I don't want any ick": Cummings to author.

——  "professional mourners": Griffin Dunne, "Farewell to My Father," *Daily Beast*, September 11, 2009.

——  "But I don't have a suit": Cummings to author.

——  "My Funny Valentine" anecdote and quotes: G. Dunne, *Fresh Air* interview.

291  he began to complain: Crowley to author.

——  purchased the last available plot: Lovejoy to author.

——  asked Mart Crowley and Jack Cummings: Crowley to author; Cummings to author.

——  fireplace fender: Stark to author.

# Bibliography

Abramson, Leslie, with Richard Flaste. *The Defense Is Ready: My Life in Crime.* New York: Pocket Books, 1998.

Clark, Marcia, with Teresa Carpenter. *Without a Doubt.* New York: Viking, 1997.

Daugherty, Tracy. *The Last Love Song: A Biography of Joan Didion.* New York: St. Martin's, 2015.

Didion, Joan. *Play It as It Lays.* New York: Farrar, Straus and Giroux, 1970.

———. *Salvador.* New York: Simon & Schuster, 1982.

———. *Slouching towards Bethlehem.* New York: Farrar, Straus and Giroux, 1968.

———. *Where I Was From.* New York: Alfred A. Knopf, 2003.

———. *The White Album.* New York: Simon & Schuster, 1978.

Dumas, Timothy. *Greentown: Murder and Mystery in Greenwich, America's Wealthiest Community.* New York: Arcade, 1998.

Dunne, Dominick. *Another City, Not My Own: A Novel in the Form of a Memoir.* New York: Crown, 1997.

———. *Too Much Money: A Novel.* New York: Crown, 2009.

———. *The Way We Lived Then: Recollections of a Well-Known Name Dropper.* New York: Crown, 1999.

Dunne, John Gregory. *Harp.* New York: Simon & Schuster, 1989.

———. *Quintana & Friends.* New York: E. P. Dutton, 1978.

Fuhrman, Mark. *Murder in Greenwich: Who Killed Martha Moxley?* New York: Avon, 1999.

Grobel, Lawrence. *Signing In: 50 Celebrity Profiles.* New York: HMH Press, 2014.

Heymann, C. David. *Liz: An Intimate Biography of Elizabeth Taylor.* Citadel Press, 1996.

Hofler, Robert. *Party Animals.* Boston: Da Capo Press, 2010.

———. *Sexplosion: From Andy Warhol to "A Clockwork Orange"—How a Generation of Pop Rebels Broke All the Taboos.* New York: It Books/HarperCollins, 2013.

———. *Variety's "The Movie That Changed My Life."* Boston: Da Capo Press, 2009.

Indiana, Gary. *Resentment: A Comedy.* New York: Doubleday, 1997.

Kellow, Brian. *Can I Go Now? The Life of Sue Mengers, Hollywood's First Super-Agent.* New York: Viking, 2015.

Kennedy, Robert F., Jr. *Framed: Why Michael Skakel Spent over a Decade in Prison for a Murder He Didn't Commit.* New York: Skyhorse.

Langella, Frank. *Dropped Names.* New York: HarperCollins, 2013.

Levitt, Leonard. *Conviction: Solving the Moxley Murder.* New York: ReganBooks, 2004.

Mulcahy, Susan, ed. *Why I'm a Democrat.* San Francisco: PoliPointPress, 2007.

Schiller, Lawrence, and James Willwerth. *American Tragedy: The Uncensored Story of the Simpson Defense.* New York: Random House, 1996.

Soble, Ron, and John Johnson. *Blood Brothers: The Inside Story of the Menendez Murders.* New York: Onyx, 1994.

Summers, Anthony, and Robbyn Swan. *Sinatra: The Life.* New York: Alfred A. Knopf, 2005.

Toobin, Jeffrey. *The Run of His Life: The People v. O.J. Simpson.* New York: Simon & Schuster, 1996.

# Filmography

*Dominick Dunne: After the Party*. Directed by Kirsty de Garis and Timothy Jolley. Road Trip Films, 2008.

*Dominick Dunne: In Search of Justice*. Directed by Clara Kupferberg and Robert Kupferberg. Wichita Films, 2007.

*Guilty Pleasure: The Extraordinary World of Dominick Dunne*. Directed by Barry Avrich. Melbar Entertainment Group, 2002.

*Making the Boys*. Directed by Crayton Robey. 4th Row Films, 2011.

*O.J.: Made in America*. Directed by Ezra Edelman. ESPN, 2016.

# *Index*

*Page numbers in italics indicate illustrations.*